INNOVATION IN MANUFACTURING NETWORKS

IFIP – The International Federation for Information Processing

IFIP was founded in 1960 under the auspices of UNESCO, following the First World Computer Congress held in Paris the previous year. An umbrella organization for societies working in information processing, IFIP's aim is two-fold: to support information processing within its member countries and to encourage technology transfer to developing nations. As its mission statement clearly states,

> IFIP's mission is to be the leading, truly international, apolitical organization which encourages and assists in the development, exploitation and application of information technology for the benefit of all people.

IFIP is a non-profitmaking organization, run almost solely by 2500 volunteers. It operates through a number of technical committees, which organize events and publications. IFIP's events range from an international congress to local seminars, but the most important are:

• The IFIP World Computer Congress, held every second year;
• Open conferences;
• Working conferences.

The flagship event is the IFIP World Computer Congress, at which both invited and contributed papers are presented. Contributed papers are rigorously refereed and the rejection rate is high.

As with the Congress, participation in the open conferences is open to all and papers may be invited or submitted. Again, submitted papers are stringently refereed.

The working conferences are structured differently. They are usually run by a working group and attendance is small and by invitation only. Their purpose is to create an atmosphere conducive to innovation and development. Refereeing is less rigorous and papers are subjected to extensive group discussion.

Publications arising from IFIP events vary. The papers presented at the IFIP World Computer Congress and at open conferences are published as conference proceedings, while the results of the working conferences are often published as collections of selected and edited papers.

Any national society whose primary activity is in information may apply to become a full member of IFIP, although full membership is restricted to one society per country. Full members are entitled to vote at the annual General Assembly, National societies preferring a less committed involvement may apply for associate or corresponding membership. Associate members enjoy the same benefits as full members, but without voting rights. Corresponding members are not represented in IFIP bodies. Affiliated membership is open to non-national societies, and individual and honorary membership schemes are also offered.

INNOVATION IN MANUFACTURING NETWORKS

Eighth IFIP International Conference on Information Technology for Balanced Automation Systems, Porto, Portugal, June 23-25, 2008

Edited by

Américo Azevedo
Universidade de Porto
Portugal

 Springer

Innovation in Manufacturing Networks

Edited by Américo Azevedo

p. cm. (IFIP International Federation for Information Processing, a Springer Series in Computer Science)

ISSN: 1571-5736 / 1861-2288 (Internet)
ISBN: 978-1-4419-3487-1
e-ISBN: 978-0-387-09492-2

Printed on acid-free paper

Printed in the United States of America.

9 8 7 6 5 4 3 2 1

springer.com

TABLE OF CONTENTS

TECHNICAL SPONSORS:

IFIP WG 5.5 COVE
Co-Operation infrastructure for Virtual Enterprises and
electronic business

Society of Collaborative Networks

ORGANIZATIONAL CO-SPONSORS:

Faculdade de Engenharia da Universidade do Porto

INESCPORTO
Instituto de Engenharia de Sistemas e Computadores do Porto
Laboratório Associado

23, 24 and 25 June 2008 - Porto, Portugal

BASYS 08

8TH IFIP INTERNATIONAL CONFERENCE ON INFORMATION TECHNOLOGY FOR

BALANCED AUTOMATION SYSTEMS

PROGRAMME CONFERENCE CHAIR
Américo Azevedo (PT)

<table>
<tr><td>

PROGRAMME CO-CHAIRS
Luís M. Camarinha-Matos (PT)
Emanuele Carpanzano (IT)
Engelbert Westkamper, (DE)
David Williams (UK)

</td><td>

STEERING COMMITTEE
Luis M. Camarinha-Matos (Chair, PT)
Hamideh Afsarmanesh (NL)
Heinz-H. Erbe (DE)
Weiming Shen (CA)

</td></tr>
</table>

REFEREES FROM THE PROGRAMME COMMITTEE

Afsarmanesh, Hamideh (NL)
Azevedo, Américo (PT)
Backhouse, Chris (UK)
Barata, José (PT)
Burns, Neil (UK)
Camarinha-Matos,L. M. (PT)
Carneiro, Luis (PT)
Carpanzano, Emanuele (IT)
Cellary, Wojciech (P)
Chituc, Claudia-Melania (RO/PT)
Copani, Giacomo (IT)
Cunha, Pedro (PT)
Faria, José (PT)
Goranson, Ted (US)
Kodratoff, Yves (F)
Kovács, Gyorgy (HU)
Molfino, Rezia (IT)

Onori, Mauro (ST)
Paralic, Jan (SK)
Pinho de Sousa, Jorge (PT)
Portugal, Paulo (PT)
Putnik, Goran (PT)
Rabelo, Ricardo (BR)
Rais, Abdur (EUA)
Rauber, Thomas (BR)
Shen, W. (CA)
Soares, A. Lucas (PT)
Smirnov, Alexander (RUS)
Tamura, Shinsuke (JP)
Valckenaers, P. (BE)
Viana, Ana (PT)
Westkamper, Engelbert (DE)
Williams, David (UK)

Innovation in Manufacturing Networks

A fundamental concept of the emergent business, scientific and technological paradigms is that of 'Innovation'. Be it in the manufacturing or the services area, innovation – the ability to apply new ideas to products, processes, organizational practices and business models - is crucial for the future competitiveness of organizations in a continually increasingly globalised, knowledge-intensive marketplace.

Responsiveness, agility as well as the high performance of manufacturing systems is responsible for the recent changes in addition to the call for new approaches to achieve cost-effective responsiveness at all the levels of an enterprise. Moreover, creating appropriate frameworks for exploring the most effective synergies between human potential and automated systems represents an enormous challenge in terms of processes characterization, modelling, and the development of adequate support tools. The implementation and use of Automation Systems requires an ever increasing knowledge of enabling technologies and Business Practices. Moreover, the digital and networked world will surely trigger new business practices.

In this context and in order to achieve the desired effective and efficiency performance levels, it is crucial to maintain a balance between both the technical aspects and the human and social aspects when developing and applying new innovations and innovative enabling technologies. BASYS conferences have been developed and organized so as to promote the development of balanced automation systems in an attempt to address the majority of the current open issues.

The BASYS'08 which was held in Porto, Portugal, is the 8th event in a series of successful conferences. Their global aim is to provide an international forum for the exchange of leading edge scientific knowledge and industrial experience regarding the development and integration of the various aspects of Balanced Automation Systems which cover the complete life-cycle of company's Product, as well as the Processes. The focus of this conference was to discuss the rapidly evolving field of the integration of human actors and emergent technologies, in addition to the multi-disciplinary approaches in relation to business ecosystems in which a myriad of networked technologies and devices, which are fully interacting with human beings, will generate, consume and relay data and knowledge in the context of a pervasive digital environment.

This book contains a set of invited keynote papers as well as a selection of the papers which were accepted for presentation at the BASYS'08 conference. The book opens with a set of interesting articles provided by several invited authors, covering perspectives such as collaborative manufacturing networks, disruptive innovation and virtual factory design environments. The remaining sections of the book include a number of selected papers, which provide a comprehensive overview of the recent advances in the various manufacturing issues.

The papers are organized in the following sections:

- *Collaborative Networks*
- *Interoperability and Collaboration Support*
- *Digital Factory*   •
- *Intelligent Machines and Sensor Networks*
- *Innovation and Entrepreneurship*

Despite the significant efforts that are required in order to make progress in the domain of the BASYS conference, as a whole, the papers in this book will prove to be a significant contribution to the already existing literature.

The contents of this book - Innovation in Manufacturing Networks- reflect the vitality of the discussion held in the plenary and parallel sessions of the BASYS'08 conference. This book is the direct consequence of extensive teamwork, resulting from the generous collaboration of all the authors, which are representatives of the academia, research and industry, the members of the organizing committee and the members of program committees who participated in terms of the selection of articles and the input of valuable comments which contributed to the quality of this project. Special thanks are due to Mr. Mark Macedo for his help during the preparation of the book and to Ms. Lidia Vilas-Boas for her valuable help, availability and deep professionalism all the time.

The editor,

Américo Azevedo
INESC PORTO, Faculdade de Engenharia
Universidade do Porto, Portugal

ADVANCES IN COLLABORATIVE NETWORKED ORGANIZATIONS

Luis M. Camarinha-Matos
New University of Lisbon
Quinta da Torre – 2829-516 Monte Caparica, PORTUGAL
cam@uninova.pt,

Collaborative networks represent a fundamental paradigm in modern industrial organizations. It is not only a survival factor or a mechanism to increase agility, but also a basis to promote innovation through collaboration. Aiming at giving a general overview of the area, this paper presents a summary of its current achievements and further research challenges.

1. INTRODUCTION

The information and communication technologies have been a fundamental "companion" of the manufacturing industry since the late 1970s. Along the last 3-4 decades many new approaches and paradigms were introduced, leading to progressive levels of integration, first inside the enterprise and lately in terms of networks of enterprises. The diagram of Fig. 1 briefly illustrates this evolution.

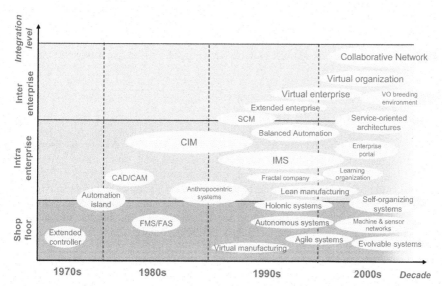

Figure 1. A brief historic evolution in manufacturing systems

Please use the following format when citing this chapter:

Camarinha-Matos, L.M., 2008, in IFIP International Federation for Information Processing, Volume 266, *Innovation in Manufacturing Networks;* ed. A. Azevedo; (Boston: Springer), pp. 3–16.

The diagram does not intend to give a precise "duration" for each paradigm, but rather an indication of the period when each topic was more "popular". As illustrated, although important challenges and activities are currently found at shop floor and intra-enterprise level, the inter-enterprise collaboration is becoming more and more important.

The need to consider the industrial developments in a more global perspective is also confirmed by prospective studies and recommendations such as the conclusions of the IMS Forum (IMS, 2006), shown in Fig. 2 (left side).

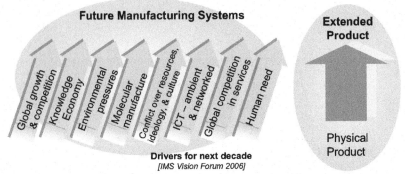

Figure 2. Manufacturing systems evolution drivers

The concept of product also evolved from the "physical product" to the notion of "extended product". This includes customized solutions to clients "embodying: intelligence as well as service capabilities in the form of real-time diagnostics, self-maintenance, security, traceability, self-direction, entertainment, convenience, responsiveness, and reciprocity" (Myers, 2006). The notions of social responsibility and sustainability also force companies to consider the full life cycle of the products / services, giving emphasis to life cycle management and end of life planning and operation. All these factors force companies to seek collaboration in order to better satisfy the market and societal demands.

2. COLLABORATIVE NETWORKS

In recent years the area of collaborative networks is being consolidated as a new discipline (Camarinha-Matos, Afsarmanesh, 2005) that encompasses and gives more structured support to a large diversity of collaboration forms. A collaborative network (CN) is a network consisting of a variety of entities (e.g. organizations, people, and even intelligent machines) that are largely autonomous, geographically distributed, and heterogeneous in terms of their operating environment, culture, social capital and goals, but that collaborate to better achieve common or compatible goals, and whose interactions are supported by computer network.

Most forms of collaborative networks, namely the cases found in industry, imply some kind of *organization* over the activities of their constituents, identifying roles for the participants, and some governance rules, and therefore, can be called manifestations of **collaborative networked organizations (CNOs)**. Other more spontaneous forms of collaboration in networks can also be foreseen. For instance, various **ad-hoc collaboration processes** can take place in virtual communities, namely those that are not business oriented – e.g. individual citizens contributions in case of a natural disaster, or simple gathering of individuals for a social cause (Camarinha-Matos, Afsarmanesh, 2008). These are cases where people or organizations may volunteer to collaborate hoping to improve a general aim, with no pre-plan and/or structure on participants' roles and how their activities should proceed. Fig. 3 shows a partial taxonomy of collaborative networks.

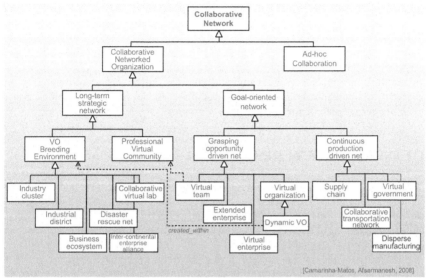

Figure 3. A partial taxonomy of collaborative networks

As shown in this taxonomy, among the CNOs it is important to distinguish between the long-term strategic networks or alliances and the goal-oriented networks. In fact many initial works on Virtual Organizations (VOs) / Virtual Enterprises (VEs) underestimated the difficulties of the creation process while advocating very dynamic scenarios. However, the agility and dynamism required for VOs are limited by the difficult process of establishing a common operational basis and building trust. The creation of long term associations of industry or service enterprises, an evolution of the industrial cluster concept, represents an approach to overcoming these obstacles and thus supporting the rapid formation of VO inspired by business opportunities. The concept of VO Breeding Environment (VBE) was introduced to represent this approach. A VBE represents an association of organizations and their related supporting institutions, adhering to a base long term cooperation agreement, and adoption of common operating principles and infrastructures, with the main goal of increasing their preparedness towards rapid configuration of temporary alliances for collaboration in potential Virtual Organizations. Namely, when a business opportunity is identified by one member (acting as a broker), a subset of VBE organizations can be selected to form a VE/VO (Afsarmanesh, Camarinha-Matos, 2005). A similar long-term organization is the Professional Virtual Community (PVC) which represents an alliance of professional individuals, providing an environment to facilitate the agile and fluid formation of Virtual Teams (VTs), similar to what VBE aims to provide for the VOs. A more comprehensive overview of the various classes of CNs can be found in (Camarinha-Matos, Afsarmanesh, 2008).

Many research initiatives and industrial developments have addressed different aspects of particular classes of CNOs during the last decades. However in most cases these initiatives corresponded to *fragmented* research and due to the funding and assessment criteria, targeted very short-term objectives, focused on solving a specific problem. A more sustainable development of the area should be based on contributions of a multidisciplinary nature, namely from the information and communication technologies, socio-economic, operations research, organizational, business management, legal, social security, and ethical areas, among others. In this direction, the ECOLEAD project was launched in 2004 with the aim to create the necessary strong foundations and mechanisms for establishing an advanced collaborative and network-based industry society. ECOLEAD addressed three main focus areas: VO Breeding Environments (VBE), Virtual Organizations (VO), and Professional Virtual Communities (PVC), as well as their inter-relationships. These areas were complemented by research on horizontal ICT support infrastructures and contribution to a theoretical foundation for CNOs.

In parallel, several other international initiatives have been contributing to the development and consolidation of the new discipline. In the following sections a brief survey of the current state in the various areas is presented.

3. ICT INFRASTRUCTURES

The ICT infrastructure plays the role of a base enabler for effective, safe and coordinated interactions among the CNO members. In other words, it acts as a CNO "operating system" or executor, hiding the details of the collaborative network "machinery". Benefiting from the rapid development of the so-called Internet technologies, this has had a fast progress during last years.

Fig. 4 illustrates the current state of the art regarding general ICT support to CNOs. This diagram is not intended to give a full account of all developments in this extensive area but just to pinpoint the main building blocks and recent progress. Examples of relevant projects contributing to the area are also included.

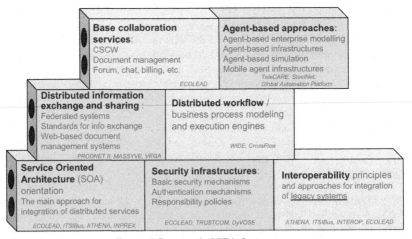

Figure 4. Progress in ICT infrastructures

While earlier efforts were focused on basic interoperability, secure communications, coordination and information sharing and exchange, current trends go towards advanced collaboration support services and semantic support.

Fig. 5 illustrates some of the challenges requiring further research in the area.

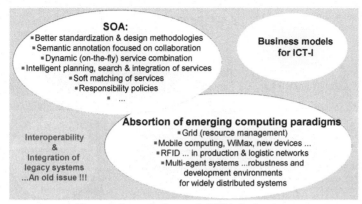

Figure 5. Some challenges in ICT infrastructures

4. VO BREEDING ENVIRONMENTS AND VO CREATION

Evolving from earlier concepts of industry cluster, industrial district or business ecosystem, the notion of Virtual organization Breeding Environment (VBE) was established as a more general concept encompassing these and other long-term strategic alliances. During last years substantial progress was achieved both in conceptual and methodological terms as well as development of support systems. Fig. 6 gives a brief summary of the main building blocks and corresponding elements developed in a number of recent projects, with particular relevance to ECOLEAD (Afsarmanesh, Camarinha-Matos, 2005).

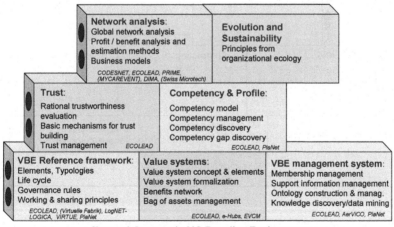

Figure 6. Progress in VO Breeding Environments

There are already a significant number of operational VBEs (Afsarmanesh, Camarinha-Matos, 2007). Nevertheless many challenges for further research have been identified, as illustrated in Fig. 7.

Figure 7. Further research challenges in VBEs

As the main purpose of these organizational structures is to make their members prepared to collaborate when a business opportunity is identified, a growing number of developments on VO creation are now conducted assuming a VBE as the underlying context. A summary of such recent developments is illustrated in Fig. 8.

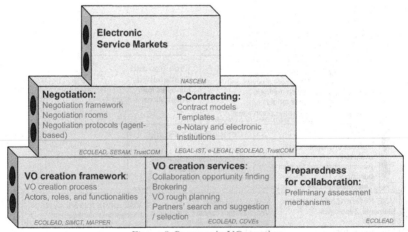

Figure 8. Progress in VO creation

It shall be mentioned that VO creation / consortia formation is one of the most addressed topics in research in the last 10 years. Nevertheless, many of the works on partner selection or negotiation, for instance, ignored the problems that are addressed by a VBE and therefore generated solutions with theoretical merit but somehow far from the actual needs in industry. More recently the efforts are becoming more focused on real business needs and new solutions, which are less automated and more in the line of decision-support tools, are being proposed.

5. VO MANAGEMENT

Substantial developments in the early days of VE/VO research were focused on supporting the operational phase of these networks, paying little attention to the other phases of the life cycle. However, being these organizations temporary, and often of a short duration, it is very important to devote attention to the creation, evolution and dissolution phases as well. More recent works have a more comprehensive scope and the area of VO management became an important research topic. Fig. 9 highlights recent developments in the topic, covering conceptual, methodological and technology developments aspects. Further research challenges are illustrated in Fig. 10.

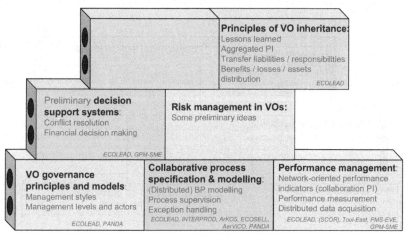

Figure 9. Progress in VO Management

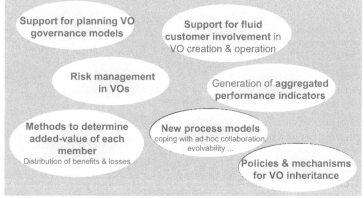

Figure 10. Some challenges in VO management

6. PROFESSIONAL VIRTUAL COMMUNITIES

The Professional Virtual Communities topic has its roots in different areas – virtual communities, communities of practice, and concurrent engineering - and thus represents an attempt to synthesize a new organizational structure based on synergies from those related areas. On the other hand, a PVC is another kind of "breeding environment" to facilitate the dynamic creation of virtual teams and thus gets inspiration on the previous developments in the area of VBEs.

As illustrated in Fig. 11, the main contributions of ECOLEAD in this area were on the conceptual and methodological side. Other projects have developed some tools and approaches for collaborative problem solving, namely in the AI and Collaborative Engineering communities, but an integrated framework and platform are still missing.

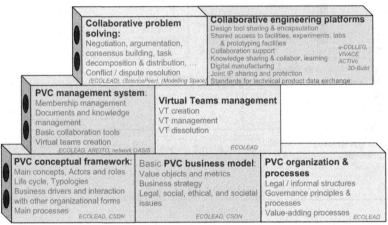

Figure 11. Progress in PVC

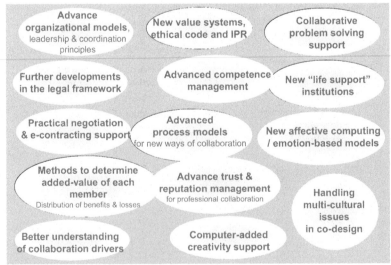

Figure 12. Examples of further research challenges in PVC

The introduction of a business dimension in these virtual communities although showing an interesting potential for knowledge workers, also raises additional challenges requiring further R&D. Examples of such challenges are shown in Fig. 12.

Another aspect requiring further work is the combination of PVCs and VBEs, i.e. PVCs composed of professionals working for the VBE organizations. This kind of hybrid structure requires specific models and support functionalities.

7. TOWARDS A REFERENCE MODEL

After an initial decade characterized by developments focused on solving particular problems and leading to fragmented solutions, in the last 5 years there is a growing awareness for the need of more holistic and sound approaches. The initial phase was also characterized by having different communities (e.g. engineering or management) addressing similar problems but with little or no interaction. Understanding that collaborative networks require contributions from multiple "adjacent" disciplines and a more structured theoretical foundation is leading to the consolidation of the area as a new discipline (Camarinha-Matos, Afsarmanesh, 2005). Some illustrative elements of this trend are shown in Fig. 13.

A major necessity is the elaboration of a reference model that could provide a general basis for understanding the significant concepts, entities, and relationships of some domain, and therefore a "foundation" for the area.

Modeling complex systems such as Collaborative Networks requires a proper framework to capture their complexity. For this purpose, ECOLEAD introduced the ARCON modeling framework (Camarinha-Matos, Afsarmanesh, 2007a, 2008). ARCON includes three perspectives: 1) Life cycle, 2) Environment characteristics, and 3) Modeling intent (Fig. 14).

The first defined perspective addresses the timing cycle of different CN life stages. This perspective captures the evolution of CNs and the diversity during their entire life cycle, represented by the vertical axis, labeled as "Life cycle stages".

The second defined perspective focuses on capturing the CN environment characteristics, represented by the horizontal axis, labeled as "Environment characteristics". This perspective further includes two subspaces (points of view) that comprehensively cover, the internal elements characteristics (labeled "Endogenous Elements") of CNs, as well as the external interactions characteristics (labeled "Exogenous Interactions") that address the logical surrounding of the CNs. For the endogenous elements perspective the following sub-dimensions are considered: Structural, Componential, Functional, and Behavioral. Under Endogenous Interactions the following sub-dimensions are included: Market, Support, Societal, and Constituency.

The third defined perspective for ARCON reference modeling is related to the different intents for the modeling of CN features, represented by the diagonal axis, labeled as "modeling intents". This perspective addresses the three possible modeling stages for CN elements, from the general representation, to the specific models (e.g. using a specific modeling approach or theory), and finally to the detailed specification of the implementation architecture for CN element.

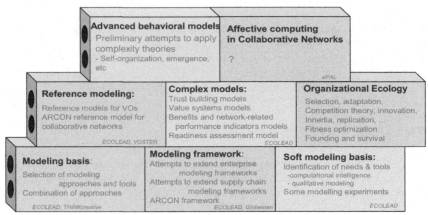

Figure 13. Progress on a theoretical foundation for CNs

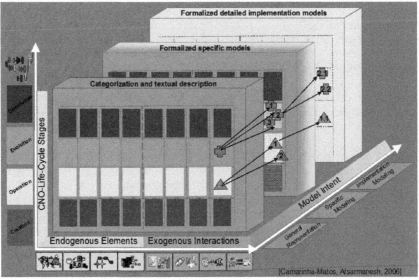

Figure 14. ARCON modeling framework

Using this framework, ECOLEAD also made a first attempt to collect and organize the most common general concepts under the endogenous elements and exogenous interactions perspectives, as briefly summarized in Fig. 15 and Fig. 16.

The framework was first applied to the CNO cases studied in ECOLEAD, namely VBEs, VOs, and PVCs. An attempt to generalize from these cases was then made, trying to identify a common set of concepts and entities, which were discussed with a wide group of experts from different fields. Nevertheless it is clear that it is not a finished job but rather a starting basis.

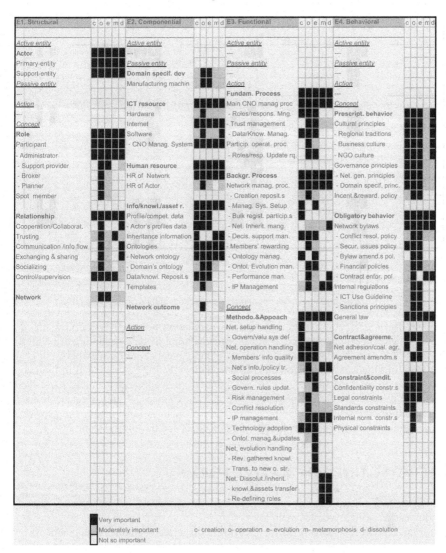

Figure 15. Contribution to a reference model – endogenous perspective

A textual description is also provided for each concept. Example:

- <u>Broker</u>   Role played by an actor when engaged in identifying and acquiring collaboration opportunities (business opportunities or others), by marketing CNO competencies and assets and negotiating with (potential) customers. Also responsible for interacting with (potential) customers, on behalf of the CNO, during the early phases of response to these opportunities. In some cases there is also the possibility of this opportunity brokerage role being played by an outside entity, as a service to the CNO.

For a complete description see (Camarinha-Matos, Afsarmanesh, 2008).

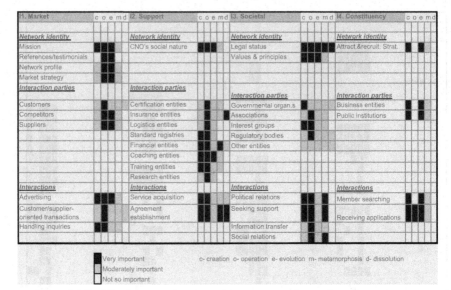

Figure 16. Contribution to a reference model – exogenous interactions perspective

Promising new directions, from a theoretical foundation perspective, are now being explored by different initiatives such as advanced behavioral models, including principles of emergence and self-organization, affective computing in collaborative networks, etc.

The ideas of Organizational Ecology (Hannan, Freeman, 1977), originated in the late 1970s are now being tried in the area of collaborative networks, e.g. to understand the emergence and survival of new organizational forms (Campos, 2007). Organizational Ecology combines the fields of sociology, ecology and organizational theories to provide a new description of the phenomena linking organizations and the environment.

8. EMERGING COLLABORATIVE FORMS

Currently the Collaborative Networks paradigm is spreading to new sectors and application cases. Some examples include:

1. Joint resource management (e.g. grid / dispersed manufacturing networks, computer grid).
2. Collaborative virtual lab (involving also remote access to lab resources).
3. Inter-modal collaboration (e.g. integrated transportation systems).
4. Collaborative e-government / network of governmental organizations.
5. Energy networks management (involving a network of producers, transporters, regulators, and even costumers with micro-production capability).
6. (Occasional) crisis management (e.g. rescue network in case of a major incident).
7. Customers involvement networks (kind of living lab).
8. Virtual institutes (e.g. a network of universities offering a joint e-learning programme).
9. Permanent crisis / social care (e.g. supporting homeless).
10. Collaborative gaming.
11. Collaborative innovation.
12. Context awareness service provision (i.e. providing services offered by different providers and that depend on the context, e.g. location of a mobile customer).
13. Machine and sensor networks (e.g. networks of robots).

Some of these cases pose new challenges and are likely to originate new classes of collaborative networks.

One interesting example is the customer involvement in innovation co-creation networks (Berger et al. 2005), (Hippel, 2002). The challenge here is to enable *collaborative innovation* involving a network of SMEs (manufacturers, designers, etc.), interfacing different entities and customers. Unlike previous works focused on interactions between one company and its customers, it is necessary to address the much more challenging scope of customer involved in networked collaboration and co-innovation, as shown in Fig. 17.

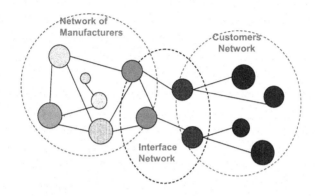

Figure 17. Customers' involvement in a CN

A great potential for innovation in collaborative networks comes thus from two different directions: 1) The application of the paradigm to new domains and scenarios, and 2) The exploration of new theories and approaches originated in different disciplines that can contribute with new insights to better understand and manage these complex systems.

9. CONCLUSIONS

The discipline of collaborative networks and particularly the collaborative networked organizations are going through an expansion and consolidation process as confirmed by the large amount of conceptual results, methodologies, support tools, and developed pilot demonstrations and applications during the last years.

Hand in hand with this progress, and especially as a result of the enlarging application base, new research challenges are being identified. Collaborative networks are nowadays applied in a large variety of sectors, including industrial manufacturing, services, logistics and transportation, energy management, education, agribusiness, government, research, elderly care, etc. The paradigm is becoming a pervasive phenomenon with a great potential. Further research and development shall materialize this potential.

On the theoretical foundation side, and complementing the first attempts to establish reference models, new approaches and theories originated in different fields are being adapted and extended to support a consolidation of this new discipline.

9.1. Acknowledgments

This work was supported in part by the ECOLEAD integrated project funded by the European Commission.

10. REFERENCES

1. Afsarmanesh, H., L. M. Camarinha-Matos. "A framework for management of virtual organization breeding environments". In: Collaborative Networks and their Breeding Environments, Springer, Boston, 2005, pp. 35-48.
2. Afsarmanesh, H., L. M. Camarinha-Matos. Towards a semi-typology for virtual organization breeding environments. In Proc.s of COA 2007 - 8th IFAC Symposium on Cost Oriented Automation Affordable Automation Systems, Habana, Cuba, 2007.
3. Berger, C.; Moslein, K.; Piller, F.; Reichwald, R. Cooperation between manufacturers, retailers, and customers for user co-design: Learning from exploratory research. European Management Review 2005; 1: 70-87.
4. Camarinha-Matos, L. M. "Emerging collaboration forms and further research needs". In Methods and tools for Collaborative Networked Organizations, Springer, 2008.
5. Camarinha-Matos, L. M.; Afsarmanesh, H. Collaborative networks: A new scientific discipline. J. Intelligent Manufacturing 2005; 16, N° 4-5: 439-452.
6. Camarinha-Matos, L.M., Afsarmanesh, H. On reference models for collaborative networked organizations. International Journal Production Research Online Publication Date: 01 January 2007 (2007a), Printed version: Volume 46, Issue 5, 2008: 1207 – 1229.
7. Camarinha-Matos, L.M., Afsarmanesh, H. A comprehensive modeling framework for collaborative networked organizations. Journal of Intelligent Manufacturing 2007b, Volume 18, Number 5 / October, 2007: 527-615.
8. Camarinha-Matos, L.M., Afsarmanesh, H. Collaborative Networks – Reference modeling. Springer, 2008.
9. Camarinha-Matos, L. M., H. Afsarmanesh, M. Ollus. Virtual Organizations: Systems and Practices. Springer, Boston, 2005.
10. Campos, P. J. Organizational survival and the emergence of collaborative networks: a multi-agent approach. PhD Thesis, University of Porto, Faculty of Economy, 2007.
11. Hannan, M.; Freeman, J. The population ecology of organizations. American Journal of Sociology 1977; vol. 82: 929-964.
12. Hippel, E. Horizontal innovation networks – by and for users. MIT Sloan School of Management, 2002.
13. IMS. Proceedings of the IMS Vision Forum 2006 (B.-W. Choi, D. Nagy, Editors). IMS International. Seoul, Korea, 2006.
14. Myers, J. (2006). Future value systems: Next generation economic growth engines & manufacturing. In: Proc. of the IMS Vision Forum 2006 (B.-W. Choi, D. Nagy, Editors). IMS International. Seoul, Korea, 2006, pp 30-47.
15. Reichwald, R.; Seifert, S.; Walcher, D.; Piller, F. Customers as part of value webs: Towards a framework for webbed customer innovation tools. Technische Universitaet Muenchen, 2005.

NEW CHALLENGES IN COLLABORATIVE VIRTUAL FACTORY DESIGN

Stefano Mottura, Giampaolo Viganò, Luca Greci, Marco Sacco
Emanuele Carpanzano

Institute of Industrial Technologies and Automation
National Research Council, Milano, Italy
stefano.mottura@itia.cnr.it, giampaolo.vigano@itia.cnr.it,
luca.greci@itia.cnr.it, marco.sacco@itia.cnr.it,
emanuele.carpanzano@itia.cnr.it

The present paper describes the results of recent and ongoing major European projects about the virtual factory design topic, highlighting in particular new challenges related to the networked collaborative design of factories layout and configuration. A pilot factory for the production of customized shoes is referred to throughout the paper as application example of the proposed methods and tools.

1. INTRODUCTION

In recent years a relevant change in factory conception, design and optimisation is ongoing, i.e. the use of digital design in many different aspects of a "production/factory/system": the intensive use of digital models and simulations (numerical and visual, also real-time), the growth of digital and virtual prototyping as tools supporting the evaluation and decision making process before the real product is released, are techniques and processes becoming more and more part of the life of a "factory product". In this paper, within the above context, a project, lead by ITIA – CNR, is presented, aimed to develop an application framework based on 3D-realtime-interactive solutions for the networked collaborative design of new factories layouts.

2. PREVIOUS WORK

The virtual factory, conceived as a system that can be digitally simulated under various points of view, has been carried on by ITIA in previous years (Böer 1996, Sacco 2000, Carpanzano 2004). The first effort on such a theme has been the Manu*F*uturing project where a deep analysis on the main aspects of a factory to be digitally represented has been executed. Discrete event simulation was used to simulate models of the production coupled with a 3D immersive virtual environment as a new interface for creating the production layout (see Figure 1).

Please use the following format when citing this chapter:

Mottura, S., Viganò, G., Greci, L., Sacco, M. and Carpanzano, E., 2008, in IFIP International Federation for Information Processing, Volume 266, *Innovation in Manufacturing Networks*, ed. A. Azevedo; (Boston: Springer), pp. 17–24.

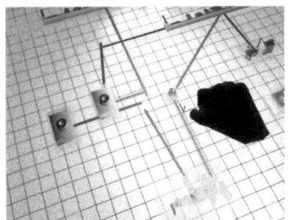

Figure 1. First example of virtual reality environment for factory layout design.

The virtual reality and advanced interfacing tools for editing the plant and/or factory layout has then been developed in the Modular Plant Architecture (MPA) Project, see also (Sacco 2004), where a more modular and enhanced designing environment was developed (see Figure 2 and Figure 3). In this new application the plant layout work was simulated by an external process simulator.

Figure 2. The virtual factory environment.

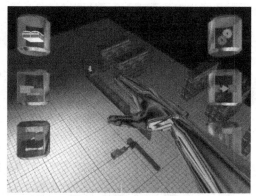

Figure 3. The user interface.

Another important step in the virtual factory design research was the simulation of the ITIA pilot factory for the customized shoes production in Vigevano, Italy (see also Sacco 2004, Carpanzano 2004). In this application the whole laboratory has been reproduced in 3D with a first-person navigation model (see Figure 4). Such an innovative factory allows consumers to order a personalized pair of shoes, different as for models, colours, materials and consumer's feet geometrical data. **Thus,** the main feature of the pilot factory is a high level of flexibility and reconfigurability. With the virtual environment the user can compose the production process by selecting the particular machines among the whole factory, as happens in real reconfiguration (see Figure 5). The movements of the machines and the flow of the semi-finished materials are simulated by an external process simulator. As shown in the figures, also the graphical quality of the environments has been enhanced, thanks to the rendering libraries developed at ITIA during last years.

Figure 4. Virtual factory of the ITIA-CNR pilot factory in Vigevano, Italy.

Figure 5. Production line configuration in the virtual factory environment.

Furthermore, the factory control system was developed through the support of digital facilities for the analysis, verification and optimisation of the automation functionalities, from the very first phases of the design life cycle (Carpanzano 2004, Carpanzano 2007). At the beginning of the design life cycle, the control and supervision system was specified by means of UML (Unified Modelling Language) diagrams; in particular use-case, class, sequence and state diagrams were used. The system architecture and functions were designed using the Function Block formalism defined by the IEC 61499 standard. The functional model obtained was analysed and optimized by means of discrete event simulations performed in the Simulink/Stateflow environment. When the functional modules had been verified, the control and supervision algorithms were developed using the SFC (Sequential Functional Chart) formalism. The SFC algorithms were analysed through closed loop dynamic simulations in the ISaGRAF environment in order to verify their correctness and to optimize their performance (Figure 6). In order to perform the closed loop simulations, simplified models of the plant devices have been represented by means of suitable SFC modules and data structures. Moreover, to simplify the analysis of the simulation results, a dedicated simple 2D graphic animation has been realized in ISaGRAF Simulations have been performed by considering typical operating conditions, i.e. typical production orders, and the results obtained show that the system is deadlock free and that the plant is well balanced, i.e. its resources are all used effectively. After the verification and optimization of the automation functions and algorithms the corresponding code was generated and implemented on the target industrial devices. Such simulation-based analysis techniques reduced the plant rump-up times and costs and improved overall system performance (Carpanzano 2007).

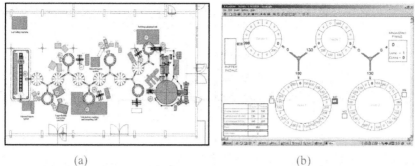

(a)   (b)

Figure 6. Layout of the Plant (a) and Simulation Graphical Interface (b).

3. THE DIFAC PROJECT

Currently, a new challenge in digital factory design is being faced: the virtual factory design within collaborative real-time networks. The idea is to invest the experiences of the past and ongoing researches by adding the feature of an environment for factory layout design in a shared networked framework. The presented ongoing research is part of the DiFac Project (www.difac.net).

The framework will be composed by a set of distributed personal computer (PC) workstations, on the PCs the factory being designed is visualized simultaneously by all different users. Just with this capability the users become participants of a networked meeting, by sharing the same virtual environment: they can interactively share the subject of their discussion and their work. The shared virtual environment allows to identify a PC as server and as leader of operations, and the other PCs as clients and active participants. The users acting on the server can manage and manipulate the virtual environment layout (that can be for example a line, a process or a whole factory) while the clients observe in real-time the proposed design and may suggest their modifications. While clients have the opportunity to modify the virtual layout, only the server has the rights to confirm and store permanently the work done during the meeting and all the related data. In this context, the set of data fields that describe a factory layout (3d models, textures, state of virtual objects, data of simulations and so on) will be called a *project*.

3.1. System architecture

Projects are stored in a database on the server and are composed by several data fields: name, identifier, original layout description, alternative layout descriptions, references to data of the virtual environment as 3d models, textures, simulation conditions and results. The core common to both server application and client application supports the following operations:

- visualize the list of available projects (the virtual layouts in progress),
- access to the representative data fields of a specific project,
- load the 3d virtual environment that represents a specific layout,
- interact with a specific layout: navigate, select and edit virtual entities.

The server retrieves data directly from the database and shares them over the network with all connected clients. So, while the server has a direct access to the database, the clients can deal with projects by interfacing though the server (see Figure 7). Let's remind here that the server is not intended merely as a database server.

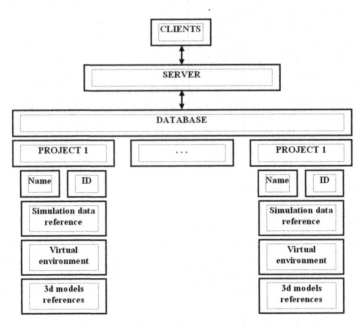

Figure 7. The server is the interface to access the projects database.

3.2. Session operation model

The execution of a collaborative virtual factory layout editing session is quite inspired to networked arcade real-time 3d games, like cars or motorbikes races. People join the game and every player sees who is connected; then, through dedicated communication channels (typically a chat embedded in the game) all the players agree on a specific circuit where to play the race (or, alternatively, the server imposes all its own decision). Afterwards, the game starts and all the players see and share interactively in real-time the same 3d race. With respect to this example, people join the shared virtual factory application and every person can see who is connected and, through dedicated communications (embedded chat, previous email and so on) all the people agree on a specific project to edit from a set of available project information broadcasted by the server. Then, the collaborative session starts, and all people can modify and propose their suggestions by acting in the same virtual environment.

With respect to the example of the cars race game (where every player runs by himself), in a project session all the players operate on the same objects and data. To do this in a coherent way, like in real human meetings, a player, before doing any operation in the virtual environment, should select the object to manage. The act of selecting locks the object for that player that has exclusive access to the object itself. The other players can see in real-time what it is happening on that object (or set of objects) in the virtual environment.

The behaviour of this logic is managed and maintained by the server application. When a client selects an object it sends to the server a request of exclusive ownership, the server receives it and checks if it is possible and then sends back the to the client the answer (see Figure 8). On the other side, relevant operations that can be done locally, and in an independent way, are the navigation in the virtual environment and project database consulting (always through the transparent interface of the server).

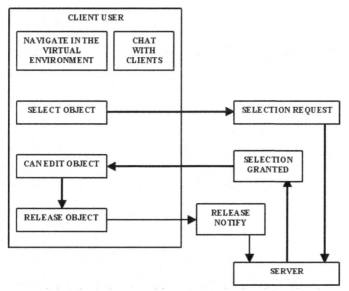

Figure 8. Collaborative logic protocol for accessing the shared virtual environment.

Once that a virtual layout is accepted by all participants, it can be saved into the database by the server side, thus it will be available for further editing for next sessions.

The selection mechanism is not the only logical operation managed by the server but it is the important one for managing an entity of the shared virtual environment. The other important behaviours handled by the server are:

- manage accesses to the underlying database of projects,
- manage the participations of a session: join/abandon; broadcast clients identificative information,
- manage potential clients limitations in the rights of editing virtual entities.

4. CONCLUSIONS

The framework under development presented in this paper is an example of integration and use of enabling technologies and techniques aimed to a collaborative virtual environment for virtual factory layout editing and design. The described platform adopts networking software techniques, virtual reality techniques, as well as collaborative means, and integrates them in a software unique application that, in the context of the DiFac Project, is aimed to the factory layout, but its potential concept obviously can be applied also in the important field of the collaborative networked product design and evaluation, where the "product" is just the object to be pushed into the market. Another relevant point is that, as for software modules and functionalities development, ITIA is managing and storing the functionalities in a programming library, that is an extension of existing ITIA's library for managing 3d real-time graphics, so that a base platform will be available and reusable for developing further shared virtual environments.

4.1. Acknowledgments

The work and research results described in this paper have been carried on by ITIA – CNR in the context of the following major projects:
Integrated Programme N° 507378 CEC-Made-Shoe "Custom, environment and comfort made shoe", 6 FP Priority IST- NMP (Manufacturing, Products and Service Engineering 2010);
EUROShoE Project, Contract G1RD-CT-2000-00343, Project N° GRD1-2000-25761; 5 FP Growth;
DiFac Project, Contract N° 035079, Digital Factory for Human-Oriented Production System, 6FP STREP.

5. REFERENCES

1. DiFac Project website: www.difac.net.
2. Sacco M, Mottura S, Greci L, Viganò G, Böer CR. "Experiences in virtual factory prototype: modular plants design and simulation". IFAC-MIM 2004, Conference on Manufacturing, Modelling, Management and Control, 2004.
3. Sacco M, Mottura S, Viganò G, Avai A, Böer CR. "Tools for the innovation: virtual reality and discrete events simulation to build the 2000 Factory". Proceedings of AMSMA 2000, pp. 458-462.
4. Böer CR, Jovane F. "Towards a new model of sustainable production: ManuFuturing". CIRP Annals STC O, 05/01/1996, pp. 415.
5. Carpanzano E. Cataldo A. Innovating Shoe Manufacturing using Advanced Simulation Techniques. ERCIM News. Special Theme: Industrial Diagnosis, Planning and Simulation 2004; N° 56: 22-23.
6. Carpanzano E., Jovane F. Advanced Automation Solutions for Future Adaptive Factories. Annals of the CIRP Vol. 56/1/2007.

03

FEELING THE PAIN: DISRUPTIVE INNOVATION IN HEALTHCARE MARKETS

David J Williams
Loughborough University, UK, d.j.williams@lboro.ac.uk
Oliver Wells
Association of British Healthcare Industries, UK, oliwells@aol.com
Paul Hourd
Loughborough University, UK, p.hourd@lboro.ac.uk
Amit Chandra
Loughborough University, UK, a.chandra@lboro.ac.uk

Healthcare is a growing market for products and services, costs are rising especially in the developed world. Disruptive innovations enable transition; less-skilled people do more sophisticated things in lower cost settings. In healthcare they promise to allow non-consumers new treatments reducing healthcare inequalities and ultimately to reduce the cost of individual treatments. A UK study shows adoption of such innovations is difficult because of the complexity of actors within the healthcare innovation network including clinical professionals, the supply chain, re-imbursement and regulatory agencies and healthcare service providers. Understanding cost containment in the overall system is key as is understanding the mechanisms and adoption conditions required to incentivise necessarily conservative service providers and clinical professionals with a busy, care driven agenda.

1. INTRODUCTION

There are many barriers to innovation in state-led healthcare systems including that of the UK: the busy care driven agenda of organizations and the individual; cost containment procurement strategies; the valley of death "chasm" between the early adopter and the early majority; the effect of regulation, clinical trials etc, etc,. This paper presents the perspective of a stakeholder group on the question "Can removing the barriers to the adoption of innovative technology – particularly disruptive technology – drive significant change in the NHS, the UK National Health Service, to the benefit of patients and to promote economic growth?". Consideration of this question should help to develop a better model for the creation of new products and consequently the introduction of a new technology into the NHS and other state healthcare systems and foster debate with healthcare commissioners about novel ways to overcoming the barriers to technology adoption including mechanisms for risk – clinical and commercial – and reward – "upside" – sharing with the supply side. Understanding innovation in a complex network is at the core of this discussion. This network is made up of users, healthcare professionals, industry and other suppliers, regulatory and reimbursement agencies including healthcare commissioners – each of which feels pain of a different form: physical, professional or financial, that drives them to innovate.

Please use the following format when citing this chapter:

Williams, D.J., Wells, O., Hourd, P. and Chandra, A., 2008, in IFIP International Federation for Information Processing, Volume 266, *Innovation in Manufacturing Networks;* ed. A. Azevedo; (Boston: Springer), pp. 25–34.

This keynote paper begins with an introduction to healthcare as a market in the UK context and innovation within healthcare with emphasis on the concept of disruptive innovation. The paper continues by reporting the results of an activity with a UK stakeholder group to determine a small number of interventions, based on a systemic view of the NHS and the other actors in the national innovation system, to encourage disruptive technologies that give opportunities for step changes in healthcare delivery performance and industry and economic growth.

2. BACKGROUND

2.1. Healthcare as a Market

Industry and business supplies healthcare delivery with the infrastructure, products and systems it requires. Healthcare is a growing market. In the western world it is important to recognize that the cost of healthcare delivery is rising, this is partially driven by changing patterns of demand, demographics, by the escalating costs of pharmaceuticals and the increasing costs of the opportunities of diagnostic instruments. These escalating costs demonstrate the scale and growth rate of the market, but bring with them the challenge of cost containment – rationing – and reducing operational costs. Regional inequalities in access to healthcare are also divisive – the western world has easy access to healthcare, this access is much more difficult in other less rich or privileged locations – this is also a challenge to business.

Healthcare is different from many other markets. The differences arise from the characteristics of the industry and its products and the range of professionals that work within it and the healthcare delivery system it serves. Two considerations shape the industry – products must be absolutely safe and ethical in their use – and much of the money that pays for them comes not from the patient that uses them, but from the healthcare system that pays the costs (the reimbursement system). The industry is carefully controlled by regulation and has to consider radical change thoroughly. People engaged in the industry come from the business and engineering professions, the life sciences including pharmacy, clinical practice and the caring professions. There are wide cultural differences between them, their backgrounds and their drivers. Business focuses on the market and finance reconciling complex conflicting objectives, engineers and physical scientists are driven to innovate in technology and have a quantitative approach, life scientists address complex biological science problems primarily from a qualitative viewpoint; clinicians and carers will always put patients – people – first.

2.2. The UK Context, the NHS and Innovation the NHS

The most significant healthcare provider in the UK is the National Health Service (NHS). The NHS was created in 1948 by the post war Labour government as the state system for the provision of healthcare with uniform, free access for all – a "universal service, based on clinical need, free at the point of delivery". Since then the NHS has grown to be one of the largest and most complex organizations in the world. There is also a complementary commercially oriented independent sector.

To the outsider and given the growing economic importance of healthcare this large and notionally integrated market place appears to be an ideal innovation opportunity for the UK economy and business to work with healthcare delivery to identify and create the new healthcare products both capable of success in world markets and of giving real patient benefit. This opportunity was formally recognized in the UK with the publication of the Cooksey Review (Cooksey, 2006).

Unfortunately innovation within this apparently favorable environment is not straight forward because of: the busy, care driven agenda of the organization and individuals; pressures on cost containment that drive procurement strategies to lowest cost, bulk buying and commoditization; continual policy and organizational churn as a consequence of political imperatives; capturing and communicating evidence and benefits across an organization of the scale and organizational complexity of the NHS; leadership and project management issues within a non-commercial care driven culture; the requirement to satisfy a regulator and for clinical trials or their equivalent; the larger than is usual "chasm" between the early adopter and the early majority as a consequence of the conservatism of clinicians and care delivery providers; as a consequence of industry structure, the significance of SMEs as technology providers to the innovation system; and the cultural gulf between industry and the NHS.

2.3. Disruptive Innovation

"Disruptive innovations enable a larger population of less-skilled people or providers with less training to do things in a more convenient, lower cost setting, which historically could only be done by specialists in less convenient settings" – Clay Christensen. (see Bower and Christensen 1995 and more particularly Christensen, Bohmer and Kenagy 2000).

Disruptive innovations are those that overturn apparently entrenched incumbent technologies. Innovations in the incumbent technologies have a product performance with time trajectory that begins to exceed the trajectory of the demand requirements of the customer. The incumbents then begin to be replaced by simpler cheaper, disruptive, innovations when the improvement trajectory of the disruptor allows its performance to match the lowest requirements of the demand. The most well known example of a disruptive technology in healthcare is less invasive medicine, particularly cardiac angioplasty and ultimately use of the stent (Hourd and Williams, 2007). Within the UK, Independent Sector Treatment Centres, which are commercially run, focused treatment centres operating in parallel to the mainstream NHS that take NHS patients, are another more service oriented instance of disruptive innovation. Disruptive technologies have three distinctive characteristics: they target non-consumers; they have a novel business model or value proposition and they drive out the incumbent in a niche where they deliver equivalent quality at a lower price.

Given the pressures on healthcare globally such approaches that have the potential to deliver radical benefits at lower cost and reduce inequalities are *very* attractive. As we will see, however, because disruptive innovations primarily target non-consumers, they will frequently increase overall system costs, while this is acceptable in purely commercial circumstances, it is harder to accommodate in an essentially finite resource state system – there are no paying customers to drive change in state run health organizations.

3. RESEARCH METHOD

As indicated above disruptive technologies are anticipated to give opportunities for step changes in healthcare delivery performance and industry and economic growth. The object of the work was to deliver a stakeholder endorsed multi-perspective "Think Piece" – essentially this document – in order to promote and inform debate and identify areas that demand more attention. The stakeholders comprised a steering group that met three times in a workshop environment and a reading group to whom documents were circulated (group members are listed in the acknowledgements). The work is based on a systemic view of the NHS and the other actors in the national innovation system and attempts to build upon a virtuous circle linking improved healthcare delivery to requirements driven technology innovation. The work was process focused and did not attempt technology foresight or road mapping or address issues associated with professional practice. The work was presented for final review at the NHS Institute Conference at the Wellcome Trust on 5th November 2007.

4. SUMMARY OF KEY RESULTS

The results of the activity fall into four key areas: cost, price and value, system cost and value; the innovation process including risk and reward sharing; requirements capture and ideas generation; and forces on disruptive innovations.

4.1. Cost, Price and Value, System Cost and Value

A simple "Boston Box" for cost and quality as used in health economics when considering product price, Figure 1, is helpful in considering some of the micro-economic aspects of the innovation process.

The "box" helpfully defines areas where the case for technology has to be made (higher quality with higher cost); a "magic kingdom" of "no-brainer" decisions (higher quality and lower cost) and the "danger zone" of lower quality and lower cost. Making the case can be easier for new and radical technologies in the independent sector. This immediately identifies some of the challenges that the state system faces.

Importantly there is a perception that the national current commercial approach is pushing the NHS into the "danger zone" and that the NHS/healthcare delivery not benefiting as quickly as it should from products in the "magic kingdom". Underlying this is the recognition that disruptive technologies that have particularly targeted non-consumers lead to increasing demand that can increase total system cost – and improve welfare – even if the technology is cost effective and of equivalent quality. This can be moderated by commercial demands for market share and consequent economies of scale leading to lower costs, and more careful consideration of system value through the life cycle. Total system cost increase may be moderated if resource is released by the substitution of the incumbent.

Technology adoption, diffusion and substitution is an intensely dynamic process. Importantly for the healthcare provider substitution and adoption requires the provision of two concurrent services and this is likely to favour the incumbent. Demand for the new technology or service may also be throttled by requirements for trials or post market surveillance. Consequently disruptive services must be introduced in partnership and show cost down and efficiency gains within a good understanding of capacity requirements. Training is key to effectiveness and reducing costs.

It is also important to recognise that legacy services within the system that have been impacted by the introduction of disruptive approaches will have to redefine their value proposition (for instance they may provide notionally the same service as the new alternative but actually deliver it to patients of multiple pathologies) to command increases in reimbursement tariff. System value must be the goal. As Porter and Tiesburg, 2006, has emphasised competing on results and value is the only alternative to shifting cost and limiting services - a zero-sum competition where one actor's gain is a loss for another. Silo thinking is not helpful!

4.2. The Innovation Process

A simple model of the innovation process (Figure 2) is also helpful in bringing a number of issues to the surface. This model of the process recognizes the iterative nature of much healthcare technology development and that there are two dominant perspectives; that of the healthcare delivery system and that of business. It also highlights: the use phase; the identification of requirements from the use phase; the resourcing of the innovation process by multiple stakeholders – the risk and reward sharing process; the technology realization phase; and the healthcare assessment phase followed by adoption. In such systems ideas generation and requirements capture is complex and technology creation often comes from integrating several underpinning technologies which are emerging in parallel with different drivers. Comparative evaluation is complex, it must take place with the correct data and stakeholders including clinical benefit, regulation, reimbursement and purchasing; and take account of adoption conditions and definitions of quality, effectiveness and cost. Navigation of the regulatory pathways requires business to have access to a library of regulatory issues and signposting to experts. Note that it is considered that international regulation always favours the incumbent technologies.

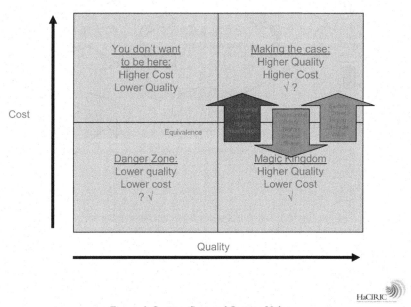

Figure 1. System Cost and System Value

It should also be noted that technology forms only a part of the innovation and that adoption requires matching all the acceptance criteria of the key stakeholders. Disruptive technologies involve much wider interactions than incremental changes. Users and beneficiaries will not be familiar with the technology. New skills may be required and supporting people may need retraining. There will be a lack of background knowledge of risks and benefits and the best ways to use the technology. Commercial organisations will also have to re-orientate their staff to sell and support the new technology.

Feedback, attrition and building the evidence base takes place as the innovation cycles around the process. A major issue within the UK is the incentivisation of health professionals to participate in all of the process cycle.

A key issue that must be recognized here is that, for business, the state national healthcare system, while large, is only part of the world market. Resourcing the innovation process and sharing financial risk and resource is complex with multiple actors including clinicians, industry; government; academics; venture and other commercial sources of funding and ultimately users (Hourd and Williams, 2006, 2008). It is clear that, even for UK based multinationals, the relative value of access to the NHS when compared with access to US clinical practice, is not sufficiently high. It is also clear that it is problematic for SMEs, especially potentially disruptive SMEs, to access the NHS (Hourd and Williams, 2008).

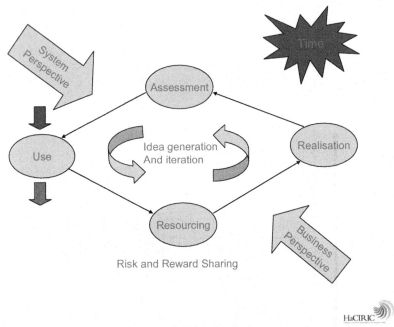

Figure 2. A simple model of the innovation process

To move forward on risk and reward sharing between industry and healthcare delivery we have to understand the commercial value of access/early access to the NHS and manage any risks of early access. Commissioning of health services should be a mechanism to incentivise innovation and may be able to address some of these issues. Disruptive technologies will require an improved understanding of the relationship between technology and service assessment processes and commissioning and reimbursement. This is just one instance of the "silo" based behaviour characteristic of large organisations that prevents actions that lead to better system value.

4.3. Requirements Capture and Ideas Generation

There are many sources for healthcare technology innovations. Some come from the inspiration of an inventor and their invention; some from an engineering tradition of problem solving. Some come from the user who has been personally touched by a healthcare problem or tragedy; some come from the healthcare professional and their demand for a more efficient tool to improve a clinical pathway; and some come from the healthcare provider and their requirement for reduced costs and service reconfiguration or a requirement to respond to the latest imperative from government. It all depends on who is feeling the pain and the kind of pain that they are feeling!

Figure 3 tries to capture some of the sources of innovations and the techniques, such as roadmapping, that might lead to a more systematic perspective on requirements capture balancing technology push with the identification of unmet needs. It is clear that the involvement of knowledge, practice and problem led healthcare professionals is required to ensure that innovations reflect a true projection of the current technology and requirements trajectory (Chatterji and Fabrizio, 2007). Given our earlier comments on incentivisation of health professionals, this involvement requires addressing in the current UK system.

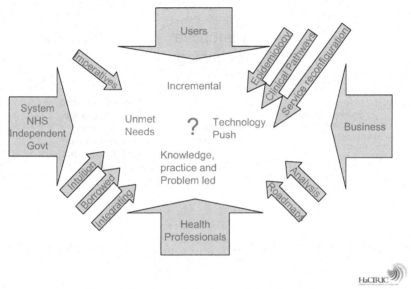

Figure 3. Requirements Capture and Ideas Generation

4.4. Forces on Disruptive Innovations

Figure 4 shows that the introduction of a disruptive technology requires the tensioning of four forces: the reaction force from the displaced technology and its suppliers; competitive pressures on the system and suppliers that drive innovation and invention; and user needs and benefits. It is intuitive that a focus on meeting user needs will stimulate improvement in performance and value. Clearly the tensioning of the four forces and the necessary responses will be associated with the level of disruption of the innovation, methods are therefore required to assess the disruptiveness of a technology in order to develop strategies to assist its adoption.

5. CONCLUSIONS

This paper has identified a number of key issues in a testing instance of innovation in networks. Disruptive technology adoption is dynamic, as are costs. Technology introduction alone is not sufficient, systems must change, these changes must happen in partnership to realize efficiency gains. For healthcare, targeting non- consumers delivers reduced inequality but inevitably drives up system cost even with lower product costs. This has two consequences: the requirement to consider the value of a technology through the whole system and lifecycle and the requirement for the incumbent technology or service to redefine its value proposition when challenged.

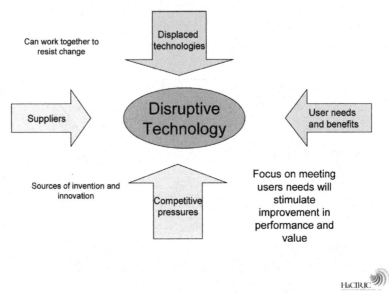

Figure 4. Disruptive Technology Forces

While there are a number of UK initiatives to promote heath technologies for patient benefit including the NHS Institute for Innovation and Improvement with its integral The National Innovation Centre, the Innovation Hubs (charged with exploiting innovations from within the health service) and the Adoption hub (charged with rolling out key promising innovations nationally), this analysis of the process of disruptive technology introduction in UK healthcare and particularly the NHS identifies some key areas for increased focus to prepare the ground for potential paradigm shifts:

- the creation of a process for the timely identification and quantification of realistic unmet needs;
- personal and organizational incentives (or perhaps reduced dis-incentives) to ensure continued involvement of clinical professionals in the whole of the innovation process;
- tools to profile the behaviors of key actors who are involved in adoption, and the development of matching strategies to overcome them;
- and, determining mechanisms for risk and reward sharing in the early introduction of technologies between the supply side and the NHS.

Access to the NHS for small and medium enterprises, SMEs, can be problematic and multinationals rarely see sufficient value from early access to the NHS and target other markets first. To move forward on risk and reward sharing we have to improve mutual understanding of the commercial value of access/early access to the NHS. This should form a core part of the evolution and realization of the healthcare service commissioning process to encourage and support the uptake of innovative technologies that are clinically effective and cost effective, a major topic of national debate, and current activities in the mapping of clinical value chains. This must include the impact of potentially increased system costs as a consequence of disruptive innovations that target non-consumers.

A recent review prepared by the HaCIRIC team at Imperial College (Barlow et al, 2007) on innovation diffusion and adoption processes in healthcare highlights that implementation is especially difficult when it changes the pattern of interdependence amongst individuals or groups and involves organizational and process change, this is inevitable with disruptive innovation. Complexity arises from the organization and its leadership; the organizational capacity and readiness for change; negotiation, power, micro-politics and local contexts; and evidence, risk and reward, perception and organizational norms. It also identifies orthodox micro-economic perspectives on innovation, such as ours here, ignore politics and power and the requirement to understand and incentivise dramatic, system level, innovation. This is another key area for focus in the future.

5.1. Acknowledgments

This work has been funded by the UK Engineering and Physical Sciences Research Council and forms part of the work of the Health and Care Infrastructure Innovation Research Centre, HaCIRIC, a collaboration of Imperial College and Loughborough, Reading and Salford Universities.

The work was carried out in collaboration with a stakeholder group, the Association of British Healthcare Industries (ABHI) and the UK NHS National Innovation Centre, part of the NHS Institute for Innovation and Improvement. Members of the stakeholder group included Richard Archer, Two BC; Chris Bantock and Bill Maton-Howarth, Department of Health; John Bessant, Imperial College; Clive Bray, MHRA; Kathryn Brown, BERR; Keith Chantler, Colin Morgan and Margaret Parton, Adoption Hub; Andrew Clark and Helen Hunt, EPSRC; Mike Craven and Steve Morgan, Nottingham University; Tony Davies, Medilink WM; Melanie Evans, Re:source Hub; Mark Fisher, Exomedica; Merlin Goldman, Technology Strategy Board; Michelle Hill-Perkins, Partnerships UK; Gareth Lloyd Jones, Medilink Yorkshire and Humberside; Geoff Morris, Medtronic; Clare Packer, Birmingham University; Tim Rubidge, Training Hub for Operative Technologies in Healthcare; Maire Smith and Brian Winn, NHS NIC; Mark Wickham, Smith and Nephew; John Wilkinson, ABHI; and Aniko Zaigon, Medicogen. We would like to thank this group for their active participation in discussions and review of documents. We would also like to thank Immanuel Sebastine for his help in the final reporting of this work.

6. REFERENCES

1. Barlow J and The Imperial College HaCIRIC Team with Chiu K, Innovation diffusion and adoption processes in healthcare – a review of the Literature, Tanaka Business School Imperial College Internal Working Paper, December 2007.
2. Bower JL Christensen CN, Disruptive Technologies, Catching the Wave, Harvard Business Review 1995; Jan-Feb: 43-53.
3. Chatterji AK, Fabrizio K, Professional Users as a Source of Innovation: The Role of Physician Innovation in the Medical Device Industry, Working Paper Fuqua and Emory Business Schools, July 2007.
4. Christensen CN, Bohmer R, Kenagy J, Will. Disruptive Innovations Cure Healthcare?. Harvard Business Review 2000; Sept-Oct: 102-111.
5. Cooksey D. A review of UK health research funding. HM Treasury Report. 2006, online at http://www.hm-treasury.gov.uk/independent_reviews/cooksey_review/cookseyreview_index.cfm.
6. Hourd PC, Williams DJ. Disruption in Healthcare, Angioplasty: An instance of disruptive innovation. Healthcare Engineering Working Paper RGC/74.1/07, 2007.
7. Hourd PC, Williams DJ. Success in Healthcare Technology Businesses: Coordination of the Value Milestones of New Product Introduction, Financial Stakeholders and Business Growth., Innovation: Management , Policy and Practice 2006; Volume 8(3): 229-247.
8. Hourd PC, Williams DJ, Results from an Exploratory Study to Identify the Factors that Contribute to Success for UK Medical Device Small & Medium Sized Enterprises. Journal of Engineering in Medicine, Part H, 2008 (*in press*).
9. Porter ME, Teisberg EO, Redefining Healthcare: Creating Value-Based Competition on Results. Harvard Business School Press, 2006.

PART 1

COLLABORATIVE NETWORKS

04

TOWARDS A METHODOLOGY TO MEASURE THE ALIGNMENT OF VALUE SYSTEMS IN COLLABORATIVE NETWORKS

António Abreu, Patrícia Macedo, L.M. Camarinha-Matos
New University of Lisbon
Quinta da Torre – 2829-516 Monte Caparica, PORTUGAL
ajfa@fct.unl.pt, pmacedo@est.ips.pt, cam@uninova.pt,

As networks are typically formed by heterogeneous and autonomous entities, it is natural that each member has its own set of values. As a result, the ability to quickly identify partners with compatible or common values represents an important element for the success of collaborative networks. However, tools to measure the level of alignment are lacking. Applying some soft modeling tools, this paper discusses some perspectives and criteria to measure the level of alignment among a set of members in the context of a VO breeding environment.

1. INTRODUCTION

A number of requirements are needed to create successful collaborative coalitions, including: sharing of goals among members, having some level of mutual trust, having created some common infrastructures, and having agreed, totally or partially, on some practices and values.

Conciliating different organizational values is a challenge faced by collaborating organizations in our days. In general, the structure of a value system, and therefore the drivers of the Collaborative Networked Organizations' (CNO) behavior, includes multiple variables / aspects. Complementarily there are other elements that strongly influence or determine the behavior of a CNO and its members, such as the schema of incentives, trust building and management mechanisms, ethical code, the CNO culture, and the contracts and collaboration agreements.

Since collaborative networks are typically formed by heterogeneous and autonomous entities, it is natural that each member has its own set of values, and thus conflicts among partners might emerge due to existence of values *misalignment* (Abreu,2006). On the other hand, it is often assumed that the alignment between values systems of members involved in collaborative processes is a pre-requisite for a successfully co-working. However, the concept of alignment of value systems is difficult to define. Nevertheless, it can be intuitively understood that when the values of one member are incompatible with the values of another, there is a misalignment and the potential for conflicts is high. When the values of a member are compatible with the values of another member, there is an alignment and the potential for emergence of conflicts is lower.

The existence of a total alignment does not imply the total elimination of conflicts. An assessment of the level of alignment thus rather implies that the causes for conflicts are better understood and thus mechanisms may be designed for the progressive resolution of

Please use the following format when citing this chapter:

Abreu, A., Macedo, P. and Camarinha-Matos, L.M., 2008, in IFIP International Federation for Information Processing, Volume 266, *Innovation in Manufacturing Networks;* ed. A. Azevedo; (Boston: Springer), pp. 37–46.

problems. Consequently, the level of alignment might work as a predictive indicator of the potential level for collaboration and also the capacity that a coalition has for getting agreements when conflicts take place during a collaborative process. The ability to quickly identify partners with a strong alignment represents an important boosting element for successful coalition formation.

Furthermore, the measurement of the level of alignment depends on the criteria that are used. In fact, there are several aspects that must be considered when we try to measure the level of alignment between two value systems. In some contexts, the alignment can be related to the existence of common values, level of shared interests or aims (ethical principles, business practices, etc...). On the other hand, there are some cases in which the level of alignment must be related to the existence of complementary values, relations among values, etc.

As the measurement of the level of alignment depends on several aspects that have an imprecise description, the adoption of soft modeling perspectives and techniques seem promising. Therefore, this paper suggests some perspectives to measure and analyze the level of alignment between value systems in a CNO context based on soft modeling techniques.

2. SOME BACKGROUND

In psychology and sociology *values* have typically been conceptualized as shared beliefs about desired behaviors and end-states, as in (Rokeach,1973). These shared beliefs concern the processes of goal pursuit and outcomes. Merton advocates that cultural objectives of an organizational unit are the "Things worth striving for" - what has outcome value in the culture (Merton,1957). *Value* has also been defined as the "relative worth, utility, or importance: degree of excellence". This definition of *value* highlights the fact that object's value depends on the "standard" that is used in the evaluation. Depending on the standard, the same object will be evaluated differently. The set of values hold by an individual or society define its *value system*.

This concept of value system has been studied and applied by diverse researchers. The philosopher Robert Hartman developed a formal Axiology, that is a branch of axiology (axiology is a general theory/science of human values, their origins, interrelations and dynamics) that attempt to use mathematical formalism to define *values* and *value systems*. Hartman (Hartman,1973) first defined the concept of value in terms of a logic-based axiom stating that *value* can be objectively determined according to a one-to-one correspondence between the properties of a given object and the meaning specifications contained in its concept. An object has value to the degree it fulfills its concept (Mefford,1997). Hartman introduced also the concept of *dimension of value* and developed the basic axioms for this concept. He defines three dimensions for value: Systematic Value, Extrinsic Value and Intrinsic Value. Hartman defends that the foundation concepts of axiology provide the framework for understanding an object's value and its valuations in precise terms of the three dimensions and their relationships to each other.

Goguen et Linde have developed, since 1978, several studies about value and value system in organizations (Goguen,2003) They proposed a method for using discourse analysis to determine a value system for an organization from a collection of stories told by members of the organization among themselves on informal occasions. The evaluative material collected from the stories is classified and represented using a formal structure called a *value system tree*. A value system tree serves as a formal summary of the interpretation that the analysts made from the collected data.

Another contribution to the study of values systems came from the Distributed Artificial Intelligence discipline, where some theories where developed using agents. (Filipe, 2003) proposed an approach based on organizational agents where it is assumed that an agent is responsible for its values. The agent's preferences with respect to norms are defined in its value system, using deontic logic. In this approach an agent can represent a member of an organization or an organization itself. Another work (Woods,2003) proposed the use of par consistent logic to reason over values.

Gordijn, Yao-Huan Tan and Kartseva (Gordijn,2000), (Tan,2004), (Kartseva,2004) have developed a methodology and an ontology called e3-value in order to define *value models* that support the business processes. The e3-value model was developed to support e-commerce business and is essentially focused on the economic value of objects and on activities and actors that create economic value.

Both perspectives of value systems (economic and socio-psychological) are relevant to performance management in collaborative networks, as discussed in (Macedo,2006). In essence the economic perspective provides a transaction mechanism between partners, assuring an equality utility between objects exchanged, and the psychosocial perspective provides a regulation mechanism to ensure social cohesion, to avoid and solve conflicts and to build performance indicators.

3. METHODOLOGY ADOPTED TO MEASURE THE LEVEL OF VALUE SYSTEM'S ALIGNMENT IN A VBE CONTEXT

The existence of a *VO breeding environment* (VBE) is assumed at the basis of the following discussion. A VBE represents an association or pool of organizations and their related supporting institutions that have both the potential and the will to collaborate with each other through the establishment of a "base" long-term cooperation agreement. Whenever a business opportunity is identified by one member (acting as a broker) a subset of these organizations can be selected and thus forming a VO. Various VOs can coexist at the same time in the context of a VBE. A breeding environment, being a long-term networked structure, presents the adequate base environment for the establishment of collaboration agreements, common infrastructures, common ontologies, and mutual trust, which are the necessary facilitating elements when building a new VO (Camarinha-Matos,2003), (Camarinha-Matos,2004). Furthermore, a sustainable VBE should have defined a common value system that "guides" its behavior as a whole. In other words, VBE represents a group of organizational entities that have developed some *preparedness* for collaboration, in case a specific opportunity arises. Industry *clusters* or industry districts are examples of such breeding environments.

In this context, a low level of alignment of the value systems of individual members of the VBE is likely to constitute an obstacle for the sustainability of the collaboration, namely in the case of incompatible values. It is therefore important to develop tools that allow estimating the level of alignment of value systems, from different perspectives, for all members. Considering the nature of the concepts here involved, a combination of various "soft modeling" approaches is suggested, as suggested, as shown in Fig. 1.

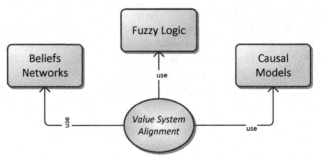

Figure 1. Suggested soft modeling techniques

The **Causal Models** approach can be applied to analyze the relations of influence between values (Greenland,2002). Based on this approach the level of alignment can be measured in terms of the structural similarity or inter-relationships between Value Systems.

Fuzzy Logic is considered to allow different degrees of inclusion/relevance of each element in a given set (Berthold,2003), it means to allow one element to belong to a given set with a bigger or smaller intensity, also known as degree of membership or degree of truth. Fuzzy reasoning also provides methods to "assemble" partial information, so in this case the partial information about compatible values and incompatible values is used in order to reason about the alignment between Value Systems.

Belief Networks capture relations (which may be uncertain, ambiguous, or imprecise) between a set of variables. Based on the set of states that each variable can have and its belief level (prior probability) it is possible to infer how the prior probability is updated by new data items (Jensen, 1996).

In this case, Beliefs Networks will be used to infer if the values of one partner, based on past behaviors, are aligned with the expected values of another partner.

4. MODELING EXAMPLES AND RESULTS

Since the concept of "alignment" is still ill-defined and shows a multifaceted nature, there are several aspects that can be considered when we try to measure the level of alignment between two value systems. In this paper we discuss three perspectives of alignment:

- *Perspective 1* - Type of relations among values.
- *Perspective 2* - Level of compatibility and incompatibility between value systems.
- *Perspective 3* - Members' past behaviors.

Perspective 1
In collaborative processes, the type of relationships between values can be seen as the seed and ingredient of a successfully co-working. Considering the premises that a member's behavior depends on:

- the way its main values are related, and/or
- potential partners having strategic values that make it consider as advantageous collaborating with them (i.e. values that provide positive impact on its own values).

Under this assumption the level of alignment could be measured in terms of the structural similarity or impact inter-relationships between value systems. For this purpose causal models can be used to model relationships among values.

In order to illustrate this idea, let us consider the following cases:

Case 1. Let us suppose there are two members in a VO, each one possessing a specific set of main values. Applying causal models the inter-relationship among values could be established and then for each causal model drawn a matrix of influence among values can be defined as shown in Figure 2.

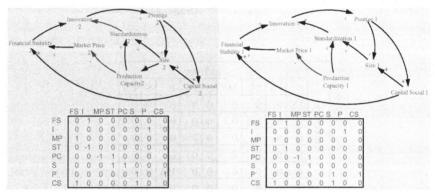

	FS	I	MP	ST	PC	S	P	CS
FS	0	1	0	0	0	0	0	0
I	0	0	0	0	0	0	1	0
MP	1	0	0	0	0	0	0	0
ST	0	-1	0	0	0	0	0	0
PC	0	0	-1	1	0	0	0	0
S	0	0	0	1	1	0	0	0
P	0	0	0	0	0	1	0	1
CS	1	0	0	0	0	1	0	0

	FS	I	MP	ST	PC	S	P	CS
FS	0	1	0	0	0	0	0	0
I	0	0	0	0	0	0	1	0
MP	1	0	0	0	0	0	0	0
ST	0	1	0	0	0	0	0	0
PC	0	0	-1	1	0	0	0	0
S	0	0	0	1	0	0	0	0
P	0	0	0	0	0	1	0	1
CS	1	0	0	0	0	1	0	0

Figure 2. Influence relationships among values

Applying the concept of Euclidean distance we can consider the level of alignment as a metric of structural equivalence. According to this perspective the level of alignment is total if the two value systems are structurally equivalent. In this case the entries in the respective rows and columns of each matrix will be identical, and thus the Euclidean distance between them will be equal to 0. On the other hand, if they are not structurally equivalent, the level of alignment decreases with the increase of the Euclidian distance.

However, this "understanding" of alignment fails when two actors, although having several common values, they believe only one can maximize its common values through a collaborative process. As such no collaborative process can emerge based on these values. In these cases, other criteria must be used, such as based on impacts between values as discussed in case 2.

Case 2. Let us suppose two members identified their sets of values and, by applying causal models they defined the impact inter-relationships between value systems. Based on these relations each one builds a matrix of impacts. Figure 3 illustrates the inter-relationships between values of two members and the matrix of impacts from the perspective of the industry member. In this example, the level of knowledge of the university can have a (positive) impact on the technological capacity of the industry when they collaborate.

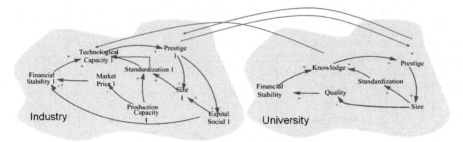

Industry

University

		Industry							
		FS	TC	MP	S	PC	P	S	CS
University	FS	0	0	0	0	0	0	0	0
	K	0	I22	0	0	0	0	0	0
	Q	0	0	0	0	0	0	0	0
	S	0	0	0	0	0	0	0	0
	P	0	0	0	0	0	I56	0	0
	S	0	0	0	0	0	0	0	0

Figure 3. Impact inter-relationships between values systems

Based on this perspective, there is high level of alignment and a potential motivation to collaborate if the sum of impacts is positive and large. On the other hand, if the sum of impacts is null or negative the level of alignment is weak.

Perspective 2
Let us suppose there are two members in a VO, each one of them possessing its own set of main values as illustrated in Fig. 4.

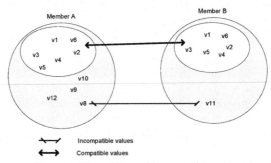

Figure 4. Compatible and incompatible values

As the perceptions of compatible and incompatible values are qualitative and deal with imprecise quantities, one approach is to apply fuzzy logic concepts. Fuzzy Logic can provide methods to "assemble" or reason about the partial information about compatible and incompatible values in order to reason about the alignment level of the value system of two members.

In order to illustrate how fuzzy logic can be applied in this scenario, let us consider the following table:

Table 1. An example

Member A in relation to B	Compatible Values	Incompatible Values	Indifferent Values	Total Number of Values
Total	6	1	3	10
Percentage	60%	10%	30%	100%

The concepts of Incompatible Values, Compatible Values and Alignment Level are modeled in a fuzzy way as shown in the Fig. 5. The two variables being analyzed can belong to various fuzzy sets with distinct membership degrees. For instance, 60% of the number of Compatible Values would be classified as "a lot" with membership of 0.6, and as "most" with membership of 0.4.

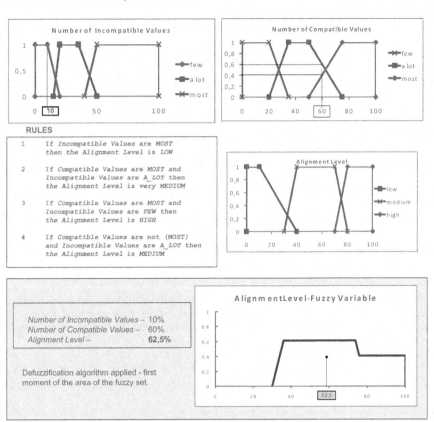

Figure 5. Fuzzy inference process

The Fig. 5 shows a simplified illustration of a fuzzy inference process which is composed of:

- **Fuzzification process** - Operation through which numeric values are translated into fuzzy sets. In this example there are two cases of fuzzification: *Compatible-Values* and *Incompatible-Values*, both modeled by a membership function as it is shown in the figure.

▪ **Fuzzy Inference**– Application of a set of inference rules. In this illustrative scenario, the inference rule associated is of the form: IF *Compatible Values* are ....AND *Incompatible Values* are ... THEN the *Alignment level* is .... Four inference rules were defined for illustrative purposes.

▪ **Defuzzification process** - Operation through which the output linguistic value, induced by the fuzzy inference is translated into a numeric value (Moment defuzzification algorithm was applied) (Kosko,1997). In this example, this operation is modeled by the membership function *Alignment-Level* as shown in the Figure 5.

In this example the alignment level calculated by the fuzzy inference process is 62% and resulted from the execution of the rules 3 and 4.

Perspective 3

Let us assume that it is possible to establish a connection between past and future behaviors, the behavior of an actor is related with its value system and no explicit representation of the value system is available.

Based on this perspective, the level of alignment can be "measured" through an inference process applying belief networks. In order to illustrate how belief networks can be applied in a VBE context, let us consider the following assumptions:

• There are records of members' past behavior at the VBE management level.
• The partners behavior is explained in terms of a set of values previously defined (principles or qualities considered worthwhile or desirable). There are a finite number of possible values that can describe a partner's behavior. For instance:

  Partner behavior = < Quality, Prestige, Lead time>

• There are a finite number of possible states associated to each value that can be chosen to measure the value.
• Each value can have a set of states and its belief level (prior probability) is expressed in terms of percentage based on past cooperative behaviors.

Let us assume an enterprise B needs to establish a network where Quality and Lead Time are two strategic values. In order to avoid undesirable partners, it is important to identify members that have a strong alignment with it (according to B's evaluation) in relation to these two values.

Based on past experiences with others partners in collaborative processes, when an enterprise B identifies another one that considered quality and lead time as strategic values, the probability that such partner in the future adopts these values as strategic, according to the beliefs of B, is 90% (prior probabilities) as shown in table 2.

Based on past records an enterprise A exhibited the following behavior in terms of quality:

• 60% of the times is considered a strategic value
• 40% of the times is considered an irrelevant value;
  and, in terms of lead time:
• 70% of the times is considered a strategic value
• 30% of the times are considered an irrelevant value.

Table 2. Beliefs of B based on past experiences

Values		Level of Alignment		
Quality	Lead Time	Strong	Medium	Low
Strategic	Strategic	0,9	0,1	0
	Irrelevant	0,6	0,3	0,1
Irrelevant	Strategic	0,2	0,5	0,3
	Irrelevant	0,2	0,3	0,5

Applying Belief Networks for these two values, enterprise B can infer the Level of Alignment in relation to partner A, as shown in Figure 6.

Base on the available data, the enterprise B infers there is a probability of 56,6% that A will adopt a behavior that considers both values strategic.

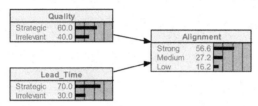

Figure 6. Alignment level inference

5. CONCLUSIONS

The measurement of the alignment level of value systems can be a useful instrument to the VBE manager, to a VO broker, and to a VBE member. This indicator can be determined for a particular collaboration process (a particular VO occurrence) or over a period of time (average values) and can be used in decision-making processes, such as the planning of a new VO. However the concept of "alignment" can have different interpretations. Therefore, various perspectives have been discussed, using different soft modeling approaches.

Some benefits of the proposed modeling approaches can be summarized as:

- The causal models are easy to understand and useful for describing in a simplified way the value system (its structure and cause-effect relations), and using simple calculus it is possible to reason about the level of alignment.
- The belief networks and fuzzy logic models have the advantage of dealing well with imprecise and partial information.
- The fuzzy logic models allow measuring the level of alignment through a linguistic form.
- The belief networks can be useful to predict the level of alignment based on past behaviors.

However, the proposed models also carry some limitations such as:

- For large problems, the collection of information to build a model can be very difficult.
- The models are not easy to maintain and modify if proper tools are not available.
- In case of causal models, if there are many interdependencies between values the calculation becomes very time consuming.
- In real application, belief networks demand a record of past behavior that might not be available.

Furthermore, to reason about the value system alignment other approaches might be useful, such as two-sorted logic, par consistent logics, and dynamic systems. Consequently the development of methodologies to measure the value systems alignment in collaborative networks still requires further work. Some preliminary steps in this direction were presented and initial results illustrate the applicability of the suggested approach.

5.1. Acknowledgments

This work as supported in part by the ECOLEAD integrated project funded by the European Commission.

6. REFERENCES

1. Abreu A, Camarinha-Matos LM. "On the Role of Value Systems and Reciprocity in Collaborative Environments". In Network-Centric Collaboration and Supporting Frameworks, Spring, ed. IFIP, Volume 224: Boston Springer, 2006.
2. Berthold MR. Intelligent Data Analysis: An Introduction. Springer, 2003.
3. Camarinha-Matos LM, Afsarmanesh (Ed.s) H. Collaborative Networked Organizations - A research agenda for emerging business models: Kluwer Academic Publishers, 2004.
4. Camarinha-Matos LM, Afsarmanesh H. "Elements of a VE base infrastructure". J. Computers in Industry 2003;51:139-163.
5. Filipe J. "The organizational semeiotics normative paradigm". In Collaborative Networked Organizations. London: Springer, 2003: 261-272.
6. Goguen J. "Semiotics, compassion and value-centered design". In Keynote lecture, in Proceedings of the Organizational Semiotics Workshop, University of Reading; UK, 2003.
7. Gordijn J, J.M. Akkermans, Vliet JCv. "Value based requirements creation for electronic commerce applications". In 33rd Hawaii International Conference on System Sciences; Hawai, 2000.
8. Greenland S, Brumback B. "An overview of relations among causal modeling methods". International journal of epidemiology, 2002.
9. Hartman R. The Measurement of Value. In; 1973, 1973.
10. Kartseva V, Gordijn J, Akkermans H. "A Design Perspective on Networked Business Models: A Study of Distributed Generation in the Power Industry Sector". In 12th European Conference on Information Systems; 2004.
11. Kosko B. Fuzzy Engineering. New Jersey: Prentice Hall, 1997.
12. Macedo P, Sapateiro C, Filipe J. "Distinct Approaches to Value Systems in Collaborative Networks Environments". In Network-Centric Collaboration and Supporting Frameworks: Springer Boston, 2006: 111-120.
13. Mefford D, Meffortd V. Values Usage Exercise (VUE) A Tool For Raising Values Awareness Concerning The Professional - Personal Values Interface. In: Conference on Professional Ethics. WASHINGTON, 1997.
14. Merton RK. Social Theory and Social Structure. The Free Press 1957;3.
15. Rokeach M. The nature of human values. New York: Free Press. 1973.
16. Tan Y-H, Thoen W, Gordijn J. "Modeling Controls for Dynamic Value Exchange in Virtual Organizations". In Berlin S, ed. Trust Management, 2004: 236-250.
17. Woods J. Paradox and Para consistency: Conflict Resolution in the Abstract Sciences. Cambridge: Cambridge University Press, 2003.

05

READINESS FOR COLLABORATION ASSESSMENT APPROACH IN COLLABORATIVE NETWORKED ORGANISATIONS

David Romero[1], Nathalie Galeano[1], Arturo Molina[2]

[1]*CIDYT - ITESM Campus Monterrey, Monterrey, Mexico*
david.romero.diaz@gmail.com, ngaleano@itesm.mx
[2]*VIDT - ITESM Campus Monterrey, Monterrey, Mexico*
armolina@itesm.mx

Collaboration is essential to develop successful Collaborative Networked Organizations (CNOs). In order to know if an organization is ready and has the needed characteristics for collaborate and participate in a CNO, either a Virtual Breeding Environment (VBE) or a Virtual Organization (VO), a set of specific elements should be evaluated. These evaluation elements are referred as Readiness for Collaboration Assessments and are the main topic of this paper. Main elements that should be considered in these assessments, especially for an organization that wants to become a VBE member are presented as a first approach that can be implemented in different Virtual Breeding Environments.

1. INTRODUCTION

Collaboration has a clear impact on business performance; therefore a wide variety of organizations are starting to join efforts and working together under a large number of collaborative models to deal with market dynamism and hypercompetitive global environments (Todeva & Knoke, 2005). Collaboration is widely recognized as a mechanism for leveraging competitiveness and thus increasing survivability in turbulent market conditions. Through different collaborative models, organizations nowadays are capitalizing on individual strengths by sharing risks and resources, and joining complementary skills and capacities, in order to gain new competitive advantages and excelling individual capabilities (focus on core competencies).

Collaboration is instituted gradually, implies mutual trust and thus takes time, effort and dedication. Collaboration can be viewed as part of a development continuum of four building blocks known as the *continuum of collaboration* (Himmelman, 2001) required to fully realize a collaborative endeavor. First building block is *networking* which involves communication and information exchange for mutual benefit among entities (e.g. organizations). Second building block, extending networking, is *coordination* which now implies in addition to exchanging information, aligning/altering of activities so that more efficient results can be achieved. Third building block, extending coordination, is *cooperation* which not only involves information exchange and adjustments of activities, but also sharing resources for achieving compatible goals. Fourth building block, extending cooperation, is *collaboration* which now represents a process where entities

Please use the following format when citing this chapter:

Romero, D., Galeano, N. and Molina, A., 2008, in IFIP International Federation for Information Processing, Volume 266, *Innovation in Manufacturing Networks;* ed. A. Azevedo; (Boston: Springer), pp. 47–56.

share information, resources and responsibilities to jointly plan, implement and evaluate a program of activities to achieve a common or compatible goal[1].

In short, *collaboration* implies sharing risks, resources, responsibilities and rewards among organizations acting as a joint entity (e.g. a collaborative network), in order to achieve a common goal that would not be possible, or would have higher cost, if attempted individually (e.g. a collaboration opportunity).

Collaborative Networked Organizations (CNOs), or simply collaborative networks can be defined as "networks of organizations that are largely autonomous, geographically distributed, and heterogeneous in terms of their: operating environment, culture, social capital and goals; nevertheless these organizations collaborate to better achieve common or compatible goals, and their interactions are supported by a computer network" (Camarinha-Matos & Afsarmanesh, 2006).

For developing successful CNOs, it is necessary that potential members are ready in advance and prepared to participate in collaborative endeavors, but how to state that an organization is ready to play a part in a collaborative effort?, this is the main research question that this paper addresses.

In order to define the term collaboration readiness in a CNO, two terms should be defined: "Readiness" and "Collaboration Readiness". *Readiness* means a state or quality of being ready and grasps the following elements: preparedness, promptness, aptitude and willingness. *Collaboration readiness* can be defined then as the evidence of *readiness* reflected in the provision of staff, budget, training, technology and other resources to support *collaboration* based-on the quality and effectiveness of past and current collaborative activities across organizational boundaries.

Mainly in collaborative networks, readiness for collaboration means organization's capability for leadership to support collaborative activities, allocate/assign resources (money, staff, technology and information) across organizational boundaries, and attach to a common ground for successful collaboration (common operating principles, common ontology, interoperable infrastructures, and cooperation agreements).

Migrating towards this collaborative environment, requires a new organizational orientation and infrastructure based-on a *collaborative culture* which can be associated to a set of primary requirements such as: openness, commitment, leadership, trust-building, self-learning, continues training, long-term & global vision, effective communication, knowledge sharing and innovation. Collaborative culture compromises all organization's beliefs, knowledge, attitudes, and customs towards a supportive and positive behavior to enhance the capabilities of others and the willingness to adapt for the benefit of all (Romero et al, 2007b).

This paper will present initial efforts towards defining a first assessment approach to evaluate organization's readiness for collaboration to participate in two CNO types: *Virtual Breeding Environments (VBEs)* and *Virtual Organizations (VOs)*.

Main research objectives are: [1] to identify critical criteria to assess collaboration readiness in VBE membership applicants to become VBE members; [2] to identify critical criteria to assess collaboration readiness in VBE members to become VO partners; and [3] to provide some guidelines for organizations that would like to continuously enhance their readiness for collaboration after becoming a VBE member.

[1] See also Camarinha-Matos & Afsarmanesh, 2006.

2. READINESS FOR COLLABORATION IN VBEs AND VOs

Virtual Breeding Environments (VBEs) represent "an association or pool of organizations and their related supporting institutions, adhering to a base long-term cooperation agreement and adoption of common operating principles and infrastructures, with the main goal of increasing both their chances and their preparedness towards collaboration in potential VOs". Virtual Organizations (VOs) represent "a temporary alliance of organizations that come together to share skills or core competencies and resources in order to better respond a collaboration opportunity, and dissolve when their goal has been achieved" (Camarinha-Matos & Afsarmanesh, 2006).

A realistic approach to materialize a truly dynamic VO creation process when a collaboration opportunity arises, and being able to cope with the time period during which an opportunity must be seized or lost, requires preparedness in potential VO partners, which can only be developed in a long-term proactive cooperation (e.g. within a VBE) (Camarinha-Matos & Afsarmanesh, 2007).

VBEs as supporting environments aim to guarantee this preparedness in their members to quickly get engaged in collaboration processes (e.g. VO creation). VBE training underlines the preparedness needs of its members to be supported and maintained during the VBE lifecycle as a strategic item to achieve genuine readiness for collaboration in the VBE members.

According to Himmelman's (2001) *continuum of collaboration*, VBEs represent networks where cooperative inter-organizational relationships are promoted and instituted. VBE members work together on long-term projects like the creation of credibility & performance records, common ontology, working & sharing principles, and interoperable infrastructures to establish the base trust for all VBE members to collaborate in VOs. Furthermore, true collaboration, occurs when VBE members relinquish some of their autonomy to jointly meet a collaboration opportunity and agree that their goal could be best accomplished together as a combined effort of all the VO partners selected.

In summary, two main issues should be evaluated in relation to the readiness for collaboration in CNOs: VBE membership applicants' readiness to become VBE Members, and VBE members' readiness of to become VO partners.

2.1. Readiness of VBE Membership Applicants to become VBE Members

VBE membership applicants refer to potential organizations that have the interest to become VBE members. Once these organizations have approved the first readiness for collaboration assessment level they become VBE members.

VBE members are those organizations that have established common interests with other VBE members, and also have complied with the general *VBE working & sharing principles* (Irigoyen, 2006). VBE working & sharing principles can be described under five perspectives: [1] *Organizational perspective* - related to the definition of VBE actors, roles, rights and responsibilities (Camarinha-Matos & Afsarmanesh, 2005); plus VBE structure, governance rules and bylaws (Romero et al, 2007b). [2] *Business process perspective* - related to the main VBE lifecycle management process (Afsarmanesh & Camarinha-Matos, 2005). [3] *Resources perspective* - related to the assets management such as: physicals, technology, staff, knowledge, and other tangible & intangible resources (Afsarmanesh & Camarinha-Matos, 2005; Romero et al, 2007a). [4] *Value systems* and *business model* (Romero et al, 2006; 2007a) *perspective* - related to membership (Sitek et al, 2007), profiling and competency (Ermilova & Afsarmanesh, 2006), trust (Msanjila & Afsarmanesh, 2006) performance (Alfaro et al, 2005), incentives and sanctions (Romero et al, 2007a), and agreements/contracts management (Camarinha-Matos & Oliveria,

2006). [5] *Interactions perspective* - related mainly with VO creation process (Camarinha-Matos et al, 2005; 2007) and potential third party interactions (e.g. supporting institutions) (Romero et al, 2006).

2.2. Readiness of VBE members to become VO partners

VO partners refer to those VBE members that have approved the second readiness for collaboration assessment level by complying with a *competency-based approach* used to search and select the most suitable VO partners, from a subset of VBE members, according to the particular competency requirements of a collaboration opportunity.

A *competency-based approach* (Boucher & Eburnean, 2005; Camarinha-Matos et al, 2005; 2007; Ermilova & Afsarmanesh, 2006) focus on searching and selecting the potential VO partners based-on the possession of the precise competencies (as a set of processes, resources and standards) to respond to a specific collaboration opportunity, plus the capabilities[+] and capacities[++] required to manufacture/execute a certain product/project in the quality[+] and quantity[++] required. In this sense, the adoption of a competency-based approach to assess the readiness for collaboration level for VBE members to become VO partners will provide an accurate description of the necessary criteria to search and select the right VO partners.

3. READINESS ASSESSMENT APPROACH

The readiness for collaboration assessment approach aims to determine both; whether an organization can be qualified to enter a particular collaborative network, such as a VBE, and when a collaboration opportunity arises, the level of preparation to participate in a VO. Alternatively, if the organization is not ready to collaborate, the assessment model will provide a development plan (e.g. feedback) for helping the organization to improve the weak points for passing the readiness assessment evaluation in the near future. Making this assessment should involve the VBE administrator to accept or reject potential VBE members, and the VO planner (business integrator) for the selection of potential VO partners.

The proposed readiness for collaboration assessment approach is based-on four levels, devoting the first three to assess VBE membership applicants' readiness to become VBE members, and the last level for VBE members' readiness to become VO partners, and all together addressing the VBE working & sharing principles (see Table 1).

Table 1. VBE Working & Sharing Principles vs. Readiness for Collaboration Assessment Approach

VBE Working & Sharing Principles		Readiness for Collaboration Assessment	
Perspective	Organizational	Corporate Governance & Enterprise Architecture (Organization)	Assessment
	Business Process	Enterprise Architecture (Processes)	
	Resources	Enterprise Architecture (Resources + Information/Knowledge)	
	Value Systems & Business Models	Enterprise Architecture (Market)	
	Interactions	Past Performance & Competency	

Following paragraphs detail the evaluation criterions for the VBE member's readiness assessment, and then for the VO partners' readiness assessment:

3.1. VBE Members' Readiness Assessment

The VBE members' readiness assessment is applied once by the VBE administrator to the VBE membership applicants. The evaluation criteria focus on stable elements (inter-organizational compatibility) to appraise the readiness for collaboration of potential VBE members. Following paragraphs detail the evaluation criterions for the VBE member's readiness assessment:

Corporate Governance Assessment. In this criterion the focus is on *strategic fit*, the objective is to find the compatibility between the VBE membership applicant interests and the VBE strategy. Associations are normally successful when partnering organizations connect with the collaboration purpose and with each other. Moreover, clarifying the *collaboration purpose* to come with a shared understanding about the collaborative goals and expected outcomes helps VBE membership applicants to settle their expectations. Preparing a written *collaboration purpose statement* by answering: What are the reasons for entering the VBE? (E.g. new market opportunities, shorter time-to-market, risk/cost sharing, access to complementary competencies) and How the potential VBE member intends to cooperate with its future partners? (E.g. sharing production capacities, sharing resources: financial, physical, human, technological, knowledge) can help to clarify which are the VBE membership applicant expectations from the benefits of joining a VBE. Reaching collaboration purpose clarity requires time, but is needed to discuss and negotiate a shared vision to concrete it in a collaboration agreement (e.g. the VBE membership).

As an extension of clarifying the collaborative purpose, discovering potential alignment areas between the VBE and the VBE membership applicant missions, strategies and values can help to agree on a common denominator of the cultural aspects, visions, and strategies for creating a basic agreement on mutually shared working & sharing principles. Taking time to identify congruency of mission, strategy, and values helps to realize drivers to build solid foundations for collaboration (shared common values, trust, and commitment) that without them collaboration cannot evolve, and therefore cannot success.

Enterprise Architecture Assessment. In this criterion, the focus is on *organizational agility*, the VBE membership applicant infrastructures are evaluated in terms of their *adaptability* - as the ability to effect changes in response (or in anticipation) to environmental conditions, *promptness* - as the ability to accomplish objectives in a short period of time, and *innovation* - as the ability to generate many solutions to a problem, towards collaboration in dynamic VOs.

The enterprise architecture assessment provides a set of elements (criteria) to evaluate and select the VBE member applicants that could belong to the VBE based-on five dimensions: market, processes, resources, organization and information/knowledge (see Table 2).

The main objective of the enterprise architecture assessment is to identify opportunity areas to implement common standards to ensure that VBE members are interoperable in a business process and a technological manner. Furthermore, common operating rules, common infrastructures and common ontology for exchanging information between VBE members (VO partners) should be defined in order to provide facilities for communication and resources sharing.

Table 2. Enterprise Architecture Assessment Dimensions

Dimension	Description	Components	Indicators
Market	This dimension deals with all the external factors of the organization (its value chain).	• *Products/Services:* or value proposition, covers all the aspects of what an organization offers to its customers, comprising not only the organization's bundles of products and services, but also the manner in which it differentiates itself from its competitors. • *Market:* organization's market scope, target segments, target customers, and strategy (business mission) to compete differently than its competitors. • *Customer:* organization's strategy to offer its customers something distinctive or at a lower cost than its competitors, focusing on reaching customers (e.g. distribution channels) and maintaining customer satisfaction and loyalty (e.g. Customer Relationship Management). • *Suppliers:* organization's strategy to surround itself with the rights partners to amplify its resources to deliver a final product to the customer (e.g. Supply Chain Management).	• New Products • New Services • Market-Share • Customers Satisfaction • Customers Loyalty • Suppliers Capability • Suppliers Capacity
Processes	This dimension deals with all the main and supporting business processes involved in the organizational value creation process.	• *Main Processes:* Input Logistics, Operations, Output Logistics, Marketing and Sales, Services. • *Supporting Processes:* Procurement, Technology Development, Human Resources Management, and Organization Infrastructure.	• Quality • Deliver Time • Deliver Speed • Deliver Certain • Flexibility • Innovation
Resources	This dimension deals with all the resources (assets) available to be allocated in order to support organizational business processes.	• *Human Capital:* in terms of staff profiles and competencies (skills, experience & knowledge). • *Technological Capital:* in terms of the production equipment capabilities and capacities for the specific application domain of the organization (physicals, machinery, information and communication technologies).	• Competency • Quality • Time • Volume • Costs • Flexibility • Environment
Organization	This dimension deals with the organizational structure by managing the different working methods that staff uses to perform their daily activities under the defined governance model.	• *Organizational Structure:* as the roles, relationships and staff responsibilities and duties definition inside the organization, under a set of arrangements that allow the effective communication and coordination of all staff allowing the organization to operate properly. • *Working Methods:* as the methods, techniques, practices and procedures followed to perform a certain task with the purpose of reaching a predetermined objective.	• Financial Ratios • Best Practices • Industry Standards
Information/ Knowledge	This dimension deals with the information databases and flow that will support and handle the organizational business processes.	• *Type of information:* in terms of structure, semi-structure and non-structure information available. • *Flow of information:* in terms of the information that allows the conformation of databases and information flows for maximize the organizational value contribution to its staff and processes.	• Quality • Integrity • Availability • Exchangeability • Confidentiality • Updatability

Past Performance Assessment: In this criterion, the focus is on *past experiences* in collaboration. Successes and failures in past collaborative activities are evaluated as significant indicators of readiness for future collaboration. Organizations ready to collaborate normally have a track record of successful collaborations. Some examples of collaborative models that can serve to this purpose are presented in Table 3.

Main focus on this criterion is to identify past experiences of an organization participating in different collaborative models, and to analyze the past performance records of these collaborative endeavors. Some questions that could be used for this purpose are: Was the collaboration successful? Why? Which were the main challenges during the collaboration process? How were these challenges overcome? Which were the main lessons learned during the collaboration process?

Table 3. Interorganisational Relationships Classification by Todeva & Knoke (2005)

Interorganisational Relationship	Description
Hierarchical Relations	Through acquisition or merger, one firm takes full control of another's assets and coordinates actions by the ownership rights mechanism.
Joint Ventures	Two or more firms create a jointly owned legal organization that serves a limited purpose for its parents, such as R&D or marketing.
Equity Investments	A majority or minority equity holding by one firm through a direct stock purchase of shares in another firm.
Cooperatives	Coalitions of small enterprises that combine, coordinate, and manage their collective resources.
R&D Consortia	Inter-firm agreements for research and development collaboration, typically formed in fast-changing technological fields.
Strategic Cooperative Agreements	Contractual business networks based on joint multi-party strategic control, with the partners collaborating over key strategic decisions and sharing responsibilities for performance outcomes.
Cartels	Large corporations collude to constrain competition by cooperatively controlling production and/or prices within a specific industry.
Franchising	A franchiser grants a franchisee the use of a brand-name identity within a geographic area, but retains control over pricing, marketing, and standardized service norms.
Licensing	One company grants another the right to use patented technologies or production processes in return for royalties and fees.
Subcontractor Networks	Inter-linked firms where a subcontractor negotiates its suppliers' long-term prices, production runs, and delivery schedules.
Industry Standards Groups	Committees that seek the member organizations' agreements on the adoption of technical standards for manufacturing and trade.
Action Sets	Short-lived organizational coalitions whose members coordinate their lobbying efforts to influence public policy making.
Market Relations	Arm's-length transactions between organizations coordinated only through the price mechanism.

The principal dimension used by Todeva & Knoke (2005) for ordering this classification is that, from bottom to top, collaborating organizations experience increasing integration and formalization in the governance of their inter-organizational relationships (e.g. working & sharing principles). Therefore, the main objective of the past performance assessment is to determine how open is the VBE membership applicant to embrace new forms of communication and cooperation to capitalize new ways of working based-on collaboration (shared goals).

3.2. VO Partners' Readiness Assessment

The VO partners' readiness assessment is evaluated each time that a VBE member is suggested to participate in a VO in order to respond to a particular collaboration opportunity with specific competency requirements. The VO planner, as the business integrator, will assess a set of potential VO partners in terms of their readiness for collaborate in a particular VO. Therefore, a *competency-based approach* is used to evaluate the competency, capability, capacity and availability of a VBE member to jointly work in a VO and handle the requirements of a collaboration opportunity.

Competency Assessment. In this criterion, the focus is on a *combined status* of competency, capability, capacity and availability when a collaboration opportunity arises and a VBE member is called to become a VO partner. The main idea is to select the most suitable VO partners based-on their core competencies in order to exploit organization's unique capabilities and strategic assets to deliver a product and/or a service within the required time-, cost- and quality frame while keeping a high level of agility to cope with the variable duration of market opportunities.

Additionally to the competency assessment approach proposed in this paper, VO partners' assessment can be complemented with the use of performance indicators like: price, delivery date, quality level, etc. depending on the VO planner preferences and the collaboration opportunity constrains (Baldo et al, 2007; Jarimo et al, 2006).

4. REMAINING READY TO COLLABORATE

The idea of remaining ready to collaborate refers to the VBE supporting nature underlining continues preparedness of its members to keep up with the emerging requirements of future collaboration opportunities in the market (e.g. Deming Cycle, or PDSA cycle, for continuous improvement). A VBE must then serve as a preparedness platform for ad-hoc collaboration (e.g. VO creation) offering different mechanisms to its members that will facilitate the management of different emerging requirements to participate in different collaboration opportunities.

One approach that can be considered by the VBE administration can be to promote and incentive one of the primary requirements of collaboration: *self-learning*[2]. A second approach is the continuous VO partnerships' assessment for discovering areas of improvement in the different collaboration elements. A third approach is the creation of a development plan as part of the VBE strategy to access and/or explore new markets in multidisciplinary sectors by recruiting new VBE members with the competencies required or training current VBE members to develop new competencies.

First approach related to self-learning (self-training) will require the establishment of incentives to promote this proactive behavior in the VBE members; benefits for investing in improving organizational competency must be clearly reflected, for example: increase VBE members chances of VO involvement, and as a result increase business activity and profit. Second approach can be carried out as a VO inheritance process; after VO dissolution an evaluation (questionnaire) must be applied to assess the VO partnership quality level in terms of the VO partners' synergy, leadership efficiency and effectiveness. Some examples of questions to include in this evaluation are presented in Table 4:

Table 4. VO Partnership Assessment Questionnaire (Suggested Questions)

Terms	Questions
Synergy	By working together... How well VO partners were able... • to respond to the customer needs and requirements within the required time-, cost- and quality frame? • to carry out comprehensive value-added activities that connects their production systems? • to clearly communicate and commit with their duties (deadlines)?
Leadership	By working together... How well VO partners were able... • to take responsibility for the VO partnership (risk sharing)? • to enhance the each other's capacity to achieve a common purpose (real collaboration)? • to communicate and share a common vision? • to foster trust, sharing and commitment?
Efficiency	By working together... How well VO partners were able... • to share, exchange and combine their skills and resources to focus in their core-competencies? • to coordinate the resources provision (money, staff, technology, and information) to support collaborative activities? • to manage collaborative decision-making (democracy)?
Effectiveness	By working together... How well VO partners were able... • to evaluate the VO participation benefits by comparing benefits vs. drawbacks? • to end with a positive experience and satisfaction from the VO partnership?

Third approach requires a strategic planning process, where the VBE administration defines a competency development plan where VBE membership applicants with specific competencies are recruited to close a VBE competency gap, or current VBE members are

---

[2] *Self-learning* - A process in which VBE members take the initiative to diagnose their own readiness for collaboration level by identifying their own gaps and/or improvement areas and formulating action-plans towards closing these gaps or continuously improve their collaboration readiness. The VBE administrator becomes a facilitator in the learning (training) process.

trained to develop new competencies to improve their capabilities and capacities in terms of their business processes to execute new value-added activities to deliver new products and/or services to access new collaboration opportunities in the market.

5. CONCLUSIONS & FURTHER RESEARCH

In today's hypercompetitive environment, collaboration is being promoted, expected, or required everywhere in order to remain competitive or perhaps survive. The readiness for collaboration assessment approach presented in this paper tries to increase the organizations readiness for collaboration in VOs by self- or assisting learning, training, evaluation means within a VBE. The approach described views collaboration readiness assessment in two perspectives, initial evaluation to become a VBE member and further development to participate in a VO. The collaboration readiness assessment itself is a collaborative process where VBE members discuss and negotiate strategic action-plans to increase their interoperability. Continuous evaluation of the collaboration readiness level of VBE members provides focus, feedback and learning to support continues improvement of organizations' capability to cooperate and collaborate.

Further research is required to build a collaboration readiness assessment methodology to attend the variety of critical success factors and barriers to be breakdown to develop a successful collaboration culture based-on best practice of a history of successful collaborations in global landscape.

The initial readiness for collaboration approach presented in this paper intents to depict a set of guidelines for describing a number of elements, for constructing in the near future a successful readiness for collaboration methodology for CNOs.

5.1. Acknowledgments

The information presented in this document is part of the results of the ECOLEAD Project (European Collaborative Networked Organizations Leadership Initiative), funded by the European Community, FP6 IP 506958. The authors wish to acknowledge the support of the Innovation Center in Design and Technology from ITESM - Campus Monterrey.

6. REFERENCES

1. Alfaro, J.; Rodriguez, R., Ortiz, A. "A Performance Measurement System for Virtual and Extended Enterprises". In Collaborative Networks and their Breeding Environments, Camarinha-Matos, L.M. et al (Eds.), IFIP, NY: Springer Publisher, 2005, pp. 285-292.
2. Afsarmanesh, H., Camarinha-Matos, L.M. "A Framework for Management of Virtual Breeding Environments". In Collaborative Networks and their Breeding Environments, Camarinha-Matos, L.M. et al (Eds.), IFIP, NY: Springer Publisher, 2005, pp. 35-48.
3. Baldo, F.; Rabelo, R.J., Vallejos R.V. "An Ontology-based Approach for Selecting Performance Indicators for Partners Suggestion" In Establishing the Foundation of Collaborative Networks, Camarinha-Matos L.M. et al (Eds.), IFIP, Vol. 243, NY: Springer Publisher, 2007, pp. 187-196.
4. Boucher, X., Lebureau, E. "Coordination of Competencies Development within Networks of SMEs". In Collaborative Networks and their Breeding Environments, Camarinha-Matos, L.M. et al (Eds.), IFIP, NY: Springer Publisher, 2005, pp. 57-66.
5. Camarinha-Matos, LM.; Silveri, I.; Afsarmanesh, H., Oliveira, A.I. "Towards a Framework for Creation of Dynamic Virtual Organizations". In Collaborative Networks and their Breeding Environments, Camarinha-Matos, L.M. et al (Eds.), IFIP, NY: Springer Publisher,, 2005, pp. 69-80.
6. Camarinha-Matos, L.M., Afsarmanesh, H. "Collaborative Networks: Value Creation in a Knowledge Society". In Knowledge Enterprise: Intelligent Strategies in Product Design, Manufacturing and Management, K. Wang et al (Eds.), IFIP, Vol. 207, NY: Springer Publisher, 2006, pp. 26-40,
7. Camarinha-Matos, L.M., Oliveria, A.I. "Contract Negotiation Wizard for VO Creation", 3rd International Conference in Digital Enterprise Technology, EST Setúbal Press, 2006
8. Camarinha-Matos, L.M., Afsarmanesh, H. "A Framework for Virtual Organization Creation in a Breeding Environment". International Journal Annual Reviews in Control, Elsevier Publisher, Vol. 31, 2007, pp. 119-135.
9. Camarinha-Matos, L.M.; Oliveira, A. I.; Ratti, R.; Demšar, D.; Baldo, F., Jarimo, T. "Computer-Assisted VO Creation Framework". In Establishing the Foundation of Collaborative Networks, Camarinha-Matos, L.M. et al (Eds.), IFIP, NY: Springer Publisher, 2007, pp. 163-178.
10. Ermilova, E., Afsarmanesh, H. "Competency and Profiling Management in Virtual Organization Breeding Environments". In Network-Centric Collaboration and Supporting Frameworks, Camarinha-Matos, L.M. et al (Eds.), IFIP, NY: Springer Publisher, 2006, pp. 131-142.
11. Himmelman, A.T. On Coalitions and the Transformation of Power Relations: Collaborative Betterment and Collaborative Empowerment. American Journal of Community Psychology, 2001; Vol. 29, No. 2.
12. Irigoyen, J.; Galeano, N.; Guerra, D., Molina, A. "Virtual Breeding Environment: Working & Sharing Principles". In Interoperability of Enterprise Software & Applications, Konstantas, D. et al (Eds.), Springer London Publisher, 2006, pp. 99-110.
13. Jarimo, T.; Salkari, L., Bollhanlter, S. "Partners Selection with Network Interdependencies". In Network-Centric Collaboration and Supporting Frameworks, Camarinha-Matos L.M. et al (Eds.), IFIP, Vol. 224, NY: Springer Publisher, 2006, pp. 389-396
14. Msanjila, S.S., Afsarmanesh, H. "Assessment and Creation of Trust in VBEs".   In Network-Centric Collaboration and Supporting Frameworks, Camarinha-Matos L.M. et al (Eds.), IFIP, Vol. 224, NY: Springer Publisher, 2006, pp. 161-172.
15. Romero, D., Galeano, N., Giraldo, J., Molina, A. "Towards the Definition of Business Models and Governance Rules for Virtual Breeding Environments". In Network-Centric Collaboration and Supporting Frameworks, Camarinha-Matos L.M. et al (Eds.), IFIP, NY Springer Publisher, Vol. 224, 2006, pp. 103-110,
16. Romero, D.; Galeano, N., Molina, A. "A Conceptual Model for Virtual Breeding Environments Value Systems". In Establishing the Foundation of Collaborative Networks, Camarinha-Matos L.M. et al (Eds.), IFIP, NY: Springer Publisher, Vol. 243, 2007a, pp. 43-52.
17. Romero, D.; Giraldo, J.; Galeano, N., Molina, A. "Towards Governance Rules and Bylaws for Virtual Breeding Environments". In Establishing the Foundation of Collaborative Networks, Camarinha-Matos L.M. et al (Eds.), IFIP, NY: Springer Publisher, Vol. 243, 2007b, pp. 93-102.
18. Sitek, P.; Seifert, M., Graser, F. "Partner Profiling to support the Initiation of Collaborative Networks". In Concurrent Innovation: An Emerging Paradigm for Collaboration Competitiveness in the Extended Enterprise, 13th International Conference on Concurrent Enterprising, 2007, pp. 213-220.
19. Todeva, E., Knoke, D. Strategic Alliances and Models of Collaboration. Journal of Management Decision, Emerald Publisher 2005; Vol. 43, Issue 1: 123-148.

06

COLLABORATIVE NETWORKED ENTERPRISES: A PILOT CASE IN THE FOOTWEAR VALUE CHAIN

Emanuele Carpanzano, Andrea Ballarino
Institute of Industrial Technologies and Automation,
National Research Council, Milan, Italy,
e.carpanzano@itia.cnr.it, a.ballarino@itia.cnr.it

Present paper describes major RTD challenges and key technologies in order to respond to the demand for consumer oriented highly flexible and networked production systems. Shoe manufacturing is considered as a pilot sector, and a factory for the production of highly customized footwear is discussed as an example of agile and balanced production system, capable of integrating and cooperating with various actors of the footwear value chain.

1. INTRODUCTION

Nowadays, manufacturing industry is facing frequent and unpredictable market changes, respectively imposed by consumer needs and expectations on one side, and by competition enlarged at global scale on the other.

In particular there is an increasing consumers' demand for products with high technological contents, capable of addressing improved quality of life at all levels. Furthermore, requested manufacturing products shall more and more be highly personalized, endowed with comfort and /or fashion contents, new functionalities, healthy for humans and sustainable for the environment.

Therefore, at production level, a new approach is needed to meet such perspective, based on new balanced manufacturing systems and on cooperative enterprises, capable of following the rapid market dynamics as well as the continuously changing consumers' attitudes and expectations.

2. THE FOOTWEAR VALUE CHAIN

2.1. The footwear sector

Footwear sector represents one of the traditional pillars of the "Made in Europe" as well as one of the most important sectors of European manufacturing.

Today, market trends tell about an exigent consumer, who is more and more searching for novelties, for stylish products and for technologies: footwear market is definitively requiring more and higher value added products on demand, in terms of comfort, health and sustainability.

However, when considering the shoe manufacturing sector, the scenario appears extremely fragmented and rigid, not capable to fully respond to market challenges.

Please use the following format when citing this chapter:

Carpanzano, E. and Ballarino, A., 2008, in IFIP International Federation for Information Processing, Volume 266, *Innovation in Manufacturing Networks;* ed. A. Azevedo; (Boston: Springer), pp. 57–66.

Footwear value chain is constituted by many specialized knowledge intensive, as well as low technology based SMEs. Each phase of the shoe production is deeply characterized by traditional approaches, often human centered, with different and opposite management policies along the footwear value chain, always oriented to batch quantities and local maximization (Pillar et al., 2003).

As already happening for other sectors, the Footwear sector is living a crucial season in the increasingly complex economic environment: new frontiers of competitiveness are being faced, in a global scenario where east and far east competitors benefit from incomparable advantages in terms of volumes and labor costs.

A huge effort is therefore necessary: major introduction of information technology and automation on one side, and integration among different actors and technologies in a network of real time collaborating enterprises on the other, are some key factors to be achieved to respond to daily challenges, and to face the global competition.

2.2. Footwear value chain actors

As mentioned before, the footwear value chain is characterized by a strong fragmentation: shoe as product is composed by an average of 20 among parts and components, different as for materials and production processes, provided by various independent actors.

Shoes are designed and manufactured along a complex process which:

- involves stylists and modelers on product design;
- has articulated interactions, at material supply chain level, with last makers, tanneries, leather and synthetic material suppliers, components suppliers (e.g. soles, which by themselves recall for several operations, suppliers and dedicated supply chain)
- is mostly based on external third party services suppliers at manufacturing level (i.e. component cutting, piece stitching, shoe assembling and product finishing before commercialization).

A general low technological level characterizes the whole production process as well as the interactions from suppliers to producers, to network distribution, up to retailers.

3. MAJOR CRITICAL ISSUES AND NEEDS

Today, the footwear sector is characterized by many specialized and low technology based SMEs. Automation level in production systems and equipment is low: basically, more than 60% of the operations and therefore of products added value is human centered. As a general remark, the production process – constituted by three main phases: cutting, stitching and assembling– is often hardly automated. All the steps involve an operator, either assisting the machine, as it happens in cutting and in some assembling operations, or directly performing the job manually, as in the stitching phase.

It can be easily understood how present human based approach negatively impacts in terms of costs on global scale competition with Far East countries, with huge low cost work force, causing phenomena like delocalization of some or of the whole production process.

Furthermore, another major critical issue can be identified in the inertia between the fast changing consumer and retailer demand and the slow responding manufacturing chain: today the time horizon for fully responding to a new market demand recalls for 2/3 months. Consumers' requests and retailers are not involved in the "real time" loop, and distribution network prove to be slow and ineffective.

In product realization, most enterprises are based by 2D design technology and related production process, which characterize as old fashioned, proprietary and closed solutions. At conception level, there is a lack of digital tools capable of integrated product design: today actors cooperating along process use different - neither integrated nor interoperable - design environments, and often base their interactions on "trial and sample" approaches. Major lacks can be registered at product information and order management levels: there is no real integration at supply chain level. Platforms necessary for traditional SME producers and retailers to catch up, do not yet exist: only legacy solutions represent state of the art, barely able to interact, if at all.

Business processes between manufacturers and their material suppliers, as well as processes between manufacturers and retailers (and consumers) are today not effectively – or at all - addressed. Lack of global standards, deeply developed and widely accepted, nowadays also represents a main issue.

In fact, standardization process in footwear sector is running slowly, both on information and on production data flows: knowledge is difficult to structure and integrate, in a global scenario where growing delocalization implies loosing the manufacturing knowledge.

4. MAJOR RTD CHALLENGES AND KEY TECHNOLOGIES

In such a situation, the conception, design and realization of production systems capable to produce always changing high value added shoe products, needs a new generation of manufacturing technologies at all factory levels, in order to build a network of cooperating enterprises, based on new balanced production and automation systems.

To achieve an agile production of consumer oriented high value added footwear, all the phases of the process must be reconceived and automated, to enhance local and global flexibility and cooperation among enterprises, based on synergies and integration along the steps of the value chain, and exploiting a manufacturing approach based on balanced production systems.

The whole path between purchase and start of production of - small batches of - shoes shall be reduced to a minimum: the revision paradigm recalls for complete integration from direct consumer ordering via web interactive services, to flexible and dynamically changing organization schemas, up to real time response in production. Point of sales, design, Enterprise Resource Planning (ERP) and Product Data Management (PDM) environments, as well as production plants shall be highly integrated, so that both the dispatching of orders and the feedback from production can be nearly immediate.

In such a direction, major RTD challenges to be faced deal with:

- *Integration of customers and retailers in the real time loop*: new dedicated concepts shall be developed respectively addressing new co-design and vending solutions.
- *Development of innovative internet and ICT based real time distribution networks.*
- *Integration of SMEs knowledge into new technologies* and improvement of their competitiveness.
- *Development of innovative open design and production solutions* based on emerging technologies.
- Development of *standards for products and processes*, to structure knowledge and integrate actors along the value chain

Specifically, in order to realize the proposed paradigm, the following key technologies are necessary:

- new *ERP-PDM tools* capable of managing minimum batch production orders up to a single sample order, so promptly responding to request for lower quantities;
- new solutions, cooperating with ERP-PDM tools, to create a *unique real time internet based network integrating manufacturers, vendors and suppliers*;
- new *planning and Manufacturing Execution System (MES) solutions* capable of scheduling and managing inbound logistics and production life cycle according to small batch production orders;
- new *3D integrated CAD-CAM software instruments* capable of rapidly and automatically adapting products designs to always changing consumers needs;
- new *shop-floor supervision and automation technologies* that implement highly agile, reconfigurable and balanced production lines;
- new *flexible operating machines and controls* capable of self-adapting their working cycles to a high variety of new different products designs.

5. ITIA-CNR RTDI FACTORY FOR PERSONALISED SHOE PRODUCTION

Proposed technologies, as well as related methodologies and tools, were developed and are currently being used in the innovative RTDI factory for the production of personalized shoes at ITIA-CNR premises in Vigevano (IT).

Such factory represents, as Manufuture best practice (Manufuture, 2005), an example of flexible paradigm in the conception, engineering and networked production of consumer oriented customized shoes (figure 1).

5.1 Consumer integration and flexibility in product order

In the factory context, consumer's integration is realized through dedicated facilities and foot measurement technologies. Consumers can directly order a personalized pair of shoes in a specifically developed Point of Sale (POS), by choosing among a variety of models, colors, materials. Order information is completed by consumer's feet geometrical data, which are computed by means of scanning devices (Carpanzano, 2006), (Chiodi et al., 2006), (Mass Customized Shoe Design and Manufacture, 2004).

As an immediate consequence, and in contrast with the mass production paradigm, production orders reflect the heterogeneity and unpredictability of customer orders: each one is unitary and different from the previous one (different models, geometries, materials, and sequences of operations).

Such heterogeneity has been managed by specifically developed tools, capable of dynamically adapting data structures to the various specific requests and by innovative production lines and manufacturing cells, capable of flexibly adapting and re-configuring.

Figure 1. RTDI factory for personalized shoes production

Figure 2 shows the overall structure of the information, coordination and production systems conceived to manage mass customized shoe production.

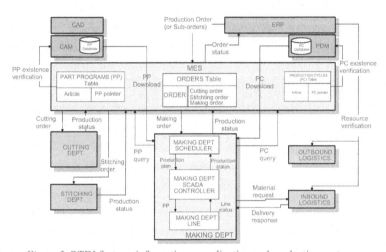

Figure 2. RTDI factory: information, coordination and production systems.

At design-time, each consumer order is processed and CAD module semi-automatically generates specific CAD data, stored into the PDM repository. To such an aim, "quick adaptation functions" were deployed in the 3D CAD system, to achieve a unique last-shoe design by merging specific model style requirements, as well as morphology of the consumer's foot and biomechanical requirements. The output of this phase is a complete "project" of the shoe and of all its components: CAM module processes such data and generates part programs plus useful information intended for various machines at plant level.

At order-time, the ERP module (among other functions) processes new Consumer Orders, collected via Internet, and generates Production Orders. After factory job scheduling (limited to departmental level), it makes Work Orders visible to the Supply Chain Management (SCM) and the MES modules, classified by productive phase or by resource. The MES module dispatches order information and technical data to each department subsystem, through SOAP message or via interactive web services, also informing the Logistics system about the overall job routing.

At conceptual level, a new order management and dispatching philosophy is prosecuted, to orientate heterogeneous processes towards common shared concepts, while, at deployment level, an introduction and harmonization of communication protocols and data-formats was realized towards a major interoperability and interchange-ability of systems cooperating in the same production chain.

Therefore, factory ERP and PDM management architectures flexibly handle concepts like models, measures, customer and production orders, operation, etc. in a commonly defined way, to underpin the network of weaved information. This ensures linear and efficient retrieval and dispatching of useful data, during order processing.

At shop-floor level, department supervisors schedule locally their operation, respecting factory job scheduling, then process the orders. Cutting, Making and external Suppliers mainly work adopting a controlled "pull" approach. This better compensates the difficulties of overall scheduling at company level, due to the uncertainty factors introduced by promoting heterogeneous and unitary orders. Stitching is actually dispatched through the overall Logistic system.

At production-time, each subsystem at plant level sends feedbacks to the MES module, which in turn informs the ERP. The SCM module collects similar information from the suppliers via an interactive web interface. Updated information is made visible to all the Intranet modules: MES, SCM (to drive job progress) and POS (to inform the Sales assistant and, possibly, the Consumer).

Such a "digital" approach allowed the integration and the cooperation of modelers and manufacturers with material and components suppliers on the challenging task of the customized shoe, where each geometry and therefore component shall be changed and undergo the whole engineering process each time.

A network of collaborative enterprises has been set up around the RTDI factory, encompassing a variety among last makers, material, components and sole suppliers, up to footwear producers, capable of "real time" interaction. Such mechanism was made possible through the realization of the SCM module, based on web and XML oriented approaches. Such SCM module offers to each external supplier a convenient interface to consult specialized views of their job-list, and possibly download the order-specific CAM technical data, to choose work orders to process, and to give a feedback about their progress.

5.2. Agile solutions for balanced production systems

As a fundamental premise, in order to fully understand the impact of customization on shoe production, the following considerations shall be made on main phases of the process:

- cutting shoe pieces: main driver of this phase is represented by material and its maximization. Materials must be optimized by nesting the pieces with the best layout, depending on the nature of the material, natural (leather) or synthetic. This heavily contrasts with the heterogeneous mix of unitary orders launched in production (material/colors combinations with always changing geometries), causing a huge complexity to manage;

- stitching shoe pieces: all the components building the upper (i.e. the shoe without the sole) are stitched together, according to a predefined sequence of operations specific to each shoe model. The nature of these operations deeply involves the human factor, so reducing the advantages of introducing automation in operations themselves;

- <u>shoe assembling</u>: main driver of this phase is the shoe construction type, meaning the specific sequence of operations (namely 20) to be executed in order to assemble the final product, involving the last, the upper, the sole and other components. Today assembly lines are specifically conceived and balanced on a reduced set of products (often one construction type), to be iteratively manufactured in series, using all sizes;

- <u>internal logistics</u>: today such phase consists of trolleys, containing and moving production batches of the same item. Such an approach contrasts with the complexity introduced by small – up to single – production lots.

In order to effectively integrate value chain actors at manufacturing level, so maximizing the advantages of the real time cooperation, new automation solutions for balanced and agile production were deployed along all process steps.

At planning level, a two hierarchical level scheduling architecture was conceived: finite capacity scheduling functionalities were developed, through the interaction between high level scheduler, responsible for the factory planning, and shop-floor schedulers, responsible for the production within each phase. Such an approach allowed the creation of mechanisms for dynamic response and re-organization of production, capable to cope with new incoming orders.

Advanced nesting and cutting solutions were developed, integrating current cutting technologies with computer aided functionalities as for automatic building of cutting sessions with always changing pieces geometries derived from 3D CAD. Furthermore, devices for automatic pieces detection and collection were deployed. Such an approach enabled to hold the traditional approach oriented to material maximization, by managing the complexity of heterogeneous production orders cut in parallel.

At shop-floor level, a flexible and agile assembly system has been deployed and currently is devoted to the simultaneous production of personalized and completely different shoe models. In the perspective of heterogeneous one pair orders, continuously and unpredictably changing, "new" objects to be produced should be sent in production without stopping the process to change parameters, setup up machines, etc.

To satisfy this goal, the assembly system is based on an innovative, modular and scalable control architecture, integrates flexible operating machines and controls able to manage and, if necessary, to re-configure to maximize the production of heterogeneous products. Each shoe is pushed along the line from a work-post to the next, following the shorter route and respecting the specific operation cycle defined for each model, independently from other concurrent orders. The result is a system where orders, completely different in terms of model to be produced, sizes, fit and components, must coexist and be produced in the most efficient way. Along the system, shoes undergo various operations performed by machines and robotic cells which continuously self-adapt to the specific CAD geometries and CAM parameters of the worked piece, by interacting with control supervising systems.

Transversal to the aforementioned phases, the automated logistic system plays a crucial role in integration of both production phases and external suppliers. Core element of the system is a tagged box, i.e. the container of shoe pair. The main goal of the internal logistic system is to avoid any rigid sequence of box dispatching in the workflow by collecting and delivering "in time" required objects.

To cope with this objective, internal logistics is handled through an aerial system: an automatic box warehouse, connected to four I/O towers (cutting, stitching, assembly and suppliers), is responsible for serving all internal departments, keeping the 'association' between production boxes and related production order, which is hence traceable during the whole process. The various components are collected in the box as they became available (from suppliers or from warehouse) and the box is then automatically moved along the various phases.

5.3. Validation of the overall system

Design and implementation of the RTDI factory were carried out in EUROShoE project (EUROShoE, 2004), within European Commission Vth Framework Programme. The RTDI factory as well as its network of cooperating suppliers, were proved in an extensive validation campaign (based on acquisition of nearly 2000 customers), during which consumers experienced the whole process, from product ordering till delivery of final customized goods.

Major elements emerging from validation are related to both conceptual and deployment levels.

At order management level, product data definition as well as a common language to identify items and to append structured data represented a crucial aspect to be solved. Though basic in the footwear sector, concepts like models, seen as family of products, articles and color/style variants are different among shoe companies: such difference implies the possibility to structure product features and related technical data in several ways, strongly conditioning the integration of internal and external actors. To deal with such heterogeneity of involved systems, the PDM solution was developed on various existent tools, integrating them by means of the Intranet and by a controlled use of the file system. A more centralized approach would have imposed some duplication of data, plus limitation in the full and coherent exploitation of each specialized tool: some of them in fact rely on their own internal database and/or directory structure. ERP logical architecture was used as a skeleton for the PDM data organization: concepts like models, variants, production orders, phases, operation, etc. were commonly defined to underpin the network of weaved information, inside the factory and with networked suppliers. This strategy ensures a linear and efficient retrieval and dispatching of useful data.

At Supply Chain Management level, traditional approach to production, based on big quantities, and materials managed by stock, could not be applied, in particular with components having geometry dependent on consumer measures, like lasts, insoles and leather soles. Furthermore, most suppliers in the shoemaking industry are small enterprises, with a poor IT equipment and low capability of adapting from big production lots to 'on demand' little orders. The Intranet SCM module helped to mitigate this burden, offering to each supplier a convenient interface to consult their job-list, and possibly download the order-specific CAM data. Some promising cooperative mechanisms have been implemented, to split the component production in sub-steps, loading the RTDI factory with the more variable 'on demand' tasks (e.g. cutting variable geometry pieces) and leaving to the supplier only the specialized manufacturing (e.g. molding the component). This working method has given good results, helping in both the production of unitary orders and in the testing activity at design-time.

At production management level, the high level scheduler provided factory planning of departmental and of external production phases, respecting sequences and production constraints. Web oriented mechanisms were deployed for production order phase advancement, giving the possibility to monitor and to update the order situation remotely.

A decoupled approach was followed, leaving to each department scheduler the task of internal production planning. This approach helped in reducing the overall complexity, so avoiding a more strict interaction between two scheduling levels, and proved effective in managing minor changes in the planning and/or in the customer order.

Besides this, "pull" mechanisms, enabling each department to ask for specific available orders, were introduced in practice, in order to correct some production dynamics, and to optimize performance of some phases, e.g. cutting.

Considering performance of the RTDI factory and its network of suppliers, production rate was calibrated in order to launch orders twice a day. Maximum reached production was in terms of hundreds pairs a day: such a limit was not stressed over some extent, due to project conditions. The overall production process requires a variable time, from a few hours to some days, depending on various factors, as: the need of custom-made specific phases, the need to involve external suppliers, the complexity of the model.

5. CONCLUSIONS

Nowadays rapid dynamics of market demand in the footwear sector, characterized by consumer growing requirements and expectations, as well as by strong industrial competition, claim for new production strategies, encompassing the whole value chain.

The complexity and fragmentation of the shoe manufacturing sector was discussed in present paper, identifying major deficiencies of a technology poor and strongly human centered sector. Major RTD challenges and key technologies for the footwear sector address in particular the integration of customers and retailers in the real time loop, the introduction of IT and automation based solutions, capable of conjugating SMEs knowledge patrimony with new technologies, and integration among different value chain actors.

Network of cooperative enterprises, capable to exploit new organization schemas, as well as agile and balanced production systems, represent a concrete solution to place competition context on value added products rather than on cost.

The RTDI factory for personalized shoe production was presented and discussed as paradigmatic case. The business model of shoe customization imposed a significant definition of the whole manufacturing lifecycle, involving the creation of innovative production tools and the design of proper IT infrastructure

The path for consumer integration was explored through new measuring and design solutions: as a consequence, the whole product design, management and production processes were completely revised. Production planning and job dispatching represented a critical aspect of the architecture, because such functionalities had to cope with the unusual mix of heterogeneous orders and the quickness required to react.

Resulting experience testifies the suitability of internet and ICT based tools in real time integration of value chain actors, as well as the possibility of developing open design and production solutions through emerging technologies (e.g. 3D CAD-CAM and adaptive factories).

Considering the cooperation along the supply chain, the RTDI factory with its networked enterprises supports new collaborative innovation experiences on both products and processes.

Nevertheless, in order to further improve footwear sector competitiveness and networking along the value chain, major efforts are mandatory in the future particularly in the development of standards for products and processes, which are today not existing at all, as well as in the structuring of sector knowledge.

6. REFERENCES

1. Carpanzano E. Process tools for made-to-measure, high quality and inexpensive shoes, Italian Applications. Federico Pedrocchi, Hublab Edition, 2006, 221-225.
2. Chiodi A., Ballarino A., Airoldi F. "Job Dispatching and Monitoring in an Agile Production System". In Proceedings of ESDA 2006: 8th Biennial ASME Conference on Engineering Systems Design and Analysis, 2006, July 4-7, Torino, Italy
3. EUROShoE – 2004, http://www.euro-shoe.net
4. Manufuture – A vision for 2020 – 2005, http://www.manufuture.org/
5. Piller, F., Tseng, M. "New directions for Mass Customization". In The Customer centric enterprise Advances in mass customisation, Springer, 2003
6. Special issue: Mass Customized Shoe Design and Manufacture, International Journal of Computer Integrated Manufacturing, 2004, Taylor and Francis, Vol 17, no.7

07

MODELING PERFORMANCE INDICATORS' SELECTION PROCESS FOR VO PARTNERS' SUGGESTIONS

Fabiano Baldo[1], Ricardo J. Rabelo[1], Rolando V. Vallejos[2]

[1]*Federal University of Santa Catarina, BRAZIL*
baldo@gsigma.ufsc.br, rabelo@das.ufsc.br
[2]*University of Caxias do Sul, BRAZIL*
rvvallej@ucs.br

In the current dynamic world where organizations are inserted in, there is no time to postpone businesses due to the lack of support that helps them to establish the required connections with other organizations agilely. In this context, one of the critical issues is the creation of Virtual Organization, when partners have to be selected. This paper addresses a very closely related issue, which is the selection of the performance indicators that should be applied to drive the partners search. Considering the complexity of this task, this paper presents the process modeling designed to support the user to find appropriated performance indicators that can be used to compare and to suggest organizations that are able to fulfill a business' requirements.

1. INTRODUCTION

Globalization has been imposing an increasing competition among companies. Looking at customers, lower costs, higher quality and shorter delivery dates keep being essential elements in the competitive matrix of companies. However, this selection is a complex problem. Part of the problem is related to the intrinsic nature of Collaborative Networked Organizations (CNO), where companies are disperse and heterogeneous at several dimensions. In more volatile alliances, like Virtual Organizations (VO), this problem is more difficult as the usual processes of making quotations and selecting partners should be carried out even faster.

In this work, a VO is seen as a dynamic, temporary and logical aggregation of autonomous organizations that cooperate with each other to attend a given collaboration opportunity (CO) or to cope with a specific need, where partners share risks, costs and benefits, and whose operation is achieved via a coordinated sharing of skills, resources and information, enabled by computer networks (Rabelo *et al.* , 2004). In this context, the right selection of suppliers/partners is simply crucial for the effective success of a VO as a wrong election can impact negatively the competitive matrix of the VO as a whole.

However, alliances of type VOs have other particularities that make this aforementioned task very hard as, per definition, a VO is something unique, i.e. partners can't be always the same even for similar COs, as it happens in traditional supply chains. A CO comes from different customers and countries, which have different cultures, different regulations, different standards, and that apply different metrics in terms of e.g. quality, manufacturing processes and environmental cares. Therefore, the search for partners that can attend all the specificities of a given VO must also involve the selection

Please use the following format when citing this chapter:

Baldo, F., Rabelo, R.J. and Vallejos, R.V., 2008, in IFIP International Federation for Information Processing, Volume 266, *Innovation in Manufacturing Networks;* ed. A. Azevedo; (Boston: Springer), pp. 67–76.

of the most suitable performance indicators (PI) that companies should respect in order to become real candidates / members of that VO. It is important to highlight that PI selection phase precedes the classical Partners Search and Suggestion/Selection phases within the VO Creation framework.

Actually, companies' profiles use to be expressed in the form of PIs. This also uses to be taken into account for internal benchmarking purposes of a VBE[1] (Vallejos *et al.* , 2006). The problem is that managers use to make the selection of PIs without any methodological support or computer assistance. In practice, this means that the selected PIs are almost the same for any CO despite the (usual) hundreds or even dozens of PIs existing in a CNOs' Performance Measurement System (PMS). On the other hand, and even due to the enormous disparity in the PIs' definitions, terminologies and meaningfulness, managers don't have time to go through PMS to analyze PIs one by one. Instead, with the hurry of the business life, they get used to pick the same set of PIs. Worse than this, in the medium-long terms, this affects the VBE quality as partners don't use to improve the PIs associated to their internal processes if they are not forced to.

As a contribution to this problem, this paper presents a process modeling for PI selection as well as the rationale of a supporting system being developed for that. The advantage of such modeling is twofold. Firstly, it helps in the understanding of this process, leaving perfectly clear which are the inputs, outputs, resources and triggers of every involved activity, the interdependences, as well as the correct sequence of activations. Secondly, it can be used for automation this process, including the information integration requirements.

This paper is organized as follows. In section 2, the problem of finding criteria for VO partners' suggestion is depicted. In section 3, the strategy of selecting criteria to suggest partners is shown. Section 4 presents the process modeling conceived to identify the most suitable set of criteria. Section 5 addresses a case study. Preliminary assessment and future works are presented at the end.

2. CRITERIA FOR PARTNER SUGGESTION

Until few years ago it was supposed that VO partners could be quickly and easily identified and selected from the open universe of existing companies. However, nowadays it is known that this is not as simple as it seems to be (Camarinha-Matos *et al.* , 2005), and that selection is more feasible and effective when carried out within the scope of CNOs of VBE type, considering that VBEs works with known enterprises and it normally has a set of common PIs settled when they are created.

One idea superseded during the last years is that costs and dates would be enough to suggest VO partners. Today it is a common sense that is necessary to use more meaningful criteria to accurately suggest appropriated organizations as VO partners (Crispim and Sousa, 2007, Jarimo and Pulkkinen, 2005). Petersen (2003) emphasizes the importance to suggest partners using well-defined set of criteria based on common attributes known by every interested organization. Following Petersen's idea, PIs can be used as part of these common set of criteria for partners' suggestion. Some authors are already applying such approach, e.g. Grudzewski et al. (2005) and Seifert et al. (2005). That is an approach that can be used by organizations that use a common PMS, e.g. organizations that belong to VBEs. Nevertheless, most of the PMS are composed of plenty of PIs, like the ones offered by the SCOR model[2]. Höbig (2002) overcomes this problem using generic and high-level PIs provided by PMS. However, to use always the same generic PIs to compare and select VO partners seem not to be useful in practice. So, it is necessary to find a way to select just the relevant ones for each specific CO. Although PMS is an area of research with several available results, a review in the literature has revealed the inexistence of any work which tries to systemize and to give a methodological support for the process of PIs selection.

In the proposed approach, the strategy adopted to select the set of relevant PIs is to filter them according to the CO's requirements. This can be seen as a problem of information matching / information retrieval because the only meaningful information in a PI is its own definition. Although being a good approach, it is too simplistic for the tackled problem. PIs are described with different words by each organization, sometimes a different PI represents the same or equivalent PI's underlying concept, and sometimes they have small but relevant differences in their scopes. Yet, they are configured in different PMS according to companies' daily jargon, which in turn not even follow standards terminology (e.g. SCOR, APICS). In other words, PIs are implemented in a different way from companies to companies (Bittencourt and Rabelo, 2005). Another aspect is that CNO requires an additional category of PIs that so far hasn't been considered, like the cooperation level, trustworthiness, and performance history in past VOs (Westphal *et al.* , 2007).

Therefore, in order to cope with this, an additional level of information is necessary to be introduced. A way to do that is introducing semantics, which can be done by means of semantic annotation using a common ontologies and mappings (Baldo *et al.* , 2007). Semantic annotation is currently considered the state-of-the-art when information retrieval is concerned. The term *annotation* refers to the use of auxiliary symbols that are used to modify the interpretation of other symbols (Dorado and Izquierdo, 2003). Semantic annotation techniques use ontologies to perform the proper annotation of the significant words included in the text (Kiryakov *et al.* , 2004).

3. PROBLEM FORMALIZATION

This section formalizes the problem of PI selection to a specific CO. This is made using sets theory, as follows.

Let's assume $P = \{1, ..., p\}$ as the set of PIs being used to measure performance in a VBE. Let also assume $R = \{1, ..., r\}$ as the set of requirements that should be fulfilled in order to create a VO to satisfy a specific CO. So, in order to figure out whether a PI i P is related to a requirement j R, the function $f($ presents the intersection's cardinality of each PI and each requirement set of *relevant terms*.

$$f(i,j) = \left| Pd_i \cap Pr_j \right|, \quad \forall i \in P \land \forall j \; \text{i} \tag{1}$$

Pd_i = set of *relevant terms* presented in the definition of a PI i P.

Pr_j = set of *relevant terms* presented in the description of a requirement j R.

A *relevant term* can be considered every word or sequence of words that contribute to the meaning of either PI definition or requirement description. Examples of *relevant terms* are substantives, nouns, verbs and adjectives.

In order to introduce more expressivity and meaningfulness in the result of equation 1, it was introduced in conjunction with *relevant terms* the notion of semantics. This was accomplished through the utilization of semantic annotations and an ontology designed specially to characterize the concepts related to PIs and COs as well as the relationship among them. Now, the *relevant terms* of both PIs and COs definitions can also be linked to a formal representation, stated in the ontology, using semantic annotations. This additional formalization enables the *relevant terms* to be *semantic relevant terms*. Both ontology and *semantic relevant terms* compose the so called PIs and COs knowledge base.

Let's define $K = \{1, ..., k\}$, that is the set of *semantic relevant terms* included into the PIs and COs knowledge base.

Due to the introduction of semantics in the PIs selection process, now a PI can also be selected for a specific CO requirement whether it has *semantic relevant terms* in common with a requirement *j* R.

Thus,   *g(* presents the intersection's cardinality of each PI and each requirement set of *semantic relevant terms*.

$$g(i,j) = |Sd_i \cap Sr_j|, \quad \forall i \in P \land \forall j \; \text{\tiny{I}} \tag{2}$$

Sd_i = set of *semantic relevant terms* in a PI *i* P found in the knowledge base *K*. It is presented in equation 3.

Sr_j = set of *semantic relevant terms* in a CO requirement *j* R found in the knowledge base *K*. It is presented in equation 4.

$$Sd_i = \{k_z \mid Pd_{i,y} = k_z, \quad \forall i \in P \land \forall y \in Pd_i \land \forall z \in \tag{3}$$

$$Sr_j = \{k_z \mid Pr_{j,y} = k_z, \quad \forall j \in R \land \forall y \in Pr_j \land \forall z \in \tag{4}$$

The objective function to find the PI that have more *relevant terms* and *semantic relevant terms* in common for a specific CO requirement is:

$$Z = \max \sum_{i=1}^{p} \sum_{j=1}^{r} (f(i,j) + g(i,j))$$

4. PROCESS MODELING

The process of selecting PIs for VO partners' suggestion presented in this paper is composed of two macro activities. The first one is carried just once and it is called *preparation phase (A1)*. It comprises the ontology and knowledge base creation as well as the PIs' description semantic annotation. The second one is executed whenever a new VO needs to be created, and it is called *operation phase (A2)*. It performs the acquisition of CO requirements and the selection of proper PIs. Figure 1 presents this process, modeled in IDEF0[3]. In rough terms, IDEF0 is a diagram used to model processes from the functional point of view. Each process is modeled as a box, and its main components are: inputs (left), outputs (right), mechanisms (bottom) and enablers (top). Both preparation and operation phases' descriptions and diagrams are shown in Figure 2 and Figure 3, respectively.

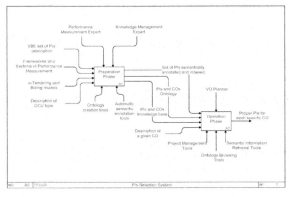

Figure 1. IDEF0 of Performance Indicators Selection Process

Preparation phase:

A1.1 **PIs and COs Ontology Creation**: This activity creates the PIs and COs ontology having literature on performance measurement literature and existing e-procurement standardization as the basis for. This formalization is driven by a knowledge management and an expert on PIs.

A1.2 **PIs and COs Knowledge Population**: This activity performs the population of PIs and COs knowledge base using information from catalogs of PIs as well as from description of CO types.

A1.3 **Automatic PIs Semantic Annotation**: In this activity it is applied an automatic semantic annotation technique, combined with PIs and COs ontology and knowledge base, to create annotations in PIs' information.

Operation phase:

A2.1 **CO Requirements Acquisition**: it is devoted to the identification of the three main pieces of information that are necessary to make the PIs selection: CO objectives, CO type and CO performance requirements.

A2.2 **Search Criteria Identification**: based on A2.1, the link between CO's information and COs' knowledge base is established in order to identify the semantic terms that will be applied in the semantic information retrieval.

A2.3 **PIs Search**: This activity performs the semantic information retrieval using the semantic terms provided by the previous activity. The list of PIs that match such semantic terms is generated as the output.

A2.4 **Result Analysis and Evaluation**: In this activity the result is analyzed and evaluated. This is done to ensure which PIs are suitable to select VO partners. This is a subjective task and it is driven by the user. Regarding its difficulty, support systems can be used to mitigate the subjectivity and to maximize the quality of the results. Even though, an expert can refine this.

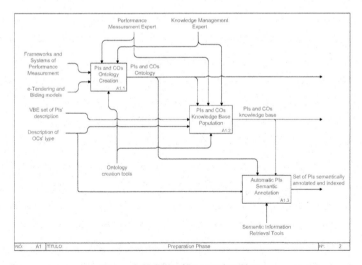

Figure 2. IDEF0 of Preparation Phase

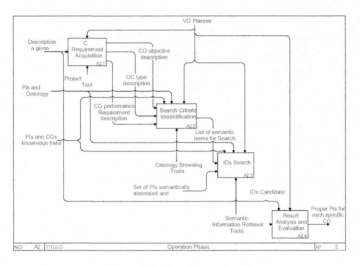

Figure 3. IDEF0 of Operation Phase

The very final output of the whole process is the set of proper PIs suggested to search for VO partners for a given CO. This output can be further used as an input to the *Partners Search and Suggestion* macro process.

5. PRELIMINARY RESULTS

In order to realize if the PIs selection process modeling works and provides better results against other methods, like SQL-based information retrieval, a preliminary case study has been conducted. A pilot from the ECOLEAD[4] project was selected and a certain CO was chosen. More than two hundred PIs were populated in the VBE's database. Having both CO description and PIs, some PIs selection performance estimation was realized regarding some classic metrics used to measure performance in information retrieval systems, which are *precision* and *recall*. The former is calculated through the division of relevant documents retrieved by the total of retrieved documents, and the latter is calculated through the division of relevant retrieved documents by the total of relevant documents (Baeza-Yates and Ribeiro-Neto, 1999).

The addition of semantics in non-structured textual information is supported by the semantic annotation technique, as stated in section 2. Therefore, in order to semantically annotate the PIs' description it is necessary to specify a comprehensive ontology that describes all the relevant concepts related to PIs' characterization in a sensible way. A preliminary version of such ontology is presented in Baldo et al. (2007).

About the CO description, the information structure exemplified below follows the basic template for CO Description and Characterization proposed in ECOLEAD (Demsar et al., (2007). This template is composed of about 200 attributes, varying from general aspects (like CO id, objectives and requirements) to more detailed ones (like work breakdown structure, required competencies and resources). A partial instance of this CO template is showed below.

> *Product Name*: Centrifuge Machine
> *Objectives*: Design and manufacturing of a centrifuge machine to separate various components of blood.
> *Sector*: Health sector
> *Type*: Collaborative Project Modality
> *Specific Requirements*:
>   - Aerodynamic compact construction for vibration free performance;
>   - Power rotor to efficient separate micro substances;
>   - Body made of strong fabricated & corrosion resistant steel;
>   - Speed range 100 to 6000 rpm and above, accuracy 1 rpm;
>   - Capable to operate continuously in a temperature of 10-40 °C and relative humidity up to 80%.

It can be noted that the main focus of this CO is *quality*, addressed by terms like *efficient, accuracy, strong* and *resistant*. Therefore, a possible complete target semantic query to retrieve PIs concerning this specific CO could be: "Look for PIs that measure *production*, with the objective of *accuracy*, considering the perspective of *quality*, in the domain of *manufacturing industry*". It is important to mention that the construction of semantic queries is driven by the human user and it is supported by a tool developed for that. Figure *4* shows a screenshot of this tool, with an example of the query and the results found out.

For comparison purposes, the semantic-based target query was decomposed into four pieces, from the smallest one ("Look for PIs that measure *production*") to the largest one (the whole semantic target query). These four semantic-based queries were compared against four correspondent SQL-based queries formed with the same terms as those used in the semantic ones. For instance, the semantic-based query "Look for PIs that measure *production*" has a correspondent SQL-based query like "*select * from PIs where PI_description like '%production%'*". This strategy was adopted in order to show that the higher the number of search terms is the better the results provided by semantic queries are, regarding other information retrieval methods. These performance tests have been performed in a set of 237 PIs where 12 were identified as relevant ones by experts, previously.

Figure 5 presents the *precision* and *recall* performance results of both semantic-based and SQL-based queries. Axis X represents each one of the four queries and axis Y the percentage of precision and recall in a) and b), respectively. In the execution of the fourth query, the semantic one retrieved 15 PIs, where 3 were not relevant (80% of precision and 100% of Recall). As can be seen in Figure *4*, "*Failure rate based on acceptation*" is an example of no relevant PI that was retrieved by semantic queries. On the other hand, SQL-based query retrieved 9 PIs, where just 7 were relevant (77% of precision and 58%).

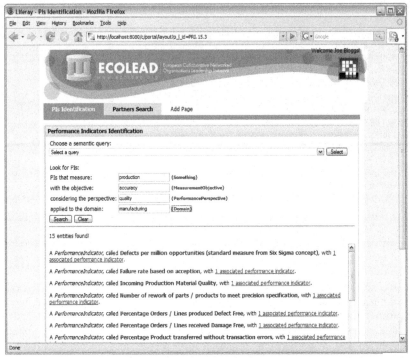

Figure 4. Screenshot of PIs Selection Tool

As the result, it can be noted that semantic queries had a slight higher precision because they have retrieved all the relevant PIs in spite of having retrieved few non-relevant PIs. On the other hand, the results achieved via SQL didn't bring even the relevant PIs. Anyway, the final decision about which PIs will be indeed used in the partners' search is taken by the human manager, who is then assisted in this process.

Considering recall, again semantic queries had a higher performance due to their ability to deal with synonymous. For instance, when considering accuracy, the PIs related to precision (correctness and error, detect or damage free) also would be retrieved. Figure 4 presents some examples of retrieved PIs that have accuracy synonymous like, "*Defect free*", "*Damage free*" and "*Without error*". This is something that most of the other information retrieval techniques don't do.

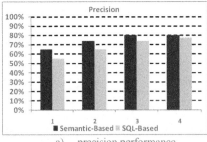
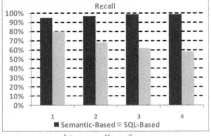

a)   precision performance   b)   recall performance

Figure 5. Performance of Semantic-based queries against SQL-based ones

6. CONCLUSION

This work has presented a contribution to the problem related to the criteria selection to suggest VO partners. To this end, the problem has been formalized and the involved processes modeled. This modeling aims at improving the user's decision concerning the selection of organizations, giving additional information about what can be used to compare the possible VO partners in a more effective way, as well as to systemize the whole process. The user can have different criteria to compare candidates for different COs. Thus, it is possible to find better partners comparing them via PIs that better represent the performance expected to this VO. Some preliminary tests have been made in the ECOLEAD project. First results showed that this model can work properly for, at least, the manufacturing industry sector (as most of the ECOLEAD partners belong to this sector).

It is an ongoing work. Although the whole model and software are already developed, validation activities will now be the focus of the work. It comprehends activities of measuring the effective usefulness of the retrieved PIs against the CO's specifications and VO's specificities. At another level, next activities consist in the deployment of the system at some ECOLEAD project's pilots and the application of the methodology in a real case scenario.

6.1 Acknowledgements

This work has been supported by CAPES Brazilian Research Agency and European Commission. It has been developed in the scope of the European IST ECOLEAD (www.ecolead.org) and of the Brazilian IFM II projects (www.ifm.org.br).

---

[1] VBE (Virtual organization Breeding Environment) represents a long-term association of organizations prepared to cooperate and to establish VOs in the right time COs are identified (Afsarmanesh *et al.* 2005).

[1] SCOR (Supply-Chain Operations Reference-Model) is a reference model for supply-chain management systems and practices (www.supply-chain.org).

[1] http://www.idef.com/idef0.html

[1] *European Collaborative networked Organizations LEADership initiative Project* aims to create strong foundations and mechanisms needed to establish advanced collaborative and network-based industry society in Europe (www.ecolead.org).

7. REFERENCES

1. Afsarmanesh, H.; Camarinha-Matos, L.M. "A Framework for Management of Virtual Organization Breeding Environments". In Sixth IFIP Working Conference on Virtual Enterprises. Valencia, Spain: Springer, 2005.
2. Baeza-Yates, R.; Ribeiro-Neto, B., Modern information retrieval. England: Addison-Wesley Harlow, 1999.
3. Baldo, F.; Rabelo, R.J.; Vallejos, R.V. "An Ontology-Based Approach for Selecting Performance Indicators for Partners Suggestion". In Eighth IFIP Working Conference on Virtual Enterprises. Guimarães, Portugal: Springer, 2007.
4. Bittencourt, F.; Rabelo, R.J. "A Systematic Approach for VE Partners Selection Using the SCOR Model and the AHP Method". In Sixth IFIP Working Conference on Virtual Enterprises. Valencia, Spain: Springer, 2005.
5. Camarinha-Matos, L.M.; Afsarmanesh, H.; OLLUS, M. "ECOLEAD: A Holistic Approach to Creation and Management of Dynamic Virtual Organization". In Sixth IFIP Working Conference on Virtual Enterprises. Valencia, Spain, 2005
6. Crispim, J.A.; Sousa, J.P. "Multiple Criteria Partner Selection in Virtual Enterprises". In Eighth IFIP Working Conference on Virtual Enterprises. Guimarães, Portugal: Spring, 2007
7. Demsar, D.; Mozetic, I.; Lavrac, N. "Collaboration Opportunity Finder". In Eighth IFIP Working Conference on Virtual Enterprises. Guimarães, Portugal: Spring, 2007
8. Dorado, A.; Izquierdo, E. "An Approach for Supervised Semantic Annotation". In Workshop on Image Analysis for Multimedia Interactive Services. 2003.
9. Grudzewski, W.M.; Sankowska, A.; Wantuchowicz, M. "Virtual Scorecard as a Decision-making Tool in Creating Virtual Organisation". In Sixth IFIP Working Conference on Virtual Enterprises. Valencia, Spain. 2005
10. Höbig, M., "Modellgestützte Bewertung der Kooperationsfähigkeit produzierender Unternehmen". In Fortschritt-Berichte VDI. Düsseldorf. 2002
11. Jarimo, T.; Pulkkinen, U. "A Multi-Criteria Mathematical Programming Model for Agile Virtual Organization Creation". In Sixth IFIP Working Conference on Virtual Enterprises. Valencia, Spain: Spring. 2005
12. Kiryakov, A.; Popov, B.; Terziev, I.; et al., "Semantic annotation, indexing, and retrieval". Web Semantics: Science, Services and Agents on the World Wide Web, 2004; 2(1): p. 49-79.
13. Petersen, S.A. "Using Competency Questions to Evaluate an Agent-based Model for Virtual Enterprises". In Fourth IFIP Working Conference on Virtual Enterprises. Lugano, Switzerland: Kluwer Academic Publishers. 2003
14. Rabelo, R.J.; Pereira-Klen, A.; Klen, E.R., "Effective Management of Dynamic Supply Chains". International Journal of Networking and Virtual Organizations, 2004.
15. Seifert, M.; Eschenbächer, J., "Predictive Performance Measurement in Virtual Organization". In Emerging Solutions for Future Manufacturing Systems, L.M. Camarinha-Matos, Editor. Springer. 2005, p. 299-307.
16. Vallejos, R.V.; Lima, C.P.; Varvakis, G. A Framework to Create a Virtual Breeding Environment in the Mould and Die Sector. in Seventh IFIP Working Conference on Virtual Enterprises. 2006. Helsinki, Finland.
17. Westphal, I.; Thoben, K.D.; Seifert, M. Measuring Collaboration Performance in Virtual Organizations. in Eighth IFIP Working Conference on Virtual Enterprises. 2007. Guimarães, Portugal: Springer.

A COLLABORATION READINESS
ASSESSMENT APPROACH

João Rosas, Luis M. Camarinha-Matos
New University of Lisbon, PORTUGAL
jrosas@uninova.pt, cam@uninova.pt

Collaboration readiness depends on "hard" factors such as competency fitness or
technological preparedness, but also on several other factors of a "soft" nature such
as organization's character, willingness to collaborate, or affectivity / empathy
relationships. A modeling approach to assess how prepared is an enterprise to join a
collaborative network is proposed. The approach is based on a notion of "character"
of the organization and the use of belief networks. An example illustrates the
proposal.

1. INTRODUCTION

In collaborative networks, members work together towards the achievement of common
or compatible goals. As collaboration goes on, they adopt patterns of behavior according
to the situations they are involved in. While most of these patterns are both acceptable and
desirable, some others might not be. Naturally, undesirable behaviors should be avoided,
as they affect collaboration and may lead to conflicts. The act of working in collaboration
is by itself considered challenging and risky. Many times, an organization works
successfully alone, but poorly in collaboration. This means that before joining networks,
organizations should be adequately prepared for collaboration.

This research proposes the elaboration of an approach for performing assessment of
the collaboration readiness of members or candidates for collaborative networks. This
assessment is mostly based on the concept of organization's character, as described in
section 2. The Bayesian Belief Network will be used to make predictions on collaboration
preparedness based on organization's character, as described in section 3. The approach is
then illustrated with a small example.

2. COLLABORATION READINESS ASSESSMENT

2.1. The character of an organization

Organizations inside networks work and interact with each other towards the achievement
of common or compatible goals. They typically manifest a variety of behaviors, according
to the peers and situations they are involved in. In this sense, behavior can be understood
as anything that an organization does involving pro-active actions and responses to
external events/requests. These behaviors typically tend to show some repetition through
time, mainly those that appear to be positive for collaboration or achievement of the goals.
This repetition usually leads to the formation of behavioral patterns. These patterns can be
associated to a set of identifiable *traits*. A trait represents a relatively stable predisposition

Please use the following format when citing this chapter:

Rosas, J. and Camarinha-Matos, L.M., 2008, in IFIP International Federation for Information Processing, Volume 266, *Innovation in
Manufacturing Networks;* ed. A. Azevedo; (Boston: Springer), pp. 77–86.

to act in a certain way or, in other words, the preponderance for the occurrence of a certain behavioral pattern. These traits, together, form what is referred to as *character*. An organization's character can therefore be seen as a composition of a set of traits that determine the behavior or nature of the organization. This underlying mapping between character traits and behavior can be used to perform behavior prediction. This means, in turn, that collaboration readiness assessments can be performed using the concept of organization's character. Basically if the predictable behavior is positive towards collaboration, then the readiness increases, otherwise it decreases. This is the approach suggested in this paper for collaboration readiness assessment. It shall be noted that the intrinsic connection between character traits and behavior has traditionally been an extensive research topic in Psychology, as expressed in (Goldie 2004) and (Webber, 2006).

Examples of research that address the behavioral aspects of collaboration can be found in (Camarinha-Matos & Macedo, 2007), which establishes a dependency of the joint behavior and the underlying value systems. In (Westphal et al, 2007) the problem of collaboration performance is addressed, using aspects, such as flexibility, reliability and commitment.. In (Romero et al, 2007) the definition of guidelines for governance rules and bylaws for behavior regulation is attempted. The idea of an organization having a character is not a completely new concept. For instance, in (Gothlich, 2003) a model for collaborative business ecosystems is presented taking some metaphors from biology, in which the behavioral patterns are described through a small number of classification traits, namely resilience and responsiveness. In (Wilkinson et al, 2005) an analogy is made between the idea of mating and sexual appealing and the idea of business mating. They describe matching factors for engaging in long term partnerships. These factors were grouped in financial issues, organizational (and strategic issues), and technological issues. In (Chun, 2005) a "virtuous ethical character" scale, composed of 6 dimensions (integrity, empathy, courage, warmth, zeal, conscientiousness) and 24 items, is described to enable an assessment of the link between organizational level *virtue* and organization's financial or non-financial performance.

2.2. Towards a collaboration readiness assessment model

The word readiness, according to the Oxford Dictionary of English (Oxford, 2003), refers (1) to the state of having been made ready or prepared for something; (2) the willingness to do something; (3) and the quality of being immediate, quick and prompt. Following this definition, an organization could be considered ready to collaborate if it is prepared and willing to work in collaboration for the achievement of common goals, performing tasks in an accurate and reliable way. This readiness concept should cover several aspects, ranging from technological and economical to behavioral and social ones. In this research, however, the emphasis is put more on aspects related to organization's behavior. Since traits represent predispositions to act in a certain way, an organization can be considered prepared to collaborate if its character traits have values that favor the predisposition of occurrence of behaviors that are desirable in a collaboration context.

In this section a number of concepts are defined in order to better understand the context and suggested approach. In the used notation it is assumed that all single attributes are named in small letters, while sets are named in capital letters. At the base, let us consider the following sets:

- $O=\{o_1, o_2, \dots \}$ – the set of organizations of a virtual organization breeding environment (VBE) (Afsarmanesh, Camarinha-Matos, 2005).
- $T=\{t_1, t_2, \dots\}$ – the set of trait identifiers that can be used to characterize an organization's character.

- $V_i=\{v_{i,1}, v_{i,2},...\}$ –the set of values that trait t_i can assume.
- $E=\{e_1, e_2, ...\}$ – the set of empathy, affectivity or attitudes assumed by one organization toward others.
- $OP=\{op_1, op_2, ... \}$ – the set of comparison operators. The operator op_i performs comparisons between the values of the set V_i (e.g. 'near(v_1,v_2)').
- $C=\{c_1, c_2,...\}$ –the set of competences required for the achievement of a collaboration opportunity.

Just as an example, these sets can be instantiated with the following values:
$O=\{net1, org2, university3\}$, $T=\{flexibility, creativity, reliability\}$, $E=\{trusts, distrusts, respects, relies, dislikes, ... \}$, $V_{reliability}=\{low, fair, high\}$, $C=\{DBA, logistics, ICT, CAD\}$,and $OP=\{'<', '>', '=', about, near, reliability\_op, prestige\_op\}$.

Definition 1 (**Organization's Behavior**) – The way in which an organization acts or conducts itself and toward others; the way it behaves in response to a particular event or situation.

Definition 2 (**organization's behavioral patterns**) – The regularities of behaviors that are observable or discernible in the behaviors of an organization.

Definition 3 (**Organization's Character**) – An organization's character can be seen as a composition of a set of traits that determine the way it behaves. It can be modeled as a tuple $OC=(o, TV)$, in which
- o - is the organization being characterized.
- $TV = \{(t_i, v_{i,k}) \mid t_i \in T, v_{i,k} \in V_i\}$ – is the trait set constituted of tuples, each one composed of a trait and a corresponding trait value.

As an example, the character of a hypothetical organization org_1, using the above definition, could be specified by the tuple (org_1, {(*reliability*, high), (*creativity*, fair), (*honesty*, high)}).

Definition 4 (**Willingness to collaborate**) – An organization is willing to collaborate whenever it perceives that (a subset of) its interests can be better satisfied in collaboration with other organizations.
These interests can include the access to new markets, access to resources, complementing its competences and skills, sharing of market risks, or increasing its own benefits. Sometimes this willingness can be negative; for instance, whenever an organization feels uneasy or when perceives important concerns in the *VO* or in the *collaboration opportunity (CO)* achievement (e.g., when it does not believe that the CO will provide the expected benefits).

Definition 5 (**Character-related Preparedness Conditions**) – The preparedness conditions related to the organization's character are represented by a set *CP* of preparedness items. Each item is a tuple that specifies the condition or value required for a given character trait of an organization. The preparedness conditions' set is formally defined as:
$CP = \{ (t_i, v_{i,k}, op_i, p_i) \mid t_i \in T, v_{i,k} \in V_i, p_i \in [0,1], op_i \in OP \}$, in which
- t_i - is the trait name
- $v_{i,k}$ - is the trait value, such that $v_{i,k} \in V_i$.
- op_i - is the operator used for comparing the values of probability p_i.
- p_i - expresses the desired probability/likelihood of the trait t_i having the value $v_{i,k}$.

As an example, a preparedness pattern would be represented by the following set $CP = \{(reliability, high, '>=', 0.7), (creativity, fair, 'about', 0.8)\}$.

Definition 6 **(Competences fitness)** – An organization fits in some collaboration scenario if it possesses adequate (or required) competences.

The competences' adequacy depends on whether the context is either a *VBE* (bringing competences that fit the general scope of the VBE) or a virtual organization (*VO*) (providing or complementing required competences for the achievement of the *VO goals*) (Camarinha-Matos, Afsarmanesh, 2006).

Definition 7 **(Preparedness for collaboration)** – An organization is considered prepared to collaborate if it can satisfy a set of character's conditions (definition 5) and possesses adequate competences (definition 6).

Definition 8 **(Affectivity/Empathy relationships)** – It is a set composed of elements that specify empathic relationships between organizations. It is formally specified as $A=\{(\ o_i,\ o_j,\ e_l,\ level)|\ o_i, o_j \in O,\ e_l \in E,\ level \in [-1,1],\ \}$. Each tuple represents a "feeling" between one organization o_i, and a peer o_j. The *level* parameter specifies the intensity of the feeling. Empathy relationships can be negative (e.g., when an organization distrusts another).

Definition 9 **(Readiness to collaborate)** - is a concept that combines the organization's preparedness (definition 7), willingness to collaborate given a concrete *CO* (definition 4), and the affective/empathic relationships (definition 8) between this organization and the other entities to participate in the CO.

Figure 1. Collaboration readiness concept

Contrary to preparedness, the concept of readiness is applied to a specific collaboration opportunity and typically defined for a short time window. Preparedness, on the other hand, is more long-term oriented.

Specific cases of readiness can be defined, e.g. Readiness to join a *VBE*, Readiness to join a VO. Past research has put considerable effort in the area of "competence fitness" (e.g. matching algorithms for partner selection). However, the other elements of Fig. 1 have received little attention so far, and yet they are important for the success of a collaboration process. In the remaining of this paper we will focus on the issue of character's related preparedness. The other aspects will be subject of future research. For this purpose, let us make the following assumption:

Assumptions – **Organization's behavior predictability**
An organization performs actions or behaviors that tend to repeat through time, leading to the formation of behavioral patterns. These patterns can be associated to a set of identifiable traits. Given the underlying correspondence between traits and behaviors, then the organization's character can be used in behaviors' prediction. Thus, the character of an organization can be used to perform collaboration preparedness assessment, in the following way:

o If the predicted patterns are seen as favorable to collaboration, then the collaboration preparedness increases.
o If these patterns are mostly positive, then in terms of its character the organization is considered prepared to collaborate.
o On the opposite side, if these patterns are considered undesirable or unfavorable to collaboration, then the collaboration preparedness decreases.
o If these patterns are mostly negative, then in terms of its character the organization is considered not prepared to collaborate.

With the above definitions together with these assumptions, it is possible to formulate the following two axioms of collaboration preparedness.

Axiom 1 - An organization *org* is prepared according to a given set of character-related preparedness conditions *PC* if for each preparedness item $p \in PC$, there is a corresponding belief *b*, such that *org*'s character complies with the preparedness item *p*.

$$\forall_{org} \forall_{PC} ((is\_prepared(org, PC) \leftarrow$$

$$\forall_p \exists_b ((belongs(p, PC) \land belief(org, p, b)) \rightarrow complies(p, b)))$$

The predicate 'belief' estimates the probability or likelihood of a given trait to have a value *b*. The 'complies' predicate verifies whether this likelihood meets the condition *p* specified in *PC*. The 'belief' predicate uses a belief network for its functionality as described in section 3.

Axiom 2 – A *VO* satisfies a given set of preparedness conditions *PC* if all its members are prepared according to *PC*.

$$\forall_{VO} \forall_{PC} ((preparedness(VO, PC) \leftarrow$$

$$\forall org ((belongs(org, VO) \rightarrow is\_prepared(org, PC)))$$

It shall be noted that often there is not enough information to perceive and characterize an organization's character. This results in traits that are unknown or specified with imprecision. This increases the uncertainty regarding behavior's prediction and, consequently, limits the collaboration readiness assessment. Therefore, the output of the assessment process should be of probabilistic nature.

3. A MODELING EXPERIMENT

3.1. Belief networks basics

A Bayesian belief network is a kind of probabilistic model that represents causal relationships on a set of variables (Fig. 2). It is composed of two parts: the structural part, which consists of a direct acyclic graph, in which nodes stand for random variables and edges for direct conditional dependence between them; and the probabilistic part that quantifies the conditional dependence between these variables. Each variable can have state values (such as, 'no', 'yes' or 'low', 'high'). If the value of a variable in a node is known, then that node is said to be an evidence node. More on belief networks can be found in (Jensen, 1996). For instance, in Fig. 2, the arc pointing from node C to node E can be perceived as C causing or influencing E. Each of the child nodes have a conditional probability table that quantifies the effects that the parents have on them. For the nodes without parents, the corresponding table only contains prior probabilities. Due to these conditional dependences, if a node becomes an evidence node, then the probabilities (or likelihood) of the other nodes change.

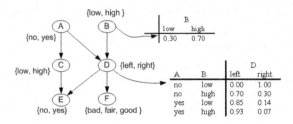

Figure 2. An example of a Bayesian belief network

For any node of the network, the computation of conditional probabilities is done using the Bayes' rule, exemplified in the next section. For the above example, the probability of variable *E* being in state *yes* or *no* is conditioned by its parent C being in state *low* or *high* and its parent *D* in state *left* or *right*. Belief networks can be used to perform queries in distinct ways:

- To perform predictions. This is useful whenever some causes are known and it is necessary to determine the probability of possible effects/consequences. For instance, when B=low and C=high, the probability of E=yes is given by the query P(E=yes | B=low, C=high).
- To perform diagnostics. For instance, when the fact F=bad is known, it is necessary to determine the likelihood of eventual causes: P(A=yes| F=bad).
- It is also possible to make queries on the joint distributions, without providing evidences. For instance, the probability of F=fair, without further evidence, is given by P(F=fair).

3.2. Modeling the predictor

In simple situations a Bayesian network can be specified by an expert and used to perform inferences, as illustrated in Fig. 3. In many cases this task is too complex to be done by hand. Alternatively, both the structure (nodes and arcs) and parameters of the local distributions can be learned from historic data, using Machine Learning techniques (Pearl, 1996), (Cheng et al, 1997), (Cheng, Greiner, 2001) and (Friedman, 1997).

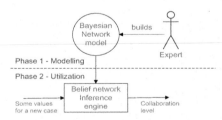

Figure 3. Belief Network modeling and utilization

In order to guide the belief network design process for this experiment, we selected a few assumptions related to members' behavior, among potential many others, which should be taken as merely illustrative. Therefore, for building a modeling example, we conjecture that:

- An organization of fragile economical condition, in order to benefit from others' competences (that usually it cannot afford to own), is more willing to accept the risks of collaboration. On the other hand, due to its fragile condition, it tends to be less reliable.

- An organization in good economical condition might be more reliable, but does not feel the same pressure, as the previous case, to collaborate and therefore tend to be more risk conservative considering collaboration/partnerships.
- A small size organization (e.g. a SME) might possess fewer competences and, with the goal of complementing them, accepts to be more exposed to the risks of collaborating with other organizations.
- The prestige of an organization, which is an attribute that is perceived by its peers, is fundamental in collaboration and adds directly to the preparedness level.
- The creativity of an organization, which can be roughly estimated by evaluating its rate of generated innovations, might also be important for collaboration, and adds directly to the preparedness level.

Certainly, these conjectures are arguable, but they are considered here only for the elaboration of an illustration. An example belief network, modeled using the above guidelines, for the inference of the organization's preparedness levels is shown in Fig. 4, using (Netica, 1997).

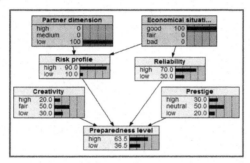

Figure 4. A Bayesian network example to assess the preparedness level

For this belief network, the joint probability distribution, from which the predictions and diagnostics can be made, is the following (showing only the initials for the nodes names):

$$P(PD,ES,RP,R,C,P,PL) = P(PD) \times P(ES|PD) \times P(RP|PD,ES) \times P(R|PD,ES,RP)$$
$$\times P(C|PD,ES,RP,R) \times P(P|PD,ES,RP,R,C) \times P(PL|PD,ES,RP,R,C,P)$$

This function can be simplified by considering the conditional independence statements implied in the belief network. For instance, the 'partner dimension' variable does not directly influence the 'preparedness level', as 'reliability' does. This is because $P(PL|PD,R)=P(PL|R)$, so PD can be removed from the above expression. In other words, PL and PD are conditionally independent given R. The same approach can be applied to the other conditional probabilities, which helps removing more variables (the shaded ones) from the above expression. This results in the expression:

$$P(PD,ES,RP,R,C,P,PL) = P(PD) \times P(ES) \times P(RP|PD,ES) \times P(R|ES) \times P(C) \times P(P)$$
$$\times P(PL|RP,R,C,P)$$

As an illustration for the given problem, and assuming most of the nodes as evidences (to reduce calculations), the probability of preparedness level PL=high, given that PD=high, ES=fair, C=high, and P=high is given by:

$$P(PL_{high} \mid PD_{high}, ES_{fair}, C_{high}, P_{high}) = \frac{P(PL_{high}, PD_{high}, ES_{fair}, C_{high}, P_{high})}{P(PD_{high}, ES_{fair}, C_{high}, P_{high})} = 0.815$$

After the belief network description, it is now possible to give more explanations about the behavior of the 'belief' predicate, used in axiom 1. This predicate, through the belief network, provides the likelihood that, for a given character, the trait t_i specified in preparedness item t (definition 6) has the value $v_{i,k}$ also specified in that item. As an illustration, let us consider the preparedness item t = (reliability, high, '>', 70) and observe the vbe_1 in table 1. This predicate would provide the values for belief b (see axiom 1 for 'b'), using the belief network, as illustrated by the following cases:

- For organization o_1, the belief that reliability=*high* is b=100%, because o_1 has the trait 'reliability' defined with value high in its character profile. It would be represented by an evidence node in the belief network of Fig. 4.
- For organization o_3, the belief that reliability=*high* is b=0%, because o_3 has low reliability in its character profile. It would be represented by an evidence node in the belief network of Fig. 4, but with different evidence (low reliability).
- For organization o_2, the belief is b=53.6%. This is because, the reliability of this organization is unknown and, therefore, this value is obtained using the query b=P('reliability=high'| known_traits(o_2)) on the belief network of Fig. 4. The predicate '*known_traits(org)*', provides the known values of an organization's traits.

3.3. An example

The example described below illustrates the estimation of collaboration preparedness based on organizations' characters, which, as mentioned before, is one of the aspects considered in the readiness assessment approach being researched.

Let us consider the existence of a virtual breeding environment composed of a group of organizations. These organizations, together with corresponding competences and character traits, are defined as shown in table 1. For illustrative purposes, the traits used in this example are the ones defined in the belief network of Fig. 4 in section 3.2. Aspects related to the orthogonality of these traits are yet to be considered in future research. As illustrated in Table 1, one important aspect to emphasize here is that, for the given organizations, some traits are unknown.

Table 1. Competences and traits of the VBE's members

VBE_1 composition							
		Organization traits					
Organization	*Competences*	*PD*	*ES*	*RP*	*R*	*C*	*P*
o_1	c1, c2	high	good	?	high	high	high
o_2	c4, c6	med	?	high	?	low	high
o_3	c2, c5	med	fair	high	low	high	high
o_4	c1, c2	?	good	high	low	?	?
o_5	c1, c3, c4	high	bad	high	high	high	low
o_6	c2, c3	low	good	high	?	high	high

(PD: partners dimension; ES: economical situation; RP: risk profile; R: reliability; C: creativity; P: prestige).

Fig. 5 illustrates two distinct cases of network joining. In the first case, organization *o_12* is a candidate to join the *VBE*. In the second, organization *o_6*, already a member of the *VBE*, is being considered to join an existing virtual organization (*VO*), namely *vo_1*.

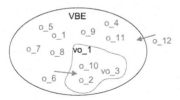

Figure 5. A Virtual breeding environment with an existing VO

As a newcomer, little information is known about o_12's character. The only known evidences about this candidate are that it is in good economical situation and is of low dimension (as illustrated in the belief network of figure 4). We can query the belief network about the probability of this organization to express a high preparedness level, using the conditional probability

P("preparedness level"=high| "partner dimension"=low, "economical situation"=good)=60.1%.

For the second case, candidate o_6 is already a member of the VBE and, as such, there is more information about its character, so its classification's certainty should increase. Taking the known traits of o_6 from table 1, the probability of this organization having a high preparedness level is obtained by the query:

P("preparedness level"=high| "partner dimension"=low, "economical situation"=good, "prestige"=high, "creativity"=high)=90.5%.

If we want to assess whether the virtual organization vo_1 is composed of members that are prepared to collaborate, we can define some preparedness conditions, supposedly adequate for a given situation or context, and run the predicate "preparedness" specified in the axiom 2. We would invoke the following query

"preparedness(vo_1, {(reliability, high, '>=', 0.7), (creativity, fair,'about',80)})"

In this case *vo_1* is not prepared according to the specified preparedness conditions, because organization *o_2* does not comply with the preparedness conditions. This organization has reliability P(reliability=high, know_traits(o_2))=0.63, which is less than 0.7, as specified in the conditions. It also fails in terms of creativity, because P(creativity=fair, know_traits(o_2))=0. In other words, its creativity level is *low* and the conditions of the query require it to be *fair*.

4. CONCLUSIONS

Collaboration can be highly beneficial and even a survival factor for industrial companies. But it can also be risky, being important to assess the readiness of potential partners. Although most works in the past were focused on "hard" factors such as competency matching or technological preparedness, the success of a collaborative process depends on several other factors of a "soft" nature such as organization's character, willingness to collaborate, or the affectivity / empathy relationships. A preliminary approach to handle such elements was introduced.

The preliminary results show that this assessment approach is feasible and promising. Nevertheless, further research is needed towards the development of a full assessment model for collaboration readiness, which is the subject of our ongoing research.

4.1. Acknowledgements

This work was funded in part by the European Commission through the ECOLEAD project.

5. REFERENCES

1. Afsarmanesh H, Camarinha-Matos LM. "A framework for management of virtual organization breeding environments". In Collaborative Networks and their Breeding Environments; eds. Camarinha-Matos, L., Afsarmanesh, Ortiz, A.; Springer, 2005, pp. 35-48.
2. Camarinha-Matos LM, Afsarmanesh H. "Creation of Virtual Organizations in a Breeding Environment". In Proceedings of INCOM'06 - St. Etienne, France - 17-19 May 2006.
3. Camarinha-Matos LM, Macedo P. "Towards a Conceptual Model of Value Systems in Collaborative Networks". In Establishing the Foundation of Collaborative Networks; eds. Camarinha-Matos, L., Afsarmanesh, H., Novais, P., Analide, C.; Boston: Springer, 2007, pp. 53–64.
4. Chun R. "Ethical Character and Virtue of Organizations: An Empirical Assessment and Strategic Implications". Journal of Business Ethics, V57, 2005, pp. 269-284.
5. Goldie P. What people will do: personality and prediction. Richmond. Journal of Philosophy 2004; 7: 11-18
6. Gothlich SE. "From Loosely Coupled Systems to Collaborative Business Ecosystems". Paper No. 573, University of Kiel (Germany), May 2003, from http://www.bwl.uni-kiel.de/grad-kolleg/de/kollegiaten/goethlich/Business%20Ecosystems%204b%201,5Z.pdf
7. Netica Application for Belief Networks and Influence Diagrams Users Guide, Norsys Software Group, 1997,http://www.norsys.com.
8. Oxford Dictionary of English. Catherine Soanes, Angus Stevenson (Ed.), Second Edition, ISBN 0-19-8613474, Oxford University Press, Oxford, UK, 2003.
9. Romero D, Giraldo J, Galeano N, Molina A. "Towards Governance Rules and Bylaws for Virtual Breeding environments". In Establishing the Foundation of Collaborative Networks; eds. Camarinha-Matos, L., Afsarmanesh, H., Novais, P., Analide, C.; Boston: Springer, 2007, pp. 93–102
10. Webber J. Virtue, Character and Situation. Journal of Moral Philosophy 2006; 3 (2): 193-213.
11. Westphal I, Thoben KD, Seifert M. "Measuring Collaboration Performance in Virtual Organizations". In Establishing the Foundation of Collaborative Networks; eds. Camarinha-Matos, L., Afsarmanesh, H., Novais, P., Analide, C.; Boston: Springer, 2007, pp. 33–42
12. Wilkinson IF, Freytag P, Young L. Business Mating: Who Chooses Whom and Gets Chosen?. Industrial Marketing Management 2005, Vol. 34: 669-80.

09

PROCESS MANAGEMENT IN COLLABORATIVE NETWORKED ORGANIZATIONS: A PERSPECTIVE UNDER THE SCOPE OF ORGANIZATIONAL MEMORY

Leandro Loss[1,2], Leonardo Leocádio Coelho de Souza[3], Ricardo José Rabelo[1]

[1]*Federal University of Santa Catarina - Brazil*
DAS – Department of Automation and Systems
GSIGMA – Intelligent Manufacturing Systems Group
loss@gsigma.ufsc.br
rabelo@das.ufsc.br

[2]*Faculdade SENAC Florianópolis – Serviço Nacional de Aprendizagem Comercial – Brazil*
Departamento de Gestão da Tecnologia da Informação

[3]*Federal University of Santa Catarina – Brazil*
EGC - Department of Engineering and Knowledge Management
leoleocadio@egc.ufsc.br

This paper presents an analysis of the relationship between Virtual Organization Inheritance and Organizational Memory. It also frames the concept of process management as being an element of Organizational Memory under the scope of Collaborative Networked Organizations (CNOs). The authors argue that the transformations occurring in processes executed by Virtual Organizations are elements of Organizational Memory and shall be stored for future use by the CNOs' members in order to improve their performance as time passes by.

1. INTRODUCTION

New ways of thinking in organizations are arising and are going to the opposite side of the bureaucracy. Bureaucracy has dominated the organizational studies in the last century, but when concerning the new world scenario nowadays it is not profitable anymore (Drucker, 2006). The organizational reconfiguration that has occurred since the beginning of the 20th, started by Taylor and Ford's ideas, where organizations were hierarchical and bureaucratic, has been changed. New approaches by which organizations work embrace new strategies like collaborative networks, including Virtual Organizations Breeding Environments and Virtual Organizations (Camarinha-Matos and Afsarmanesh, 2006).

Despite the foundations coined in the beginning of the last century have been innovative for that time, they are not, only by themselves, adequate enough to the customers' requirements and expectations nowadays (Friedman, 2005). Actually, such requirements and expectations have increased due to many factors. It is possible to cite some: people's interconnectivity (throughout the Internet), the reduction of customs

Please use the following format when citing this chapter:

Loss, L., Leocádio de Souza, L. and Rabelo, R.J., 2008, in IFIP International Federation for Information Processing, Volume 266, *Innovation in Manufacturing Networks;* ed. A. Azevedo; (Boston: Springer), pp. 87–94.

barriers, higher participation of women in the society, as well as the rising of the Eastern Asian economies in the commercial scenario just to mention some.

As one alternative to face this new reality and the changes that are day by day faster than the day before, organizations are looking for new approaches, like working in strategic alliances with other organizations or in collaborative networks, as argued in ECOLEAD (2006).

The discipline of Collaborative Networks has risen as the answer to coordinate, manage, and arrange tasks, as well as processes among all agents that are part of the value chain. It means that this approach involves Information and Communication Technologies (ICTs), processes, organizations, individuals, and the learning related to this kind of relationship between organizations and the market.

The rationale behind this paper is that <u>processes</u> are part of the Organizational Memory and processes also foster organizational learning. Such learning may help to provide further reconfigurations in business opportunities that may be shared and used by all actors taking part of the Collaborative Networks. It is seen that processes in Collaborative Networks have not been explored so far as one element of Organizational Memory. Taking this idea into consideration, the paper also investigates the relationship between the assets that may be re-used (inherited) in alliances among organizations (see section 2) and the foundations related to the discipline of Organizational Memory.

In this sense, this research was done as an exploratory and descriptive investigation. Despite processes management and Collaborative Networks (a branch of strategic alliances) be relevant topics in industry and academia (Pereira-Klen *et al.*, 1999; Camarinha-Matos and Afsarmanesh, 2007), both communities do not approach in deep the relationship of organizational memory, inheritance, and processes management altogether, characterizing an exploratory investigation. On the other hand, it is descriptive because it identifies and describes process management in Collaborative Networks under the scope of Organizational Memory.

In order to support this research, studies about strategic alliances, virtual organizations, organizational memory, and processes management were done. It allowed a conceptual analysis and the identification of relevant information to this work.

The content of this paper is divided as follows: section 2 stresses the importance of alliances among organizations, mainly represented by Collaborative Networks; section 3 presents the discussion about Virtual Organization Inheritance and Organizational Memory. The relationship between Organizational Memory with Process Management is shown in section 4; finally section 5 provides the final considerations.

2. ALLIANCES AMONG ORGANIZATIONS

According to Charim (2004), partnership shall be any agreement among organizations, even if it is a relationship of buying-selling. As a result, partnerships are the seeds to a higher interaction among organizations. Gaspareto (2003) argues that the main activities executed in partnerships, under a traditional view, may be represented by *joint ventures, holdings, consortia, outsourcing* and *strategic alliances*.

Regarding the topic of strategic alliances, Child (2003) also argues that the term *Strategic alliance* refers to cooperation between entities in order to improve their objectives. Strategic alliances may range from contract-based joint ventures to less formal collaboration forms (Child 2003), like Collaborative Networks.

The authors of this paper recognize that under the scope of strategic alliance is framed the discipline of collaborative networks. Collaborative Networks that have some kind of organization, like ethical code, rules, and roles, are called as Collaborative Networked

Organizations (CNOs) and comprise a variety of entities. Such entities may be either organizations or individuals (Camarinha-Matos and Afsarmanesh, 2006) and most of them are autonomous, geographically distributed, and heterogeneous. This heterogeneity also considers different environments and the culture of the involved entity (Camarinha-Matos and Afsarmanesh, 2007).

In a slightly different way, when compared to other kinds of networks, the collaboration process under the CNOs' scope is an intention that derives from shared believes. Members of a CNO may achieve common objectives that would not be feasible due to high costs and lack of knowledge in specific issues if they would be done by a single organization (Camarinha-Matos and Afsarmanesh, 2006). There are many manifestations of collaborative networks, for a detailed overview about this topic see Camarinha-Matos and Afsarmanesh (2006).

This paper explores only the CNOs' manifestations known as Virtual Organizations Breeding Environment (VBE) and (Dynamic) Virtual Organization (VO). The former stands for a set of organizations that are willing to collaborate with each other and, as such, establishes a long-term cooperation agreement aiming the sustainability of this network (Camarinha-Matos and Afsarmanesh, 2006). The main objective of the VBE is to enable the creation of (dynamic) VOs. The latter (VO) is characterized as temporary alliances among organizations. These alliances are created in order to share skills or core competencies and resources as well as to better respond to collaboration opportunities. Usually VOs are supported by computer networks (Rabelo and Pereira-Klen, 2004).

However, despite VOs increase agility, flexibility, and provide an efficient utilization of resources and knowledge among organizations when facing new business opportunities, they are not continuous. The aspect of temporary arrangements brings some challenges (Karvonen *et al.* 2004), like loss of information, loss of knowledge and other values (Karvonen *et al.* 2007). It composes the assets that can be used to create value in the future, not only to one specific organization, but also to all entities taking part of the VBE and improving its *preparedness* for future collaborations in the forms of VOs.

Hence, these assets must be gathered, stored, properly handled and managed, and retrieved when it is necessary either by other VBE members or by other VOs. Based on that, VO inheritance (VO-I) has emerged as the practice for dealing with issues related to how the information, knowledge, devised practices, products and services may be managed accordingly (Loss *et al.*, 2006). Loss *et al.*, (2006), Karvonen (*et al.* 2007), and Picard (2007) have explored this topic. It is believed that VO-I is closely related to the Organizational Memory (Walsh and Ugson, 1991; Huber, 1991; Nilakanta *et al.*, 2006), however the literature about VO-I have not yet explored this intersection so far. Next section frames the characteristics of VO-I under the scope of the Organizational Memory.

3. VIRTUAL ORGANIZATION INHERITANCE AND ORGANIZATIONAL MEMORY

According to Karvonen *et al.*, (2007) and Loss *et al.*, (2006), VO inheritance is related to the practice of transmitting the experience and other non-proprietary assets that were created in a collaboration process. Karvonen *et al.*, (2007 p. 254) coined the term VO heritage to describe the contents of the VO-I. VO heritage is defined as "the different assets which are inherited from a VO to a VBE".

The rationale behind the VO-I is that after VOs accomplish their tasks, the lessons learned and the useful outcomes of a certain VO shall return to the VBE, so that the VO-I shall: i) improve preparedness of the VBE; VOs can be created and started faster, and better managed as well; ii) VOs may be more effective and reliable regarding time and costs, as well as ensure the quality of its products; iii) VO management efforts are reduced and trust relationships reinforced. It is argued therefore that VO-I contributes to the "VBE bag of assets". The VBE bag of assets is defined as "all valuable elements that different VBE Members may wish to share with others and which are available to all VBE members" (ECOLEAD 2006 p. 16).

Likewise the VBE bag of assets, the Organizational Memory (Walsh and Ungson, 1991; Huber, 1991) seeks for keeping both tangible and intangible assets produced by organizations, working in strategic alliances or not. Walsh and Ungson, (1991) argue that Organizational Memory is structured in five "retention bins", namely: i) individuals; ii) culture; iii) transformations; iv) structures; and v) ecology. Furthermore, they recognize that Organizational Memory also resides in "external archives". These external archives are identified as former employees, clients, suppliers, and so forth. Consequently, both organizational memory and VBE bag of assets are constituted not only by human memory, but also by retention elements.

Bringing these research fields together, VO-I and VBE bag of assets could be framed under the conceptualization of Organizational Memory. ECOLEAD (2006) elected different forms of assets that may be inherited by the VBE, the three main types are: i) financial capital; ii) intellectual capital; and iii) social capital. Under the perspective of Organizational Memory these forms of assets are classified as:

Financial Capital corresponds to the retention bin called *Transformations*. Transformations correspond to the "logic that guides the transformation of an input (whether it is a raw material, a new recruit, or an insurance claim) into an output" (Walsh and Ungson, 1991 p. 65). Financial Capital is seen as a *Transformation* because the profit of a certain VO was produced by processes and tasks executed by the VO members. Even being a tangible asset (money or equipments), common procedures or tools used to generate this asset shall be recorded/stored and are part of the organizational memory, but in an inter-organizational context.

Intellectual Capital corresponds to both retentions bins called *Individuals* and *Culture*. According to ECOLEAD (2006), Intellectual Capital is split into:

- *Human Capital* – it is nearby to the retention bin called *Individuals* that retain information and knowledge based on their own experiences and competences (tacit knowledge, skills, and so forth) and their capacity in creating new value; and
- *Structure Capital and Innovation & Learning Capital* – they are related to the retention bin called *Culture*. Culture comprises the way of "thinking and feeling about problems that is transmitted to members in the organization" (Walsh and Ungson, 1991 p. 63). It comprises quality standards, management systems, as well as the understanding of the marked conditions, business and technological solutions.

Social Capital corresponds to the retention bin called *External Archives* because it refers to the relations and logistic channels that an organization maintains with its clients, suppliers or other organizations. Social Capital is also related to the retention bin called *Structure* due to the influence and the perception of the activities executed by certain people and the roles concerning employees, customers and other organizations.

The retention bin called *ecology* is related to the physical structure (setting and design) and it is not covered neither by the VO-I nor by the VBE bag of assets. An illustration about VO-I and Organizational Memory can be visualized in Figure 2.

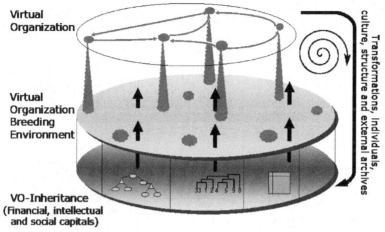

Figure 1. VO-Inheritance. Source: Loss *et al.*, (2006)

As a result of this framing, VO-I can be seen under the scope of Organizational Memory. It also goes beyond the limits of human knowledge (tacit or explicit) as argued by Loss *et al.* (2006). VO-I is not stored in one single spot, indeed it is split over the members and distributed across the organizations.

On the other hand, it is observed that neither VO-I nor Organizational Memory are approaching the management of processes (distributed or not) when dealing with CNOs. Although the research about VO-I and Organizational Memory has been intensified, aspects related to process management are not yet characterized. It is believed that the characterization of process management is an important facet that must be taken into consideration because processes store and provide vital information to the VO's functioning (Pereira-Klen *et al.*, 1999) and thus, they might be seen as one element that is part of the VO-I, and as a consequence, part of the Organizational Memory. Consequently, it is important to study the role of process management under the scope of CNOs as an element of Organizational Memory. Next section gives special attention to this issue.

4. PROCESS MANAGEMENT

In order to formulate and/or change the organizational behavior and become more competitive, organizations shall fulfill certain prerequisites. Some of these prerequisites are closely related to choices in organizational strategies, for example, working in a Collaborative Networked Organization-like, the evaluation about resources availability, as well as working either in a vertical or in a an horizontal (organized by processes) way.

It seems that organizing duties by processes is an interesting alternative in order to provide some level of standard to the inputs and to the outputs in a value chain. Process management, when seen as a organizational methodology, gives the opportunity to enterprises to reach higher efficient rates than the traditional approaches when providing goods and services, adapting themselves to the market changes, leading to efforts integration, and the capacity to learn (Gonçalves, 2000). It implies to represent organizations as a set of processes in order to facilitate the comprehension and increasing business performance, customer relationships, and market share to the stakeholders.

Under the context of CNO, VOs may work based on processes. It means that organizations, being part of a certain VO, are responsible for a set of processes. In this way each organization plays the role of either client (receiving inputs) or supplier (providing outputs) for a certain process, as shown in Figure 3. The whole Collaboration Opportunity will result in a value chain producing and delivering goods or services to the final client.

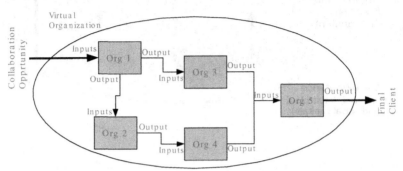

Figure 2. Processes in a Virtual Organization

Hence, processes (represented in Figure 3 by each organization[1]) may be understood as "any activity that receives an input, performs transformations in order to add value, and produces an output to an internal or external client" (Harrington, 1993). As such, the creation of concrete results will depend on resources availability and their use by the VO members.

Wearing the lenses of Organizational Memory, processes and the retention bin called *transformation* are alike. Processes have embedded the knowledge and resources to transform an input into an output, similarly as stated by Walsh and Ungson (1991). These transformations are important to be remembered in the future and may be re-used by other VBE members in another collaboration opportunity, so that it shall constitute one more element of the VO Inheritance (Karvonen *et al.*, 2007).

It is argued that all duties in a VO could be executed as processes and thus, it is possible to realize how the duties are executed. As a result, process management break functional barriers and embrace into the VO management model the final client, goods or services, and the workflow executed by the VO itself.

Once duties are split into processes, it is possible to monitor the VO members (owners of the processes) like "black boxes" with their inputs and outputs. The operations on "how the tasks that compose a process are executed" may be inherited by the VBE and be further improved or re-used. At the same time, these "black boxes" deliver products or services according to a specified criteria.

In order to measure "how good" or "how bad" is the inherited content (process), benchmarking tools and performance indicators might be used. Once a process is an agreed and formal procedure in the organization, it is possible to recognize its level of success.

---

[1] One organization may be responsible for one or more processes.

5. FINAL CONSIDERATIONS

This paper highlighted the relationship between Virtual Organization Inheritance (VO-I) and Organizational Memory and framed the process management as one element of VO-I. It also conceptualized the financial, intellectual, and social capitals pointed as elements of VO-I by ECOLEAD (2006) according to the "retention bins" of Organizational Memory proposed by Walsh and Ungson (1991).

As a result, one may consider the following relationship:

- Financial Capital is related to the retention bin called Transformation;
- Intellectual Capital is related to the retention bins called Individual and Culture; and
- Social Capital is related to the retention bins called Structure and External Archives.

The retention bin called Ecology is related to the physical structure and is not approached under the scope of CNOs, mainly when dealing with Virtual Organizations because VOs do not have a physical venue.

Process management was framed as the retention bin called *transformation* due to the inputs are processed and returned as outputs (goods or services). It means that the processes are the learning instruments used to produce knowledge represented by either tangible or intangible assets. This knowledge may be reused in the future collaboration opportunities.

Next steps include a deeper investigation of this study in order to characterize the retention bin *transformation* in a wider context. It is believed that *transformation* is part of all other retention bins and it aggregates values from all other retention bins.

5.1 Acknowledgments

This work has been partially supported by the Brazilian councils of research and scientific development – CNPq (www.cnpq.br) and CAPES (www.capes.gov.br), as well as FAPEMA (www.fapema.br). It has also been developed in the scope of the Brazilian IFM project (www.ifm.org.br) and the European IST FP-6 IP ECOLEAD project (www.ecolead.org). Special thanks to Ms. Andrea Steil for her comments and contributions.

6. REFERENCES

1. Camarinha-Matos, L.M., Afsarmanesh, H. "Collaborative networks: Value creation in a knowledge society". In PROLAMAT conference, eds. Wang, K., Kovács, G. L., Wozny, M. J., e Fang, M., vol. 207 of IFIP, Boston: Springer, 2006, pp 26–40.
2. Camarinha-Matos, L.M., Afsarmanesh, H. A Comprehensive Modeling Framework for Collaborative Networked Organizations" Journal of Intelligent Manufacturin 2007; 18:529-542.
3. Charim, M.Aliança empresarial no setor de transportes: estratégia para dinamizar o transporte de encomendas em ônibus. Tese de doutorado, Depto de Eng. de Produção – UFSC, 2004.
4. Child, J.Learning Through Strategic Alliances. Eds. Dierkes, M., Antal, A. B., Child, J., e Nonaka, I., Handbook of Organizational Learning and Knowledge. Oxford University Press Inc., 2003, pp 657-680.
5. Drucker, P. F. Classic Drucker – The new society of organizations. Harvard Business School Press, 2006, pp 127-138.
6. ECOLEAD. European Collaborative Networked Organizations Leadership Initiative. Technical report D21.4a - Characterization of VBE Value Systems and Metrics, March 2006.
7. Friedman, T. L. The World Is Flat: A Brief History of the Twenty-First Century Farrar, Straus and Giroux, 2005
8. Gaspareto, V. Proposta de uma Sistemática para Avaliação de Desempenho em Cadeias de Suprimentos. Tese de doutorado, Depto de Eng. de Produção – UFSC, 2003.
9. Gonçalves, José Ernesto Lima. Processo, que processo? Revista de Administração de Empresas, São Paulo, v.40, n.4, p. 8-19, out./dez. 2000.
10. Harrington, H. J. Aperfeiçoando Processos Empresariais. São Paulo: Makron, 1993.
11. Huber, G. P.Organizational learning: The contributing processes and the literatures. Organization Science, 1991, pp 88–115.
12. Karvonen, I., Jansson, K., Salkari, I., Ollus, M., "Challenges in the management of virtual organizations". In Camarinha-Matos, L. (Ed.), Virtual Enterprises and Collaborative networks (Kluwer Academic Publishers), 2004, pp 255-264.
13. Karvonen, I., Salkari, I., Ollus, M. "Identification of Forms and Components of VO Inheritance". In IFIP, Vol 243. Establishing the Foundation of Collaborative Networks; eds. Camarinha-Matos, L., Afsarmanesh, H., Novais, P., Analide, C. (Springer), 2007, pp 253-262.
14. Loss, L., Pereira-Klen, A. A., Rabelo, R. J. Virtual Organization Management: An Approach Based on Inheritance Information In: Global Conference on Sustainable Product Development and Life Cycle Engineering. Oct 03-06. São Carlos, SP, Brazil, 2006.
15. Pereira-Klen, A. A., Rabelo, R. J., Spinosa, L. M., Ferreira, A. C. "Distributed Business Process Management". In IFIP International Federation of Information Processing, Networking Industrial Enterprises, eds. Camarinha-Matos, L., Afsarmanesh, H., KAP, 1999, pp. 241-258
16. Nilakanta, S., Miller, L. L., Zhu, D. Organizational Memory Management: Technological and Research Issues. Journal of Database Management. Jan-Mar 2006; 17, 1 ABI/INFORM Global pg 85.
17. Picard, W. "Continuous Management of Professional Virtual Community Inheritance Based on the Adaptation of Social Protocols". IFIP International Federation of Information Processing, vol. 243. Establishing the Foundation of Collaborative Networks; eds. Camarinha-Matos, L., Afsarmanesh, H., Novais, P., Analide, C. (Springer), 2007, pp 381-388.
18. Rabelo, R. J., Pereira-Klen, A. A. "A Brazilian Obseratory on Global and Collaborative Networked Organizations". In Collaborative Networked Organizations: A Research Agenda for Emerging Business Models (eds) Kluwer Academic Publishers, Norwell, MA, 2004, pp 103-112.
19. Walsh, J. P., Ungson, G. R. Organizational memory. Academy of Management Review 1991; 16(1).

10

AUTOMATING TRUST ASSESSMENT FOR CONFIGURATION OF TEMPORARY PARTNERSHIPS

Simon Samwel Msanjila, Hamideh Afsarmanesh

University of Amsterdam, (msanjila, hamideh)@science.uva.nl

Owing to advances in digital technology, emerging breakthrough solutions responding to market needs are becoming increasingly innovative and complex. Large amount of resources, competencies, skills, etc. are required to accomplish such solutions, usually beyond the capabilities and capacities of a single organization. The emergence of co-innovation networks as breeding environments for creation of temporary partnerships has enhanced the possibility of success for organizations and facilitating their collaborations. One obstacle to configuration of such partnerships as well as collaboration has been the difficulty in assessing the trust level of potential partners. So far, trust level assessment has been performed manually by organizations and in ad hoc manners, which is both time consuming and hardly produces accurate results. Consequently, formation of collaborative initiatives has become more challenging and organizations are reluctant to work with each other. This paper addresses the supervised automation of the assessment of trust level of organizations in co-innovation networks. It presents the design and development of Trust Management system, addressing its specifications and architectures to facilitate its implementation.

1. INTRODUCTION

Establishing trust relationships among organizations has proved to enhance the efficiency of collaborative processes (e.g. collaborative designing of a new product, etc.) which involve a number of organizations. Organizations are now encouraged to trust others in order to jointly address the need for sharing large amount of resources, competencies, skills, etc. required to respond to a larger opportunity, which none of them could do alone. However, finding trustworthy partners for such collaborations is becoming more challenging.

Traditionally, trust is seen as subjective aspect and thus its evaluation has been opinion-based. Applying subjective based trust analysis, such as opinion-based trust, in collaboration is too risky due to the fact that it can be biased and difficult to formally reason. Approaches for rational trust analysis are needed. We define trust of an organization, as it is applied in VBEs, as the objective-specific confidence of a trustor organization to a trustee organization based on the results of fact-based assessment of trust level of the trustee (Msanjila and Afsarmanesh, 2007c). Thus objective based trust creation refers to the process of creating trust among organizations based on the results of the fact-based assessment of their trust levels. Only measurable or numeric data are applied to the assessment and the resulted trust levels can be supported with some formal reasoning applied during the assessment of trust level, which in turn enhances the reasoning of the established trust relationships.

Please use the following format when citing this chapter:

Msanjila, S.S. and Afsarmanesh, H., 2008, in IFIP International Federation for Information Processing, Volume 266, *Innovation in Manufacturing Networks;* ed. A. Azevedo; (Boston: Springer), pp. 95–104.

A priori to jointly addressing market/society opportunities organizations must both trust each other and prepare themselves for sharing and exchanging the required resources and information, establishing necessary infrastructure for co-working, etc. To address the need of preparing themselves and increase their chances of collaboration, organizations join co-innovation networks that have emerged as breeding environments for the formation of temporary partnerships, such as virtual organizations (VOs). One popular form of co-innovation networks is the VO Breeding Environment (VBE). A VBE is defined as an alliance of organizations and related supporting institutions, adhering to a base long term cooperation agreement, and adopting common operating principles and infrastructures, with the main goal of increasing both their chances and preparedness towards collaboration in potential VOs (Afsarmanesh, et al 2007). VBEs support the preparation of organizations by: (1) maintaining common and sharing principles, (2) providing interoperable infrastructure, (3) facilitating common understanding with a maintained ontology, (4) providing definition of value systems and performance metrics, (5) supporting the assessment of trust level of organizations, etc.

In practice, organizations have been manually assessing trust level of each other both in ad hoc manners which are inefficient, hardly accurate and time consuming. Furthermore, to match the need of quickly responding to opportunities, processes related to assessment of trust level of organizations must now be (semi-) automated. This paper presents an approach and a system for supervised automation of Trust Management to assist the administration of co-innovation networks and specifically VBEs with handling such processes. We define the Trust Management (TrustMan) system which aggregates our previous introduced models and approaches appeared in (Msanjila and Afsarmanesh, 2007a & 2007b), and automates the processes related to the management of trust among organizations in VBEs.

1.1. Assessing trust level of organizations in co-innovation networks

Perceptions of trust have been in line with the nature of purposes for its applications as well as involved actors. Thus purposes for establishing trust differ among the practices. For each specific practice in which a particular group of actors is involved trust is differently interpreted and perceived as compared to others. In our research, we classify trust aspects into five perspectives: Technological (Tech), Social (Soc), Structural (Str), Managerial (Man), and Economical (Eco) (Msanjila and Afsarmanesh 2007c). Furthermore, to address variation of trust perceptions, a *rational* approach is required for measuring trust level and reason on the results.

To "*rationally*" assess trust level of organizations a series of fact-based trust criteria can be applied. With the empirical study of co-innovation networks as well as survey of the past research, we have identified a good number of measurable criteria that act as indicators of trust assessment (Msanjila and Afsarmanesh 2007c). However, we have also identified that the influence of a trust criterion on the trust level can be either positive or negative depending on its behaviour. Furthermore, the behaviour of each trust criterion changes in time, and causally influences others. Causal influences can be studied by applying concepts from system dynamics (Kirkwood, 1998). Results can be translated into mathematical equations reflecting inter-relations of trust criteria (Msanjila and Afsarmanesh 2007c). The formulated equations comprise the base for our designed mechanisms for assessment of trust level of organizations (Msanjila and Afsarmanesh 2007a). Basically, mechanisms developed for TrustMan implement three forms of equations. The 1st form of equation is applied to calculate the final comparative scores of trust level of organizations as an average of weighted scores of all perspectives (equation 1). In all equations the following are applied: **TL** (trust level), **S** (score), **per** (trust perspective), **IF** (intermediate factor), **W** (weight), and **Avg** (average).

$$TL = Avg[(W_{Tech} * S_{Tech}),(W_{Soc} * S_{Soc}),(W_{Str} * S_{Str}),(W_{Man} * S_{Man}),(W_{Eco} * S_{Eco})]\ldots(1)$$

The score for each trust perspective is calculated as weighted average of score for all intermediate factors as shown in equation (2) which represents the 2nd form.

$$S_{per} = \frac{1}{n}\sum_{i}^{n} W_{IF_i} * S_{IF_i} \ldots\ldots\ldots\ldots\ldots\ldots\ldots(2)$$

The score for intermediate factors is calculated as a function of trust criteria and known factors as shown in equation (3) which represents the third form.

$$S_{IF} = f[rust\_criteria, known\_factors] \qquad Where\, 0 < W_i < 1, and \sum_{\forall i} W_i = 1 \ldots\ldots(3)$$

2. SPECIFICATION OF TRUSTMAN SYSTEM

The system supports five main kinds of user (Table 1) and based on their requirements the related functionalities are specified as addressed in section 2.1.

Table 1: Specification of users and their requirements for TrustMan system

User 1: VBE administrator	This user group has the highest administrative rights. They can view, and execute all the functionalities in the system. The requirements for this user include system's support to: (1) Assesses trust level of membership applicant and VBE members, (2) Define and provide rights to other users, (3) Support other users to evaluate trustworthiness of trustees (3) Manage trust related data, and (4) Update trust criteria.
User 2: VO planners	This user group gets temporary administration right to perform administrative tasks using. The fundamental requirements for this user group include system's support to: (1) View the trust criteria applied to the system, (2) Select specific trust criteria, and (3) Evaluate specific trustworthiness.
User 1: VBE members	The users in this group possess non-administrative rights and thus they can only access the system to manipulate their own trust related data. Their requirements include support to: (1) Accesses its base trust level records, (2) Updates its trust related data, (3) View the trust criteria applied to the system.
User 3: Membership applicants	This user group possesses the very basic rights to support itself with interactions related to its application submission. The requirement for this user group is to get support provided to submit the trust related data for the assessment of base trust level.
User 4: Ext. stakeholder	This user group includes customers, and invited organizations. Requirements for this group are s support: (1) Customers to create trust to the VBE, and (2) Invited organizations to trust the VBE.

2.1. Specification of functionalities

TrustMan system implementation adopted the web services technology. It provides web functionalities for human user and web services for system users (Table 2).

Table 2: Specification of functionalities provided by TrustMan system

S1	**For assessing base trust level of organizations:** When customizing the TrustMan system, in a specific environment, the VBE administrator selects the minimum set of trust criteria - base trust criteria - that reflects the characteristics of the specific domain of the VBE and suits the needs of the environment. The results of the assessment that apply the base trust criteria are referred to as "*base trust level*". The *service for assessing base trust level* supports the assessment of the trust level of organizations based on the base trust criteria.
S2	**For evaluating specific trustworthiness of organizations:** This service aims at measuring how trustworthy an organization is for a specific trust objective, i.e. inviting a VBE member to participate in a VO, etc. The trustor selects a specific set of trust criteria and defines ratings for values of trust criteria to classify different levels of trust. TrustMan system applies the selected trust criteria and ratings to evaluate the organizations' trustworthiness.
S3	**For establishing trust relationships among organizations:** The approach suggested to facilitate *establishing trust relationships* among organizations is through measuring their historical data for both their trust records. To create trust among organizations, they can be provided with relevant information queried from the data stored in the TrustMan system, which will enable them trusting others. The challenge for the information provision is related to the four questions of: "*who*", "*when*", "*why*" and "*how*" (Msanjila and Afsarmanesh, 2007d).
S4	**For creating trust to the VBE:** This service supports external stakeholders (invited organizations, and customers) to create trust to the VBE. They need to access information that will assist them with trusting the VBE in relation to their businesses. This service guides them to access information which fits their trust purposes and perceptions.
S5	**For managing trust related data:** This service supports VBE: membership applicants, members, and administrator. Applicants will use this service to submit trust related data to facilitate the assessment of base trust level for the evaluation of their application towards joining VBEs. Members will use the service to update trust related data. Administrator will use the service to manage the trust related data, i.e. ensuring its updated, valid, etc
S6	**For managing the assessment mechanisms:** The equations applied for the development of mechanisms (section 1.1) for assessing trust level of organizations incorporates weights for the applied parameters. The weights can be changed from time to time when it is needed using this services. The service is accessed by the administrator only.

3. ARCHITECTURAL DESIGN OF TRUSTMAN SYSTEM

Based on the specifications above, we present the architectural design of TrustMan system addressing the operational architecture and the componential architecture.

3.1. Operational architecture

TrustMan system is one of the subsystems that together constitute the so-called VBE management system (VMS). The VMS is designed to assists the VBE administration with semi-automatically handling of managerial tasks (Afsarmanesh, et al 2007). TrustMan system assist the VBE administration with handling the tasks related to managing trust among organizations in the VBE. In order to properly and comprehensively provide the required services the TrustMan system interacts with others sub-systems (Figure 1) for four purposes, namely for: *(1) acquiring the trust related data, (2) providing results of the trust level assessment, (3) accessing ICT-Infrastructure (ICT-I) basic services, and (4) supporting human access.*

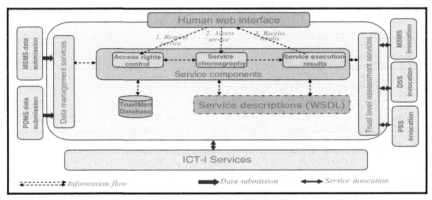

Figure 1. Operational architecture for TrustMan system

(a)   Interactions for assisting the acquisition of trust related data

Two sub-systems namely: *Membership Structure Management System (MSMS) and Performance Data related Management System (PDMS)* interact with TrustMan for submitting trust related data. MSMS is developed to assist the VBE administration with handling the registration of new VBE members, and defining their roles and rights. One fundamental information necessary for the VBE administration to decide about acceptance of the VBE membership applicant is the base trust level. The MSMS interacts with TrustMan to facilitate applicants submit trust related data to the TrustMan system. The interactions are based on service invocations.

While the VBE is in operation phase its members participate in activities, both within the VBE and in configured VOs. Thus their trust related data must be continuously updated. The main source of trust related data is the organizations' performances achieved in those activities. The PDMS interacts with TrustMan to assist the VBE actors with updating the trust related data based on the collected organizational performance. The PDMS includes management systems for VO information, inheritance, and VBE's activities related performance.

(b)   Interactions related to accessing results for trust level assessment

Some VMS subsystems need to invoke a number of services provided by TrustMan system to access the records of trust level of organizations. The trust levels of organizations in this case are used as input towards providing the required services by those subsystems to their respective users. Three VMS subsystems are identified which need to invoke services provided by TrustMan, namely: *MSMS, Decision Support System (DSS), and Partner Search and Suggestion (PSS)* (Figure 1).

MSMS shall invoke the service for assessing base trust level of membership applicant for the aim of analyzing whether the applicant organization meets the specified minimum level of trust in the VBE. Thus the MSMS uses the resulted trust level and other relevant information to provide services which support the VBE administrator on deciding about acceptance of the application.

DSS supports the VBE administration to make decisions on a number of issues but mainly in relation to controlling and alarming member organizations for: *the VBE competency gap, the organization's lack of performance, and the organization's low trustworthiness.* Specifically for this case, in order to analyze the evolution of trust level of the organization the DSS shall invoke the services provided by TrustMan system for assessing base trust level of organizations. The interactions take place in scheduled manner and thus the organizations whose trust level is deteriorating can be alerted and advised on enhancing their trustworthiness.

PSS assists the VO planner with selecting suitable VO partners among the VBE members. One key activity during the selection of suitable VO partners is the evaluation of their specific trustworthiness. The PSS interacts with the TrustMan to facilitate the VO planer with evaluating the trustworthiness of VO partners.

(c)   Interactions to access the ICT Infrastructure (ICT-I) basic services

The TrustMan system needs to invoke some basic services provided by the ICT-I to effectively provide required services. There are a number of basic services provided by the ICT-I developed in the ECOLEAD project (www.ecolead.org). TrustMan needs to invoke two basic services from the ICT-I, namely the service for: *data access, and security management* (Rabelo, et al 2006). The service for data access supports the TrustMan system with handling trust related data in its database, such as the related interactions with MSMS and PDMS for data acquisition. The service for security management supports the TrustMan system to authenticate remote users.

(d)   Interactions related to the human access of the TrustMan system

The interactions between human users and the TrustMan system are facilitated and achieved through the web interface. In addition to providing web services which are invoked by other remote systems, such as MSMS, DSS, PSS, etc., TrustMan system provides functionalities which can be accessed by human users on the web interface.

3.2. Componential architecture

Componential architecture of TrustMan system adopts the standard definitions of web service technology and specifically addressing the classification of layers.

(a)   **Layer 1: Presentation layer**

The presentation layer (Figure 1) handles the delivery of information from the process layer to the web interface in a format that is readable by humans. The layer also handles the transformation of data submitted by human user to the format that is acceptable by various modules at the process layer. As such, it relieves the process layer of concerns regarding syntactical differences in data representation which is understandable by the human end-user based on the web format (Field and Hoffner, 2003). The presentation layer is the only layer where people can care about what they are sending at an advanced level than a bunch of ones or zeros (Rhody, 2002).

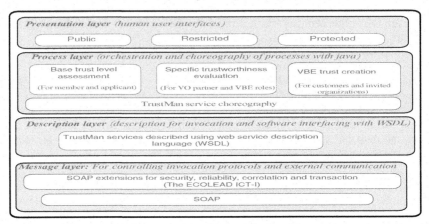

Figure 2. Componential architecture for TrustMan system

TrustMan manages, and deals with sensitive information which in most cases the VBE members consider as confidential such as strategic business data. In TrustMan system, at this layer, the web interface that facilitates the accessibility of information as well as the execution of various supported functionalities applies user rights as addressed in "*service 3*" in section 2.1, namely: *public, restricted and protected interfaces*. Modules for public interface belong to the group of result provisional components in the operational architecture. Modules for restricted and protected interfaces constitute components that belong to both components for "access right control" (user rights and roles) and components for "service execution results" (presenting records) in the operational architecture as shown in Figure 1.

(b)   **Layer 2: Process layer**

In daily life, activities are scheduled in a way that each one is known when it will be performed; following which activity, and which activity will follow soon after the preceding activity is completed. Similarly, when a service is invoked, processes that must be executed shall be organized. The process layer is responsible for defining the logic of execution of various processes (modules) to provide the requested service. The process scheduling constitutes of *orchestration and choreography*.

Orchestration refers to the logic (the sequence and flow) of execution of functions within one system process (Papazoglou and Georgakopoulus, 2003). For example, in java programming this refers to the logic of the execution of functions within one object. Figure 3 shows orchestration of several processes integrated in one choreography process, e.g. system control, trustworthiness evaluation, etc.

Choreography represents the logic that will be followed to execute various modules including invoking other services in order to provide a single integrated service (Peltz,

2003). Several web services were choreographed to provide required integrated services. To exemplify in this paper, we present the choreography of an integrated service for evaluating specific trustworthiness of organizations. Figure 3 represents the choreography of a set of services constituting the evaluation trustworthiness and thus represents a partial processes' architecture of the TrustMan.

The process layer is the only layer which constitutes the services that are scheduled and executed by users and thus all components in this layer belong to the group of components for "service choreography" in the operational architecture.

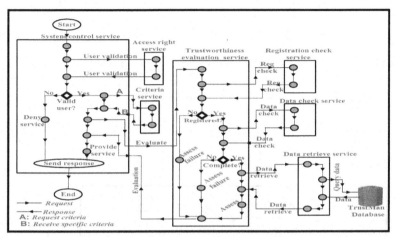

Figure 3. Choreography of a service for evaluating specific trustworthiness of organizations

(c)   Layer 3: Description layer

The description layer handles the provision of grammatical specifications of services available at a certain site. From definition as applied in web service technologies the description of a service applies WSDL (web service description language). WSDL describes four fundamental parts of the service. The first part is *Public interface,* which describes the public operations that are visible to external partners. The second part is *data type information for all message related to requests and responses* that describe the data types for the variables that should be passed to access each service. The third part is *binding information related to the transport protocol,* which defines the protocols necessary to access the service and facilitate external communication. Lastly is the *address information for locating the specified service,* which describes the server location, and how it is discovered in the UDDI.

WSDL files for java web services are generated from the respective java classes. A number of WSDL files describing the services provided by TrustMan system were generated. This layer represents similar aspects as the service description part in the operational architecture as shown in Figure 1.

(d)   Layer 4: Message layer

Message layer defines the protocols for communication, credential information, and it sends that information across the network so that a receiving server/client can be able to interpret it (Peltz, 2003). The standard communication protocol for web services is SOAP (Simple Object Access Protocol). On top of the standard SOAP protocol, addition mechanisms can be added to enhance: security, reliability, adaptability, etc. The

ECOLEAD project has developed the so-called ICT infrastructure (ICT-I) for providing the necessary measures to enhance interactions among services for supporting the collaborations in the VBE (Rabelo. et al 2006).

4. IMPLEMENTATION OF TRUSTMAN SYSTEM

Main functionalities provided by TrustMan system are developed using java-programming language. A number of classes were implemented in different "java project packages" which were logically classified based on the global view of the system's modules. Figure 4 shows modules of TrustMan system and each module constitutes a number of classes as presented below addressing their purposes.

Module for trust level assessment: This module constitutes classes which provide basic algorithms for assessing trust level of an organization. It constitutes classes which implements generic algorithms for assessing organization's trust level.

Module for static assessment: The classes in this module extend the classes included in the module for trust level assessment to reuse the implemented basic algorithms. The classes implemented in this module provide algorithms to assess trust level of an organization based on static set of trust criteria for all perspective. In this case the trust criteria to be applied to all cases are known and fixed.

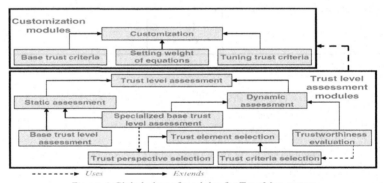

Figure 4. Global view of modules for TrustMan system

Module for base trust level assessment: The classes in this module extend the classes included in the module for static assessment to reuse the implemented algorithms. The assessment of base trust level applies the set of trust criteria selected by the VBE administrator a priori to the VBE establishment. Thus these trust criteria are known to the system. In this module additional classes are implemented to support the rating and generalization of trust level of an organization.

Module for dynamic assessment: The classes in this module extend the classes included in the module for trust level assessment to reuse the implemented basic algorithms. The classes implemented in this module provide algorithms to assess trust level of an organization based on dynamic set of trust criteria. In this case the trust criteria to be applied for the assessment are selected by the user. Thus dynamic assistance for selecting and applying the trust criteria for the assessment of trust level of organizations is implemented in this module.

Module for trust element selection: This module constitutes classes which provide algorithms for selecting trust elements for supporting dynamic trust level assessment. The classes in this module are inherited by classes in two other modules, namely: (1) Module for trust perspective selection which supports the dynamic selection of trust perspective, and (2) Module for trust criteria selection supporting dynamic selection of trust criteria.

Module for trustworthiness evaluation: The classes in this module extend the classes included in the module for dynamic assessment. The classes in this module constitute algorithms for evaluating specific trustworthiness of an organization. Also, this module uses the classes in the module for trust criteria selection.

Module for specialized base trust level assessment: The classes in this module extend classes in both modules for dynamic and static assessment. The classes in this module extend the classes in the module for dynamic assessment to reuse the algorithm for supporting the assessment of trust level of organizations adapting the dynamic selection of trust perspectives. When trust perspective is known all the trust criteria becomes static and thus classes implementing static algorithms are inherited. This module uses the classes in the module for trust perspective selection.

5. ADAPTABILITY AND REPLICABILITY OF TRUSTMAN

In our approach for assessing the trust level of organizations a large comprehensive set of trust criteria is defined and applied. Each VBE however may apply a different set of "*base trust criteria*" which constitutes those criteria that are selected by the VBE administrator, during the customization stage of TrustMan system. The selection of base trust criteria depends on the preferences and perceptions of trust perspective of both "VBE administrator and VBE members". Furthermore, as in daily life, these preferences and perceptions may also change with time. To handle such situations, TrustMan system must be replicable and easily adaptable to support easy customization such as the following modules of TrustMan system (Figure 4).

- *Module for customizing trust criteria:* The mechanisms for assessing trust level of organizations are designed based on mathematical equations (section 1.1). The adaptation and replication of TrustMan system is enhanced by facilitating the possibility to change the set of base trust criteria, without modifying the implemented mechanisms. Thus all general trust criteria are supported in the system, but only the selected set of base trust criteria are applied in assessing organizations' trust level. "*Logical operations*" are implemented in the module to ease the change of constituents of the set of base trust criteria for each VBE.

- *Module for customizing the weights of elements in the equations:* As described in section 1.1 the implemented mathematical equations consists of weights for each applied parameter, such as each trust criteria. The setting of these weights also depends on the domain and specific preferences of the VBE environment. This module supports the VBE administrator to modify the weights of equations.

- *Mechanisms for supporting tuning of trust criteria:* The set of trust criteria applied in the design of mechanisms for assessing trust level of organizations is identified in collaboration with the VBE networks participated in ECOLEAD project. Since the set is generalized avoiding the specificity of different networks, the identified trust criteria may need to be tuned for VBEs when some conditions changes, such as the emergence of new trust objectives. The TrustMan provides mechanisms for defining new trust criteria its tuning.

6. CONCLUSION

This paper addresses the automation of processes related to the assessment of trust level of organizations in VBEs. It contributes to both the formalization and architectural development of a formal trust management system. The presented system applies formal mechanisms, which are based on mathematical equations for assessing the trust level of organizations. Thus the presented mechanisms can be used to support rational reasoning about the assessed trust level of organizations. Furthermore, the system is designed and implemented based on web services technology, and therefore its adaptability, replicability and sustainability are also technologically supported. Moreover, the modules developed for supporting the customization of TrustMan system in different VBE environments, enhance the ease of its adaptability and replicability.

6.1. Acknowledgement

This work was supported in part by the ECOLEAD project funded by the European Commission. The authors thank for contributions from partners in the ECOLEAD consortium.

7. REFERENCES

1. Afsarmanesh, H., Camarinha-Matos, L., Msanjila, S.S. "Virtual organizations breeding environments: key results from ECOLEAD". In the proceedings of International conference on Cost Effective Automation in Networked Product Development and Manufacturing, 2007.
2. Field, S., Hoffner, Y. Web services and matchmaking. International journal of networking and virtual organizations, Inderscience 2003; Vol. 2, No. 1: 16-32.
2. Kirkwood, C. W. System Dynamics Method. Ventana System Inc. 1998.
3. Msanjila, S.S., Afsarmanesh, H. Trust Analysis and Assessment in Virtual Organizations Breeding Environments. International Journal of Production Research, ISBN (print) 0020-7543, Research, Taylor & Francis, 2007a, pg. 1-43
4. Msanjila, S.S., Afsarmanesh, H. Modeling trust relationships in Collaborative Networked Organizations. International Journal of Technology Transfer and Commercialization, ISBN (print): 1470-6075, Inderscience, 2007b, Vol. 6, No. 1, pg. 40-55.
5. Msanjila, S.S., Afsarmanesh, H. "HICI: An approach for identifying trust elements – The case of technological perspective in VBEs". In proceeding of International conference on availability, reliability and security (ARES-2007), Vienna, 2007c, pg. 757-764.
6. Msanjila, S.S., Afsarmanesh, H. "Specification of the TrustMan system for assisting management of VBEs". In the lecture notes of computer science series, LNCS 4657, Springer, 2007d, pg 34-43.
7. Papazoglou, M.P., Georgakopoulus, D. Service-Oriented Computing. Communications of the ACM 2003; Vol 46, No. 10.
8. Peltz, C. Web services orchestration and choreography. IEEE computer 2003; Vol. 36, No. 10.
9. Rabelo, R.J., Gusmeroli, S., Arana, C., Nagellen, C. "The ECOLEAD ICT infrastructure for collaborative networked organizations". In: Camarinha-Matos, L., Afsarmanesh, H., Ollus, M. (eds.) IFIP International Federation for Information Processing. Network-Centric Collaboration and Supporting Frameworks, 2006, vol. 224, pp. 161–172.
10. Rhody, S. Why web services. Web services journal, 2002; vol. 2, issue 2.

11

A MODEL FOR DYNAMIC GENERATION OF COLLABORATIVE DECISION PROTOCOLS FOR MANAGING THE EVOLUTION OF VIRTUAL ENTERPRISES

Marcus V. Drissen-Silva, Ricardo J. Rabelo
Federal University of Santa Catarina, BRAZIL
drissen@das.ufsc.br, rabelo@das.ufsc.br

Many problems use to take place during the virtual enterprises (VE) execution and they must be properly handled in way VE goals can be achieved. However, the VE nature imposes tougher requirements as decisions shall be taken in a distributed and decentralized manner, regarding that members are autonomous and independent. Besides agility, quality is extremely important. This means that such decision-making should be somehow assisted in order to provide managers with means to evaluate the feasibility and impact of decisions at each member, for every VE enterprises they are involved in. This paper presents a model where decision protocols are generated on the fly to guide managers towards more effective solutions.

1. INTRODUCTION

The increasing competitiveness has persuaded companies to participate in strategic alliances to reduce expenses, increase capacity, broaden markets and to improve themselves with the knowledge acquired in businesses. Nowadays, the research field that has gathered studies about the variety of kinds of strategic bonds is Collaborative Networked Organizations (CNO). Its manifestations include supply chains, extended enterprises, virtual enterprises, virtual organizations, virtual organization breeding environments, professional virtual communities, and others (Camarinha-Matos and Afsarmanesh, 2004).

This work focuses on Virtual Enterprises (VE). A VE is a dynamic, temporary and logical aggregation of autonomous enterprises that cooperate with each other to attend a given business opportunity or to cope with a specific need, where partners share risks, costs and benefits, and whose operation is achieved by a coordinated sharing of skills, resources, information and knowledge, mostly enabled by computer networks (Rabelo et al., 2004), offering a group of services abroad as they were an only organization (Camarinha-Matos et al., 2005).

There are four major phases in the VE life cycle: *i)* the creation phase, when all the objectives are settled and partners are selected to make the required tasks; *ii)* the operation phase, which manages the execution of such tasks; *iii)* the evolution phase, where *any* kind of changes necessary to be done in the VE plan and schedule are handled; and *iv)* the VE dissolution phase, which manages all actions when the VE goals are achieved. This work focuses on the VE evolution phase.

Please use the following format when citing this chapter:

Drissen-Silva, M.V. and Rabelo, R.J., 2008, in IFIP International Federation for Information Processing, Volume 266, *Innovation in Manufacturing Networks;* ed. A. Azevedo; (Boston: Springer), pp. 105–114.

In the evolution phase, different *operational* problems should be managed. For example: the anticipation or delay on parts/products delivery, partners performance below to the established metrics, collaborative tasks not accomplished or not as expected or out of the specifications, alteration on the initial product's specification, partners replacement, among many others.

Many decisions have to be taken to (try to) solve such problems. However, in a VE scenario, and especially considering the autonomy, geography dispersion and heterogeneity of working methods, is not possible to handle the problems traditionally, as an enterprise does internally, typically applying classical hierarchical mechanisms. Actually, a CNO scenario imposes different requirements to management methods (Table 1).

Table 1. Comparison of traditional management and VE management models

	Traditional Model	CNO/VE
Decision scope	*Intra-organizational*	*Inter-organizational*
Decision	*Typically centralized*	*Preferably decentralized*
Information sharing among partners	*No or eventual*	*Yes*
Decision transparency	*No or Low*	*Yes*
Quality decision evaluation	*No or Low*	*Yes*
Decision process rigidity	*Inflexible / Workflow*	*Flexible / Ad-hoc*
Information integration between partners	*Low / Medium*	*High / Very High*
Trust among partners	*Implicit*	*Explicit*
Decision objective	*Best local result*	*Feasible global result*
Mutual help level between partners	*Cooperation*	*Collaboration*

Decision-making in a CNO scenario comprises the execution of a number of activities, which starts with the identification of the problem and its severity, passing by the reasoning about the involved partners and the affected product's components, and ends with the application of the right procedure and the final problem resolution. One of the main problems in this scenario is not only to be able to react and to trigger actions towards the problem solving, but also to be agile in this.

Another fundamental aspect that should be noted is that a VE is something unique. This means that the way a problem was solved in a given/past VE is not necessarily valid for another VE. A business opportunity (BO) that generates a VE comes from different customers and countries, which have different cultures, different regulations, different idioms and jargons, different standards, and that apply different metrics in terms of e.g. quality, manufacturing processes and environmental cares. Considering that enterprises are often involved in several VEs simultaneously and that some of them are inter-related, it is not difficult to realize how ample and complex a decision-making in CNO is.

Handling these issues properly is likely impossible to be made by a human. If it was considered that most of CNO companies are composed of SMEs, this difficult is even harder. Despite the technological complexity it represents, current approaches to deal with this fail in not offering the comprehensive, flexible and holistic environment where all these CNO-related requirements and elements – from the VE *evolution* phase perspective – can be embraced and handled. Such approaches usually provides some good supporting elements but only to the "VE manager" (or equivalent), who is considered the only one allowed to have the global map and information about the situation, and who takes the decision, centralized, just informing the other companies about it. On the other hand, a decentralized scenario imposes the need of having several discussions through the network, which, in practice, is not efficient as they use to be conducted without much organization and it is very easy to lose the focus of the discussion. As a consequence, the decision-making is slower and potentially has lower quality.

In this context, the presented paper focuses on how discussions among the VE partners – and further decision-making – can be carried out more effectively. In general, the idea is to provide a supporting methodology, which can systematize and guide the discussions about a given problem within a VE towards its resolution. This methodology is represented as decision protocols, which are generated on the fly in order to cope with the various specificities of each VE and problems' states.

This paper is organized as follows. Chapter 1 presented a general analysis of the requirements for VE management and the complexity to deal with this in the evolution phase. Chapter 2 gives an overview on the management theories and methodologies that have being used in distributed management activities. Chapter 3 introduces the proposed model and framework. Chapter 4 gives an example of the envisaged dynamic generation of protocols. Chapter 5 presents some conclusions and next steps.

2. VIRTUAL ENTERPRISE MANAGEMENT

Managing the planning, execution and control of the organizations gathered to attend to a new market demand is not new and solid works have been developed around this. This chapter presents a general view of relevant issues that are directly related decision-making problem in a distributed scenario.

2.1. Virtual Enterprise as a Project

One of the most relevant foundations to support this is the *Project Management Body of Knowledge*, or just *PMBOK* (PMBOK, 2004). PMBOK states that "a project is a temporary effort to create a unique product or service", whereas a VE is a "dynamic and temporary alliance of organizations that share abilities, competencies and resources to attend a business and to offer valuable products and services ..." (Camarinha-Matos et al., 2005). As it can be noted, managing a VE seems equivalent than managing a project from the PMBOK point of view. Jansson et al. (2005) advocate that VE management is more than managing a project, as the creation of a VE requires a long and previous preparation. However, focusing on VE evolution, it seems quite acceptable to state that a VE have equivalent features than a project, as both are temporary and unique in view of the creation of a product or service.

From the project management perspective, VE evolution management comprises verification, measurement, planning and discussion. More concretely, it requires three important aspects: *i)* performance monitoring (via e.g. *BSC, SCOR* and *OLAP*); *ii)* performance evaluation (e.g. via modeling *simulation, queue theory* or *analytical modeling*); and *iii)* collaborative discussion (e.g. via mechanisms like *HERMES, Delphi,* and *groupware*).

The mentioned methods are just examples. The existing project management reference models are generic to be instantiated with any managerial models (Karvonen et al., 2005).

2.2. Virtual Enterprise Management and Decision Protocols

VE management "designates arrangement, allocation and coordination of the resources and their tasks, as well as their inter-organizational premises, to reach the VE goals, respecting time, cost and quality" (Jansson et al., 2005). VE evolution management is defined in this paper as "the decision process expressed as management knowledge that tries to offer the right direction to human decision-makers in applying adequate problem-solving techniques and computational support to handle unexpected events that happen in a VE and that modifies its initial plan, in such way VEs' goals are kept".

In terms of generation of decision protocols, three previous works can be mentioned as they are the only ones found out in the literature that cover this. ILMSS (Rabelo et al., 1998), DBPMS (Rabelo et al., 2000) and SC^2 (Rabelo and Pereira-Klen, 2002) are systems that deal with the VE evolution phase and that assist managers on decision making. However, they use a pre-defined, fixed and general decision-protocol.

Another system, the VOM Toolkit (Pěchouček and Hodík, 2007), is an integrated environment that has been developed to help the so-called VO manager in doing several activities, such as VO performance monitoring, alert about possible changes in the expected performance, and rescheduling and reconfiguration simulation to optimize the VO performance. However, as in those other three systems, it leaves to the VO manager to implement the necessary corrections to better solve the conflict. No guidelines or supporting methodology is offered to help him in these activities. As it was stressed in the previous chapter, managing the VE evolution requires several other features.

2.3. Project Management Reference Models

PMBOK model consists on the application of knowledge abilities, tools and techniques in favor of reaching the decided goals in the beginning and planning (PMBOK, 2004). It is a comprehensive model but too general in the part that deals with how changes in a project should be managed. The *Capability Maturity Model Integration* (CMMI, 2006) has been mostly used in software development. It assists organizations in the improvement of their processes and their capacity to manage the development, acquisition and maintenance of products and services. The *Agile Project Management (APM)* model faces the changing need as an adaptation in the exploration of alternatives that can fit to new scenes (Leite, 2004). There are other management models, such as the *ECM - Engineering Change Management* (Tavčar and Duhovnik, 2005), *CC - Configuration Control* (Military Handbook, 2001) and *CM – Change Management* (Weerd, 2006), which are used to analyze a project, covering phases of problem identification; demanding the necessary change; verification; analysis and change approval; implementation; and maintenance of the results of changes. Elements of these models shall be used as the basis for the envisaged VE evolution management framework.

2.4. Collaborative Discussion

In terms of computing support for discussions over the network, groupware tools only cope with a partial part of the problem. The matter is not only to make partners talking to each other, but rather to globally coordinate their discussions, integrating information for further auditing, giving transparency to the whole process, and regulating partners' involvement and information access as long as decisions are taken. Four works have been considered useful to give some support to the desired discussion environment.

HERMES is a support system to collaborative decision making by means of argumentation. It helps in the solution of non-structured problems, coordinating a joint discussion among decision makers (Karacapilidis, 2001). It offers an online discussion about one or more specific subjects, where each participant can suggest alternatives to the problem or simply point out their pros and cons in relation to current alternatives.

Delphi is a much known method (Dalkey and Helmer, 1963) created with the purpose to find the most reliable opinions without argumentations. This method collects all the participants' opinions individually, elaborates a summary and sends them back without any identity exposure. Participants provide their vision along diverse rounds about their initial judging until a consensual agreement among all the participants is reached.

Sowa and Sniezynski (2007) developed a security framework that controls information access dynamically according to partners' roles in a VE. Ratti and Rabelo (2007) present an integrated communication infrastructure including a set of groupware services (e-mail, forum, chat, etc.) tailored to VEs.

The combination and some adaptations in these works is seen a feasible starting point to support the envisaged conversation scenario.

3. PROPOSED MODEL

To delineate the scope of the model it is essential to also delineate the basic actions involved in each phase of the VE life cycle. Figure 1 illustrates the authors' vision about that. In general, this means that VE operation comprehends the monitoring of a VE after its creation, whereas the VE evolution is responsible for the analysis, management and implementation of eventual changes in the VE along its execution. These actions in turn request an interaction with the VE creation phase when the solution of a given conflict involves the replacement of partners.

In order to attend the previously mentioned requirements, the proposed model is based on four pillars. The *Organizational* pillar comprises the issues related to both intra and inter-enterprises processes that should be involved in a decision-making. The *Human* pillar endows managers with user-friendly and comprehensive decision environment where they can check and intervene (using supporting techniques and experience) along the process. The *Knowledge* pillar is related to "all" information, knowledge and management tools (methods, techniques, etc.) that can be used to support the decision-making. The *Technological* pillar refers to information and communication technologies (ICT) that support an easy and secure communication among VE members.

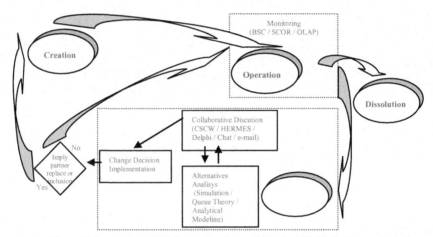

Figure 1. Interaction of VE Evolution phase within the VE life cycle

In the proposed model, project management reference models have provided the basis for the definition only of the macro phases that should be pursuit to solve a problem in a VE. This is because these models are (naturally) too generic to be ready used in a given concrete VE scenario when a problem takes place.

In general, the proposed model takes and partially automates such macro steps. The idea is to make VE members to follow some solid "guideline", which drives the discussions' evolution as long as partial solutions are achieved. During the discussions (via Internet), members can consult a group of available supporting methods that may help them in the solution as well as can check some effects of potential decisions on their companies. This creates a collaborative decision-making environment where all the involved partners can check such effects at the same time, validating or aborting a decision much faster and with more reliability.

The proposed model doesn't intend to automate the resolution of every different problem of every different VE. Instead, it intends to create a distributed/decentralized and integrated "cockpit" environment, where decision-making can be driven by a flexible and "open" protocol that offers *knowledge* to *human* managers to go through *organizational* processes using *technological* means (see the four pillars mentioned before).

A protocol is a sequence of steps that describes the activities that should be executed. Each activity should be expressed in terms of *what, why, where, when, who* and *how* it should be done towards the problem resolution. In other words, the so-called dynamic generation of decision protocols refers to taking those *reference* macro phases and to *instantiate* them according to the problem / VE. However, there is not an "engine" for automating the protocols' steps execution. This is a crucial difference to other approaches. Managers are the ones who should trigger the steps while discussing about the problem and possible alternatives, allowing them to use their experience and managerial feeling. Figure 2 shows the proposed reference protocol.

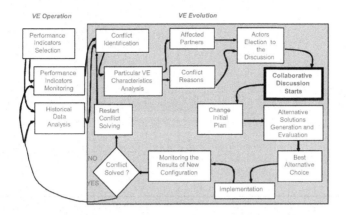

Figure 2. Reference decision protocol model for VE evolution management

The protocol instantiation varies from VE to VE and from problem to problem. This means that although the steps may be the same, the methods, number of required interactions among partners, sub-steps, etc., can be different, and the resulting solution can be different as this also depends on partners' opinions and agreements. Yet, depending on the case, steps can be even suppressed or tackled in a very simple or more complex way. Another aspect is that only part of the protocol involves activities related to conversation among partners. Other steps refer to analysis, visualizations, etc.

Performance evaluation through simulation gives an outline of which strangulation points are in the process, delays, etc. Performance evaluation techniques through performance measurement systems can be used to identify hidden or imminent problems. Therefore, decisions tend to be taken based on some foundation. This facilitates argumentations between partners and hence turns decisions faster and potentially more reliable to help a VE in reaching its goals.

A problem is not necessarily solved at once and a problem may be constituted of many sub-problems. Each sub-problem can demand diverse rounds of exchange of information, computer-aided analysis and managers' opinions. The process ends when a considered good/feasible alternative is found. In the case no solutions are found, the situation is passed to the tactile and strategic levels (which are out of scope of the proposed model) in such way decisions like negotiation with customers, cancellations, etc., can be evaluated and taken.

The protocol and underlying approach cope with the main requirements for decision-making in VEs, supporting agile collaborative decisions, respecting partners' autonomy, process transparency, offering theoretical supporting managerial framework, and providing means for some guided conversation.

4. THE DECISION PROTOCOL: AN EXAMPLE

In order to generally illustrate the protocol generation, it is possible to imagine a VE that has been created to transform five regular cars into personalized vehicles to an automotive fair. In this case, there would be different partners responsible for each of the following tasks: bodywork and painting, audio and video equipment, tires supply, engine adaptation and calibration. As partners are in different cities, not more than 100 km away from each other, which would be the best way to solve a one-week delay in one of the necessary engines? Which tasks have to be delayed? Which partners were affected? Is it possible to simulate tasks rescheduling in order to minimize the delay? Wouldn't it be better to get this engine from another supplier? Answers for these and other related questions can be expressed in a sequence of general steps to follow helped by a collaborative discussion support.

If the problem was caused by a fail in the product's specification, what sequence of tasks shall be executed to solve the problem? In the VE *operation* phase the manager would have used *OLAP cube* to measure the VE indicators performance and to identify the problem. After this - so now within the VE *evolution* phase - a particular protocol to guide the problem resolution is generated using the reference protocol, as roughly exemplified below.

1. *When a problem emerges, the first evaluation is how deeply this would affect the VE operation. If its necessary, ask for solution;*
2. *Depends on the VE particularity, different steps and tools should be used;*
3. *The VE manager and the partner responsible for the product out of specification identify the others partners affected by this problem, specially in view of tasks delayed;*
4. *In parallel, they intensively try to find the reasons of the problem;*
5. *At this point the affected members have to be invited to discuss together about the problem and on how it can be solved;*
6. *Starting the discussion that would be conducted through / assisted by a system (something like a merged HERMES system and Delphi method);*
7. *Two different solution might emerge: suggest the partner to redo the component following the correct specification (if there is trust and time to do it), or to keep discussing if this is not possible;*
8. *In the second case, it is necessary to inform that the changes should consider the VE initial goals and plan;*
9. *The VE manager and partners would use a simulation tool to see which different scenarios could be acceptable and evaluate which is the best one to solve the problem. The affected partners should exchange results.*
10. *Once agreed, this solution is settled in the VE plan and partners can monitor the VE execution again. This means that evolution is over and now the VE management goes back to the* operation *phase.*

Figure 3 shows the multi-level model, illustrating the sequence of a protocol instantiation with the reference initial protocol related to the problem (regarding the specificities VE), passing by the generation of a particular protocol, the sequence used in the discussion phase, and the different tools that would be used to help in each protocol's step.

5. CONCLUSIONS

This paper has presented an approach to assist VE members in the problem solving when conflicts take place in the VE evolution phase. A decision protocol, which is automatically and dynamic generated taking a reference protocol into account, essentially represents this approach. If on one hand the protocol is relatively generic, on the other hand it is a concrete mean to enable partners to be guided and assisted during the problem-solving, giving the potential for a faster and more reliable, feasible and collaborative decision-making. Actually, this protocol intends to face the new requirements in terms of management brought up with the VE concept, in particular the fact that decisions shall be taken collaboratively and distributed, with transparency, preserving the autonomy and independence of each VE member.

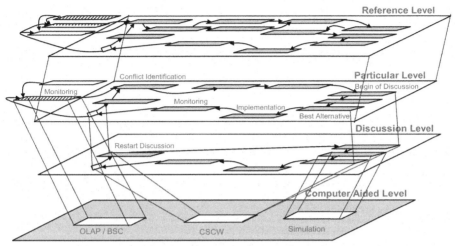

Figure 3. Example of the Reference Protocol instantiation

It is argued that a protocol shall be somehow generic to accommodate the different ways of solving a problem from different groups of managers, depending on the VE's specification, its goals, and its partners.

The protocol is focused on the VE evolution phase and it only embraces problems at operational level. Its steps were fundamentally devised based on the most relevant project management reference models.

In terms of partners' communication and information exchange, this work assumes that a VE is created from a *VBE* (Virtual Organization Breeding Environment) so partners have already some trust built. Besides that, it is assumed that the sort of supporting information and methods for problems solving are available in the VBE as this is a usual asset VBEs have.

This work is at its initial phase. The focus of the research has been put on the model and the protocol. There is not any implemented prototype so far, although a sort of services and methods are expected to be got from the ECOLEAD partners and the open-source community. Other modules should probably be implemented to attend the features of the envisaged scenario. Yet, the current version of the protocol cope with only part of the requirements identified in Chapter 1.

One important consideration about this work is the fact the decision-making can be not as fast as expected depending on the chosen techniques (e.g. simulation). However, it may be a price to pay to comply with the VE requirements.

Next steps of this work will mainly cover: the extension the protocol and computer assistance to support the other VE requirements; a prototype implementation (especially the part related to the mixing of Delphi method, HERMES system and CSCW integrated services); and the election of which performance evaluation techniques and tools should compose the "knowledge box" to support a more robust decision-making environment.

5.1. Acknowledgments

This work has been partially supported by CNPq – The Brazilian Council for Research and Scientific Development (www.cnpq.br), and it has been developed in the scope of the Brazilian IFM project (www.ifm.org.br) and the European IST IP ECOLEAD project (www.ecolead.org).

6. REFERENCES

1. Camarinha-Matos, LM, Afsarmanesh, H. Collaborative Networked Organizations – A Research Agenda for Emerging Business Models. United States: Kluwer Academic Publishers, 2004; pp. 7-10.
2. Camarinha-Matos, LM, Afsarmanesh, H, Ollus, M. "ECOLEAD: A Holistic Approach to Creation and Management of Dynamic Virtual Organizations". In Collaborative Networks and Their Breeding Environments, L. M. Camarinha-Matos, H. Afsarmanesh, A. Ortiz, Eds, Springer, 2005; pp. 3-16.
3. CMMI. "CMMI for Development Version 1.2". Tech. Report DEV, V1.2. Pittsburgh: Carnegie Mellon – Software Engineering Institute, 2006.
4. Dalkey, NC, Helmer, O. An experimental application of the Delphi method to the case of experts. Management Science 1963; 9: 458-467.
5. Jansson, K, Eschenbaecher, J. "Challenges in Virtual Organisations Management – Report on methods for distributed business process management". Tech. Report D32.1. ECOLEAD – European Collaborative networked Organizations LEADership initiative. FP6 IP 506958, 2005.
6. Karacapilidis, N, Papadias, D. Computer supported argumentation and collaborative decision making: the HERMES system. Information Systems 2001; 26 (4): 259-277.
7. Karvonen, I, Salkari, I, Ollus, M. "Characterizing Virtual Organizations and Their Management". In Collaborative Networks and Their Breeding Environments L. M. Camarinha-Matos, H. Afsarmanesh, A. Ortiz Eds. United States: Springer, 2005; pp. 193-204.
8. Kengpol, A, Tuominen, M. A framework for group decision support systems: an application in the evaluation of information tech. for logistics firms. Int. J. of Prod. Economics 2006; pp. 159-171.
9. Leite, M. M. "Implementation requirements of CRM strategies in SMEs: an approach based on Project Management" [in Portuguese], PhD Thesis, Federal University of Santa Catarina, 2004.
10. Military Handbook. Configuration Management Guidance. MIL-HDBK-61A(SE) Department of Defense – United States of America, 2001.
11. Pěchouček, M, Hodík, J. "Virtual Organisation Management eServices version 1". Tech. Report D34.5. ECOLEAD Project, www.ecolead.org, 2007.
12. PMBOK. A Guide to the Project Management Body of Knowledge. Project Management Institute Standards Committee, 2004.
13. Rabelo, RJ, Pereira-Klen, AA, Spinosa, LM, Ferreira, AC. "Integrated Logistics Management Support System: An Advanced Coordination Functionality for the Vitual Environment". In Proceedings IMS'98 - 5th IFAC Workshop on Intelligent Manufacturing Systems, 1998; pp. 195-202.
14. Rabelo, RJ, Pereira-Klen, AA, Ferreira, AC. "For a Smart Coordination of Distributed Business Processes". In Proceedings BASYS'2000 – 4th IEEE/IFIP International Conference on Balanced Automation Systems, Berlin, Germany, 2000; pp. 378-385.
15. Rabelo, RJ, Pereira-Klen, A. "A Multi-agent System for Smart Co-ordination of Dynamic Supply Chains". In Proceedings PRO-VE'2002, 2002; pp. 312-319.
16. Rabelo, RJ, Pereira-Klen, A, Klen, ER. Effective management of dynamic supply chains. Int. J. Networking and Virtual Organisations 2004; Vol. 2, No. 3:193–208.
17. Ratti, R, Rabelo, R. J. "ICT-I Reference Framework". Technical Report Deliverable D61.1c, in www.ecolead.org, 2007.
18. Sowa, G. Sniezynski, T. "Technical Report Deliverable D64.1b – Configurable multi-level security architecture for CNOs", in www.ecolead.org, 2007.
19. Tavčar, J, Duhovnik, J. Engineering change management in individual and mass production. Robotics and Computer-Integrated Manufacturing 2005; 21 (3): 205-215.
20. Weerd, van-der-Inge "Meta-modeling Technique: Method Engineering 05/06". <http://en.wikipedia.org/wiki/Change_management_process#_ref-4>, Accessed in Nov 28, 2007.

12

PARTNER SELECTION IN
VIRTUAL ENTERPRISES
AN EXPLORATORY APPROACH

José António Crispim,
Universidade do Minho
crispim@eeg.uminho.pt

Jorge Pinho de Sousa
INESC Porto, Faculdade de Engenharia da Universidade do Porto
jsousa@inescporto.pt

Partner selection in virtual enterprises (VE) can be viewed as a multi-criteria decision making problem that involves assessing trade-offs between conflicting tangible and intangible criteria. In general, this is a very complex problem due to the dynamic topology of the network, the large number of alternatives and the different types of criteria. In this paper we propose an iterative and interactive exploratory process to help the decision maker identify the companies that best suit the needs of each particular project. This is achieved by using cluster analysis to distinguish companies according to some selected features. We present an example to illustrate this approach.

1. INTRODUCTION

A virtual enterprise (VE) can be defined as a temporary alliance of independent and geographically dispersed companies set up to share skills or core competencies and resources, in order to respond to business opportunities, the cooperation among the enterprises being supported by computer networks (Camarinha-Matos and Afsarmanesh, 2003). The partner selection problem arises in many other research contexts such as supply chain design, agile manufacturing, network design, dynamic alliances, and innovation management production. In a virtual enterprise (VE) this question is difficult to handle because of the short life-cycles of these organizations (temporary alliances) and because of the lack of formal mechanisms (contracts) to assure participants responsibility. According to Mowshovitz (1994), the functioning of virtual enterprises follows the *switching principle* since connections among members are switched on and off whenever needed. Reactivity and flexibility are the major benefits but, at the same time, the main problems of VEs (Gunasekaran et al. 2008).

The creation of a VE is usually triggered by a market opportunity, giving rise to a "project" that is generally decomposable in relatively independent sub-projects or activities. The work needed to "fulfil" a project involves a set of collaborative activities and the cooperation relationships established can be represented by an activity network. Based on previous experiences the network members can rapidly set up a VE if some organizational structure already exists. This leads to the concept of Virtual Breeding Environment (VBE) which is a long-term networked structure with common operating

Please use the following format when citing this chapter:

Crispim, J.A. and Pinho de Sousa, J., 2008, in IFIP International Federation for Information Processing, Volume 266, *Innovation in Manufacturing Networks;* ed. A. Azevedo; (Boston: Springer), pp. 115–124.

principles and infrastructures, common ontologies, and mutual trust (Afsarmanesh & Camarinha-Matos, 2005).

The VE configuration process is a difficult problem due to the complex interactions between the different entities and to the highly dynamic structure of the network (resulting from the connections activation/disactivation), and because the expression of preferences may be based on incomplete or non-available information. To deal with this problem under a multi-criteria perspective, we allow several types of information (numerical, interval, qualitative and binary) in order to facilitate the expression of the stakeholders' preferences or assessments about the potential partners. This is an important requirement in practice as the multiplicity of factors considered when selecting partners for a business opportunity, such as cost, quality, trust and delivery time, cannot be expressed in the same measure or scale (Crispim and Sousa, 2007).

In the selection of partners it is very common to use ranking approaches (see e.g. Gülçin et al. 2007), but according to Munda (2005) rankings are not always trustable, because the results obtained depend for example on the quality of available information, on the set of criteria/indicators used to represent reality, on the direction of each objective/indicator, on the relative importance of these indicators and on the ranking methods adopted. The choice of the method is in fact very important to guarantee consistency between the assumptions considered by the decision maker and the obtained ranking. The quality of the decisions depends crucially on the way the methodology takes into account the various dimensions (social, political, economical, technical, etc.) considered when structuring process. This is the reason why Roy (1996) claimed that what is really important is the decision process and not the final solution.

The companies in a network may be very different from each other, and each company is characterized by a set of attributes that can be large in number. Moreover, these companies may be organised in quite different networks, depending on the particular considered criterion (see figure 1). Collecting and handling the associated data may therefore be a complicated task and require a considerable effort just in structuring the problem.

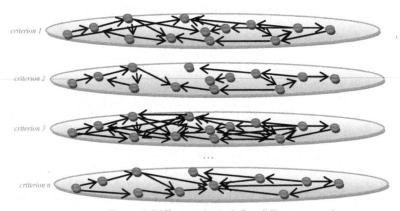

Figure 1. Different criteria define different networks

One company may be more effective, feel more secure or reliant when collaborating with a specific company or group of companies. This requires that the selection of partners follows pre-determined directions of search which demand additional knowledge about the network. In practice, it is often desirable that the companies that will perform a specific project are similar with respect with some issues (for example, organizational culture or IT usage) and complementary with respect to others (for example, leadership skills, market knowledge or technological strengths). Therefore, we claim that decision support should combine an exploratory process about enterprise's relationships with an algorithm that ranks alternative VE configurations.

The approach taken in this work is quite different from those described in most of the "partner selection" literature in VE (see e.g. Ma et al. (2007) for genetic algorithms, Ng (2007) for linear programming, Li and Liao (2007) for fuzzy theory). Its focus is rather on the *exploratory phase*, performed with the aim of obtaining relevant information about the network. This information is then intended to be used in the subsequent phase of optimally selecting each partner.

The remainder of the paper is organized as follows. In Section 2 the problem is described, in section 3 the exploratory process is presented, in Section 4 an illustrative example is described and finally, in Section 5 some preliminary conclusions are presented.

2. PROBLEM DESCRIPTION

The VE configuration process can be described as follows. Assume a VBE network A representing all potential partners (companies) and their relationships. A specific entity is responsible for the VE formation process (this entity is here referred to as the Decision Maker or DM). Entities and relationships are characterised by a set of m attributes, some assigned to the nodes and some assigned to the edges of the network. These attributes will be used to express the criteria used for evaluating solutions (i.e. VE configurations). The first step in this modelling process is to carefully define what attributes are going to be considered in both subsets.

We consider that the attributes assigned to each node comprise the company's resource availability that will be assessed according to project constraints (e. g. *time windows, minimum amount of resources* required) and other company's characteristics relevant to the decision process (e.g. firms' size or financial stability). In the selection process we can consider hard or soft constraints (i.e. we can define strict or loose thresholds for some measures), so that the process does not exclude too many potential candidates in its earliest phases. For example, a good candidate that does not fully respect the time window constraints will still be eligible if there is some slack to re-schedule activities.

The edge attributes include variables that characterise the links between pairs of companies (e.g. assessment of past relationship experiences, distance, level of trust, costs, etc...). We consider that the network is a directed graph because there is the possibility that, for example, the degree of trust between two firms is not reciprocal. From the two sets of attributes (edge and node attributes) it should be possible to derive the organizational characteristics required to achieve the project objectives. The decision maker can give weights to these organizational attributes according to his/hers believes about their relative importance for the project under consideration.

In real-world decision problems we have to handle information that is uncertain, incomplete and/or missing (Li and Lao, 2007). Furthermore, there are many decision situations in which the attributes cannot be assessed precisely in a quantitative form, due to their particular nature (e.g. trust) or because either information is unavailable or the cost of their computation is too high. In these situations an "approximate value" may be acceptable and so the use of a qualitative approach is appropriate (Herrera et al., 2004).

"Linguistic variables" will be used to represent qualitative aspects, with values that are not numbers but words or sentences in a natural language, thus making it easier to express preferences. *The linguistic term set*, usually called S is a set of linguistic values that are generally ordered and uniformly distributed. For example, a set S of five terms could be defined as follows: S = {s_0 = very low; s_1 = low; s_2 = medium; s_3 = high; s_4 = very high}, in which $s_a < s_b$ if a < b. The semantics of the elements in the term set (the meaning of each term set) is given by fuzzy numbers defined on the [0, 1] interval and described by membership functions. For the same attribute, the cardinality of S may vary depending on the decision maker's knowledge about the companies (it may be more detailed in some cases or vaguer in others). Therefore, we allow several types of criteria: numerical, interval, qualitative and binary.

The network is formed by a set of *n* companies (nodes) connected with each other, capable of performing activities and of providing a finite amount of resources that are available over specific intervals of time. We also assume that project *P* involves *k* activities that demand a specific amount *Q* of resources and have to be performed within a given interval of time *S*. These activities have some precedence relationships and therefore form an activity network.

The partner selection problem consists in choosing the best group of companies to perform all *k* activities of project *P* taking into account a set of evaluation criteria based on the *m* attributes established for the network. In this problem, the alternatives correspond to groups of enterprises that have the resources and skills needed to carry out the project. Given the multi-criteria nature of the problem, there is generally no "optimal" alternative, and a good "trade-off" solution must therefore be identified.

3. EXPLORATORY PHASE

The exploratory process takes place at an initial phase of the whole decision support process. This phase enables the DM to test various scenarios in which the companies are grouped in different ways, and/or different levels of importance are assigned to the different criteria.

In this work we use cluster analysis to somehow better structure the interesting knowledge about the network. This knowledge can be used to create or avoid some alternatives (potential groups of firms that have the resources and skills needed to carry out the project) or to confine the search to a given cluster of companies.

This approach has been applied in the supply chain area, namely as follows: Ha and Krishnan (2008) to compose a portfolio of suppliers using quantitative criteria; Bottani e Rizzi (2008) to reduce the problem dimension by grouping suppliers based on their similarities (even if they cannot control the number of elements in the clusters); and Sarkar and Mohapatra (2006) to group the selection criteria into long- and short-term categories.

A VE implies the existence of cooperation at several levels, such as R&D, production, marketing or distribution. This requirement can lead to the selection of companies belonging to the same cluster (for example, group of companies with similar (high) technical skills) or to the selection of companies belonging to different clusters according to the specific activities to be allocated (for example, for activities related to distribution choose the companies in the cluster that are stronger at this function).

In spite of the additional computational effort required by this interactive learning process when compared with a less guided search (which may be significant if the network size and/or the number of criteria considered is high), it adds the possibility of identifying different solutions, possibly closer to the DM ideals.

3.1 Criteria selection - dimensions

In order to simplify the decision process, we use in this work the concept of "dimensions". Here a "dimension" is viewed as a small set of criteria, considered together as a way to obtain a simpler representation of all network characteristics. Attribute selection is an important issue in the VE configuration process as the selected attributes should be able to explain the data, provide significant information and be not redundant.

This process of finding out which attributes should be kept (i.e. identifying attributes that are relevant to the decision making process) often provides valuable structural information and is therefore important in its own right. Moreover, if we take into account the dynamic nature of the network, relevant attributes for one project (VE) may be inappropriate for another.

It is important to notice that only some of the criteria are useful to characterize the enterprise for each dimension (e.g. financial stability), so one key task of the decision maker is to carefully define what criteria are going to be considered (e.g. ROE, Debt/Assets, Cash Flow, etc.). Moreover, these criteria have to be statistically analysed before they can be considered suitable for inclusion. For example, it would be incorrect to consider criteria that are highly correlated.

3.2 Clustering

Cluster analysis (CA) is a popular data mining technique (see e.g. Olafsson et al., 2008) that involves the partitioning of a set of objects into a set of mutually exclusive clusters such that the similarity between the observations within each cluster (i.e. subset) is high, while the similarity between the observations from the different clusters is low. In our case, this technique is useful to determine clusters of companies that can be viewed as related with the others, according to specific dimensions.

Clustering may be categorized in various ways such as hierarchical or partitional, deterministic or probabilistic, hard or fuzzy. The general approaches to clustering are: hierarchical clustering and partitional clustering (e.g. Samoilenko and Osei-Bryson, 2008). Hierarchical clustering forms clusters through agglomerative or divisive methods. The agglomerative method assumes that each data point is its own cluster, and with each step of the clustering process, these clusters are combined to form larger clusters, which may be combined to form a single cluster. The divisive method of the hierarchical clustering, on the other hand, starts with one single cluster containing all data points within the sample and proceeds to divide it into smaller dissimilar clusters.

In partitional clustering, the k-means procedure (Kim and Ahn, 2008) is a simple way to classify a given data set through a certain number of clusters (assume k clusters) fixed a priori. The main idea is to define k centroids, one for each cluster. The centroid of a cluster is the average point in the multidimensional space defined by the criteria, i.e., the cluster's center of gravity. These centroids should be placed as much as possible far away from each other.

The next step is to take each point belonging to a given data set and associate it to the nearest centroid. After all points have been grouped, new centroids are re-calculated and the points are grouped again. This process is repeated until centroids do not change. The k-means algorithm aims at minimizing an objective function, in this case the euclidian distance between each data point and the cluster centre.

Thus, k-means clustering will produce k different clusters of greatest possible distinction. In our work, since we want to explore the data and we do not know the number of clusters in advance, we will use hierarchical clustering.

4. ILLUSTRATIVE EXAMPLE

Assume we would like to form a VE to perform a project decomposed in 5 activities.

Consider a network with 100 candidates (companies) characterized by 20 attributes (10 nodes attributes and 10 edge attributes) expressed in four different types of information: numerical, percentage, binary and linguistic (table 1). Some attributes are chosen to define clusters of candidates according to several dimensions such as organizational culture, management capability, financial stability or market knowledge. It is reasonable to assume that the group of companies that will perform the project will match better together if they have similar cultures, even if we do not have preferences for a specific culture. On the other hand, the VE may have a better performance if with respect to other characteristic (e.g. leadership, managerial competencies) its companies are complementary.

Table 1. Criteria characteristics

criteria	type	edge attribute	cardinality (for linguistic)	Organizational culture	Competencies
c1	linguistic	yes	5	-	-
c2	number	yes	-	-	-
c3	lingustic	no	7	✓	-
c4	number	no	-	-	-
c5	number	no	-	✓	-
c6	percentage	yes	-	-	✓
c7	linguistic	yes	5	-	-
c8	linguistic	no	5	✓	-
c9	percentage	no	-	-	-
c10	binary	no	-	-	-
c11	linguistic	yes	7	-	✓
c12	number	no	-	✓	-
c13	number	no	-	-	✓
c14	linguistic	yes	5	✓	-
c15	linguistic	yes	3	-	-
c16	number	no	-	-	✓
c17	binary	yes	-	-	-
c18	linguistic	no	7	-	✓
c19	binary	yes	-	-	-
c20	linguistic	no	7	-	-

Notes:c3: attitude towards uncertainty/risk
c5: power distance (# of hierarchical levels from top to bottom of organization)
c8: individualism vs collectivism
c12: age of the organization (years)
c14: masculinity vs. femininity
c6: market entrance capability
c11: managerial skills
c13: productivity
c16: cost (per unit)
c18: technical expertise

In our example we will sequentially use two illustrative dimensions - organizational culture and competencies - following the postulation in section 3. Figures have been randomly generated and the algorithm was implemented in C++ with the use of the SPSS software to perform cluster analysis.

The DM maker will carry out a two steps analysis: first, he/she will partition the companies into groups with similar organizational cultures, and then he/she will distinguish the companies selected in the previous step according to their competencies.

Taking a set of variables based on the Hofstede (2002) framework to define organizational culture (attitude towards uncertainty/risk, masculinity[4] vs. femininity[5], individualism vs collectivism, small[6] vs. large[7] power distance) and the age of the organization, we have obtained the clusters presented in figure 2 and in table 2.

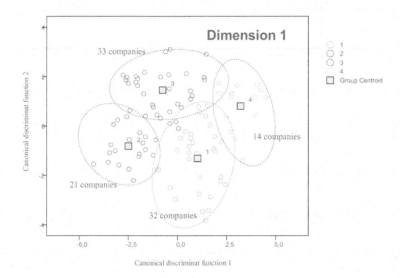

Figure 2. Clusters formation of Dimension 1

The centroid of a cluster is the average point in the multidimensional space defined by the criteria, i.e., the cluster's center of gravity.

It is very important that the DM describes each cluster carefully in order to verify if the results are valid: cluster 1 includes companies which are neutral towards uncertainty/risk, have in average 6 hierarchical levels, have a individualist culture, are relatively old (approximately 15 years in average) and are neutral in relation to masculinity/femininity. The same kind of analysis must be performed regarding the other clusters.

---

[4] Based on traditional male values (e.g. competitiveness, assertiveness, ambition)

[5] Based on traditional female values (e.g. relationships orientated)

[6] People relate to one another as equals regardless of formal positions

[7] There is a formal hierarchy accepted by all

Table 2. Clusters data of Dimension 1

criteria	Cluster			
	1	2	3	4
attitude toward uncertainty/risk	neutral	neutral	keen	keen
power distance	6	6	2	2
individualism vs collectivism	individualist	neutral	collectivist	neutral
age of the organization (years)	14,69	17,57	6,76	5
masculinity vs. femininity	neutral	feminine	neutral	masculine

Notes: a) attitude toward uncertainty/risk ={extremely adverse, very adverse, adverse, neutral, keen, very keen, totally keen}
b) power distance = {9, 8, 7, 6, 5, 4, 3, 2, 1}
c) individualism vs collectivism ={very individualist, individualist, neutral, collectivist, very collectivist}
d) masculinity vs. femininity = {very masculine, masculine, neutral, feminine, very feminine}

The DM may (or may not) prefer one of these clusters. Let us assume, for the purpose of this example, that the DM thinks the organizational culture represented by cluster 1 suits the project better. In this case, companies belonging to the other clusters will be excluded from subsequent analysis.

In the next step, he/she divides the 32 companies from cluster 1 according to their competencies (see the resulting clusters in figure 3 and table 3).

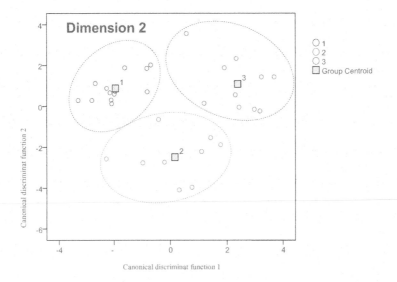

Figure 3. Clusters formation of Dimension 2

Table 3. Clusters data of Dimension 2

criteria	Cluster		
	1	2	3
market entrance capability	39%	35%	74%
managerial skills	positive	neutral	positive
productivity	57,77	31,89	39,80
cost (per unit)	6,46	7,31	7,56
technical expertise	large	large	large

Notes: a) managerial skills = {none, very negative, negative, neutral, positive, very positive, total}
b) technical expertise = {none, very small, small, neutral, large, very large, total}

In this dimension the DM is looking for complementary competencies, so he/she will choose companies from cluster 1 to perform production tasks, and companies from cluster 3 to perform marketing and managerial activities.

In a real situation, involving more companies, the DM may use optimization or a multicriteria ranking algorithm to select the best companies from each cluster (Crispim and Sousa, 2007).

5. CONCLUSIONS

The selection of partners is a critical issue in the formation of a virtual enterprise, the basic problem consisting in choosing the entities to be involved in an emergent business opportunity, according to their attributes and interactions. This paper tries to emphasise the need to obtain knowledge about the network before starting to search best candidates. This exploratory phase demands some interactivity with the DM and can be enhanced by using of cluster analysis. The potential of this approach was demonstrated by a small illustrative example. This example shows the feasibility of the method that allows directional searches in order to identify different types of solutions, hopefully closer to the DM's expectations or to the project specific requirements.

6. REFERENCES

1. Afsarmanesh, H, Camarinha-Matos LM. (2005). A framework for management of virtual organization breeding environments. In:. Camarinha-Matos L M, Afsarmanesh H and Ortiz A, eds. IFIP International Federation for Information Processing. Collaborative Networks and their Breeding Environments. Springer, Boston. 2005; 207: 35-48.
2. Bottani, E and Rizzi, A. An adapted multi-criteria approach to suppliers and products selection—An application oriented to lead-time reduction. International Journal of Production Economics, 2008; 111 (2): 763-781.
3. Camarinha-Matos LM Afsarmanesh H. Elements of a base VE infrastructure. Computers in Industry 2003; 51: 139–163.
4. Crispim, J and Sousa, JP. Multiple criteria partner selection in virtual enterprises. In Camarinha-Matos LM, Afsarmanesh H, Novais P and Analide C, eds. IFIP International Federation for Information Processing. Establishing the Foundation of Collaborative Networks. Springer, Boston. 2007; 243: 197-206.
5. Gülçin B, Orhan F and Erdal N. Selection of the strategic alliance partner in logistics value chain. International Journal of Production Economics, 2007, DOI:10.1016/j.ijpe.2007.01.016.
6. Gunasekaran A, Lai K-H and Cheng E. Responsive supply chain: A competitive strategy in a networked economy. Omega, 2008; 36:4: 549-564.
7. Ha SH and Krishnan R. A hybrid approach to supplier selection for the maintenance of a competitive supply chain. Expert Systems with Applications, 2008; 34(2): 1303-131.
8. Herrera F, Martinez, L and Sanchez PJ. Decision Aiding Managing non-homogeneous information in group decision making. European Journal of Operational Research, 2004; 166 (1): 115-132
9. Hofstede, Geert. Culture's Consequences, Comparing Values, Behaviors, Institutions, and Organizations cross Nations, Sage Publications; Second Edition 2003.
10. Li Y and Liao X,. Decision support for risk analysis on dynamic alliance. Decision Support Systems, 2007; 42: 2043– 2059.
11. Ma, X, Han, J, Wei, Z. and Wang, Y. An improved adaptive Genetic Algorithm in optimization of Partner Selection. Eighth ACIS International Conference on Software Engineering, Artificial Intelligence, Networking, and Parallel/Distributed Computing, SNPD 2007. Volume 3, 30 July 2007- 1 Aug. 2007: 455 – 460.
12. Mowshovitz, A. Virtual organizations: A vision of management in the information age, Information Society 1994, 10: 267–288.
13. Munda G. Multiple Criteria Decision Analysis and Sustainable Development. In Figueira, J, Greco, S, Ehrgott, M. eds. Multiple Criteria Decision Analysis: State of the Art Surveys, 2005, New York, USA, Springer 78: 953-989.
14. Ng W.L. An efficient and simple model for multiple criteria supplier selection problem. European Journal of Operational Research, 2007; DOI:10.1016/j.ejor.2007.01.018.
15. Roy,B. Mulcriteria Methodology for Decision Aiding. Netherlands, Kluwer Academic Publishers, 1996.
16. Samoilenko, S Osei-Bryson K-M. Increasing the discriminatory power of DEA in the presence of the sample heterogeneity with cluster analysis and decision trees. Expert Systems with Applications; 2008; 34 (2): 1568-1581.
17. Sarkar, A and Mohapatra, PKJ. Evaluation of supplier capability and performance: A method for supply base reduction. Journal of Purchasing and Supply Management, 2006; 12(3): 148-163.
18. Olafsson S, Li X, Wu S. Operations research and data mining. European Journal of Operational Research, 2008; 187(3): 1429-1448.

PART 2

INTEROPERABILITY AND COLLABORATIVE SUPPORT

13

EBXML – OVERVIEW, INITIATIVES AND APPLICATIONS

António Pereira, Frederico Cunha, Pedro Malheiro, Américo Azevedo
Inesc Porto, FEUP - Faculdade de Engenharia
Universidade do Porto
Rua Roberto Frias S/N, 4200-465 Porto, Portugal
e-mail: {ee01260, ee01069, ee0113, ala}@fe.up.pt

This paper describes ebXML. It gives an overview on its background and architecture, approved under the ISO/TS 15000. It also analyzes implementations of the standards' modules as well as initiatives concerning its development and adoption. Other frameworks' efforts on convergence with ebXML are discussed as well as expectations on its place in the future for electronic business.

1. INTRODUCTION

The globalization of the business markets brought new opportunities for business and business collaborations. Discovering the most suitable partners will give any company an advantage on its business. However, how can different enterprises, spread worldwide, overcome geographical and cultural differences, find each other and initiate business transactions?

The Internet can now connect virtually every place on the globe therefore the challenge is to provide a framework that would be widely accepted throughout all business areas.

Initially, numerous organizations decided to develop new frameworks to connected their businesses and allow an electronic base for their networks. The most successful, at a point, was Electronic Data Interchange (EDI) which had a number of problems. From the need for a private network and its high implementation costs to the fact that it was not horizontally used as the common framework throughout companies around the world, EDI had disadvantages that kept it from a wider implementation (Mertz, 2001).

With the appearance of XML, during the 1990s, the technology rapidly was adopted in various areas due to its high simplicity, flexibility, extensibility and ubiquity (R. Glushko & J. Tenenbaum & B. Meltzer, 2007). The Organization for Advancement for Information Standards (OASIS) – a non-profit organization that develops, encourages and supports information standards – and the United Nations body for Trade Facilitation and Electronic Business (UN/CEFACT) decided to join forces and create a new framework for electronic business using the general-purpose extensible Markup Language: ebXML. Apart from the known influence of the UN/CEFACT, OASIS' decisions have, as well, great influence on the definition of used standards around the world as it has more than 600 organizations as members, namely SUN Microsystems, SAP, IBM, Primeton, EDS and BEA Systems, Inc.. Both the needs for uniformity and convergence of the dispersed and often competing efforts of many organizations to create electronic business frameworks led to the decision

Please use the following format when citing this chapter:

Pereira, A., Cunha, F., Malheiro, P. and Azevedo, A., 2008, in IFIP International Federation for Information Processing, Volume 266, *Innovation in Manufacturing Networks;* ed. A. Azevedo; (Boston: Springer), pp. 127–136.

of creating ebXML. The vision of ebXML's founders was to enable enterprises of any size, in any global region, to conduct business using the Internet (ebXML, 2007).

After the release of the OASIS approved standards, the International Standard Consortium Technical Committee (ISO/TS) followed. In spite of this, work in improvements and development is ongoing, in a fast rate as the standards' adoption.

This article will make an overview on the ebXML's concepts followed by examples of actual implementations. Initiative concerning the growth of the framework will be presented, making the link to the final discussion on what to expect in the future for business networking.

2. ebXML CONCEPTS AND ARCHITECTURE

The ebXML Work Group has developed architectural modules that cover all areas needed to ensure reliable and global interoperability among businesses. These Standards were developed by ebXML Technical Committees and, in 2004, approved by ISO and published as technical specifications ISO/TS 15000. Each part of the ISO specifies one of the modules of ebXML's suit of standards.

2.1. ebXML Specifications and ISO/TS 15000 Standard

The standard covers only five of the frameworks' elements: Collaboration protocol Profiles and Agreements (which will be presented in more detail than the others for it is key to understand the framework's objective and how it works), Messaging Service, Registry Information Module, Registry Services Specification and Core Components.

The main purpose of the module described under ISO 15000-1, is, basically, to specify how companies do business. Each company must create their own Collaboration Protocol Profile (CPP). Here lie descriptions of the business capabilities of an individual party, how it exchanges information, how its business processes are and what kind of relations it's interested in engaging. Figure 1 exemplifies how a CPP is built.

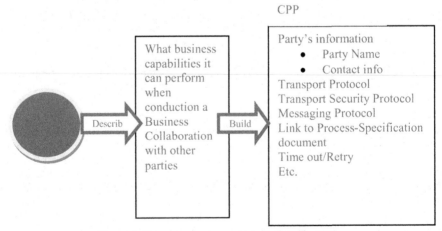

Figure 1. Steps a company must take to build its CPP

By specifying the enterprise's business needs and capabilities in a universal form (XML), the process of searching for suitable business partners is greatly simplified. With a common database storing all the CPPs, a simple query will identify any company compliant with the desired restrictions. A company can file multiple CPPs with the registry, thus expecting to create various business agreements.

When compatible CPPs are found, a Collaboration Protocol Agreement (CPA) is automatically created. This CPA describes the form in which the business collaboration will occur, the type of messages being sent and how. To clarify the concept, if a CPP declares "Company A can do X", a CPA will then define "Company A and B will do X together" (Mertz, 2001). Figure 2 shows how two parties' CPPs are negotiated into a CPA.

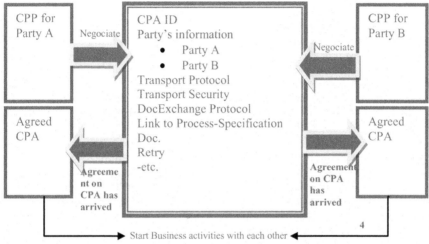

Figure 2. The creation of a CPA through CPPs

Once a CPP is filed, it cannot be changed for this action would put in risk all the CPAs previously created.

Described in the ISO/TS 15000-2 is the ebXML Messaging Service module version 2.0.

In order to enable the actual information exchange between enterprises, security and reliability are critical factors, especially considering that the communications may be made through means as unsecure as the Internet. To overcome this issue a XML based messaging service was designed so it would be robust and simple to use on enterprises' trading messages. To perform as a universal framework, it runs over various communication protocols such as HTTP, SMTP and FTP. Never forgetting the top goal of being a framework available to everyone, its XML-based characteristic allowed it to be a low-cost solution, when compared with existing EDI solutions. The ebMS enveloping not only makes the message secure but it also allows transfer of both XML-based and non XML-based data, covering all cases where additional information is part of the business. This is possible through ebMS's flexibility and independence of the actual payload being sent. Recently a new version, v3.0, of ebMS was approved by OASIS although v2.0 is still the most used.

The third module of the standard, ISO/TS 15000-3, is the specification of the Registry Information Model. A secure information repository, the Registry, where information accessible to everyone is one of the core features of the ebXML framework.

Sharing enterprises' CPPs will allow any other company to easily locate compatible business partners. Additionally, the availability of the registry allows the integration of any new enterprise in the ebXML system through a simple submission of its CPP. Apart from searching and submitting, the database also allows enterprises such operations as managing, retrieving and removing, all made through the registry interface. Storage in the registry is not limited to XML schemas and documents, it also supports submission of UML models and software components (ISO/TS 15000-3, 2004).

The registry is responsible not only for the storage but also for the safekeeping of all its information, which simplifies enterprises' operations but, on the other hand, enhances the database's needs in security issues. Registry Information Model specification was approved under the ISO/TS 15000 Part 3 in 2004 although it was already widely used as an OASIS approved standard.

The ISO/TS 15000 Part 4 defines how communications with the registry are made. All the services provided by the registry are also described in normative form. To better distinguish, ebRIM provides a High level, conceptual definition of what the registry is and how it works, while the ebRS contains detailed and technical information on how every operation designed by the ebRIM is performed.

One of its most important functions is to regulate the users' access to the registry. Who can perform which operations and how must be well defined with the ebRS. In addition to this, by applying all these rules to the Registry, security level within the ebXML system is greatly raised.

The 5th and final part of the ISO/TS 15000 standard, entitled "Core Components Technical Specification" addresses the difficulty of connection and interoperability between different software. By following this standard, applications will be able to understand each others' business semantics thus enabling information exchange between different enterprises, governmental agencies or any other kind of organization. It is not a standard for a specific business area, therefore it can, in fact, be applied in any environment where business information exchange is required. "ISO/TS 15000-5:2005 will form the basis for standards development work of business analysts, business users and information technology specialists supplying the content of and implementing applications that will employ the UN/CEFACT Core Component Library (CCL)" (ISO/TS 15000-5, 2005).

Another specification of ebXML not found in the ISO/TS 15000 but developed by OASIS is the Business Process Schema Specification (BPSS). It's used to describe standard B2B business processes by defining choreography of activities amongst business partners. It usually refers to standard business documents that are exchanged in the business process.

2.2. Use Case Example

The first step for an enterprise, willing to integrate in the ebXML system should be to question the registry for documentation regarding Core Library, i.e., information on how it can initiate its own ebXML implementation. After creating a standard CPP, company A must file it with the ebXML registry for sharing, storing and safekeeping. This action will fully integrate the company in the ebXML framework, enabling it to query the database for compatible CPPs.

Once two (or more, if the business process was defined like that) compatible CPPs are found, a CPA is automatically created, which defines collaborative specifications between the parties.

After this point, actual business transactions are completely set-up, leaving only legal restrictions to finalize, which are obviously outside the ebXML's range of competencies.

Figure 3 shows this sequence of steps taken by a company, in order to do business through the ebXML framework.

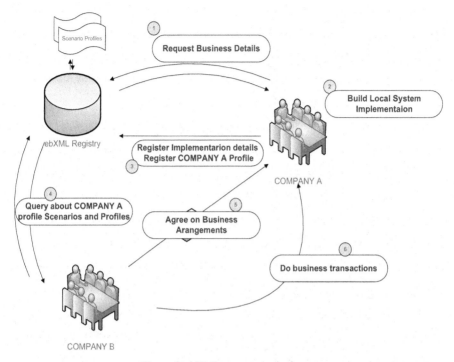

Figure 3. ebXML use case scenario

3. INITIATIVES AND APPLICATIONS

Nowadays, ebXML standards are adopted by many companies. In the majority of the cases just part of the standards are implemented. Some companies try to use ebXML parts as plug-ins on their existing solutions. Others try to redesign their architecture for using the ebXML standards.

In any case, and due to its success in enterprise integration and interoperability in collaborative businesses, several research projects and technology infrastructures based on ebXML are appearing (Chituc & Azevedo, 2006).

As the ebXML specifications mature and are upgraded, its use is extended to even more areas, thus heading to the ebxml's vision.

3.1. ebXML – A Generic Framework

Although it was originally designed to support electronic business, ebXML is a generic framework for collaboration between several entities. "It is equally suited to e-Government and e-Health integration as it is for e-Commerce" (van der Eijk, 2007).

ebXML is being deployed worldwide: in the Agriculture, Chemical, Telecommunications and Automotive Sectors, in Governments and Healthcare Services and in non-government organizations, Universities and Research Centers. Next are briefly exposed some deployments where this generic framework was adopted: in a Japanese food retail industry, in the Norwegian Healthcare Service and in a German mobile communications company.

The Kasumi B2B Integration Project is an initiative in the Japanese food retail industry that aims to augment the added value of services instead of improving efficiency by automating processes. This project develops communication protocols for real B2B collaborations. The adoption of Internet B2B standards reduces the costs needed to develop solutions for B2B collaboration. This project is one of many to use ebXML MS module as a communication protocol for messaging over the Internet.

Kasumi runs a supermarket chain and has several business partners. The aiming at augmenting added value of services improves the quality of information exchange and therefore provides benefits to suppliers and retailers.

A key advantage of using ebMS to enable B2B collaboration is that it doesn't demand a highly developed infrastructure (Hayashi & Mizoguchi, 2003).

Fig. 4 shows an example of an ebXML document exchange between a retailer and a manufacturer from the Kasumi project. This is a XML document that a supplier would send to a retailer when requesting product registration (the information in the document can be of one or more products). The retailer accesses the document through a web page and a negotiation between the two parties occurs through phone or e-mail. Finally the document is updated, stored in the database and sent back to the supplier.

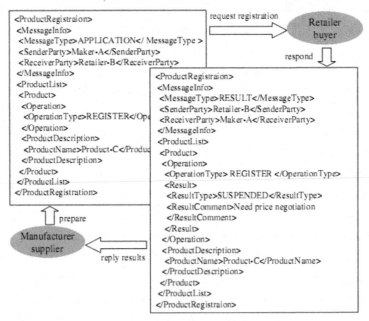

Figure 4. ebXML document used in Kasumi

A second example is the Norwegian Healthcare Service. It's managed by the National Insurance Administration (NIA) of Norway. The Healthcare Service had an EDI-based communications infrastructure between the NIA and their business partners: pharmacies, hospitals and general practitioners.

But the NIA decided that an upgrade was necessary. The main reasons for this upgrade were the security and reliability of the messages as well as increasing the administrative processes which led to a better service provided and reduced manual handling.

Another issue in the upgrade was the choice of using open standards solutions in the new architecture. The NIA and her partners chose the ebMS standard for their message transport protocol, mainly due to the secure and reliable messaging of arbitrary payloads that it provides.

The main reason for using open standard solutions is the level of interoperability it allows. The responsibility of implementing these standards is strictly of the business partners. In fact, each one can implement its own solution, one that suits their business requirements, with the only concern that the solution uses the chosen standards. (van der Eijk, 2005)

Another example of ebXML's application is T-Mobile Communications Company. This is a German company that has business collaboration with suppliers, distributors, wholesales, customers and other business partners involved in the supply-chain. Their business interactions create large amounts of information and, therefore, massive exchanges of messages. A main concern of T-Mobile, when selecting the B2B standard to use, was for the overall system to have a more capable and standard-based B2B interface that would work for all business domains. Other requirements concerned the ability to exchange business data in any format, in a reliable and secure way among the several parties, using open standard solutions. T-Mobile found in ebXML MS and ebXML CPP/A the solution that best met their requirements. One key advantage that T-Mobile noted with their overall experience while using ebXML was, that besides being a powerful tool, at the same time it was very easy to implement and to integrate in existing enterprise applications with limited, or even no changes, to back-end solutions.

By deploying a generic solution for business collaboration, T-Mobile facilitates future connections to new partners (van der Eijk, 2007).

3.2. ebXML's Adoption by RosettaNet

More and more solutions are developing their standards adopting or approaching to ebXML due to the generic and simplicity nature of its use. So, these adoptions of ebXML standards aim at a better final solution.

In 2001, the widely known RosettaNet announced that future versions of RosettaNet Implementation Framework (RNIF) would include support for ebXML Messaging Service Specification. RNIF serves as a guide for e-business process development and implementation and, by supporting ebMS, hopes to achieve interoperability goals across industries. This way, RosettaNet ensures that their vertical supply-chain standards are supported by a horizontal, universally accepted messaging service (RosettaNet press release, 2007).

In 2003, RosettaNet formally adopted ebXML BPSS for expressing business collaborations involving RosettaNet PIPs (OASIS news, 2003). RosettaNet used an error prone manual for configuration, but now their software can install BPSS schemas and be configured correctly on the first try.

RosettaNet's configuration of the system connectivity contains information about the identity of their partners, security certificates and network endpoints. The exchange of this information is done in an informal manner (e.g. e-mail exchanges). Here the ebXML CPP/A can be adopt to automate all the process, reduce error and make the exchange of information easier (Jauhiainen & Lehtonen & Ranta-aho & Rogemond, 2006).

3.3. freebXML

freebXML is an initiative that promotes the growth, development and adoption of ebXML technologies and software solutions. The objective of freebXML.org is to be a center for information sharing and a repository of 'free' ebXML code and applications (freebXML, 2007).

freebXML.org is sponsored by the Center for E-Commerce Infrastructure Development and the Department of Computer Science & Information Systems at the University of Hong Kong. It has several projects: ebMail, freebXML BP, freebXML CC, freebXML Registry, Hermes Message Service Handler and Webswell Connector. Next is a briefly description of three of these projects:

ebMail is a Graphical User Interface (GUI) system that enables users with limited knowledge of ebXML to engage in B2B activities. The user interface is an ebMS-based mail client that allows communications with business partners. The messages exchanged are read in a GUI form which makes it simple to use and with no requirements concerning integration. Plug-in modules provide excellent flexibility and extensibility for adding new business document types and to incorporate advanced functions.

freebXML BP is the project name for the ebBP Editor tool. This tool was designed for helping the user in creating business process specification based on BPSS. This project is realized within the scope of IST-2103 Artemis project supported by the European Commission, DG Information Society and Media, eHealth Unit. The ebBP Editor implementation is based on an XML Schema Editor and is this editor that creates the XML segments of BPSS.

Hermes is a Message Service Handler that provides standardized, reliable and secure infrastructure for exchanging business documents. It uses the ebMS standard and supports secure messaging functions through Internet-based technologies and transport protocols to suit different needs and business requirements. Hermes has been successfully deployed and is being used by two enterprises (a buyer and a seller of office supplies) in Hong Kong.

4. CONCLUSIONS

Today, CEOs face numerous problems while trying to increase their enterprises' markets from which standards to use for deploying the business solution to the level of information shared between partners. All agree that, in order to broaden businesses markets, there are common requirements for the solutions. An electronic mean for displaying business processes in a simpler and less expensive way for inter-integration, as well as ways for supporting and represent business processes independently from technical solutions.

Previous frameworks specified separate and incomplete solutions. EDI provided a runtime data structure, routing specification tools, but didn't provide support for bilateral negotiations, business process modeling or APIs. The universal standard XML is not a communications solution, doesn't define business semantics and doesn't have a transaction registry. Web Services Description Language (WSDL), provides simple ways for identifying services' name, their parameters and identifies Business Processes. As seen before in this article, ebXML provides tools and methods to address these issues.

Limitations still exist in the ebXML standard. It does not provide support for runtime alterations on CPP & CPA. Human decisions are still not directly integrated in the framework.

4.1 Expectations

Business-to-Business integration, by electronic means, will continue to increase, as will the need for higher levels of interactions. The development of new tools and methods is dependent from this increase. To support these increases and the adoption of e-business, ebXML has been considered for native integration within Linux, through organizations such as the Open Source Development Lab (OSDL). "The rapid acceptance of LINUX worldwide and especially in high growth countries such as China, India and Japan, should fuel dramatic growth in the ebXML infrastructure" (Webber, 2007). The development of uniform infrastructures for sharing information between the front-office and the back-office, will also lead to a rapid adoption of ebXML in business model. In the near future, ebXML will provide methods for implementing Radio Frequency Identification (RFID) and mobility through wireless solutions. These methods will always be based upon the core definitions of ebXML. ebMS module will continue to evolve, enabling new tools for system designers to deliver a higher quality of service at a greater logical level.

5. REFERENCES

1. Campbell, S. "ebXML technology", January-February 2006.
2. Chituc, C.-M., Azevedo, A.L. "Business Networking – the Technological Infrastructure Support." In Knowledge and Technology Management in Virtual Organizations, Putnik, G., Cunha M. ed., Chapter 16, 2006, Idea Group Publishing, pp. 334-353.
3. ebXML, http://www.ebxml.org
4. freebXML, 2007. Available online at: http://www.freebxml.org/ (accessed December 10, 2007).
5. Frømyr, J. "The users of ebXMLWho is using ebXML – a review of the global adoption of ebXML." Presentation at the CEN/ISSS ebXML Market Survey Event Lisbon, February 1, 2006.
6. Hayashi, K., & Mizoguchi, R. (2003). Document Exchange Model for Augmenting Added Value of B2B Collaboration. Available online at: http://www.ei.sanken.osaka-u.ac.jp/pub/miz/ICED_CR_submit_hayashi_3.pdf (accessed October 15, 2007).
7. ISO/TS 15000, International Standards Organization, 2005
8. Jauhiainen, S., Lehtonen, O., Ranta-aho, P., Rogemond, N., 2006. Available online at: http://www.soberit.hut.fi/T-86/T-86.161/2005/B2Bi-final.pdf (accessed December 10, 2007).
9. Maijala, V. "MASTER'S THESIS Outlook of Information Security in E-Business". February 17, 2004.
10. Mertz, D., 2001. "Understanding ebXML". Available online at: http://www.ibm.com/developerworks/xml/library/x-ebxml/. (accessed November 9, 2007).
11. OASIS news, 2003. Available online at: http://www.oasis-open.org/news/oasis_news_10_20_03.php (accessed November 30, 2007).
12. OASIS. http://www.oasis-open.org
13. Pigaga, A.. "Business Process Modeling Using ebXML: Case Study". In http://www.sts.tu-harburg.de/pw-and-m-theses/2003/piga03.pdf. May, 2003
14. Pro, S. "What is ebXML" In Presentation at the CEN/ISSS ebXML Market Survey Event Lisbon, February 1, 2006.
15. Robert J. Glushko, Jay M. Tenenbaum and Bart Meltzer "An XML framework for Agent-based E-commerce". In "Communications of the ACM", Vol.3, No3, March 1999
16. RosettaNet press release, 2001. Available online at: http://www.rosettanet.org/cms/sites/RosettaNet/News/PressReleases/2001/modules/rn_news/rn_news_0011.html (accessed December 10, 2007).
17. Shin, Sang - ebXML Presentation. In http://www.javapassion.com/webservices/, April, 2004
18. Tellmann, R., & Maedche, A. "Analysis of B2B Standards and Systems" Version: 1.3, February 28, 2003
19. van der Eijk, P. (2005). Norwegian e-health infrastructure based on XML, ebXML and PKI: Trygdeetaten case study. Available online at: OASIS, http://www.oasis-open.org/casestudies/Trygdeetaten-A4.pdf (accessed November 4, 2007).
20. van der Eijk, P. (2007). T-Mobile International ebXML B2B Gateway Solution: Adoption of the ebXML Messaging Service and ebXML Collaboration Protocol Profiles and Agreements OASIS Standards. Available online at: OASIS, http://www.oasis-open.org/casestudies/tmobile-A4.pdf (accessed December 10, 2007).
21. Webber, D., 2007. "The Benefits of ebXML for e-Business". Available online at: http://www.idealliance.org/proceedings/xml04/papers/44/webber.htm. (accessed November 10, 2007).

14

AN ANALYTICAL APPROACH FOR COMPARING COLLABORATIVE BUSINESS FRAMEWORKS

Claudia-Melania Chituc[1,2], Américo Azevedo[1,2], César Toscano[1]

[1]INESC Porto; [2]Faculty of Engineering of the University of Porto, Portugal;
{cmchituc, ala}@fe.up.pt and ctoscano@inescporto.pt

Several collaborative business frameworks have been developed in order to support organizations to attain interoperability in today's networked business arena. However, the diversity of frameworks generates selection problems. The goal of this article is to present an analytical method supporting the comparison of collaborative business frameworks, which may also be used by decision makers in the framework selection process. The results obtained by comparing four collaborative business frameworks are discussed.

1. INTRODUCTION

Due to recent developments of information and communication technologies (ICTs) and turbulent market conditions, businesses have migrated from traditional practices to e-business, which represents an enabler for interoperability in a collaborative networked environment (CNE), e.g., (Chituc, Toscano, Azevedo, 2007a).

Although active research is pursued in the area of interoperability in a CNE and on the emergence of collaborative business frameworks and standards, few studies aiming at comparing them are available.

The objective of this article is to present an analytical method for collaborative business frameworks comparison, which may also be used by decision makers (DMs) in the framework selection process.

The rest of the article is organized as follows: the next section presents four relevant collaborative business frameworks. An analytical method for collaborative business frameworks comparison is introduced in section three. Then, the comparison results are discussed.

2. COLLABORATIVE BUSINESS FRAMEWORKS

2.1. Introduction

In this article, the term collaborative business framework represents a fundamental structure which allows the definition of a set of concepts to model an organization or a network of organizations while performing e-business. Several cross-industry and industry-specific collaborative business frameworks have been proposed by industry and interest organizations, e.g., CIbFw, ebXML, RosettaNet, papiNet.

Please use the following format when citing this chapter:

Chituc, C-M., Azevedo, A. and Toscano, C., 2008, in IFIP International Federation for Information Processing, Volume 266, *Innovation in Manufacturing Networks*; ed. A. Azevedo; (Boston: Springer), pp. 137–144.

2.2. Collaboration Interoperability Framework

The Collaboration Interoperability Framework (CIbFw) aimed at supporting seamless interoperability in a CNE has been introduced by (Chituc, Toscano, Azevedo, 2007b). The CIbFw has been elaborated to answer the general requirements for interoperability and the gap analysis presented in (Chituc, Toscano, Azevedo, 2008). It comprises six elements: (1) a messaging service, which assures communication among organizations; (2) a collaboration profile/ agreement definition and management service, responsible for the definition and management of the organizations' collaboration profiles and agreements; (3) five main clusters of collaborative business activities, which model inter-organizational activities; (4) a centralized repository; (5) a set of business documents and supporting documents; (6) a performance assessment service. The CIbFw relies on the concept of Business Enabler, which is an entity from the CNE with the sole purpose of easing organizations in performing e-business by providing different services, e.g., messaging, performance assessment. The CIbFw supports two types of communication over the Internet: through the messaging service provided by the BE's system, or directly on P2P basis.

The specifications of the CIbFw serve as basis for the development of two ICT platforms targeting two industry sectors in Portugal: the footwear, and textile, cloth and yarn industries. The ICT platforms are implemented within the scope of TECMODA R&D national project (www.tecmoda.org) pursued in partnership with the Portuguese Technological Transfer Associations (CITEVE, CTCP, ANIVEC) and INESC Porto. The messaging service relies on ebXML messaging specifications, ebMS.

2.3. ebXML

ebXML (www.ebxml.org) is a modular suite of specifications aimed at enabling e-business over the Internet, targeting enterprises of all sizes and from any sector. It comprises the following elements: messaging (ebMS); registry/ repository; business process specification schema; collaboration partner profile/ agreement; and core components. It offers a strong conceptual base and the number of software implementations is relatively high (e.g., Hermes MSH: www.cecid.hku.hk). The ebMS defines a standard communication protocol for the reliable and secure exchange of messages between e-business partners over the Internet and uses the SOAP.

2.4. RosettaNet

The RosettaNet consortium (www.rosettanet.org) develops universal standards for the high-tech and electronics industry global supply chain, and supports their implementation and adoption. It consists of a multiple messaging service, Partner Interface Processes (PIPs) and PIP Directory; dictionaries and RosettaNet Implementation Framework (RNIF). RosettaNet's standards are XML-based, defining message guidelines and business process (BP) interfaces.

2.5. papiNet

papiNet (www.papinet.org) is an international paper and forest industry e-business initiative. It provides a set of standard electronic business documents which facilitate the flow of information among parties engaged in buying, selling and distributing paper and forest products. The papiNet interoperability guidelines are based on the ebMS. It includes a common terminology and standard business documents to use in both domestic and international electronic transactions.

3. COMPARATIVE ANALYSIS

3.1. Related Work

Most of the research studies on collaborative business frameworks are more descriptive than comparative, e.g., [Shim *et al.*, 2000], [Li, 2000]. A general and component-based comparison of eCo, RosettaNet, BizTalk and e-speak frameworks has been elaborated by (Kim *et al.*, 2003). However, this comparative analysis only tackles technical aspects related to interoperability. Several studies focus only on standardization in general, such as: conceptual framework targeting vertical e-business standards; standards developing organizations, e.g., (Zhao *et al.*, 2005).

For the properties of the XML-based e-business frameworks, three technical variables have been identified by (Medjahed *et al.*, 2003), (Numilaakso, Kotinurmi, 2004), and (Numilaakso *et al.*, 2006): business documents, BPs, and messaging. The comparison results obtained illustrated that most of the e-business frameworks complement each other in some aspects (e.g., ebMS is a complement of papiNet), competing in others (e.g., ebMS and RNIF).

However, to compare and assess collaborative business frameworks better, an analytical model is necessary. Research in this area is scarce. A comparison and evaluation of ebXML and RosettaNet based on a decision model specified for small and medium sized enterprises (SMEs) has been introduced by (Pusnik, Juric, Rozman, 2002). A general overview and a formal comparison of ebXML and RosettaNet is available in (Pusnik *et al.*, 2003). The two frameworks have been compared based on a 'utility function'. This study has two main limitations. Firstly, the criteria identified are limited. Secondly, the presented model does not admit a hierarchy of preferences. Also, some of the criteria may be useful to compare technologies, but they are not adequate to compare frameworks.

3.2 Criteria Definition

A set of twenty two criteria has been identified to support the analytical comparison of the collaborative business frameworks. These criteria and their scale definitions are presented in *Table 1*. Seven groups of criteria have been determined: (1) Description and Publication; (2) Search/ Browse Information; (3) Collaboration; (4) Management; (5) Performance Assessment; (6) Specifications; (7) Implementations.

The selection of these criteria is based on an extensive literature review, the views and attributes for seamless interoperability and the general requirements for interoperability presented in (Chituc, Toscano, Azevedo, 2008).

Table 1. Criteria description and scale definition

Criterion Id	Name	Description	Scale definition
C1	Description	It evaluates the ability of a framework to address aspects related to the description of an organization (e.g., specification of the information to be included in an organization's collaboration profile).	1 – Yes/ 0 – No
C2	Publication	It evaluates the ability of a framework to address issues related to the publication of an organization's collaboration profile.	1 – Yes/ 0 – No
C3	Identification of potential business partner/ opportunity	It evaluates the ability of a framework to address issues related to the identification of potential business partner(s), or opportunity (e.g., search for a potential business partner in a centralized repository).	1 – Yes/ 0 – No
C4	Messaging	It evaluates the ability of a framework to address issues related to the communication between two organizations/ systems, e.g., message exchange.	1 – Yes/ 0 – No
C5	Inter-organizational collaborations	It evaluates the ability of a framework to address issues related to the description/ specification of inter-organizational collaborations.	1 – Yes/ 0 – No
C6	Negotiation and agreements	It evaluates the ability of a framework to address issues related to the negotiation and establishment of a collaboration agreement between two organizations in order to perform e-business.	1 – Yes/ 0 – No
C7	Semantics	It evaluates the ability of a framework to address issues related to semantic interoperability, e.g., cross- and intra-industry semantic interoperability.	2 – Cross- & intra-industry semantic interoperability/ 1 – Intra-industry semantic interoperability/ 0 – It does not tackle interoperability issues.
C8	Information management	It evaluates the ability of a framework to address issues related to information management.	1 – Yes/ 0 – No
C9	Conflict solving	It evaluates the ability of a framework to address issues related to solving potential conflicts.	1 – Yes/ 0 – No
C10	Rights and obligations	It evaluates the ability of a framework to address aspects related to the rights and obligations of an organization in a CNE/ CN (e.g., access rights).	1 – Yes/ 0 – No
C11	Roles/ Tasks fulfillment	It evaluates the ability of a framework to address aspects related to organization's roles/ tasks fulfillment.	1 – Yes/ 0 – No

Table 1. Criteria description and scale definition (cont.)

Criterion Id	Name	Description	Scale definition
C12	Learning	It evaluates the ability of a framework to address aspects related to an organization's/ CN's ability to learn.	1 – Yes/ 0 – No
C13	Performance assessment	It refers to the ability of a framework to address issues related to performance assessment.	1 – Yes/ 0 – No
C14	Technical specifications	It evaluates the amount of supporting literature and examples (e.g., technical reports, scientific articles) available, which facilitate the learning and understanding of a framework.	3 – High number/ 2 – Average/ 1 – Low number/ 0 – Zero.
C15	Comprehensibility	It evaluates the effort (e.g., time, work) neecesary to understand all the features of a framework.	3 – Low effort/ 2 – Average/ 1 – High amount of effort.
C16	Generality	It characterizes the degree of generality of a framework (e.g., considering the possibility to adapt it to the requirements of a certain industry).	3 – High/ 2 – Average/ 1 – Low.
C17	Targeted enterprises (by size)	It refers to the type of enterprises targeted by a framework.	3 – Supporting enterprises of all sizes/ 2 – Mostly for SMEs/ 1 – Only for large enterprises.
C18	Maturity	It evaluates the maturity or recognition of a framework, based on the number of years since the first technical specification has been published.	Number of years since the first specification has been published or presented.
C19	Policy	It characterizes the degree in which the specifications of a framework follow national/ international legislation and recommendations.	3 – High/ 2 – Average/ 1 – Low.
C20	Accessibility	It characterizes the degree in which the specifications of a framework are available for different organizations.	3 – High/ 2 – Average/ 1 – Low.
C21	Tools support	It refers to the quantity of support tools designed and implemented to facilitate the development of infrastructures considering a certain framework as basis.	3 – High number/ 2 – Average/ 1 – Low number/ 0 – Zero.
C22	ICT platforms	It refers to the quantity of ICT platforms developed by following the specifications of a framework.	3 – High number/ 2 – Average/ 1 – Low number/ 0 – Zero.

3.3. Interoperability Characterization Function

A weight coefficient may be assigned to each criterion since a certain enterprise manager or DM may prefer certain criteria over the others. With these considerations, an interoperability characterization function C_f has been defined to support the analytical comparison of collaborative business frameworks, as follows:

$$C_f : F \to \mathfrak{R}^*_+ \text{, and } C_f(F_j) = \sum_{\substack{i \in I \\ \max(ci(Fj)) \neq 0}} \frac{C_i(F_j) * w(c_i)}{\max(c_i(F_j))} + \sum_{i \in P} c_i(F_j) * w(c_i)$$

where: C_i is criterion i, and $i \in N^*$; F_j is the framework alternative, $F_j \in F$ (F is the set of frameworks) and $j = \overline{1, n}$; $n \in N^*$ is the total number of frameworks to be compared; $w(c_i)$ is the weight associated to criterion i and $w(c_i) \in [0,1]$; $I = \{7, 14, 15, 16, 17, 18, 19, 20, 21, 22\}$ and $P = \{1, 2, 3, 4, 5, 6, 8, 9, 10, 11, 12, 13\}$

Table 2 portrays the results obtained by the comparison of four frameworks: CIbFw, ebXML, RosettaNet and papiNet. For simplicity, the weight assigned to each criterion was 1, that is: $w(c_i) = 1 \ \forall \ i \in N^*$. This means there is no preference of one criterion over the others.

4. DISCUSSION

The value obtained for the C_f is higher for ebXML when compared to the other three frameworks. It is followed by CIbFw. The lowest value has been obtained with papiNet.

Analyzing the results attained for each group of criteria, the CIbFw specifications tackle better the first five groups of criteria. In fact, the CIbFW is the only framework addressing G5) Performance Assessment. However, ebXML provides more detailed technical specifications and a higher number of implementations (reflected by G6 and G7). Concerning the number of implementations (e.g., tools, ICT platforms), the lowest values have been obtained by CIbFw. This can be explained by the fact that ebXML, RosettaNet and papiNet are more mature initiatives (e.g., RosettaNet specifications have been published eight years before the first presentation of CIbFw specifications).

The mean values and the standard deviation have been calculated. The standard deviation (5,17) illustrates a relatively high distribution of the data from the mean value (12,2). Also, the coefficient of variation is 42,37 %, which shows a relatively high degree of data heterogeneity.

The results attained must be carefully interpreted, since the selection of the comparison criteria is based on the definition of seamless interoperability proposed by (Chituc, Toscano, Azevedo, 2008), and the requirements for interoperability identified. Also, the weighted values associated to each criterion were considered to be constant. Thus, the values obtained for the C_f are specific to the numerical values assumed for the parameters. For example, C17 may have a different weighted value in different countries. In Europe, the industry is dominated by SMEs, so for the European industry it might be of higher relevance to have a framework targeting SMEs rather than one supporting enterprises of all sizes.

Different values can be assigned to the weight associated to each criterion $w(c_i)$, considering, for instance, $w(c_i)$ between 0,1 and 0,9. The results obtained for four simulation experiments are illustrated in Figure 1. This model may be used by a DM in the selection of a collaborative business framework: the framework for which the highest value of the C_f has been obtained is selected. However, the value obtained for the C_f depends on the importance associated to each criterion. For example, a certain DM may assign a higher importance to criteria related to specifications or implementations, than to management. This situation is reflected by *Case B* (Figure 1), where the highest value of C_f is obtained for ebXML. For the *Case D*, where higher importance has been assigned to performance assessment and management, the CIbFw should be selected.

Table 2. Results for frameworks comparison

Criterion		C_f(ClbFw)	C_f (ebXML)	C_f(RosettaNet)	C_f(papiNet)
G1) Description and Publication		**2**	**2**	**0**	**0**
C1	Description	1	1	0	0
C2	Publication	1	1	0	0
G2) Search		**1**	**1**	**0**	**0**
C3	Identification of potential business partner/ opportunity	1	1	0	0
G3) Collaboration		**4**	**4**	**2,5**	**2,5**
C4	Messaging	1	1	1	1
C5	Inter-organizational collaborations	1	1	1	1
C6	Negotiation and agreements	1	1	0	0
C7	Semantics	2	2	1	1
G4) Management		**3**	**1**	**0**	**0**
C8	Information managemet	1	1	0	0
C9	Conflict solving	1	0	0	0
C10	Rights and obligations	0	0	0	0
C11	Roles/ tasks fulfilment	0	0	0	0
C12	Learning	0	0	0	0
G5) Performance Assessment		**1**	**0**	**0**	**0**
C13	Performance assessment	1	0	0	0
G6) Specifications		**4,44**	**6,88**	**4**	**4,11**
C14	Technical specifications	1	3	2	2
C15	Comprehensibility	3	3	2	2
C16	Generality	2	3	1	1
C17	Targeted enterprise (by size)	2	3	1	2
C18	Maturity	1 (2006)	8 (1999)	9 (1998)	7 (2000)
C19	Policy	2	3	1	1
C20	Accessibility	3	3	2	2
G7) Implementations		**0,66**	**2**	**1,33**	**0,66**
C21	Tools support	1	3	2	1
C22	ICT platforms	1	3	2	1
Interoperability Characterization Function		**16,1**	**16,88**	**7,83**	**7,27**

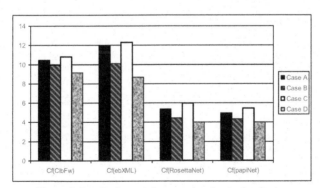

Figure 1. Results for weights associated to each criterion

5. CONCLUSIONS

Several collaborative business frameworks and standards have been developed, based on which different ICT platforms have been implemented. The relatively high number of collaborative business frameworks proves their importance. At the same time it creates selection problems for decision makers.

Research aiming at the comparison of collaborative business frameworks is challenging. The challenges are related to the difficulty in tracing the adoption of these initiatives, frequent changes on the specifications of a specific framework, the disappearance of a certain initiative and the emergence of new approaches.

The analytical comparison performed based on the twenty two criteria and the C_f proposed showed a slight advantage of ebXML over the CIbFw, RosettaNet and papiNet, when the weighted values associated to each criterion were equal. However, these results have to be interpreted carefully, since the obtained values are specific to the associated numerical values. This model may be useful for decision makers in the process of selecting a collaborative business framework. Further work will be pursued to validate the proposed model with real data from industry.

5.1. Acknowledgments

The first author acknowledges FCT for PhD grant BD/SFRH/19751/2004.

6. REFERENCES

1. Chituc, C.-M.; Azevedo, A. "Business networking -- the technological infrastructure support". In Knowledge and Technical Management in Virtual Organizations, Putnik, G.; Cunha, M. eds., Chapter 16, Idea Publishing/ IGI Global, 2006, pp. 334-353.
2. Chituc, C.-M.; Nof. S.Y. The Join/ Leave/ Remain (JLR) decision in collaborative networked organizations. Computers & Industrial Engineering Journal 2007; 53: 173-195.
3. Chituc, C.-M.; Toscano, C.; Azevedo, A. E-business and collaborative networks: a service oriented architecture for the footwear industry. Proc. IEEE INDIN 2007a, pp. 591-597.
4. Chituc, C.-M.; Toscano, C.; Azevedo, A. "Towards seamless interoperability in collaborative networks". In Establishing the Foundation of Collaborative Networks, Camarinha-Matos, L.; Afsarmanesh, H.; Novais, P.; Analide, C., eds., vol. 243/ 2007, 2007b, pp. 445-452.
5. Chituc, C.-M.; Toscano, C.; Azevedo, A. Interoperability in Collaborative Networks: independent and industry specific initiatives – The case of the footwear industry. Computers in Industry (accepted for publication) to appear in Vol. 59, Issue 5, May 2008 (DOI:10.1016/j.compind.2007.12.012).
6. Kim, D.J.; Agrawal, M.; Jayaraman, B.; Rao, H.R. A comparison of B2B e-service solutions. Communications of ACM 2003; 46(12): 317-324.
7. Li, H. XML and industrial standards for electronic commerce. Knowledge and Information Systems 2000; 2(4): 487-497.
8. Medjahed, B.; Benatallah, B.; Bouguettaya, A., Ngu, A.H.H.; Elmagramid, A.K. Business-to-business interactions: issues and emerging technologies. VLDB Journal 2003; 12: 59-85.
9. Nurmilaakso, J.-M.; Kotinurmi, P. A review of XML-based supply chain integration. Production Planning & Control 2004; 15 (6): 608-621.
10. Nurmilaakso, J.-M.; Kotinurmi, P.; Laesvouri, H. XML-based e-business frameworks and standardization. Computer Standards & Interfaces 2006; 28(5): 585-599.
11. Pusnik, M.; Juric, M.B.; Rozman, I. Evaluation of technologies for business process automation. Informatica 2002; 26: 373-380.
12. Pusnik, M.; Juric, M.B.; Hericko, M.; Rozman, I.; Sumak, B. "A comparison of ebXML and RosettaNet", 2003.
13. Shim, S.; Pendyala, V.; Sundaram, M.; Gao, J. "Business-to-business e-commerce frameworks". In IEEE Computer, 33(10), 2000, pp. 40-47
14. Zhao, K.; Xia, M.; Shaw, M. "Vertical e-business standards and standards developing organizations: a conceptual framework". In Electronic Markets 15(4), 2005, pp. 289-300

15

SUPPORT OF KNOWLEDGE CREATION PROCESSES IN A COMPUTER-BASED COLLABORATIVE SYSTEM

Ján Paralič, František Babič
Centre for Information Technologies, Technical University of Košice, Slovakia,
{jan.paralic, frantisek.babic}@tuke.sk

This paper presents a particular approach how to support the knowledge creation processes that are based on innovative idea of trialogical learning. The key task in trialogical learning is to understand how the "weaker" forms of knowledge are used and made explicit in a meaningful way in collaborative processes. Trialogical learning provides mechanism by which tacit knowledge is conceptualized in collaborative systems. Within the "Knowledge-Practices Laboratory" (KP-Lab)[1] project suitable tools and practices for support of trialogical learning are being designed, implemented and evaluated. The KP-LAB platform offers, except of others, also facilities for discovering, managing and visualization of some tacit knowledge. We present in this paper one particular approach how to this is supported with proposed awareness features

1. INTRODUCTION

One important aspect of collaborative systems (virtual learning environments, computer-based collaborative systems, etc.) is awareness support that provides information about performed activities, about user's behavior, relations between participants or between participants and environment, reasons of decisions, etc. This information is can be viewed as a kind of tacit knowledge that could be expressed and used for identification of innovative ideas and re-use it in future processes.

Tacit knowledge are described as knowledge that people carry in their minds and therefore it is difficult to access. Tacit knowledge is regarded more valuable because it provides context for situations, ideas or experiences. This concept is widely used in various disciplines, such as knowledge management, artificial intelligence and psychology. In the field of knowledge-based systems researchers have been, in the last decades, mainly concerned about making (some) tacit knowledge explicit.

In the field of knowledge management, Nonaka and Takeuchi (Nonaka and Takeuchi, 1995) introduced a paradigm shift by developing a practical aspect of tacit knowledge. This approach considers tacit knowledge as non-linguistic non-numerical form of knowledge that is highly personal, context specific and deeply rooted in individual experiences, ideas, values and emotions. This approach suggests that tacit knowledge has to be captured and communicated in organisations in order to enhance knowledge creation processes.

Nonaka and Takeuchi's work as well as other two theoretical approaches to knowledge creation are briefly described in the following section 2, together with

---

[1] www.kp-lab.org

Please use the following format when citing this chapter:

Paralič, J. and Babič, F., 2008, in IFIP International Federation for Information Processing, Volume 266, *Innovation in Manufacturing Networks;* ed. A. Azevedo; (Boston: Springer), pp. 145–152.

a generalized view of knowledge creation as a trialogical learning process and a way how this approach is followed within the KP-Lab project from the technological perspective. Section 3 focuses on one important aspect of the KP-Lab technological platform, namely awareness support that in our opinion provides a kind of tools supporting both, tacit knowledge capture and reuse, as well as support of collaborative knowledge creation processes as such.

2. KNOWLEDGE CREATION

Knowledge creation is one of the core aspects of trialogical learning and of the knowledge development in general (this includes also knowledge adoption, distribution, review and revision) within an organization. From the methodological point of view the knowledge creation processes have been studied in different contexts (Paavola et al., 2004):

- Carl Bereiter's knowledge building approach has emerged from cognitive studies in the educational context (Bereiter and Scardamalia, 1993),
- Yrjö Engeström's theory of expansive learning is based on Activity Theory (Engeström, 1999), and
- Nonaka and Takeuchi's model of organizational knowledge creation originates from the analysis of work in Japanese companies (Nonaka and Takeuchi, 1995).

Tacit knowledge can be seen as an important aspect of these models although with different interpretation in particular approaches:

- Bereiter emphasizes conceptual artefacts and ideas which are collaboratively developed,
- Engeström emphasizes practices and activities which are reflected and transformed in collective processes, and
- Nonaka & Takeuchi emphasize personal hunches and insights which are explicated for the use of the community.

Tacit knowledge are based on the idea that knowledge is not something expressed in symbolic or declarative means but on various other meanings, signs, and structures embedded in visual representations, practices, concrete artefacts, diagrams, etc. The key task for trialogical learning is to understand how these "weaker" forms of knowledge are used and made explicit in a meaningful way in collaborative processes.

2.1. Trialogical learning

Trialogical learning is a relative new approach in CSCL (Computer-supported Collaborative Learning) and CSCW (Computer-supported Cooperative Work) domain. Theoretical as well as practical aspects of this innovative approach started to be researched and developed in Finland, at the University in Helsinki. From this institution the idea is being distributed now in the (not only) European educational community, e.g. within the Knowledge Practices Laboratory (KP-Lab) project.

Trialogical learning has emerged from the theories that are mentioned thereinbefore. Trialogical learning is not supposed to be a "super-theory" on the basis of these background theories but it pinpoints certain kinds of phenomena which are prevalent and central nowadays: how people organize their work for developing some shared, concrete "objects" (like conceptual artefacts, practices, products), see Figure 1.

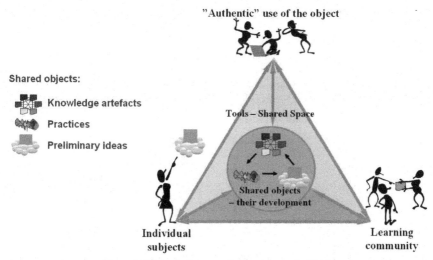

Figure1. Trialogical approach (Paavola et al., 2004)

Trialogical learning (Hakkarainen and Paavola, 2007) refers to the process where learners are collaboratively developing shared objects of activity in systematic fashion. It concentrates on the interaction through these common objects (or artefacts) of activity, not just among people or within one's mind.

2.2. Knowledge Practices Laboratory

One of the main goals of KP-Lab project is to research and develop relevant technologies that support trialogical learning. The essential way how to design and develop supporting collaborative technologies is a co-evolution process of researchers, technological developers and users. It is organised as follows. Trialogical learning theory, which is being developed by theoretical partners, is a fundament that needs to be transformed into real practice. This is only possible with carefully designed tools that will use together with innovative knowledge practices. We believe that one possible way how to achieve this transition from theory to practice can be the following: the pedagogies, grounded in the newly formed trialogical theory, produce scenarios and use cases that become the base for technological development.

KP-Lab technology builds on emerging technologies, such as semantic web, real-time multimedia communication, ubiquitous access using wireless devices, and interorganisational computing. There are also non-technological tools as the change laboratory (the idea is to arrange on the shopfloor a room or space in which there is a rich set of instruments for analyzing disturbances and for constructing new models for the work practice).

The multinational consortium integrates expertise from various domains, including pedagogy, psychology and engineering as well as end-users and key representatives from the corporate/business sector to provide authentic environments for research and piloting. The project involves 22 partners from 14 countries, as well as many schools, universities, companies and work places and other prospective end-users.

2.3. KP-Lab platform

The KP-Lab platform is based on interoperability of the integrated tools and on a support of semantic web models and standards. It provides the technology mediation for innovative knowledge creation processes and allows the objects exchanges between applications with their specific appliance domains.

KP-Lab platform provides working environment to support cooperative and collaborative work or leaning between registered users. This environment integrates many supporting tools, e.g.

- Shared Space: a virtual collaboration space offering facilities for interacting with knowledge artefacts, knowledge process models, users and the shared space itself:
  - o working with the knowledge artefacts, e.g. creating, editing, storing, sharing, commenting, annotating semantically, disseminating, discussing;
  - o managing the knowledge processes, e.g. creating, changing and executing process models;
  - o managing the shared space itself (e.g. configuring the tools available).
- Map-It: a tool that supports synchronous discussions within any group of users and semi-automatic generation of a "discussion map" and a comprehensive and organized set of discussion documentation;
- Change Laboratory: an intervention method for systematically developing work practices. It is based on the framework of developmental work research that provides reflective feedback of participant work;
- Semantic multimedia annotation tool: a tool that provides functionalities for single or collaborative annotation of multimedia clips.

One of the main purposes of such performing activities is to use tacit knowledge in the collaborative creation of shared objects of activities. Therefore, the KP-LAB platform offers facilities for discovering, managing and visualization of tacit knowledge. This knowledge in the background of the practices will be better visualized and brought forward with the new awareness features. So Awareness services will be implemented as a part of the KP-Lab platform and will work with information/data from it.

The Awareness services enable to explicate the traces through; for example, graphical views to participant's relations, patterns of sequences and actions, suggested reading and tags, etc. These features provide more explicit traces of the tacit process knowledge that is embedded in the practices of the members of the group/community, bringing it more into the open to be perceived and making it easier to consciously acknowledge and analyse it when collaboratively developing the shared objects of activity.

3. AWARENESS SUPPORT

3.1. Theoretical background

Collaborative systems require awareness support to ensure collaborators know about the activities of others in order to coordinate their work, support their collaboration, identify potential problems and prevent conflicts and misunderstandings. In order to achieve a proper interpretation on on-going and past actions in a computer-based collaborative system, one needs to take into account not only what has been the content of actions of the others, but also the context and semantic relations of the actions performed by the participants of a collaborative process.

One definition of awareness that is especially relevant in a domain of collaborative systems could be: "Awareness is an understanding of the activities of others which provides a context for your own activity "(Dourish and Bellotti, 1992).

Several informal definitions of distinct awareness types have been collected by Drury (Drury et al., 2002) from previous works:

- *Informal awareness* - the general sense of who is around and what others are up to. This is important as a prerequisite for "group structural awareness" and a baseline for informal collaboration.
- *Peripheral awareness* - where people know what others are doing.
- *Social awareness* - information about the presence and activities of people in a shared environment.
- *Group structural awareness* - knowledge of roles and responsibilities, their positions on an issue and process information (Begole et al, 1999).
- *Conceptual awareness* – knowledge about rules of activity and emerging norms of virtual collaboration (Morch et al., 2005).
- *Task awareness* - how to complete a common task (such as learning assignments) as well as understanding the purpose of the task.
- *Workspace awareness* - the up-to-the-minute knowledge a person holds about the state of others' interactions with the environment, which should reduce efforts needed to coordinate common tasks and actions relative to shared objects (Gutwin and Greenberg, 1998).

Our solution will include support of several types of awareness, e.g. we will provide status information about each user (informal awareness), present and past actions of a user (peripheral and social awareness), interaction between users and between users and environment (workspace awareness) etc.

Result information of awareness can be presented to end-users (collaborators) in a passive or active way. In the first case it is the responsibility of the user to explicitly look for the information he/she needs. In the case of active systems, the user will be notified automatically about changes in the awareness information. The first approach has the advantage that the user is in control of when and what information is displayed, avoiding information overload by these means. Nevertheless, the disadvantage is the fact that in order to monitor the change in the state of a person, the user has to access that information repeatedly.

3.2. Log-based awareness (LBA)

Log based (History) awareness is an asynchronous functionality that builds on persistent storage of events representing activities performed by users of various end-user tools in KP-Lab platform and based on them supports analysis and discovery of tacit knowledge from previous activities. The results can be used as inputs for the design of the tools, content and GUI adaptation for personalization.

We will provide two levels of awareness information from this module. The first level will give answers to basic questions, e.g.:

- When each member has logged in lastly?
- Recent changes: Knowing who made what changes to which object, when?
- What kinds of resources (internal or external) students have used?
- A list of all activities that the members have done (not only in actual session).
- Who is the most active/responsible user? etc.

In cooperation with other services developed in KP-Lab (Smrz et al., 2007) and utilization of artificial intelligence techniques (e.g. various data mining techniques: clustering, association rules mining, etc.) following advanced analyses capabilities may be provided. Various statistics and graphs reflecting selected activities in the system from different points of view, present graphical view (maps) that show how the participants are related to the shared artefacts as well as to each other, discovery of interesting patterns within sequences of actions, and possibly others.

3.3. Implementation of LBA

LBA (Babič and Wagner, 2007) is based on generic log storage and query service to which every end-user tool will send various high-level events. These events will be defined by tools, because tools know what type of actions are important for users and may be useful to be logged and analyzed to infer knowledge from the actual working practices later on.

As an example of LBA exploitation we present communication with end-user tool called Knowledge Process Service (Babič and Paralič 2007) (also developed in our Centre). KPS is integrated as web service into the Shared space and provides a set of features and interfaces necessary for creation, management, and annotation of knowledge processes composed from various elements. Some of the KPS functions are the following:

- Create, view, update and reuse such process elements as Task or Milestone.
- Set-up description of the element – metadata. For example: name, actor, starting and ending dates for a task etc.
- Set-up relationships between process elements. For example: prerequisites mean tasks that need to be completed before actual task will start.
- Execution of a process: User can follow current state of a process by defined timeline.
- Change elements setting on the fly: User can flexibly make changes in description of relevant elements based on her/his user rights.
- Structure of the full process is visualized as Gantt chart.

This tool can generate several types of events as Modification of object metadata, Modification of object itself (create, delete) and Modification in process structure. If e.g. a user wants to be notified about changes in a particular Task (this means any change of Task properties metadata), the process is the following (see Figure 2). The user subscribes via KPS his/her interest to be notified when a particular Task changes (*Subscription of Task changes* in Figure 2). This subscription will be stored in the Awareness repository (*Saving in database*). Whenever any user makes a modification of this particular task, KPS issues an event to be logged (*Modification of Task - Event*) into the Awareness repository. LBA service will provide required operations and all matching subscriptions (result of *Queries* in Figure 2) will lead to notifications (*Notification of realized event*) to all their subscribers. Moreover, this event will be taken into account whenever a relevant analysis of logged events will be performed by a user or a tool (*Perform History Analysis*, *Queries*, and *Provide results of Analysis in Figure 2*).

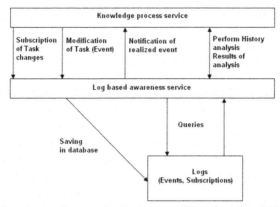

Figure 2. The schema of communication between KPS and envisaged LBA services

4. CONCLUSION

This paper presented one particular approach to support knowledge creation processes via awareness support within the KP-Lab collaborative environment. This functionality is required by participants of pilot courses in order to provide simple notifications as well as advanced analyses of processes. First prototype of LBA will be finished in September 2008 and will be ready for autumn field trials (pilot courses). Based on results of this test phase the LBA functionality may further be extend with e.g. additional analytical features.

4.1. Acknowledgments

The work presented in this paper was supported: by European Commission DG INFSO under the IST program, contract No. 27490; by the Slovak Research and Development Agency under the contract No. APVV-0391-06 and by the Slovak Grant Agency of Ministry of Education and Academy of Science of the Slovak Republic under contract No. 1/3135/06.

The KP-Lab Integrated Project is sponsored under the 6th EU Framework Programme for Research and Development. The authors are solely responsible for the content of this article. It does not represent the opinion of the KP-Lab consortium or the European Community, and the European Community is not responsible for any use that might be made of data appearing therein.

5. REFERENCES

1. Babič, F., Paralič, J. "Knowledge practices Laboratory (KP-Lab) Project". In: Znalosti 2007, VŠB-TU Ostrava, Czech Republic 2007, ISBN 978-80-248-1279-3, pp. 364-367.
2. Babič, F., Wagner, J. "Awareness service based on events logs". 2nd Workshop on Intelligent and Knowledge oriented Technologies 2007, Kosice, Slovakia. ISBN 978-80-89284-10-8, pp.106-109.
3. Begole, J., Rosson, M.B., Shaffer, C.A. Flexible Collaboration Transparency: Supporting Worker Independence in Replicated Application-Sharing Systems. ACM Transactions on Computer-Human Interaction 1999; Vol. 6: 95-132.
4. Bereiter, C., Scardamalia, M. Surpassing ourselves: An inquiry into the nature and implications of expertise. La Salle, IL: Open Court, 1993.
5. Dourish, P., Bellotti, V. "Awareness and Coordination in Shared Workspaces". In Proceedings of the AMC Conference on Computer Supported Cooperative Work (CSCW'92), Greenberg S. ed., Toronto, Canada: AMC Press, 1992, pp. 107-114.
6. Drury, J., Williams, M.G. "A framework for role based specification and evaluation of awareness support in synchronous collaborative applications". In Proceedings of the 11th International Workshops on Enabling Technologies for Collaborative Enterprises (WETICE02), Carnegie Mellon University, Pittsburgh, IEEE Computer Society Press, 2002, pp. 12–17.
7. Engeström, Y. Innovative Learning in Work Teams: Analyzing Cycles of Knowledge Creation in   Practice. Cambridge, MA: Cambridge University Press, 1999.
8. Gutwin, C., Greenberg, S. "Design for individuals, design for groups: Tradeoffs between power and workspace awareness". In Proceedings of CSCW'98 ACM Conference on Computer Supported Cooperative Work, Seattle, Washington, 1998, pp. 207-216.
9. Hakkarainen, K., Paavola, S. "From monological and dialogical to trialogical approaches to learning". A paper at an international workshop "Guided Construction of Knowledge in Classrooms", February 5-8, 2007, Hebrew University, Jerusalem, 2007.
10. Mørch, A., Jondahl, S., Dolonen, J. Supporting Conceptual Awareness with Pedagogical Agents. Information Systems Frontiers, special issue on Computer Supported Collaborative Learning Requiring Immersive Presence 2005; 7(1): 39-53.
11. Nonaka, I., Takeuchi, H. The Knowledge Creating Company. Oxford University Press, New York, 1995.
12. Paavola, S., Lipponen, L., Hakkarainen, K. Models of Innovative Knowledge Communities and Three Metaphors of Learning. Review of Educational Research 2004; 74(4): 557-576.
13. Smrz, P. et al. "Specification of the SWKM Knowledge Evolution, Recommendation, and Mining services". KP-Lab public deliverable D5.3. September, 2007.

16

EFFICIENT EVENT HANDLING IN SUPPLY NETWORKS USING Q-LEARNING AND K-MEANS CLUSTERING

Andre Doering
Fraunhofer ALB Paderborn, andre.doering@alb.fraunhofer.de
Wilhelm Dangelmaier
Heinz Nixdorf Institute, University of Paderborn, whd@hni.upb.de
Christoph Laroque
Heinz Nixdorf Institute, University of Paderborn, laro@hni.upb.de

Modern value-added processes will be globally cross-linked through outsourcing and reduction of real net output ratio. Therefore logistical planning and control processes become more complex. Events in supply networks and their consequences to the partners in the supply network will be hardly to overlook without using computer based decision support systems. This paper describes such a decision support system, learning the rules used to control the production network. In details the system architecture will be described, requirements to such a system will be identified and a solution developed at the Heinz Nixdorf Institute and Fraunhofer ALB (application center for logistic-oriented business administration) in Paderborn will be presented. The solution is based on a q-learning approach supported by a k-means clustering algorithm.

1. INTRODUCTION

Modern value-added processes in the European Automotive Industry will be globally cross-linked through outsourcing and reduction of real net output ratio to reduce production costs (Fraunhofer, 2004). Therefore logistical planning and control processes become more complex, because more cross-linked processes cause higher co-ordination effort for planning and controlling such heterogeneous supply networks (Baumgaertel, 2006).

Especially the handling of events, causing direct effects to the supply network and its production systems, must be handled very efficient. To optimize such control processes in their efficiency and reliability, automated systems are used to support human production planners in their daily complex decisions making processes. But the complexity of the event handling task in supply networks limits the usage of classical operation research methods and their algorithms: adequate models to model the problem will cause NP-hard optimization problems and long algorithm runtimes (Suhl, 2006).

The handling of an event needs fast reaction, at best case in real-time (Doering, 2007). Therefore, the usage of *intelligent* methods for production network control like artificial learning systems is in the focus in applied production research both in applied scientific projects (AC-DC) and in industry (Diedrichsen, 2007). Despite their specific

Please use the following format when citing this chapter:

Doering, A., Dangelmaier, W. and Laroque, C., 2008, in IFIP International Federation for Information Processing, Volume 266, *Innovation in Manufacturing Networks;* ed. A. Azevedo; (Boston: Springer), pp. 153–160.

implementation the objective of such intelligent systems is mostly to learn rules supporting human or automatic event handling by selecting possible reaction measures.

An event is defined as a state of a production plan offering a restriction violation in this production plan after an unexpected change of customer demands, suppliers or capacity supply or demand change, e.g. usage of safety stock after an increased customer demand. Reactions to events are here defined as the usage of specific change panning strategies, implemented by specific change planning algorithms for solving occurring lacks in production plans efficiently (Heidenreich, 2006).

Event-based rules have been defined to select applicable planning strategies enabling a fast reaction to the event (Ibid.). But the complexity of the supply networks generates many possible event states, which requires many rules to cover all possible or relevant event situations. It is obvious, that a human planner is not able to formulate all rules for implementing an efficient rule based event handling system. Also the usage of experience causes problems, because experience may not cover all respectively future events and is hardly to extract objectively using knowledge engineering techniques (Görz, 2003).

Therefore, this work deals with using machine learning techniques based on Q-learning (e.g. Mitchell, 1997 or Sutton, 1998) to learn such rules automatically and though efficiently.

For the implementation of such a learning system, several tasks are to be fulfilled. The complexity of the state space is a problem causing nearly unlimited exploration times for the Q-learning algorithm. Moreover, the learning function for Q-learning reward calculation must be defined, regarding the objective of a supply network based learning task. Thirdly, an efficient training algorithm must be developed to train the learning system efficiently.

This paper will focus on the definition of such a learning system and outline a concept for state reduction and the calculation of rewards. Forthcoming problems for training and testing will be discussed briefly.

The paper will start with brief definition of the learning problem and the requirements to the learning system in detail in chapter. 2. Chapter 3 outlines an overview of the state of the art. Chapter 4 introduces the concepts and drafts first results. The paper closes with a summary of the achieved work and an outlook to forthcoming research activities.

2. PROBLEM DEFINITION

2.1. Co-ordination in supply networks

The basic character of an automotive supply network is the breakdown of value adding processes to several production stages staring at *tier-n* up the Original Manufacturer (OEM), which finishes the value adding process by the final assembly of the car. Most production stages are based on serial production, which is mainly planned by lot scheduling algorithms (Heidenreich, 2006).

In the production system model language MFERT (Schneider, 1996) (see Figure 1) every stage of a supply network can be modeled as combination of capacities $(CON)^1$, processes $(PN)^2$ and an incoming edge for material out of a buffer $(AON)^3$, e.g. stock. The stages are connected between an edge from a PN to an AON.

---

[1] Capacity object node

[2] Process node

[3] Assembly Object Node

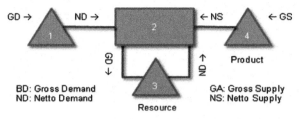

Figure 1. Basic MFERT Model

Considering a network consisting of several connected stages, the material flow generally starts from the tier-n up to the OEM. The information flow, consting of demands for material in a certain time period, is directed upwards and downwards the network, depending on the specific type of information exchange. Upward flowing information is called supply[4]. It contains information about part supplies based on values, that will be procured to the earliest possible period of a production pan in the next stage. Downward information flow will consist of demand figures representing a latest point in time for delivering a part to the production stage, where the demand is generated.

A plan consists of a number of periods t starting from now (t_0) until a pre-defined last period $PH : t \in 1, \ldots, PH$. Every period of a plan is, depending whether it is an AON or CON, allocated with a stock value or capacity value called lots. Every plan for an AON/CON will generally be represented by a vector p* allocated with a lot to consisting periods of a plan denoted by vector $p^*(t)$.

Every period will be restricted by a maximum and minimum value representing the maximum space of a buffer respectively the minimum safety stock or the maximal utilization of a modeled capacity. Between every production stage the flow of material is limited to a min or max value. Additionally, the upward procurement process between production stages can be managed in recurring cycles or at any point in time.

If a min/max-restriction is violated, the corresponding plan is called 'not consistent' and a change planning process has to be started, in order to generate a new consistent plan. The coordination during those change planning processes in the supply network is organized in a decentral way. In the implementation of the learning system, every production stage is an autonomous agent, that coordinates only by communication with the prior or succeeding production stage agents by sending gross or supply figures. For every type of change planning coordination a specific planning algorithm has been classified, that reschedules a local plan or globally sends requests of demands or supplies to corresponding agents of other production stages by demanding a minimum of plan changing steps to finish the rescheduling process.

Human defined rules are used to choose a change planning algorithm, based on certain feasible system states to assure a fast recovery to a consistent plan without the need for many planning cycles.

Such a system consists of an exponential growth of states, depending on the size of the network, the number of planning horizons and the min/max-restriction of every period. So the definition of control rules, based only on state/action-pairs, will lead to a tremendous number of rules and cannot be generated e.g. by a human planner anymore.

---

[4] ⁴Supply can be split into *netto*(NS) and *gross*(GS) supply depending on the point in the MFERT model where it is consumed by a node (see figure 1)

2.2. Requirements for a production control rule learning system

Wanting to be able to learn those rules in such an enormous state space, several problems arise. At first, the learning system must be able to search the state space efficiently and reduce its runtime to an acceptable time period. Secondly, the learning task itself must be based on an intuitive learning function, since the usage as a decision support system, the acceptance of the learned rules will rely on their intuitive understanding by human planners. At last, the training process of such learning system learning on a distributed and interrelated network planning model must be well defined to prevent the extension of runtime duration through never-ending planning processes.

Therefore, Q-Learning is a suitable solution for learning rules, because the reward function, which fulfills the learning task, can be specified in a problem oriented and intuitive way. For convergence, Q-Learning must search an unlimited amount of time through the state space (Mitchell, 1997). Therefore the state space must be reduced, in order to make Q-Learning efficient while assuring convergence of the Q-values.

Clustering, especially k-means clustering function has been identified in former and is described in a published paper, using a problem-oriented clustering (Doering, 2007 p. 487-497).

The training process must combine both, clustering and Q-learning, to an efficient learning system. The training process should deal with learning episodes based on a change planning negotiation process and restricted by clear stopping rules. This requirement prevents the unlimited duration of a learning episode and the learning task itself. The whole training process will coordinate the learning episodes and stops the training, when successful.

moreover, the quality of the original data, used in the learning process is of a high importance. Only real data, e.g. extracted from ERP-Systems, or realistic generated data must be used to ensure a problem oriented learning task.

In general the learning task could be described as:

> *Learning of production system control rules will be enabled by a problem oriented and intuitive mathematical assessment of change planning actions (reward). The rules will be represented by sorted list of Q-values where every Q-value represents a proposal for a suitable change planning action based in a specific state. The training process must rely on problem-specific real or realistic original data to make the learning process must efficient.*

In sum, the core question for a learning task is illustrated in Figure 2. Can an event be handled locally e.g by reducing safety stock (1), or should the gross demand of supplier 1 (2) or supplier 2 (3) be reduced to handle this event. Every learned rule will propose a solution for such a question.

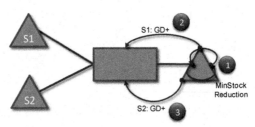

Figure 2. Draft of the learning problem

Therefore, the next chapter will shortly summarize the state of the art in Q-learing of production rules. The clustering part is also covered by (Döring, 2007 p 487-497).

3. STATE OF THE ART

In general, only few applications in Q-Learning deal with learning in distributed network models. Stegherr (Stegherr, 2000) developed a Q-Learning approach, used for control of anticipated job control in production systems. This system is based on learning local decision and therefore not suitable for this learning task.

Stockheim et. al. (Stockheim, 2003) conceptualized a learning approach for supply chain management. The learning task is to plan local lots for production charges and generate from this a secondary demand for the next production stage. The production system model used in this work is not sufficient for this learning task, because of its high granularity.

Cao et. al. focused on learning fabrication fulfillment figures for a 2-stage production system not equivalent to a supply network. Mahadevan et. al. developed a learning concept called SMART learning rules for machine maintenance in factories. This concept could be used in addition to a change planning learning approach, but is actually not sufficient for usage in this work.

4. LEARNING PRODUCTION CHANGE PLANNING CONTROL RULES

For learning control rules using Q-Learning support by *k-means* clustering the architecture proposed in Figure 3 is used.

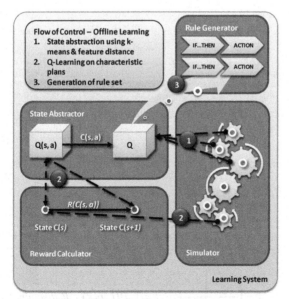

Figure 3. Learning System Architecture

The architecture consists of four modules. The *State Abstractor* module implements the clustering methods used to reduce the state space efficiently (Döring, 2007 p. 487-497). The Q-values are assigned to admit state/action pairs on cluster level, while each cluster is represented by a characteristic state. This state, called Centroid, represents the characteristic course of all assigned single states.

The R*eward Calculator* module assesses the state/action-pairs during the training process and calculates the Q-values. Each observed state will be mapped to its cluster, the Centroid is taken as origin data for the event handling change planning process. Then the resulting state is again mapped to its cluster and the reward between *C(s,a)* and *C(s+1)* will be calculated and the Q-value of *C(s)* will be updated.

The *Simulator* module provides the learning system with original data based on real data or realistically generated data. Furthermore, this module controls the training process and its learning episodes.

The *Rule Generator* Module generates, based on a specific algorithm, the rules from the preordered Q-values of each clusters stat/action pair.

4.1 Concept of the reward calculation function

To calculate the reward in an intuitive way, factors used for the decision taking by production planner should be considered. Based on the general approach of assessments in economics, a cost function will be used as a basis for the reward calculation.

Main costs factors in production networks are that are regarded for assessment of plans are (Gudehus, 2004):

- *Preparation costs:* In AON materials must be provided for transformation in the production process. This could be assessed by this preparation costs eg. including fix costs (stock etc.) and variable costs (e.g. employees).

- *Procurement costs:* If material is not available from stock, it will be procured from suppliers respectively every procurement process causes costs. These costs are based on specific agreement between a supplier and a customer based e.g. on the value and regularity of parts that are procured.

- *Resource costs:* To transform material resources, e.g. machine capacity, is needed. The performed work can be assessed by costs.

- *Restriction violations:* Every plan restriction violation, namely an event, causes overhead for its handling e.g. through the demand of troubleshooters, who deal with those topics in their daily works. This overhead can be represented by costs.

A plan will be assessed based on its periods and their values and restrictions. To get a normalized reward value the assignment of plan periods costs are normalized and limited to the interval *[0..1]*, while *0* represents no costs and *1* maximal costs caused by restriction violations in one period.

Based in the assumption, that events occurring in nearer future have more impact than events occurring later the costs will be reduced to the end of the planning horizon by a discount factor *DF(p(k))*:

$$DF(p(k)) = \left(\frac{1}{1+discount}\right)^k, k = 1..PH, p(k) \in P, discount \in 0..1$$

The sum of the costs of all periods in a plan is equal to the costs caused by this plan, called penalty costs *PC(P)* in state *s*.

$$PC(P_s) = \sum_{k=1}^{PH} DF * PC(p(k))$$

Based in this the reward can be generally defined as the difference between the penalty costs in state *s* and state *s+1* after a processed change planning.

$$R(P_s, a_i) = PC(P_s, a_i) - PC(P_{s+1})$$

The main task is to calculate the detailed penalty costs of each period as the basis for the reward calculation. Despite the differences between global and local change planning Figure 4 shows the general concepts that is used.

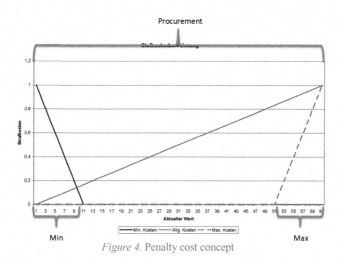

Figure 4. Penalty cost concept

A period is restricted by a minimal and maximal restrictions while values above or below this restriction cause a restriction violation and an event. Therefore this could be assessed by a specific cost function. Also general costs for procurement occur in each period raising to the value of material procured. This could also be assessed by a cost function. The full penalty costs can then be calculated from the sum of the specific cost type in each period. To get comparable costs those cost types are normalized to an interval between *[0..1]*.

5. SUMMARY

This paper discussed the requirements for a rule learning system to control change planning processes in production networks. Learning system architecture has been introduced, based on k-means clustering and Q-Learning.

The general approach for calculation of rewards based on cost functions and the storage of the Q-values have been drafted out.

Further work will specify the detailed cost functions for local and global change planning processes and detail the training process. An implementation of the system will be carried out to validate the learning architecture and the effects of clustering to its convergence.

6. REFERENCES

1. AC-DC Automotive Chassis Development for 5Day-Cars. European Integrated Research Project Sixth Framework Program. Contract No. 031520. http://www.acdc-project.org
2. Baumgaertel H.; Hellingrath B.; Holweg M., Bischoff J. Automotive SCM in einem vollständigen Build-to-Order-System. Supply Chain Management. 2006; 1: 7-15.
3. Cao H, Smith SF. "A Reinforcement Learning Approach to Production Planning in the Fabrication/Fulfillment Manufacturing Process". In Proceedings of the Winter Simulation Conference, Chick s, Sanchez PJ, Ferrin D, Morrice DJ. 2003.
4. Diedrichsen K, Nickerl, RJ. Interview: Intelligenter als das reine Event. Logistik Heute. 2007; December. 16-18.
5. Doering A, Dangelmaier W, Danne C. "Using k-means for clustering in complex automotive production systems to support a Q-learning-system". ICCI In Proceedings of the 6th IEEE International Conference on Cognitive Informatics Zhang D, Wang Y, Kinsner W (ed.). 2007; 487-497.
6. Doering A, Dangelmaier, W, Laroque C, Timm T. "Simulation-aided process coverage for delivery schedules under short delivery schedules using real-time event based feedback loops". In Proceedings of the 6th EUROSIM Congress on Modelling and Simulation. 2007; Vol 1.
7. Fraunhofer Gesellschaft, Mercer Management Consultants. Future Automotive Industry (FAST) 2015. Mercer Management Consultants. 2004.
8. Goerz G, Rollinger C, Schneeberger J (ed.). Handbuch der künstlichen Intelligenz. Oldenbourg Wissenschaftsverlag. 2003.
9. Gudehus T. Logistik. Springer Berlin Heidelberg. 2004.
10. Heidenreich J. Adaptive Mengen- und Kapazitätsplanung in kollaborativen Produktionsnetzwerken der Serienfertigung. Dissertation. University of Paderborn. 2006.
11. Mahadevan S, Marchalleck N, Das TK, Gosavo A. Self-improving Factory Simulation using Continuous-time Average-Reward Reinforcement Learning. Techreport IRI-9501852. Department of Computer Science and Engineering University Of Floriada. 1997.
12. Mitchell TM. Machine Learning. McGraw-Hill Bool Co. 1997.
13. Schneider U. Ein formales Modell und eine Klassifikation für die Fertigungssteuerung. Dissertation. Universität GH-Paderborn. 1996.
14. Stegherr T. Reinforcement-Learning zur dispositiven Auftragssteuerung in der Variantenreihenproduktion. Herbert Utz Verlag. 2000.
15. Stockheim T, Schnwind M, Koenig W. "A reinforcement learning approach fior supply chain management". In 1st European Workshop on Multi-Agent Systems. 2003.
16. Suhl, L. Mellouli T. Optimierungssysteme. Modelle, Verfahren, Software, Anwendungen. Springer. 2006.
17. Sutton RS, Barto AG. Reinforcement Learning: An Introduction. Bradford Book – MIT Press. 1998.

17

ONTOLOGY DEVELOPMENT IN HOME AUTOMATION USED IN AUTOMATIC VE FORMATION

Orlando Ribas Fernandes, Ana Paula Rocha, Eugénio Oliveira
LIACC – NIAD&R, Faculty of Engineering, University of Porto
R. Dr. Roberto Frias, 4200-465 Porto, Portugal
orlando.ribas@gmail.com, arocha@fe.up.pt, eco@fe.up.pt

Ontologies are crucial in B2B electronic commerce in general and in the Virtual Enterprise scenario in particular, enabling the mutual understanding between multiple business participants. This paper considers the development of a specific ontology in the home automation business area, illustrated in the Virtual Enterprise formation process. The ontology developed for the home automation (domotics) domain enumerates different products, its attributes, mutual relations and implicit business rules. A case study is presented based on a real scenario where business participants are represented by multiple agents in the electronic market.

1. INTRODUCTION

The main goal of the research project behind this paper was the development of a specific ontology in the home automation business area, illustrated in the Virtual Enterprise formation scenario.

The Virtual Enterprise (VE) is a flexible organizational structure, composed by autonomous and individual enterprises committed between them in temporary associations in order to answer new market requirements (Fischer et al., 1996) (Norman et al., 2004). Since these individual enterprises are heterogeneous and probably unknown to each other, the regularization of its joint activity is a crucial issue. This task can be effectively done by the so called Electronic Institution (EI), by imposing norms and rules on the cooperative behaviour of their participants.

In our approach, the EI is modelled through an open Multi-Agent System (MAS), where agents represent both enterprises and customers of the electronic market (Cardoso et al. 2005). Like the institutions that regulate the way citizens interact in human societies, the EI concept represents the virtual counterpart of real-world institutions (Arcos et al., 2005) (Cardoso et al. 2005). Besides that normative framework, the EI also provides a set of institutional services that helps in the effective coordination between agents which represent different entities of the real-world, and interact for the establishment of business relationships. These institutional services include: i) appropriate negotiation algorithms enabling the selection of the most suitable VE partners according to current needs (Rocha et al. 2005); ii) the establishment and monitoring of electronic contracts (Cardoso et al. 2005), and iii) ontology services that ensure the interoperability between heterogeneous agents with their own languages and ontologies (Malucelli and Oliveira, 2005). Although the EI also includes ontology services ,these will not be used in the present work, since it

Please use the following format when citing this chapter:

Fernandes, O.R., Rocha, A.P. and Oliveira, E., 2008, in IFIP International Federation for Information Processing, Volume 266, *Innovation in Manufacturing Networks;* ed. A. Azevedo; (Boston: Springer), pp. 161–168.

is not the goal's work. In this paper, we will therefore assume that agents have similar ontologies.

We intend to use our Electronic Institution framework with a specific ontology developed in the home automation area, to illustrate the VE formation stage. The developed ontology includes the enumeration of different products of the home automation domain, its attributes, relations and the implicit business rules.

The rest of the paper will unfold as follows. In section 2 we discuss the ontology concept empathizing on the ontology development process. In section 3, we present the Virtual Enterprise concept. Next, section 4 describes an ontology implementation in the home automation domain, and presents a case study where this ontology is used in our framework to illustrate the Virtual Enterprise formation process. Finally, section 5 presents our conclusions.

2. ONTOLOGIES

Ontology is a popular topic in the Artificial Intelligence domain with relevance in areas like: Knowledge Engineering, Natural Language and Multi-Agent Systems. But ontologies aren't limit to the Artificial Intelligence domain, being also applied, for example, in the community World Wide Web (WWW).

In the area of the computer science many and arguable definitions exist for the word "ontology". The more widely accepted in the context of Artificial Intelligence is the one of (Gruber, 1993) that defines ontology as an explicit specification of a conceptualisation. "Conceptualisation" is basically the idea of the world that a person or a group of people may have; "explicit" means that the type of concepts and restrictions about their use are explicitly defined.

Another very accepted definition in the scientific community is the one of (Uschold and Jasper, 1999) which states that, although ontologies may have several forms, always includes a specific vocabulary and some specifications as far as their meaning is concerned. Ontologies include definitions and relations of how the concepts are interrelated, which imposes a collective domain structure and restricts the possible interpretations of the existing terms.

Several studies and methodologies exist regarding the ontology development task. According to these studies, the ontology development can be decomposed in four steps (Denny, 2002):

— Domain knowledge acquisition: Sources of knowledge and expertise are collected in a structured way in order to formally describe the domain knowledge.
— Ontology organization: Identification of the main concepts related to the domain, its properties. Relations between concepts are also identified.
— Ontology instantiation: Individual instances are added following the concepts and relations already named.
— Verification: Ontology syntax and semantic is verified (sometimes in an automatic way) in order to detect and correct inconsistencies.

The ontology developed and reported in this work follows the issues just mentioned.

3. VIRTUAL ENTERPRISE

Ontologies are crucial in B2B electronic commerce in general, and in Virtual Enterprise in particular, enabling the mutual understanding between multiple business participants. A Virtual Enterprise (VE), according to Fischer (Fischer et al., 1996), is defined as a voluntary cooperation of some autonomous and heterogeneous enterprises that are, possibly, geographically distributed. All enterprises that are members of the cooperation provide its resources, abilities, capacities and knowledge, for the attainment of a service or product with base in a common agreement. The VE is also an agile structure, and so has the ability to dynamically reconfiguration in reaction to environment changes.

This new concept of enterprise entity enables the reduction of individual enterprises' processes for main abilities that try to get with the maximum quality and profit. Thus, individual enterprises can become a niche of ability in a specific area of its domain. The formation of corporations allows the share of such abilities, costs, resources (of capital, intellect and technological), and still the reduction of the complexity of the problem.

The VE life cycle comprises four phases (Fischer et al. 1996):
- Identification of needs: Appropriate description of the product or service to be delivered by the VE, which guides the conceptual design of the VE;
- Formation (partners selection): Automatic selection of the individual enterprises (partners), which, based in its specific knowledge, skills, resources, costs, and availability, will integrate the VE;
- Operation: Control and monitoring partners' activities, including resolution of potential conflicts, and possible VE reconfiguration due to partial failures;
- Dissolution: Breaking up the VE, distributing the obtained profits, and storing relevant information for future use.

Although not being the focus of this paper, it should be said that our framework includes a specific negotiation protocol to select the participants that, based on its capabilities and availability, will be able to make the optimal deal according to its own goals (the second phase of the VE life cycle). This is an iterative multi-attribute negotiation between potential VE partners and the VE organizer that includes a reinforcement learning capability in the formulation of participants' counter-proposals (Rocha et al, 2005).

In this paper, we will illustrate, based in a real business scenario, how the VE formation can be accomplished using our own framework.

4. CASE STUDY IN HOME AUTOMATION

In our scenario, Enterprises and Customer Agents meet in a market place where they cooperate to form a Virtual Enterprise with the objective of supply/get goods according to their own goals and preferences. These goods under negotiation are described by each agent using their private ontologies. As mentioned before, in this work the agents use the same ontology. The current version of our EI platform does not include the ontology services, although this module is currently being integrated in it.

The ontology developed in the current work is related with the home automation area. For its development, we selected the Protégé tool (Protégé 3.2, 2007) as the ontology editor. This choice is justified by the high usability of Protégé that offers an excellent development environment, with multiple third parties plug-ins that allows the use of several services for varied ends.

The language chosen for the ontology representation was Ontology Web Language (OWL). The OWL is a marking language for definition, publication and allotment of ontologies in the Internet , and is recommended by the W3C[1] since 2004. Being OWL based on XML, gets all the advantages of this language, stands out the fact that the information can also be changed between different types of systems (operative systems and languages of applications).

4.1. Home Automation Ontology

The first step on the ontology development process is the "Domain Knowledge Acquisition". The data supplied by the domain experts is analysed and discussed with them which allows knowing in depth the domain of interest. In this work, the data was supplied by a home automation company, "Central Casa".

The second step on the ontology development process is the "Ontology Organization". The data collected in previous step is organized into concepts (classes) that specify the products commercialized by the home automation company.

Figure 1 illustrates the structuralized organization of the created concepts (classes), using the Protégé tool. It is understood that the Products class would be the superclass of the existing products in the data received from the company. These products concern cameras, remote controls, micromodules, X10 modules and security equipment. Packs class will contain a set of other products.

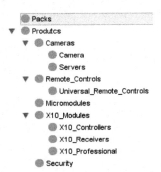

Figure 1. Ontology classes

In an ontology, properties or attributes can be of two types: Object properties or Datatype properties. Object properties connect one instance to another, and Datatype properties assign a value to an instance. In this ontology, we consider both Object and Datatype properties that are the following: *Applications, Characteristics, Description, Informations, Price, Quantity, Ref* and *belongPack..*

The properties *Applications, Characteristics, Description, Informations* and *Ref* are Datatype properties. The necessity to include these properties was found during the data analysis process. Products commercialized by the company had several textual information related to different issues, which are now enumerated in these properties.

The properties *Price* and *Quantity* are also Datatype properties. This information did not exist in the data received originally, but it was added as a necessity to the electronic negotiation that will go to elapse in the process of the VE formation.

The property *belongPack* is an Object property. It is used to indicate that an instance belong to a specific pack (*Packs* is a concept of this ontology).

---

[1] The recommendations of W3C are understood by the industry and the scientific community as standards Web

The next step in the ontology development process is the "Ontology Instantiation", where concepts considered in the ontology are now instantiated. As an example of it, Figure 2 illustrates the instantiation of the concept "Packs".

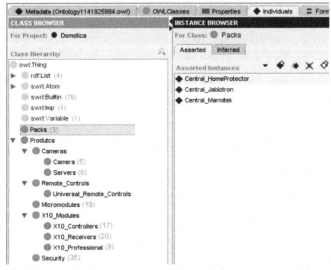

Figure 2. "Packs" instantiation

In this step, properties and relations are also filled in. Figure 3 illustrates the property *belongPack* in a particular case where two instances (*Motion_detector* and *Smoke_detector*) are considered elements of the pack *Central_Homeprotector*.

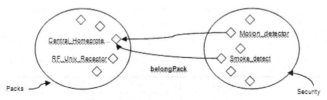

Figure 3. Relations between instances

The final step in the ontology development process, "Verification", was done in conjunction with the domain experts through a manual analysis of the developed ontology. Finally, the ontology was saved in OWL format, in order to be used by our EI framework.

4.2. Case Study Discussion

The following stage of the project consisted on the addition of a new module to the Electronic Institution platform, which allows the creation, edition and storage of proper ontologies on the intervening agents, so that they can be used on future interactions.

In the current platform, each agent in the EI has its own window. In this window it is possible to configure the agent abilities (if it is an enterprise agent that sells goods) or needs (if is a client agent that wants to buy goods), as well as to visualize its activity in the market.

The problem of VE formation is, essentially, a problem of competitive negotiation, where the different enterprise agents compete among themselves for the selection (by the client agent) as members of the VE. The negotiating strategy of each enterprise agent is the adoption of the action plan that leads the agent to his objective, which usually translates into maximizing its utility function. Enterprises and client agents will engage in a round of proposal and counterproposals. In each round, enterprises agents try to improve their proposals in order to beat concurrent enterprises and be selected by the client agent. The trading ends when the client agent receives an adequate proposal (a proposal that has a utility value higher than a pre-defined threshold), or when a time limit is reached.

The negotiation process that leads to the VE formation is done through the negotiation of the values of some properties of the instances in discussion. The values of these properties (the ones that are negotiable) can have two ranges: the domain values and the preferable values. The domain values are the ones that the agent accepts during the negotiation. The preferable values are the one the agent will prefer among others in discussion (the preference values are a subset of the domain values)

In the scenario presented, the client wants to equip its house with a safety system for detecting intruders and detecting fire. The correct solution to this particular client is the product *Central_Marmitek* pack as defined in the ontology. This product is composed by other five products: *Remote_Control-MaxiControl, Alarm-HomeGuard, Smoke_detector-MaxiControl, Pocket_Control-MaxiControl* and *Sirene_PowerHorn-MaxiControl*.

In this scenario the client agent (named *Central_Casa*) is interested in five products. The process of selecting partners for the VE includes, therefore, five parallel negotiations, one for each product. In each of these negotiations are involved different enterprise agents (Ent_Form_1 to Ent_Form_10) with responsibility for the provision of the respective component. Each enterprise agent assigns different domain values to the negotiable properties

We consider as negotiable properties the *Quantity* and *Price* properties. The domain and preferable values that the *Central_Casa* agent assigns to the negotiable properties are enumerated in Table1. In this case, is specified a large range for the attribute *Quantity*, in order to better analyze the behavior of each agent in the negotiation process.

Table 1. Preferred Values – Cental_Casa Agent

Components	Atributes	Preferred
Remote_Control-MaxiControl	Quantity	1-3000
	Price	1-35
Alarm-HomeGuard	Quantity	1-3000
	Price	1-70
Smoke_detector-MaxiControl	Quantity	1-3000
	Price	1-60
Pocket_Control-MaxiControl	Quantity	1-3000
	Price	1-50
PowerHorn - MaxiControl	Quantity	1-3000
	Price	1-75

After the negotiation, limited in this scenario to 5 rounds, the client agent *Central_Casa* selected the VE partners Ent_Form_2, Ent_Form_1, Ent_Form_1, Ent_Form_9 and Ent_Form_3 to supply the products *Comando Remoto, Alarme HomeGuard, Sensor de Fumo – MaxiControl, Comando de Bolso – MaxiControl, Sirene PowerHorn – MaxiControl* respectively. These partners were selected because they presented the best proposals concerning the negotiable properties *Quantity* and *Price* when the negotiation ended. Figure 4 shows the utility value obtained by the client agent with the proposals of each one of the selected partners.

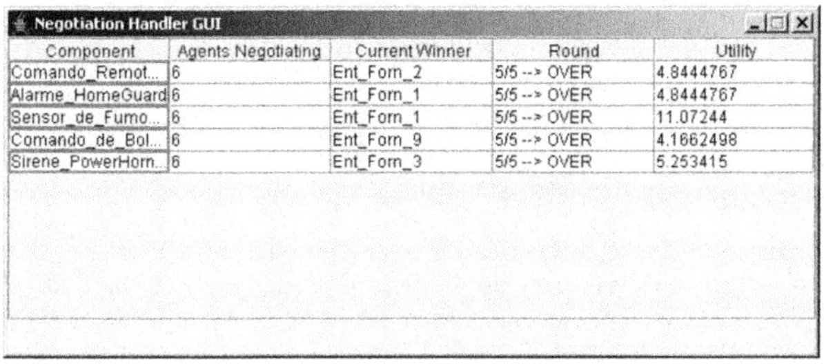

Component	Agents Negotiating	Current Winner	Round	Utility
Comando_Remot...	6	Ent_Form_2	5/5 --> OVER	4.8444767
Alarme_HomeGuard	6	Ent_Form_1	5/5 --> OVER	4.8444767
Sensor_de_Fumo	6	Ent_Form_1	5/5 --> OVER	11.07244
Comando_de_Bol...	6	Ent_Form_9	5/5 --> OVER	4.1662498
Sirene_PowerHorn	6	Ent_Form_3	5/5 --> OVER	5.253415

Figure 4. Agents that are in VE

5. CONCLUSIONS

Due to the necessity to get competitive advantage in the electronic market, it becomes crucial to make better and different than competitors, and mainly to have the capacity to create the single value for customers. It was considered, as a main goal of this work, the presentation of a realistic case in the home automation area, related to the Virtual Enterprise formation process. Thus, and with the support of the CentralCasa home automation company, ontology was developed in the business area of the home automation. We used the Protégé tool in the ontologies edition and modulation. The VE formation is one of the main phases of the VE life cycle, and an adaptive multi-attribute negotiation protocol (presented in (Rocha et al., 2005)) was used in the scenario presented here.

The already existing Electronic Institution platform was updated with the capacity to read and recognize ontologies developed using the Protégé tool. These ontologies are written in OWL.

This work can be improved in the future by including new functionalities in the current EI platform, namely the use of commitments and social intentions as well as trust and reputation mechanisms. These two topics are of great interest in B2B e-commerce in general, and VE scenario in particular, and are currently under development. Other future topics of research include:

- The development of more specific ontologies in the home automation area, and the inclusion of real Central Casa suppliers;
- The development of ontology services capable to support the formation and monitoring of the VE in an electronic market. Such services include generic processes for the creation of specific ontologies and services of translation for pre-existing ontologies.

5.1. Acknowledgments

We thank CentralCasa home automation company for providing the data used in our scenario.

4. REFERENCES

1. Cardoso HL, Malucelli A, Rocha AP, Oliveira E. "Institutional Services for Dynamic Virtual Organizations". In Collaborative Networks and Their Breeding Environments – 6th IFIP Working Conference on Virtual Enterprises, L.M. Camarinha-Matos, H. Afsarmanesh, A. Ortiz (eds.): Springer, Valencia, Spain, 2005: 521-528.
2. Denny, Michael. "Ontology Building: A Survey of Editing Tools", Technical report, O'Reilly XML.com, 2002.
3. Fischer K, Muller JP, Heimig I, Scheer A. "Intelligent Agents in Virtual Enterprises". In 1st International Conference on the Pratical Application of Intelligent Agents and Multi-Agent Technology, London, UK, 1996.
4. Gruber, Thomas R.. "Toward Principles for Design of Ontologies Used for Knowledge Sharing". In N. Guarino, R. Poli (eds.), Formal Ontology in Conceptual Analysis and Knowledge Representation, Kluwer Academic Publishers, 1993.
5. Malucelli A., Oliveira E. "Using Similarity Measures for an Efficient Business Information-Exchange". In IEEE/WIC/ACM International Conference on Intelligent Agent Technology (IAT 2005), Compiègne, France, 2005.
6. Malucelli, A., Oliveira, E. "Ontology-Services Agent to Help in the Structural and Semantic Heterogeneity". In Virtual Enterprises and Collaborative Networks, L. M. Camarinha-Matos (ed.), Kluwer Academic Publishers, 2006: 175-182.
7. Norman TJ, Preece A, Chalmers S, Jennings NR, Luck M, Dang D, Nguyen TD, Deora V, Shao J, Gray A. Fiddian N. "Agent-based formation of virtual organisations". In Int. J. Knowledge Based Systems 17, 2004: 103-111.
8. Uschold M, Jasper RA. "Framework for Understanding and Classifying Ontology Applications". In VR Benjamins (ed.), IJCAI'99 Workshop on Ontology and Problem Solving Methods: Lessons Learned and Future Trends (KRR5), Stockholm, Sweden, 1999.
9. Arcos JL Marc Esteva, Noriega P, Rodriguez-Aguilar JA, Sierra C. "Engineering open environments with electronic institutions". In Engineering Applications of Artificial Intelligence, 2005: 18:191–204.
10. Protégé 3.2. The Protégé Ontology Editor and Knowledge Acquisition System, Stanford Center for Biomedical Informatics Research, Stanford University School of Medicine, 2007.
11. Rocha AP, Cardoso HL, Oliveira E. "Contributions to an Electronic Institution supporting Virtual Enterprises' life cycle". In Virtual Enterprise Integration: Technological and Organizational Perspectives, G. D. Putnik & M. M. Cunha (eds.), Idea Group Inc., 2005: 19:229-246.

18

TOWARDS AN ONTOLOGY MAPPING PROCESS FOR BUSINESS PROCESS COMPOSITION

Célia Talma Martins[1,2], Américo Azevedo[3,4], H. Sofia Pinto[5], Eugénio Oliveira[1,3]

[1]*LIACC-NIAD&R, Faculty of Engineering, University of Porto*
R. Dr. Roberto Frias, 4200-465 Porto, Portugal
[2]*ISCAP, Rua Jaime Lopes Amorim, s/n, 4465-004 S. Mamede de Infesta*
[3]*Faculty of Engineering, University of Porto*
[4]*INESC Porto, Portugal*
[5]*INESC-ID/IST, Rua ALves Redol, 9, 1000-029 Lisboa*
talma@fe.up.pt; ala@fe.up.pt; sofia@inesc-id.pt; eco@fe.up.pt

Business Processes Composition in dynamic and semantic heterogeneous environments as Electronic Institution or Virtual Breeding Environment it's an actual research topic.
We propose a solution based on ontology mapping to solve the semantic heterogeneity problem that the composition of business processes raises in these environments.

1. INTRODUCTION

Business Processes Composition in dynamic and semantic heterogeneous environments as Electronic Institutions or Virtual Breeding Environments it is an actual research topic. The Semantic Heterogeneity Problem occurs in business processes composition in such semantic heterogeneous environments as it is the case of the Electronic Institution (EI) or a Virtual Organizations Breeding Environment (VBE), which is a community of enterprises that maintain a set of social relations, based on trust, having some common strategic goals. A further level of cooperation and collaboration happens when enterprises belonging to this VBE, take advantage of this situation to catch up business opportunities by engaging temporarily in a so called Virtual Enterprise (VE). The design of Inter-Organizational Business Processes (IOBP) in a VBE it is the main concern of our research. As enterprises have different ontologies and languages to define their own business processes this raises the semantic heterogeneity problem.

In order to solve this problem, we will apply an ontology mapping service included in a multi-agent system platform facilitating B2B interoperability during a VE lifecycle (Malucelli, 2006).

Section 2 presents an overview of business processes in Breeding Environments, section 3 presents the semantic heterogeneity problem and section 4 presents our solution to the problem and the state-of-the-art in the field. Finally section 5 presents some conclusion and further research work.

Please use the following format when citing this chapter:

Martins, C.T., Azevedo, A., Pinto, H.S. and Oliveira, E., 2008, in IFIP International Federation for Information Processing, Volume 266, *Innovation in Manufacturing Networks;* ed. A. Azevedo; (Boston: Springer), pp. 169–176.

2. BUSINESS PROCESSES in BREEDING ENVIRONMENT

2.1. Business Processes overview

Nowadays enterprises achieve their goals through their business processes, e.g. they are process-oriented. Processes are the very heart of every organization because they are the means through which companies create value for their customers. A process-based organization always starts with the identification of the key processes of the company (Vanhaberbke and Torremans, 1999).There are several definitions of business processes such as: "is a structured, measured set of activities designed to produce a specific output for a particular customer of market"(Davenport, 1993) or "...a business process as a collection of activities that takes one or more kinds of input and creates an output that is of value to the customer" (Hammer and Champy, 1993).

We see a business process as a collection of sub-processes (activities) that have one or more inputs, objectives, and one or more outputs.

Process-oriented enterprises have their key business processes identified so they can announce them in the VBE in order to participate in a future VE formation/creation.

These days enterprises are starting to cooperate with other in VE. The lifecycle of these VE has four phases: creation, operation, evolution and dissolution.

2.2. Business Processes Composition

We think that business process composition is very similar to semantic web services composition. Like web services, business processes have an input, and output and a transformation function. However business processes are more complex, because they also have objectives, a process name, clients, costumers, actors and the process flow itself. Nevertheless, in it's most basic form, a business process has one or more inputs, objectives and one or more outputs.

Although there are many web services repositories available on the web, sometimes just one web service is not enough to do a functionality required by a user or a software agent. So there should be a way to combine existing services together in order to fulfill the request. This trend has triggered a considerable number of research efforts on web services composition both in academia and industry. Similarly the same happens with business processes: sometimes one business process alone cannot fulfill a business opportunity by itself, so we need to combine in some way existing business processes of the VBE in order to fulfill a client's business opportunity request, thus forming a new VE for that particular business opportunity. There is the need to define a methodology to chain the different business processes of the different enterprises into an inter-organizational business process that satisfies a particular Business Opportunity. This is our main research issue: how to achieve the right sequence of the different enterprise's business processes in order to fulfill that particular Business Opportunity.

Based on the definition of the generic IOBP we will make the selection of business processes that satisfy that particular business opportunity. For this selection we will search in the VBE enterprises for the business processes and sub-business processes that are previously defined in the generic IOBP. In the end we will get a final VE as we can see in Figure 1, which responds to our business opportunity and a composition of business processes that will form the IOBP that responds to the business opportunity. The search for business processes can involve a basic negotiation if more than one process is found that satisfies the process we are looking for. In this case, we will select the one that has the lowest price.

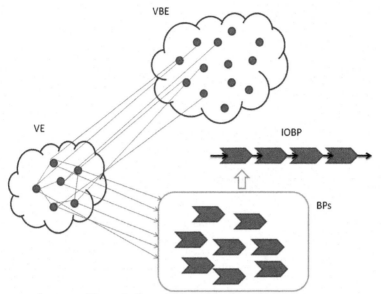

Figure 1. Composition of Business Processes

If the enterprises that belong to the VBE agree on a common ontology there are no misunderstanding problems while searching of similar business processes. However, the enterprises that belong to the VBE usually use different ontologies to represent their own business processes, so the semantic heterogeneity problem will occur.

3. SEMANTIC HETEROGENEITY PROBLEM

3.1. Ontology Mapping

Ontologies were developed in order to facilitate knowledge sharing and reuse. An ontology is an explicit formal specification of the concepts in the domain and the relations among them (Gruber, 1993). An ontology defines a common vocabulary for researchers who need to share information in a domain.

Ontology mapping is the process of finding correspondences between concepts represented in different ontologies. If two concepts correspond they should mean the same or closely related things (Dout et al, 2003). Ontology mapping uses similarity measures to see if two terms representing a concept, are either equal or mean exactly the same or have a strong similarity or are not similar at all. The same applies to both relations and properties as well as to all the entities included in the ontologies. Mapping is important once different enterprise software agents using different ontologies have to exchange and possibly combine their own business processes. There is thus a need for comparing if two business processes are equal, mean exactly the same, have a strong similarity or are not similar at all.

A business process has a name, inputs and outputs, and the name, inputs and outputs are composed of concepts that need to be compared. We have some problems that may occur:

- two business processes may have the same name but different inputs and outputs and so have completely different meanings
- two business processes may have the same name, equal inputs and outputs and so are exactly the same business process
- two business processes may have different names but have equal inputs and outputs and so are exactly the same business process
- two business processes may have different names, inputs and outputs and so have no similarity

So Ontology Mapping is a possible solution to resolve the semantic heterogeneity problem.

3.2. Ontology and Business Process Management – state-of-the-art

A method for agents to develop local consensus ontologies is proposed in (Williams et al., 2003) to aid in the communication in a business-to-business multi-agent system. They also compare variations of syntactic and semantic similarity matching to form local consensus ontologies with and without the use of a lexical database. This approach allows to find syntactic and semantic similarity by comparing two ontologies at a time with each other without the use of a global common ontology. It then merges these ontologies into a local, consensus ontology. If one agent determines that another agent's concept is similar, or equivalent, to its own concept either syntactically or semantically, it can add this concept and its associated relations to its local consensus ontology.

An approach for (semi)-automatic detection of synonyms and homonyms of process element names is presented in (Ehrig et al., 2007) in order to support semantic process model interconnectivity and interoperability by measuring the similarity between business process models semantically modelled with the Web Ontology Language (OWL). The authors further show in this paper, that by using the three similarity measures, syntactic, linguistic and structural, they can compute similarity degrees between a pair of process element names and between a pair of process models. The syntactic similarity degree is computed by comparing the number of common characters in the element names (e.g., confirmation vs verification). In order to measure similarity between two strings, the (Levenshtein) edit distance method is used. The linguistic similarity degree relies on a dictionary to determine synonyms. In this case, WordNet was used. However syntactic and linguistic similarity measures by themselves do not exploit the context of the names. That is done with structural similarity measures, which helps to detect primarily homonyms.

In (Malucelli et al., 2005) it is combined the use of ontologies and agent technologies to help in solving the semantic heterogeneity problem in e-commerce negotiations. Thereby, the focus is on ontologies, whose specifications include a concept (item/product), its characteristics (attributes) with the correspondent data types, a natural language description explaining the meaning of the concept, and a set of relationships between these concepts. This approach aims at creating a methodology that assesses a lexical and semantic similarity among concepts represented in different ontologies without the need to build a priori a shared ontology. The lexical measures are used to compare attributes and relations between concepts.

The authors in (Mtatskin et al, 2005) describe their own method for Web Services (WS) selection and composition based on Linear Logic. According to the authors the complexity of selecting and composing web services arises from two sources: it is not always easy to define selection criteria for a WS; WS can be developed by different organizations, which provide different offers, so, the ability of efficient integration of possibly heterogeneous services on the web becomes a complex problem. Their approach to WS Composition is based on a logic and marketplace system architecture that supports agent communication, negotiation and semantic reasoning. The authors claim that the use of marketplaces provides a support for composition of services based both on flow models and AI planning. The innovation of the presented work lays on the novelty that networks of marketplaces may allow to specify more flexible WS process and data flows with decentralized control than traditional workflow models. The composition of services is based on a functional specification, without taking into account low level details, such as operational environment or communication protocol.

The author's in (Berardi and Giacomo, 2005) envision an advanced Web Service registry providing support for semantic discovery, i.e., where the WS search is done by considering user specification involving WS capabilities and behaviour. The fundamental idea is to enable organizations to seamlessly compose BPs and dynamically integrate them with the partners' processes, by means of lightweight workflow-like technologies. Therefore, the WS composition framework will form a conceptual basis to define how internal BPs can be dynamically integrated with those of other organizations as value-added WS.

In (Paolucci et al, 2002) The authors claims that the location of web services should be based on the semantic match between a declarative description of the service being sought, and a description of the service being offered. An automatic matching algorithm is proposed for the automatic dynamic discovery, selection and interoperation of web services. DAML-S was adopted as the service description language because it provides a semantical view of web services.

In (Gómez-Peres et al, 2004) it is proposed a framework for design and (semi) automatic composition of semantic web services at a language-independent and knowledge level. This framework is based on a stack of ontologies that (1) describe the different parts of a SWS; and (2) contain a set of axioms that are really design rules to be verified by the ontology instances. Based on these ontologies, design and composition of SWS can be viewed as the correct instantiation of the ontologies themselves.

3.3. Proposed Solution

Our work is inserted in the configuration phase which precedes the operation phase.

We will focus on the definition of the Inter-Organizational Business Processes for a particular Business Opportunity, and for that we must select and choose the right business processes of the enterprises that belong to the breeding environment in order to fulfill that Business Opportunity.

We are assuming that a first iteration of the VE formation process has already been achieved (Macedo, 2001), e.g., we have a first set of enterprises that have been selected based on criteria such as their specific competencies and prices for a particular Business Opportunity (BO).

Following that preliminary stage there is the need to identify all the business requirements which are important for the definition of the generic IOBPs (involving all the selected partners) which will be considered as an input in the problem to be solved. This will be done by the management people, because this a decision support system that helps the management people take a decision, e.g., the main idea is to know if we can articulate the business processes of the different enterprises of the VBE to respond to that

BO. The enterprise management people designs the IOBP that will satisfy a particular business opportunity, and this IOBP is an input of our problem.

The enterprises announce their competencies, skills, resources and public business processes in this dynamic heterogeneous environment. However, it's not probable that they all have the same ontology. So when a business opportunity arises, the management people define a generic inter-organizational business process (IOBP) which is an input of our problem. Based on this IOBP we will select the most appropriate sub-business processes of the IOBP in the VBE that satisfy the IOBP. But, as already mentioned the different business processes of the different enterprises do not have a common ontology, so this raises the so called Semantic Heterogeneity Problem.

We have two degrees of complexity in our problem. First we will assume that all the enterprises have the same ontology to define their public business processes.

Let us present an example:

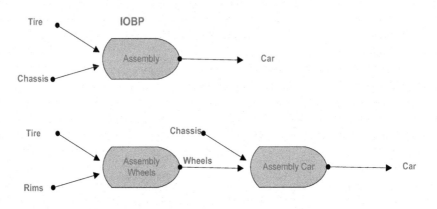

Figure 2. Business Process Composition – same ontology

In Figure 2 we can see that for we respond to the IOBP we have to gather the two upper sub-business processes: Assembly Wheels and Assembly Car, because the two business processes together have the same inputs and outputs than the generic IOBP. We are supposing that Assembly Wheels and Assembly Car are processes from different enterprises. We can respond to the business opportunity because we can gather two business processes from two different enterprises that satisfy the business opportunity. As we already mentioned, this will be done through the development of an algorithm that composes sub-business processes based on some constraints. For example one of this constraint-based rules indicates that I may only compose two business processes if the output of the first is the input of the second.

Now suppose that the enterprises have different ontologies and so implying that their business processes are differently described. The same example above would be described as follows in figure 3:

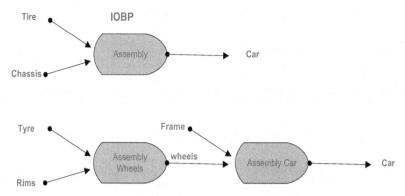

Figure 3. Business Process Composition – different ontologies

How should the system know that Tire means the same that Tyre and that Frame means the same as chassis? This is a more complex problem, which we call semantic heterogeneity problem. How can one ensure that the processes from the different enterprises have the same understanding regarding the issues that are subject to the composition of business processes?

And in order to solve this problem, we think that the use of ontology mapping will help us dealing with this problem. We must have a mapping algorithm between the two ontologies that tell us that Tire means the same as Tyre and that Chassis means the same as Frame.

4. CONCLUSIONS AND FURTHER RESEARCH

We think that the use of ontologies, more precisely ontology mapping, will help us resolving the semantic heterogeneity problem, in order to compose the right business processes that are defined through different ontologies.

To see if two business processes are similar we will use an ontology matching algorithm that is based on a previous work (Malucelli, 2006). This work uses semantic similarity measures to compare if two terms are equals.

We need to develop an algorithm that will lead us to a soundness composition of business processes considering their inputs, outputs and objectives.

Another interesting issue would be to learn from previous compositions.

5. REFERENCES

1. Malucelli A. Ontology – based Services for Agents Interoperability, Phd Thesis, Faculdade de Engenharia, Universidade do Porto, 2006.
2. Vanhaverbeke, W., Torremans, H. Organizational structure in process-based organizations", Knowledge and Process Management 1999; Vol. 6 No.1: 41-52.
3. Davenport, Thomas. Process Innovation: Reengineering work through information technology, Harvard Business School Press, Boston, 1993.
4. Hammer, Michael and Champy, James, Reengineering the Corporation: A Manifesto for Business Revolution, Harper Business, 1993.
5. Gruber, T.R. A Translation Approach to Portable Ontology Specification. Knowledge Acquisition 1993; 5: 199-220.
6. Dou D., Mcdermott D., Qi P., Ontology Translation on the Semantic Web. In Proceedings of International Conference on Ontologies, Databases and Applications of Semantics (ODBASE 2003). LNCS 2888, Springer-Verlag. Berlim Heidelberg, pp. 952-969,2003.
7. Andrew Williams , Anand Padmanabhan , M. Brian Blake, Local consensus ontologies for B2B-oriented service composition, Proceedings of the second international joint conference on Autonomous agents and multiagent systems, July 14-18, 2003, Melbourne, Australia, 2003.
8. Marc Ehrig, Agnes Koschmider, Andreas Oberweis, Measuring Similarity Between Semantic Business Process Models, in Proceedings of the 4th Asia-Pacific Conference on Conceptual Modelling (APCCM 2007), Ballarat, Victoria, Australia, 2007.
9. Andreia Malucelli, Daniel Palzer, Eugénio Oliveira, Combining Ontologies and Agents to help in solving the Heterogeneity Problem in E-Commerce Applications, in International Workshop on Data Engineering Issues in E-Commerce (DEEC 2005), IEEE Computer Society. pp. 26-35. Tokyo, Japan. April 2005.
10. M. Matskin, P. Küngas, J. Rao, J. Sampson, S. A. Petersen. Enabling Web Services Composition with Software Agents. In Proceedings of the Ninth IASTED Int. Conference on Internet and Multimedia Systems and Applications, IMSA 2005, Honolulu, Hawaii, USA, August 15-17, 2005, ACTA Press, pp. 93-98, 2005.
11. Berardi D., Giacomo G., Automatic Composition of Process-based Web Services: a challenge, in Second European Conference on Semantic Web , May 10-14, Chiba – Japan, 2005
12. Paolucci, M., Kawamura, T., Payne, T. R. and Sycara, K. Semantic Matching of Web Services Capabilities. In: International Semantic Web Conference (ISWC), 9 - 12 June, Sardinia, Italy. 2002.
13. Asunción Gómez-Pérez, Rafael González-Cabero, and Manuel Lama. A Framework for Description, Composition, and Evaluation of Semantic Web Services. IEEE Intelligent Systems. Special Issue on Semantic Web Services. 2004
14. Macedo A.P., Metodologias de Negociação em Sistemas Multi-Agentes para Empresas Virtuais. Tese de Doutoramento. Faculdade de Engenharia, Universidade do Porto, 2001.

19

USING CONCEPT MAPS FOR ONTOLOGY DEVELOPMENT: A CASE IN THE WORK ORGANIZATION DOMAIN

António Soares* and Cristóvão Sousa**

Faculty of Engineering of the University of Porto,
Electrical and Computer Engineering Department (FEUP/DEEC) and INESC Porto
e-mail: als@fe.up.pt

** *Institute for Systems and Computer Engineering of Porto (INESC PORTO)*
e-mail: cpsousa@inescporto.pt

Ontologies are a technological key factor regarding the knowledge management domain. This paper presents a graphical-based knowledge representation approach using concept maps towards creating a formal work organization ontology, which was translated into a Content Management System in order to manage the work design information. Some aspects related with the advantages of visual approaches for collaborative development of ontologies are discussed.

1. INTRODUCTION

Organizational performance depends on process efficacy and quality of life at work. A common understanding of how work should be realized based on an effective management of high skills, high trust and high quality is a key factor for business process efficacy, which demands for new forms of work organization. The implementation of new forms of work organization is a complex development process that implies an interaction between work design, individuals and groups.

Technical and organizational innovation processes e.g., business process reengineering and work redesign are normally loosely coupled leading to a sub-optimal socio-technical system. Closer interaction between these design processes is needed which calls for multi-disciplinary development teams sharing knowledge and competencies. Multidisciplinary cooperation is a new challenge and a new category of methodological tools supported by modern knowledge management technologies is needed in order to make feasible such complex development processes. In this context ontologies play a key role by providing a shared conceptual model of a specific domain, that means, it provides the vocabulary which can be used in the work organization domain, which entails the type of objects and concepts that exist and their properties and relations.

The goal of this paper is the characterization of work within and between organizations regarding the organizational concepts, types of relationships and the new trends of work organization through the use of ontologies' engineering. An approach to collaborative work design of individuals and groups, using graphical-based tools will be adopted.

Please use the following format when citing this chapter:

Soares, A. and Sousa, C., 2008, in IFIP International Federation for Information Processing, Volume 266, *Innovation in Manufacturing Networks;* ed. A. Azevedo; (Boston: Springer), pp. 177–186.

This paper is organized as follows. In the next section some visual approaches for graphical representation of ontologies will be briefly presented. Section three focuses an approach to the knowledge representation through the creation of ontologies with conceptual maps. The fourth section presents the work organization ontology developed with concept maps in the CmapTools COE authoring environment. Section five discloses a practical and possible application scenario of the developed ontology. All the steps needed to build a hierarchically set of folders and files into a Content Management System (CMS) according to the ontology exported in OWL, are described. Some directions for further work are addressed in section six.

2. VISUAL APPROACHES FOR ONTOLOGY DEVELOPMENT

Ontological level of knowledge representation is based in conceptualization. Conceptualization comprises a simplified vision of the objects, concepts, and other entities that are assumed to exist in some area of interest and the relations among them (Gruber, 1993). The use of graphical knowledge representation formalisms with a representational vocabulary agreement of terms of conceptualization of the universe of discourse is a new high potential approach in the knowledge management context. Semantic networks, conceptual graphs, rdf, topic maps and concept maps are the graphical knowledge representation formalisms briefly presented, which may also be used for ontology development.

Visually, a semantic network is a set of nodes which represent concepts and instances, connected by arcs which represent relations between nodes. According to (Gordon, 2000), semantic networks are a powerful knowledge representation system because they are easy to understand by humans and can be used in automated processing systems which means that they can also became a vehicle to archive organization knowledge. While visual tools for ontology construction, semantic networks provide the conceptual representation of a domain allowing the explicit representation of concepts, relations and instances. Semantic networks have also mechanisms for formal representation of knowledge. However, the interpretation of a semantic network may cause some confusion. No distinction is made between different types of links and the distinction between concepts and objects is not clear (Baader, 1999). Due its lack of formal semantic characteristic, there are many variances of semantic networks.

Conceptual Graphs (CGs), by its turn, is a formal logic-based knowledge representation developed by John Sowa. CGs are, in fact, a variation of semantic network combined with logic! CGs are a very powerful and versatile tool for knowledge representation. They are human readable and machine process able. Nevertheless it is not possible to draw a CG without having a basic knowledge of logic and CGs itself.

Resource Description Framework (RDF) is a framework for representing information in the web. RDF has the capability to formal express the data meaning allowing interoperability and provides an integration environment between different patterns of metadata[1]. RDF language was created to represent a simple data model based on XML and using vocabulary based on Uniform Resource Locator (URL). The data model is graphically represented through triples which consist in three types of objects that describe relationships between resources regarding properties and values. In terms of ontology representation, RDF allows the explicit representation of resources (concepts), properties and statements. RDF expresses the meaning of data allowing interoperability in the web. It is therefore a knowledge representation formalism which provides the structure

---

[1] htpp://www.w3c.org/TR/rdf-concepts

that is used to represent data models for objects and their relations. However it needs RDF Schema in order to provide mechanisms to declare properties and define relations between properties and resources. RDF Schema is used to describe, semantically, properties, classes of web resources and the type of data for the property values. It extends RDF with new vocabulary allowing the knowledge to be represented through ontologies.

Regarding Topic Maps (TM), they have a great expressive power. In some sense they are a reformulation of semantic networks and conceptual graphs. Additionally they offer a new and standard way of encoding and exchanging knowledge. Technically a TM is formed by three concepts: topic name, association and occurrence. A Topic can be everything - an object, as person, a concept, etc. The association indicates how a topic is related with other topics. Each topic involved in an association, is said to play a rule (Pepper, 2000). For example: from an Organizational point of view, "Work organization defines work practices". In this case there are two topics – WorkOrganization and WorkPractice and there is an association between them, where WorkOrganization plays the rule of the one that defines the WorkSystem. In terms of ontology representation TM can represent facts, procedures, concepts and complex relations between concepts and real world occurrences. It is possible to represent knowledge in a formal way. However, and despite of TM's flexibility, they are very difficult to manage.

Conceptual Maps (Cmaps), are able to represent meaningful relationships between concepts linked by words to from a semantic unit (Canãs, 1999). The concepts are included in circles or boxes while relations between concepts are represented by links connecting the boxes. The links are labelled, describing the relation between two concepts. Propositions result from the phrases composed by the concepts and the link label (concept - verbal phrase - concept). According to (Garcia et al., 2006) Cmaps are very useful in facilitating the visualization and discussion, and in providing domain experts with a tool that could be used to declare the primary elements of their knowledge. Cmaps' simplicity and explicitly make them very useful in several areas namely: Knowledge organization and creation; Collaborative learning; Domain summarization; Browsing tool.

3. USING CONCEPT MAPS FOR ONTOLOGY DEVELOPMENT

Regarding the use of Cmaps for ontology development it was analyzed the ontology development process (shown in figure 1) and ontology development requirements in order to evaluate the suitability of Cmaps as ontology development tool.

Figure 1. Ontology development process

Ontology development is not a static process but an iterative task that crosses several stages such as: Argumentative process; Collaborative process; Iterative process; Evolution and evaluation process. This means that when creating an ontology, domain experts and knowledge engineers argue about terms and relationships (Stevens, 2000). Therefore collaborative interaction of arguments increase the amount of information attached to the concepts or relationships (Stevens, 2000). The arguments derived from discussions can be commentaries, files or even other maps. In general, discussions take place at forums, e-mail messages, chats, etc, and become necessary for knowledge engineer to filter the messages and formalize that knowledge. This task is certainly hard to perform and, for sure, not all information can be retrieved.

By other hand methodologies or tools for ontology building must address Collaboration Support and Argumentative Support according to the ontology development process. According to (Gruber, 2006), domain experts are the central performer on ontology elicitation process, because they have the experience and knowledge about a specific area. Grounding support can be achieved in two ways. Methodologies and tools can use fundamental design patterns of foundational ontologies to provide guidance to domain experts. The second approach is to use a foundational ontology as a base model for the definition of more specific domain (Gruber, 2006). Cognitive support is used to leverage innate human abilities, such as visual information processing, to increase human understanding and cognition of challenging problems (Walenstein, 2002). As argued in (Gruber, 2006), cognitive support for ontology development is required in order to facilitate the useful/exchange of information and at the same time record the entire process. In terms of ontology development, Cmaps allow explicit specification of concepts, relations, constraints, prepositions. Allow explicit representation of consensual knowledge and are very good for conceptualization enhancing cognitive support. Even though Cmaps only allow the representation of informal knowledge, CmapTools Ontology Editor (COE) software provides via Cmaps a complete collaborative and argumentative environment, based on graphical direct manipulation and representation to facilitate the continuous exchange of information among domain experts. COE was developed in order to give CmapTools more interoperability and formalized notations meeting ontological agreements. COE allows the capture of knowledge structures using templates which can be dropped directly onto ontology map. The templates are graphical representations for commonly used OWL structures. With COE, the lack of Cmaps capability for representing formalized knowledge is solved in spite of some interoperability problems still remaining. Combining Cmaps with COE, which provide collaborative and argumentative support and formal knowledge representation based on templates, we have an interesting approach for ontology development. This particularly approach was selected to be followed in the work organization ontology development presented in the next section

4. A WORK ORGANIZATION ONTOLOGY

The work organization ontology was developed in the context of a national project called COllaboration and DEmocratic work design in Virtual Organizations (CODEwork@vo). CODEwork project joined sociologists and engineers in an attempt to find out a work organization model considering both technical and social perspective. A visual approach was needed due the heterogeneity of backgrounds of the experts in domain conceptualization and ontology development. At the same time, mechanisms of communication, discussion and argumentation were desirable which leaded to the selection of CmapTools COE to support the creation of the ontology in the work organization domain.

The ontology development in the work organization domain had several steps; the next figure shows the process that we perform for creating the ontology.

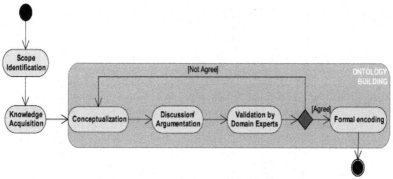

Figure 2. Ontology development methodology

The first phase was the definition of the ontology scope. Knowledge acquisition was the next phase, where all terms about the domain within the scope range were collected. Explicit definitions and descriptions were made and the competency questions were formalized in order to see if our ontology fulfilled the main scope. Later, Cmaps were created freely, without any formal restriction. The created Cmaps represented only a particular view of the problem. The next steps were to put the map on the server for collective discussion and validation. The team argued about the conceptual map trough notes, forum or other maps, files, links…, until it is reached a common understanding. After the cmap had been validated, it was converted in a formal notation. This formal notation was achieved by using COE templates.

4.1. Ontology goal and scope

The main goal of the work organization ontology is to provide a better understand of work organization design process, in order to better refine organization orientation strategies, helping employees with some decision making roles. At the same time provide a common understanding about work, avoiding communication gaps among individuals in an environment where the organizations are increasingly dependent from each other. The ontology scope is focused in the understanding of the main concepts related with the process of work design and organizational design in a human resource management perspective within and between organizations.

4.2. Ontology high level description

Work organization can be defined as a multilevel concept, divided in 3 levels of context: External Context, Organizational Context, and Work Context (Sauter et al., 2002). We cannot do much about external context. The most immediate thing we can do is to predict what will happen next and act according to it. The main management challenge is to organize/optimize all work and resources of an organization in order to endow enterprises the ability to easily adapt to market changes. The figure 3, presented below, shows the conceptualizations of work organization in a concept map. That cmap emphasize the following assumptions:

1. Work Organization can be defined as the result of work design process or organizational design process implementations.

2. Work organization has a direct impact over people and their skills, the processes and the overall work system[2], in view of the fact that it refers to the (re)organization of those concepts.

3. Regarding work design, we can consider two main different scenarios according to the boundaries of work system, thus we can have a work design process based in a vertical division of work, which the components of work are distributed inside organization among one or more hierarchical levels (Sinha, 2005). By the other hand we have the case in which the components of work are distributed across many organizational units of one or many firms and, in these case, we have a work design process based in a scenario of vertical division of work (Knublauch et al., 2004).

4. Organizational design has a set of structural dimensional, structural determinants and design models that drive the implementation process in an organization.

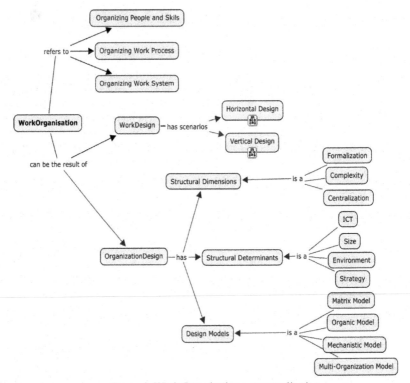

Figure 3. Work Organisation conceptualisation

In order to encode the ontology, COE software was used and the result is shown in figure 4.

---

[2] Work system is composed be 5 elements: individuals, tasks, tools and technologies.

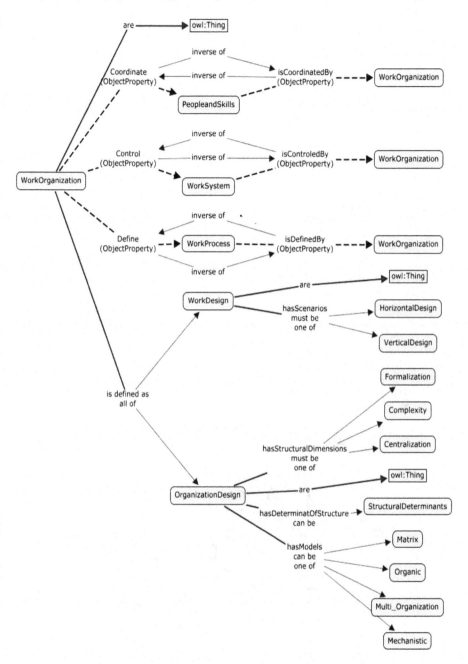

Figure 4. Work Organisation ontology map (partial map)

5. APPLICATION SCENARIO: MANAGING WORK DESIGN INFORMATION

Technically, information management can be performed through the implementation of content management systems (CMS). CMS are practical translations of Knowledge Management and Information Management approaches.

In this section we will describe how to set up Plone CMS content based on OWL ontologies. The objective is to reach a simple manageable hierarchical distribution of folders and files trough a web portal, according to the concepts and relations, which compose the work organization ontology. The steps performed to achieve that goal are presented in the figure 5.

Step 1: Development of work organization ontology in COE.
Step 2: Convert owl ontology to UML trough the Protégé UML plug-in and create UML composition relations. In OWL it is not possible to specify composition relations. With Protégé UML plug-in we specified that JobAnalysis concept was composed by three other concepts namely: JobSpecification, JobDescription and JobPerformane, then we transformed the ontology into and UML project.
Step 3: This step is optional. We opened the project with ArgoUML in order to see if the UML model converted within Protégé is consistent. At this step we may apply stereotypes specifying which object types (e.g. folder, file, special folder, discussion thread, image, etc.) our classes will assume within Plone.
Step 4/5: Using ArchGenXML utility, our UML model is converted into a valid Plone product which can be installed trough Plone administrator interface.

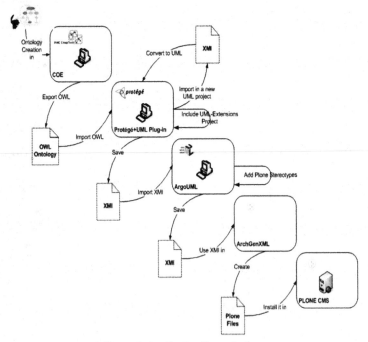

Figure 5. Application Scenario Steps

As result of the previous steps, we obtained a web portal where we are able to manage work design information according with the concepts and relations figured in the ontology.

6. CONCLUSION AND FURTHER WORK

The knowledge is not only in the ontology engineers heads, thus it is highly recommended the specification of a knowledge model supported by simple knowledge representation formalisms that allow domain specialists to discuss together about a certain domain in order to be obtained a set of concepts and its relations according with the experience, know-how and surveys of the right people without having the concern about knowledge representation technical issues. In the first step of knowledge acquisition, Cmaps do fairly the job due its informal characteristics. However, an easy knowledge formalism is not sufficient by itself to support the construction of a knowledge model. Thence came into existence the CmapTools Software by IHMC providing a complete collaborative knowledge representation environment based on CMs.

By definition ontology has formal constraints, so it is necessary to transform cmaps into a formal notation. A framework that implements a solid methodology for cmaps translation into COE formal conventions with validation mechanisms is needed.

We also foresee cmaps and Ontologies as a solution for today's' new programming challenges. Nowadays, all people access to the internet to rapidly retrieve information from several different sources either for professional or personal use. This new situation asks for new ways to develop and present web content. A possible future approach could be based on concept maps as a tool to set up a CMS for implementing e.g., a web portal. At the same time, it would be interesting to have the reverse synchronous standard mechanism in which the content created in a CMS could be used to maintain and evaluate ontologies(e.g., delete/add new instances to the ontology). Interoperability Semantic Web could be the answer at a short/medium term.

7. REFERENCES

1. Gruber TR. Toward principles for the design of ontologies used for knowledge sharing. In Nicola Guarino, Ed., International Workshop on Formal Ontology, Padova, Italy, 1993.
2. Gordon JL."Creating Knowledge Maps by Exploiting Depend Relationships", Knowledge Based Systems 2000; vol. 13: 71-79.
3. Baader F. "Logic-Based Knowledge Representation," in Artificial Intelligence Today: Recent Trends and Developments, vol. 1600/1999, Lecture Notes in Computer Science: Springer Berlin / Heidelberg, 1999 pp. 13.
4. Pepper S. "The TAO of Topic Maps," presented at XML Europe 2000, Paris, France, 2000.
5. Garcia A, Norena A, Betancourt,Ragan M. "Cognitive support for an argumentative structure during the ontology development process," in 9th Intl. Protégé Conference. Standford, California, 2006.
6. Stevens R, Goble C, Bechhofer S. "Ontology-based Knowledge Reresentation for Bioinformatics," Briefings in Bioinformatics 2000; vol. 1: 398-416.
7. Gruber A, Westenthaler R, Gahleitner E. "Supporting domain experts in creating formal knowledge models (ontologies)," presented at I-Know'06: 6th International Conference on Knowledge Management, Graz, Austria, 2006.
8. Walenstein A, "Foundations of cognitive support: toward abstract patterns of usefulness." In: 14th Annual Conference on Design, Specification, and Verification of Interactive Systems (DSV-IS'2002), Rostock, Germany, 2002.
9. Sauter S, Brightwell W, Colligan M, Hurrell J, LeGrande D, Lessin N, Lippin R, Lipscomb J, Murphy, L, Peters R, Keita G, Robertson S, Stellman J, Swanson N, Tetrick L. The Changing Organization of Work and the Safety and Health of Working People, Knowledge Gaps and Research Directions, National Institute for Occupational Safety and Health, 2002, pp. 1-43.
10. Sinha K, Van de Ven A, Designing Work Within and Between Organizations, Frontiers of Organization Science, Laguna Beach, CA, 2005.
11. Knublauch H, Fergerson R, Noy N, Musen M. "The Protégé OWL Plugin: An Open Development Environment for Semantic Web Applications", 3rd International Semantic Web Conference, Hiroshima, Japan, 2004.

PART **3**

DIGITAL FACTORY

20

DEMAND FORECAST METHOD FOR BUILD-TO-ORDER PRODUCTS USING ESTIMATE INFORMATION AS A LEADING INDICATOR

Atsushi Shimoda
Hitachi, Ltd., atsushi.shimoda.jw@hitachi.com
Hidenori Kosugi
Hitachi, Ltd., hidenori.kosugi.px@hitachi.com
Takafumi Karino
Chubu High-Technology Service, Ltd., takafumi.karino@itg.hitachi.co.jp
Norihisa Komoda
Osaka University, komoda@ist.osaka-u.ac.jp

A method for forecasting the number of parts shipments is proposed for build-to-order products using pre-sales estimate information as a leading indicator. Since the target number of parts shipments changes irregularly and over a short lifecycle, it is difficult to forecast with conventional methods. The method uses Kalman filter to correct for the noise associated with the leading indicator and to facilitate the practical application. The method was evaluated using 78 different parts of an electronic product. Experimental result revealed that the method is useful for forecasting the target shipping number.

1. INTRODUCTION

Recently, the demand for increased product variety and short delivery time has strengthened as customer needs have become more diverse. For manufacturers therefore, access to inventory has become essential in order to satisfy these demands. Conversely, short product life cycles and the concomitant increase in the obsolescence of parts due to technical improvements act to increase the need for shorter inventory periods. Consequently, reducing the parts inventory while avoiding stockout risk is an important problem for manufacturers trying to secure earnings. To resolve this problem, a variety of improvements to the supply chain have been implemented, including improved demand forecast accuracy, implementing short-term planning cycles, and bringing the stock point closer to the market (Suguro, 2006).

Build-to-order manufacturing has traditionally been limited to products with long delivery dates and with relatively low requirements such as industrial machines. However, in recent years, build-to-order manufacturing is increasingly being applied to products with a short delivery date and with high requirements such as electronics products. Consequently, it has become necessary to forecast requirements accurately to minimize inventories while ensuring short delivery dates. In this study, any product that has short delivery date requirements and which is mass produced according to order specifications on an assembly line using parts held in stock is referred to as a mass customized product. For these products, the number of parts shipments often varies markedly as the number

Please use the following format when citing this chapter:

Shimoda, A., Kosugi, H., Karino, T. and Komoda, N., 2008, in IFIP International Federation for Information Processing, Volume 266, *Innovation in Manufacturing Networks;* ed. A. Azevedo; (Boston: Springer), pp. 189–196.

and type of parts that need to be installed vary in response to the customer specifications. In addition, the mass customized products such as electronics products often have short life cycles. Taken together, these factors complicate the process of forecasting part shipments.

Many demand forecast methods have been proposed to date, including time series analysis (Kitagawa, 2005), the method for estimating the required number of parts employing Kalman filter (Ohta, 1974), and the method for estimating the required number of parts using neural networks (Araki, 1996). However, the restrictions associated with these methods are that data changes with some rules and that enough data is necessary to be able to statistically analyze before forecasting, making it difficult therefore to apply these methods when forecasting the number of part shipments, which is the aim of this study.

A method is therefore proposed for forecasting the number of individual parts. The method corrects for the delay associated with order probability and shipping time, which is variable, using estimated order information as a leading indicator with which to solve the aforementioned problem. It also applies to forecasts of the number of electronics product of part shipments and demonstrates the effectiveness of the method.

2. FORECAST PROBLEM: NUMBER OF PARTS SHIPMENTS

2.1. Feature of Forecast Object

The mass customized product targeted in this paper is one with two or more combined parts. The decision to install parts in the product and how many pieces to actually install depend on customer specifications. By stocking each part, it is possible to ship products immediately after assembly without the procurement lead-times of parts, even if assembly was initiated after the order has been finalized. Mass customized products therefore have the advantage of being able to make various products in a short time.

For mass customized products, because prices differ depending on the type of part installed, the estimate becomes an important consideration in the order process. Figure 1 is a schematic drawing of a certain order process. The horizontal axis represents time, and each row refers to the various parties concerned. First, the sales person makes an estimate based on the specifications that the customer presented. The number of parts to be installed in the product at the stage is decided and the order is confirmed through price negotiation. Then, parts being stocked by the factory are installed in the product and the product is shipped to the customer.

Mass customized products are manufactured according to monthly or weekly production plans. In every plan cycle, the number of parts shipments, the number of parts coming in, and inventory figures for each part are calculated, with additional parts ordered so as not to cause stockout. However, in case of mass customized products such as electrics products, losses due to unsalable stock and those that arise due to differences between current low prices and those initially procured from the supplier can occur easily because the life cycle of products is short and parts of those products become obsolete fast. Therefore, forecasting the number of part shipments while ordering the minimum number of parts to avoid stockout is particularly important.

However, the number of part shipments can fluctuate because orders for products equipped with the same part may occur with a relatively narrow period even though the orders themselves are random. In addition, since the parts of products are updated between different generations, the data for of each part only applies to one product generation. Consequently, since the number of forecasted part shipments for parts fluctuate irregularly over the short term, it is difficult to apply forecasting techniques such as time series analysis because the data period is short and there are no periodic changes.

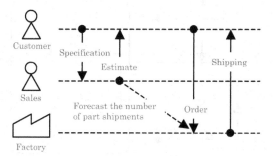

Figure 1. Ordering process

2.2. Forecast model

Based on the order process shown in Figure 1, the number of part shipments can be accurately determined when the order is fixed, when it is too late to control procurement. Conversely, while the number of parts included in the estimate is not final at the time of shipping, it is known early enough to control procurement. Therefore, estimate information is used as a leading indicator in this research. The total number of parts included in the estimate, compiled during the plan cycle, is defined as a leading indicator of the number of shipments. All of the electronic data in the estimate is compiled in the plan cycle and collected, and the number of each part is totaled. This leading indicator is referred to as the estimated number in this paper. In addition, the number of forecasted part shipments for an object is totaled using a procedure similar to that employed for the leading indicator. All of the electronic data related to the shipment slip is produced in the plan cycle and collected, and the number of each part is totaled. The number of part shipments required for this forecast will henceforth be referred to as the number of shipments.

Comparisons of the waveforms for estimate and shipment number, revealed that the shape of both numbers is similar to each other and that the number of estimates precedes the number of shipments for one or two terms, and indicates that the number of estimates is a useful indicator for forecasting. However, the height of the peak position and the amount of shift between those two waveforms differ depending with respect to time, indicating the existence of noise in the ordering process. For example, the made estimate being not received an order, a similar estimate made repeatedly, and the time required from the time at which an estimate made to the shipment varies by a single order correspond. Therefore, to use estimate information as a leading indicator, correcting this noise factor becomes a problem.

Figure 2 shows the approach employed by this study regarding the above-mentioned problem. The number of estimates is assumed to be an input into the system and the number of shipments to be an output, as shown at the left of Figure 2. The parameter that converts the input into the output is assumed for the state to be preserved at the subsequent period though changes for the long term. At this time, if the above-mentioned noise factor can be corrected using the I/O relationship, and if the parameter of the order production system can be presumed, then the output wave type can be predicted for any arbitrary input wave. The assumptions made using the above-mentioned parameter and predictions derived using the parameter are described further in Chapter 3.

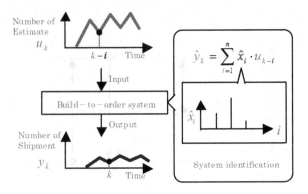

Figure 2. Basic concept of the proposed method

3. METHOD OF PREDICTION IN WHICH ESTIMATE INFORMATION IS SEQUENTIALLY CORRECTED

3.1. Predictive Model of Using Estimate Information as the Leading Indicator

In this chapter, the order production system presented Figure 2 is formulated according to the idea described in the preceding chapter. When considering the lifespan of an order, from the time an estimate is made to when it is shipped, there are rare instances in which the shipping of an order occurs immediately after the estimate has been made, or, conversely, when the estimate is made a long time before the shipment. This means that the lump of the shipment exists at a point that passes the time that is after making the estimate, which can be defined as an order probability. Then, shapes of the overlapping waves from the estimates shown in Figure 2 are assumed to correspond to the number of shipments in each period. This means that the number of shipments is an impulse response to the number of estimates, and that the number of shipments can be described as a convolution of the number of estimates and the order probability as

$$y_k = \sum_{i=1}^{n} x_i u_{k-i} + \upsilon_k \tag{1}$$

Here, y_k is the number of shipments at plan cycle k, u_k is number of estimates, and the coefficients x_i are the order probabilities of converting the number of estimates into the number of shipments. The order probability is a function of delay i, and the degree is assumed to be n. υ_k is the tabulation error for the number of shipments, obtained by subtracting the number of shipments unrelated to estimates. Here, if order probability x_i is obtained, the number of shipments at plan cycle k is predictable by the input of the number of estimates before cycle k of the plan to expression (1). However, the subscript that refers to the kind of part in this expression is omitted (it is similar in the following expressions). Here, at $k-i < 0$, it is $u_{k-i} = 0$.

3.2. Noise Correction Method Using the Kalman Filter

To accurately estimate the order probability $x\{\ \}$ of expression (1), correcting the noise that the order probability in Figure 2 possesses, is problematic. The noise associated with this order probability is considered to have a normal distribution because it is led from a lot of mutually irrelevant orders, and which is why it is corrected with Kalman filter (Katayama, 2000). To apply the Kalman filter, expression (1) is described by the following state equations (2) and observation equations (3):

$$x_{k+1} = x_k + \omega_k \tag{2}$$

$$y_k = H_k x_k + \upsilon_k \tag{3}$$

where, x_k is order probability vector, ω_k is the order probability noise, and H_k is the number of estimates.

$$x_k = \left[x_1(k), \cdots\cdots, x_n(k) \right] \tag{4}$$

$$\omega_k = \left[\omega_1(k), \cdots\cdots, \omega_n(k) \right] \tag{5}$$

$$H_k = \left[u_{k-1}, \cdots\cdots, u_{k-n} \right] \tag{6}$$

Here, the normal distribution type noise ω_k of the mean value vector 0_n and the covariance matrix $\sigma_\omega^2 I_{n\times n}$ ($I_{n\times n}$ is a unit matrix of 0_n) and υ_k of the mean value 0 and variance σ_υ^2. The next expression is obtained by applying Kalman filter to expression (2) and (3).

$$\hat{x}_{k|k-1} = \hat{x}_{k-1|k-1}$$

$$\hat{x}_{k|k} = \hat{x}_{k|k-1} + K_k \left(y_k - H_k \hat{x}_{k|k-1} \right) \tag{7}$$

$$K_k = \hat{P}_{k|k-1} H_k^T \left(1 + H_k \hat{P}_{k|k-1} H_k^T \right) \tag{8}$$

$$\hat{P}_{k|k-1} = \hat{P}_{k-1|k-1} + \frac{\sigma_\omega^2}{\sigma_\upsilon^2} I_{n\times n}$$

$$\hat{P}_{k|k} = \hat{P}_{k|k-1} - K_k H_k \hat{P}_{k|k-1} \tag{9}$$

Here, Kalman gain K_k and $\hat{P}_{k|k}$ exhibited covariance matrix of the assumed error margin, and was assumed to be $\hat{P}_{-1|-1} = \varepsilon_0 / \sigma_\upsilon^2 I_{n\times n}, \varepsilon_0 > 0$. The order probability vector $\hat{x}_{k|k-1}$ can be derived by sequential calculation of (7), (8), and (9). Then shipments of k periods y_k can be predicted from the number of estimates until the $k-1$ period.

$$\hat{y}_k = H_k \hat{x}_{k|k-1} = \sum_{i=1}^{n} \hat{x}_i u_{k-i} \tag{10}$$

4. EVALUATION

The proposed method was evaluated using real data for electronic components. A subset of equipments consisting of 78 different parts obtained by numerous shipments was selected. The evaluation period was taken as 32 terms, which exceeded the product life cycle of this product. In the evaluation, the short-term forecast was used to forecast the number of shipments based on the number of estimates and shipments until a previous period of time. For comparison, the exponential smoothing method (Goodrich, 1992) was performed under the same conditions. The exponential smoothing method is suitable for short-term forecasts as it tracks short-term changes relatively well than other known forecast method. The first-order method is adopted, and a coefficient is selected to minimize a past prediction error by the least squares method.

The evaluation condition can be described as follows: The degree of the order probability was assumed to be three, because most products were shipped within three periods after it had been estimated. While it is preferable to set an initial value for the order probability of each part, but initial values are not be understand beforehand. Therefore, once all common values for the different parts were assumed and then an individual order probability for each kind of part is estimated by an initial forecast calculation. That is, the period from term 1 to term 5 was taken as the settling period and the period from term 6 to term 32 was taken as the evaluation period for the prediction error (Table 1).

In Table 1, the 78 parts are classified by their average rate of change. Here, the average rate of change is an index that shows the degree of change in the shipment number pattern, which can be calculated using the following expression:

$$R = \frac{1}{m-1}\sum_{k=1}^{m-1}\frac{|y_{k+1} - y_k|}{y_k} \tag{11}$$

The performance was evaluated using the mean and the maximum MAPEs (mean absolute percent error (Mentzer, 1995)) for each range, which were calculated for the proposed method and the exponential smoothing method, which were then compared. In general, demand forecasting is useful when the error is less than 20% error; less than 30% is within the permissible range for practical use (Munekata, 2005).

To remain within a range that could account for 64% of the parts whose average rate of change is ≤0.4, the MAPE for the proposed method is ≤30%, while that of the exponential smoothing method is 35.8%, which exceeds the 30% that is permissible for practical use. In addition, the MAPE of the proposed method is 32.0% while that of the exponential smoothing method is 60.2% paying attention to the maximum value of the error. The proposed method exceeds 30% in the range for the change rate to exceed 0.4 but it is more excellent than the exponential smoothing method in each condition.

Table 1. Evaluation results

Average rate of change	Number of parts types	Average of mean absolute percent error (%)		Maximum of mean absolute percent error (%)	
		Proposed method	Exponential smoothing method	Proposed method	Exponential smoothing method
~0.2	7	21.8	20.4	25.1	30.3
~0.3	27	23.2	26.0	26.9	56.8
~0.4	16	28.2	35.8	32.0	60.2
~0.5	19	34.3	40.2	40.1	63.8
~0.6	9	41.5	45.9	48.0	63.3

Figure 3 shows the example of the forecast result. The horizontal axis represents the plan cycle and the Y-axis shows the number of parts. The predicted results for the proposed method and the exponential smoothing method are displayed overlapping with the number of shipments. The prediction error increases for the period where there is a large rate change because the result of the exponential smoothing method follows the change in the number of shipments after a delay of almost one term (MAPE is 23.6%). On the other hand, the result of proposed method synchronizes with the change in the number of shipments after four terms of settling period. Compared with the exponential smoothing method, the prediction error of the proposed method is improved as a result (MAPE is 20.0%).

The above-mentioned result shows that the proposed method is effective for use as a predictive technique using in this paper.

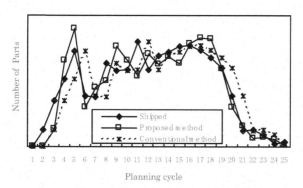

Figure 3. Example of forecasted result

5. SUMMARY

A demand forecasting method for predicting the number of parts, which change irregularly in the short term, that need to be ordered for a mass production product. The proposed method employs peculiar estimate information as a leading indicator for ordering product, sequentially corrects the noise that the order probability possesses by Kalman filter to assume the prediction error to be minimum, and accurately forecasts the number of part shipments.

The method was applied to the problem of forecasting 78 different parts for an electronic product as an actual example. The experimental results demonstrate that the method can be used to predict shipments up to change rate of 0.4 for an associated error margin of 28.2%, which is permissible for practical use.

6. REFERENCES

1. Araki, H., Kimura, A., Arizono, I., Ohta, H. Demand Forecasting Based on Differences of Demands via Neural Networks. Journal of Japan Industrial Management Association 1996; Vol.47, No.2: 59-68.
2. Goodrich, Robert L. Applied Statistical Forecasting. Business Forecast Systems, 1992.
3. Katayama, Toru. "Applied Kalman Filtering". Asakura Shoten, 2000.
4. Kitagawa, Genshiro. "Introduction to time series analysis". Iwanami Shoten, 2005.
5. Munekata, S., Saito, K. "A New Demand Forecasting Method for Newly-Launched Consumer Products Based on Estimated Market Parameters". Hitachi Tohoku Software technical report 2005, Vol.11, pp.34-39.
6. Ohta, H., Noda, H., Kase, S. Forecasting by Adaptive Kalman Filter. Journal of Japan Industrial Management Association 1974; Vol.25, No.1: 39-43.
7. Suguro, Takao et al. Stock management of site departure. Communications of JIMA 2006; Vol.16, No.5: 263-309.
8. Mentzer, John T. et al. Forecasting Technique Familiarity, Satisfaction, Usage, and Application. Journal of Forecasting 1995; Vol.14: pp.465-476.

21

AN ONTOLOGY FOR A MODEL OF MANUFACTURING SCHEDULING PROBLEMS TO BE SOLVED ON THE WEB

Maria Leonilde Rocha Varela[1], Sílvio do Carmo Silva[2]

School of Engineering, University of Minho, Portugal
leonilde@dps.uminho.pt[1], scarmo@dps.uminho.pt[2]

In this paper we describe an ontology for a model of manufacturing scheduling problems to be solved on the web, through several different scheduling methods made available by a web scheduling decision support system.

This approach aims enabling to share scheduling knowledge and methods, in a globally distributed context, in order to facilitate solving these problems, either in the industry or in the academic and research context.

The proposed ontology is described in terms of basic objects, the scheduling problem attributes, in the form of problems characterization parameters; problem classes or types of scheduling problems and relations among problem classes; and problems instances.

Finally, a sample of methods is presented for solving some well known problems arising in the scope of manufacturing scheduling through the web.

1. INTRODUCTION

The scheduling activity in an organization seeks to optimize the use of available production means or resources, ensuring short time to complete jobs and, in addition, to satisfy other important organization objectives. Thus, it can highly contribute to good service to customers and to high profitability of an organization.

Manufacturing scheduling may be defined as the activity of allocating tasks to production resources, or vice versa, over time. The result of this is usually expressed in a production schedule.

With this work we make a contribution for the better resolution process of scheduling problems by means of a decision support system on the web, based on a proposed ontology for a model of manufacturing scheduling problems description. Therefore, the system requires, first of all, the specification and identification of each problem to be solved and, then, the access to resolution methods, which are available for solving them. When there are different methods available we can obtain alternative solutions, which should be evaluated against specified criteria or objectives to be reached. Thus, we are able to properly solve a problem or closely related problems, through the execution of one or more scheduling methods and, subsequently, select de best solution provided by them. These methods can either be local or remotely accessible through the web.

The main objective of this paper consists on presenting the proposed ontology for a model of manufacturing scheduling problems, which consists on a classification framework for scheduling problems. This classification framework is represented through

Please use the following format when citing this chapter:

Varela, M.L. and Carmo-Silva, S., 2008, in IFIP International Federation for Information Processing, Volume 266, *Innovation in Manufacturing Networks;* ed. A. Azevedo; (Boston: Springer), pp. 197-204.

XML (eXtended Markup Language) on the web scheduling decision support system due to some important advantages, for instance allowing to specify scheduling problems and easily identifying methods for their resolution and to establish the necessary communication for the execution of the implemented scheduling methods through the web by using a web service (Papazoglou *et. al.*, 2003), (Varela *et al.*, 2002a,b; 2003).

This paper is organized as follows. In chapter 2 describes the proposed ontology for a model of manufacturing scheduling problems. Therefore, in section 2.1 we present a brief definition of manufacturing scheduling problems. In section 2.2 the scheduling problem attributes are presented through the main underlying characterization parameters. Section 2.3 presents and describes some well known scheduling problem classes and relations among them and in section 2.4 refers to scheduling problem instances, where an example is given. In section 3 we briefly present the web-based scheduling decision support with a list of available methods for solving some closely related and well known manufacturing scheduling problems. Finally, in section 4 we present some conclusions.

2. SCHEDULING PROBLEMS ONTOLOGY

2.1. A brief definition of manufacturing scheduling problems

The manufacturing scheduling activity may be defined as the activity of allocating production resources to tasks or vice versa, during a certain time period. Therefore, a proper production schedule enables a company to make good use of available resources and efficiently achieving operational objectives (Conway *et al.*, 1967).

The process of scheduling problem solving is essentially concerned with finding the sequence in which jobs should be processed. Sometimes, however, we may need also to know the scheduled start and finishing times of every job operation on each machine. This information completely defines a schedule or scheduling plan.

Good schedules strongly contribute to increase companies' success. Among other ways, this is achieved through deadlines satisfaction for the accepted orders, low flow times, few ongoing jobs in the system, high resource utilization and low production costs. These objectives can be better satisfied through the execution of the most suitable scheduling methods available for solving each particular problem under consideration and for doing that we need to clearly specify the problem to be solved.

2.2. Characterization parameters

Scheduling problems have a set of characteristics that need specification.
Some important processing requirements that frequently have to be taken into account for processing jobs have to do with resources other than machines, i.e. operators, tools, handling devices buffers and others.

This parameters can be expressed through a "$\alpha|\ \beta|\ \gamma$" nomenclature. Our proposed nomenclature is based on some well known nomenclatures described in the scheduling domain (Varela *et al.*, 2002a) and consists on an expanded form that can be represented by "$\alpha 1, \alpha 2\ |\ \beta 1, ..., \beta 18\ |\ \gamma$".

The first class of factors, which we call the α class, characterizes the production environment, i.e. the system and machines available. Another, the β class, deals mainly with characterization of jobs, resources and processing requirements.
Finally, the third γ class specifies the performance measure or evaluation criterion.
All the classification parameters are summarized in Tables 1, 2 and 3 below.

Table 1. Manufacturing environment characterization parameters

Class	Parameter	Designation	Value	Default value
α	α_1	Production systems types: Geral flexible system with multi-processor jobs/ operations, GFM: Single-stage GFM (GFM/f1). Single-stage GFM with parallel processors (GFM/f1/P), with: identical parallel processors (GFM/f1/PI); uniform parallel processors (GFM/f1/PU) or unrelated parallel processors (GFM/f1/PN). Multiple-stage GFM (GFM/fm): Jobshop or pure jobshop GFM (GFM/fm/J or JP) Flowshop or pure flowshop (GFM/fm/F or FP) Openshop or pure openshop (GFM/fm/O or OP). General flexible system, GF: Single-stage GF: Single-stage single processor GF (GF/f1) or Single-stage parallel processors GF (GF/f1/P): Identical parallel processors GF (GF/f1/PI) Uniform parallel processors GF (GF/f1/PU) Unrelated parallel processors GF (GF/f1/PN). Multiple-stage GF: Jobshop or pure jobshop (GF/fm/J or JP) Flowshop or pure flowshop (GF/fm/F or FP) Openshop or pure openshop (GF/fm/O or OP). General system with multi-processor jobs, GM: Single-stage GM: Single-stage single processor (GM/f1). Single-stage parallel processors GM (GM/f1/P): Identical parallel processors GM (GM/f1/PI) Uniform parallel processors GM (GM/f1/PU) Unrelated parallel processors GM (GM/f1/PN). Multiple-stage GM: Jobshop or pure jobshop (GM/fm/J or JP) Flowshop or pure flowshop (GM/fm/F or FP) Openshop or pure openshop (GM/fm/O or OP). General system, G: Single-stage single processor G (G/f1) Single-stage parallel processors G (G/f1/P). Identical parallel processors G (G/f1/PI) Uniform parallel processors G (G/f1/PU) Unrelated parallel processors G (G/f1/PN). Multiple-stage G: Jobshop or pure jobshop (G/fm/J or JP) Flowshop or pure flowshop (G/fm/F or FP) Openshop or pure openshop (G/fm/O or OP).	GFM, GFM/f1, GFM/fm, GFM/f1/P, (PI, PU, PN GFM/fm/J, GFM/fm/JP, GFM/fm/F, GFM/fm/FP, GFM/fm/O, GFM/fm/OP. GF, GF/f1, GF/fm, GF/f1/P, (PI, PU, PN) GF/fm/J, GF/fm/JP, GF/fm/F, GF/fm/FP, GF/fm/O, GF/fm/OP. GM, GM/f1, GM/fm, GM/f1/P, (PI, PU, PN) GM/fm/J, GM/fm/JP, GM/fm/F, GM/fm/FP, GM/fm/O, GM/fm/OP. G, G/f1, G/fm, G/f1/P, (PI, PU, PN) G/fm/J, G/fm/JP, G/fm/F, G/fm/FP, G/fm/O, G/fm/OP.	1
	α_2	Number of processors.	$\varnothing$, variable, m	$\varnothing$

Regarding the α class of parameters, the main manufacturing environment characterization factors are expressed by "G", representing general shops, where jobs may have no precedence relations among its operations. "F" stands for flexible manufacturing environments, meaning that the system may have two or more alternative processors for executing a given operation on some job. When jobs may require two or more processors simultaneously this is expressed by the multi-processor factor "M". A single stage manufacturing system, where each job includes only one processor, i.e., $nj=1$ $\forall j$: $j=1, ..., n$, is represented by factor "f1" and a multi-fase manufacturing system, where each job may have two or more operations: $nj \geq 2$ $\forall j$: $i=1, ..., n$, is expressed by "fm".

A single stage manufacturing system may include two or more parallel processors, and this is represented, generally, by "P". If the parallel processors are unrelated processors then the corresponding characterization factor is "PN", otherwise, in case of uniform processors this is represented by "PU" and identical processors are expressed by "PI".

There are additional factors corresponding to well known manufacturing systems like jobshops ("J"); pure jobshops ("JP"); flowshops ("F"); pure flowshops ("FP"); openshops ("O") and pure openshops ("OP"), which may or may not appear combined with the previously introduced factors "G", "F" and "M", forming a variety of manufacturing environments that may occur in several different manufacturing scenarios arising in industry or in academic context.

Table 2. Jobs characterization parameters

Class	Parameter	Designation	Value	Default value
β	β_1	Jobs preemptions	$\emptyset$, pmtn, free-pmtn, comp-pmtn	$\emptyset$
	β_2	Jobs precedences	$\emptyset$, prec, tree: intree, outtree, chain, sp-graph	$\emptyset$
	β_3	Jobs ready-times	$\emptyset$, r_j, r_{ij}, r_{jl}, r_{ijl}	$\emptyset$
	β_4	Jobs processing times restrictions	$\emptyset$, $t_j=1$, $t_{ij}=1$, $t_j=p$, $t_{ij}=p$, $t_{i(j)} \in \{a,b\}$, $t_{min} \leq t_{i(j)} \leq t_{max}$,...	$\emptyset$
	β_5	Jobs due dates	$\emptyset$, d_l, d_j, d_{ij}, D	$\emptyset$
	β_6	Batch processing	$\emptyset$, batch	$\emptyset$
	β_7	Families processing	$\emptyset$, fam	$\emptyset$
	β_8	Complex jogs processing	$\emptyset$, compj	$\emptyset$
	β_9	Jobs quantity	n, n_j, n_l	n
	β_{10}	Jobs priorities	$\emptyset$, w_j, w_{ji}, w_{jl}	$\emptyset$
	β_{11}	Multi-processor tasks	$\emptyset$, mpt_j, mpt_{ij}, mpt_{jl}	$\emptyset$

Table 3. Machines and auxiliary resources characterization parameters

Class	Parameter	Designation	Value	Default value
β	β_{12}	Machines elegibility	$\emptyset$, M_k	$\emptyset$
	β_{13}	Machines availability	$\emptyset$, $avail_k$	$\emptyset$
	β_{14}	Auxiliary resources	$\emptyset$, aux_k	$\emptyset$
	β_{15}	Critical resources	$\emptyset$, crt_k	$\emptyset$
	β_{16}	Machines setup	$\emptyset$, s_{jk}, s_{ijk}, s_{lk}, s_k	$\emptyset$
	β_{17}	Intermediate buffers	$\emptyset$, $buffer_k$, no-wait	$\emptyset$
	β_{18}	Multi-purpose machines	$\emptyset$, mpm_k	$\emptyset$

Regarding the performance measurement parameters, we think that objectives can be put together into one parameter (γ) and the proposed manufacturing classification nomenclature allows users to add their own domain specific performance measures to be considered on each particular case.

Typical examples of such measures are the maximum flow time (Fmax), the makespan (Cmax) and the mean and maximum lateness of jobs (Lmean, Lmax), among many others, namely: $\gamma \in \{$Fmax, Cmax, Σ Cj, Σ (wjCj), Lmean, Lmax, Σ Tj, Σ (wjTj), Σ Ej, Σ (wjEj), Σ NTj, Σ(wjNTj),...(*)$\}$.

2.3. Problem classes and relations among them

The problem characteristics previously described in section 2.2 may be combined in different ways, resulting in many distinct scheduling problem classes. Table 4 presents a sample of problem classes and references about some well known methods for solving them.

Table 4. Sample of problem classes and solving methods

Problem class	Method reference	Observations
G/fm/F,2 | n | Cmax	Johnson (1954)	Maximal polynomially solvable Without preemption
G/fm/F,2 | n, rj | Cmax	Lenstra et al (1977)	Minimal NP-hard Without preemption
G/fm//F,2 | n, rj; no-wait | Cmax	Roeck (1984)	Maximal polynomially solvable With no wait
G/fm/F,3 | n, pmtn | Cmax	Gonzalez & Sahni (1978) Cho & Sahni (1981)	Maximal polynomially solvable With preemption
G/fm/F,m | n, pji=1; prec | Cmax	Leung et al (1984) Timkovsky (1998)	Minimal NP-hard Without preemption
GM/F | n=3 | Cmax	Kraemer (1995)	Minimal NP-hard With multiprocessor task
GF/fm/F,3 |n | Cmax	Garey et al (1976)	Minimal NP-hard With multipurpose machines
GF/fm/F,m | rj; tji=1| Cmax	Brucker et al (1997)	Maximal polynomially solvable With multipurpose machines

For example of use of this notation is "G/fm/F,2|n|Cmax" which reads as: "Scheduling of non-preemptable and independent tasks of arbitrary processing time lengths, arriving to the system at time zero, on a general flowshop, with 2 machines, in order to minimize the maximum flow time or makespan.

Regarding Table 4 we can realize that the problems are related in terms of problem classes and subclasses. For example, class G/fm/F,2|n|Cmax previously described consists on a subclass of the general class G/fm/F,m|n|Cmax, since this last one refers to a flowshop including any number of machines besides the first one refers only to a flowshop integrating only two machines.

The proposed specification nomenclature provides a general framework of scheduling problems and related concepts, and consequently a way of describing each particular problem enabling to easily associate each problem to appropriate solving methods and specifying each problem instance to be solved. Problems are associated to methods by matching problem classification parameters, according to the proposed nomenclature, to scheduling methods inputs and additional information about given problem instances has to be specified for solving them when using the developed scheduling decision-support system (Varela *et al.*, 2002b, 2003).

00202

Innovation in Manufacturing Networks

2.4. Problem instances

One of the most critical success factors for implementing shop floor scheduling systems is the possibility of dealing with various constraints on each kind of production process (Wu, 1999).

In defining job release orders it is necessary to express a hierarchy of elements and attributes about the problems, such as item, quantity, location or destination, due date, processing time, and so on, as previously represented on section 2.2.

Therefore, in manufacturing scheduling problems a job represents an action that has certain time duration. During that time, the job changes status of inventories of corresponding items, occupying or loading some particular resources. The jobs need some resources and produce some outputs. Production resource means workstations, machines, equipments, tools, labors, and so on.

An example of a scheduling problem instance consists on processing a set of ten non-preemptable and independent jobs, with unit processing time lengths, arriving at time zero, on a general flowshop, with 5 machines, in order to minimize total completion time of all jobs or makespan (G/fm/F,5|10,p=1|Cmax).

3. SOLVING SCHEDULING PROBLEMS ON THE WEB

The manufacturing scheduling problems can be solved through a web decision support system developed based on the proposed ontology for specifying these problems, previously presented.

Figure 1 shows the automatically generated interface, based on XML and related technology for specifying scheduling knowledge about problems and solving methods (Varela *et al.*, 2002a,b; 2003). This figure shows a list of related scheduling problem classes that include characteristics specified according to the proposed problem classification nomenclature. From this list the user may select one or more of those closely related problem classes. This multiple choice is important when the user does not know exactly which class of problems he/ she wants to solve or even to enlarge the set of possible solving methods to be found for solving a problem.

Class	Complexity	Context	Problem characteristics	Select
F2|n|Cmax	Maximal Polinomially Solvable	≥	[(system_type, F), (machines, 2), (jobs, n), (measure, Cmax)]	☑
F2|rj,n|Cmax	Minimal NP-hard	≥	[(system_type, F), (jobs, n), (arrivals, rj), (machines, 2), (measure, Cmax)]	☐
F2|rj,n,no-wai	Maximal Polinomially Solvable	≥	[(system_type, F), (machines, 2), (jobs, n), (arrivals, rj), (buffers, no-wait), (measure, Cmax)]	☐
F3|rj,n|Cmax	Minimal NP-hard	≥	[(system_type, F), (machines, 3), (jobs, n), (arrivals, rj), (measure, Cmax)]	☐
F3|n|Cmax	Minimal NP-hard	≥	[(system_type, F), (machines, 3), (jobs, n), (measure, Cmax)]	☑
Fm|n|Cmax	Minimal NP-hard	≥	[(system_type, F), (machines, m), (jobs, n), (measure, Cmax)]	☑
Fm|prec,pji=1	Minimal NP-hard	≥	[(system_type, F), (machines, m), (jobs, n), (precedences, prec), (times, pji=1), (measure, Cmax)]	☐

Problem types for the general problem characteristics: [system_type=F, jobs=n, measure=Cmax]

Figure 1. List of closely related problem classes

Once the user specifies the problem classes he/ she wants to consider another automatically generated interface of the developed scheduling web system presents a list of suitable methods for solving them, as presented in Figure 2.

ID	Prob. Class	Method name	Implementation location	Reference	Complexity	Protocol	Select
				Available methods for solving the problem classes: [class=F2|n|Cmax, class=F3|n|Cmax, class=Fm|n|Cmax]			
1001	Fm|n|Cmax	BranchBoundIS	http://localhost:6002/RPC2	Ignall and Schrage, 1965	NP-hard	XML-RPC	⊙
32	F2|n|Cmax	Johnson	http://localhost:6002/RPC2	Johnson, 1954	Polynomial	XML-RPC	○

Figure 2. List of methods for solving scheduling problems

The user may select one of the given methods for solving a specific problem instance, for example, the branch-and-bound method proposed by Ignall and Schrage (Conway *et al.*, 1967), which is a NP-hard method for the general G/fm/F,m|n|Cmax (or simply, Fm|n|Cmax) class of scheduling problems and which was implemented in the developed web scheduling system through a web service based on the XML-RPC communication protocol (Terziyan and Zharko), (Varela *et al.*, 2003), (Wu, 1999).

4. CONCLUSIONS

In production enterprises, it is important nowadays, as a competitive strategy, to explore and use software applications, now becoming available through the Internet and Intranets, for solving scheduling problems. This paper proposes an ontology for solving manufacturing scheduling problems using a web based decision-support system developed based on a proposed ontology for expressing manufacturing scheduling problems.

The main importance of the proposed ontology consists on enabling to properly represent scheduling problems in order to seek for appropriate available methods for solving them.

As we referred previously it becomes necessary to use the proposed ontology and underlying nomenclature for clearly specifying the main scheduling problem characteristics to consider when we are interested in solving a given problem instance.

This nomenclature was developed based on some important ones put forward by several different authors in the scheduling domain and was extended in order to include some additional problems characteristics, which are essential for properly specifying real problem arising from diverse industrial and academic scenarios.

Besides the proposed nomenclature may appear very extended, in practice a problem classified according to this framework rarely becomes very complex, because a problem class consists on a kind of model which only has to consider the main problem characteristics to be representative for properly solving a given problem.

5. REFERENCES

1. Conway, R. W.; Maxwell, W. L.; Miller, L. W. Theory of Scheduling. England: Addison-Wesley Publishing Company, Inc., 1967.
2. Papazoglou, M.P.; Krämer, B.J.; Yang, J. "Leveraging Web-Services and Peer-to-Peer Networks". In Proceedings of Advanced Information Systems Engineering, 15th International Conference, CaiSE, Klagenfurt, Austria. June 16-18, 2003, pp. 485-501.
3. Terziyan, V.; Zharko, A. Semantic Web and Peer-to-Peer: Integration and Interoperability in Industry, Industrial Ontologies Group, MIT Department, University of Jyvaskyla, Finland (http://www.cs.jyu.fi/ai/vagan/papers.html).
4. Varela, L. R.; Aparicio, J. N.; Silva, C. S. "An XML knowledge base system for scheduling problems". In Proceedings of the Innovative Internet Computing System Conference, I2CS'02, Kuhlungsborn, Germany. Springer-Verlag in the Lecture Notes in Computer Science series, 2002a; 61-70.
5. Varela, M. L. R.; Aparício, J. N.; Silva, S. C. "Developing a Web Scheduling System Based on XML Modeling". In Knowledge and Technology Integration in Product and Services – Balancing Knowledge and Technology in Product and Service Life Cycle, BASYS'02, Cancun, Mexico. Kluwer Academic Publishers, 2002b, pp. 61-70.
6. Varela, M. L. R.; Aparício, J. N.; Silva, S. C. "A Scheduling Web Service based on XML-RPC". In Proceedings of the 1st Multidisciplinary International Conference on Scheduling: Theory and Applications, MISTA'03, Nottingham, UK. ASAP, The University of Nottingham. 2003, pg. 540-551.
7. Wu, J. Distributed System Design. New York: CRC Press, 1999.

22

EVOLVABLE ASSEMBLY SYSTEMS: FROM EVALUATION TO APPLICATION

Mauro Onori, Daniel Semere
KTH,
Stockholm, Sweden
{onori, dte}@ipp.kth.se

José Barata
UNINOVA / UNL,
Quinta da Torre, 2829-516 Caparica, Portugal
{ldr,jab,pcm}@uninova.pt

Presented in 2002, and applied within the EUPASS and A3 projects, Evolvable Assembly Systems proposes a novel way of applying assembly systems in industry. The essence of EAS resides not only in the ability of system components to adapt to the changing conditions of operation, but also to assist in the evolution of these components in time such that processes may become more robust. The main features of Evolvable systems include distributed control, a modularized, intelligent and open architecture, and a comprehensive and multi dimensional methodological support that comprises the reference architecture. The work has been, and is being, implemented through large European research projects. Evolvability being a system concept, it is envisaged to address every aspect of an assembly system throughout its life cycle, i.e., design and development, operation and evolution. Furthermore, integration of legacy subsystems and modules have been addressed in the methodology. This article will present the latest developments, applications and conclusions drawn to date.

Key words: *Evolvability, System Architecture, emergence, modular*

1. INTRODUCTION

According to the Observatory of European SMEs [1], 93% of all employees in Europe operate within companies with less than 10 workers/employees, and over 120 million people are directly employed in the European SME sector. Being the real giants of the European economies, their particular needs will need to be highlighted. Furthermore, it must be noted that due to the fact that manufacturing is becoming ever more customised, and the product lifecycles continue to decrease, the underlying needs of manufacturing become identical for both small and large enterprise. The bottom line is that almost 31% of the workforce in Europe is currently employed in the manufacturing industry, which means roughly 34 million employees or 1550 million € in value adding activities.

The addition of the service sectors directly dependent on this manufacturing industry magnifies the figure significantly, and one is still not including the major European corporations!

According to the results attained by many roadmaps ([2],[3],[4],[5],[6]), one of the most important objectives to be met by European industry is sustainability, which is multifaceted:

Please use the following format when citing this chapter:

Onori, M., Semere, D. and Barata, J., 2008, in IFIP International Federation for Information Processing, Volume 266, *Innovation in Manufacturing Networks;* ed. A. Azevedo; (Boston: Springer), pp. 205–214.

- the solutions need to be sustainable from an economical point of view as the companies need not only acquire the manufacturing technology, but also maintain it.
- there are ecological aspects linked to sustainability [7]: minimise use of resources & materials, waste disposal, pollution, etc.
- social aspects: as the technologies in question need to support and sustain the societies and economies being affected by them.

The obvious conclusion is that future manufacturing solutions will have to deal with very complex scenarios.

Evolvable Assembly Systems ([8], [9]) represents one of the paradigms proposed as an opportunity to solve such threats. It has, to date, resulted in several demonstrators and offered methodologies and architectures in support. This article will summarise the main achievements, but it is relevant to recall the reader that EAS is mainly a new paradigm and not a finalised, ready-to-use solution. This is of some importance as reconfigurability and flexibility have, after more than two decades of efforts, not produced any commercially successful results. Hence the need to explore new approaches.

2. BACKGROUND APPROACHES

The major problems incurred by companies dealing with assembly all relate to uncertainty. First of all, it is very difficult for companies to predict the type and range of products that will have to be developed. The second uncertainty regards the production volumes and lifespans reached by these future products.

For these reasons, in the process of development of a new product (or even a variant), companies need to optimise:

- the cost
- the Time-to-Market/ Time-to-Volume

In the case of a product-specific traditional assembly system, we have high initial costs and long assembly system development time, thus shortening the actual production lead times. Furthermore, each time a new product is required, investments tend to rise dramatically since the assembly system has to be adapted or exchanged.

The overwhelming reaction to these problems has been to attempt to develop extremely flexible assembly machines. In the late eighties and early nineties, the general trend in precision assembly was to develop Flexible Assembly Systems (FAS) and Flexible Automatic Assembly (FAA) cells (or Hyper Flexible Automatic Assembly, going a bit further with stepwise automation, standard assembly machines and sub-batch principle).

The goal was to have general flexibility, but the actual assembly processes were not studied in depth, therefore resulting in unstable / non-robust or badly adapted solutions. They were fairly adequate to many different product types, but failed to be very performing in any domain. The high cost of such installations was another heavy problem, especially for smaller companies. Flexibility, instead of the actual assembly process, has been the core issue of most of these developments. As shown in the Figure 1, the lower a component is positioned in the hierarchical structure, the more flexibility is necessary to ensure a certain flexibility to the whole system; this means even a system with low flexibility needs a very flexible control: this may imply that FAA solutions also failed because they never provided flexible/agile control systems!

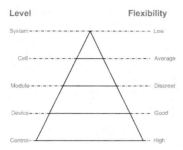

Figure 1. Possible levels of flexibility according to the hierarchical structure containing he component

The next attempt at finding a solution was Re-configurable Assembly Systems (RAS). In this case the focus was on the principle that innovative product design must not be limited by assembly process constraints.

In RMS, the Assembly System design starts from the "**New Product Requirements**". The product to be assembled is analysed in order to find all the "**Assembly System Requirements**", which means that *the driver of the whole process is the Product.* In such an approach there are no links between the Product Design process and the successive steps: it leaves the maximum freedom to the designers, but this is not always the right strategy for the company success.

2.1. EAS

Basically, the real objectives should not have been flexibility or reconfigurability. These are characteristics, not objectives. The real objective is system adaptability, which EAS targets with the following four points:

1. Optimised functionality: the assembly equipment is kept as simple as possible by deriving small, dedicated, process-oriented modules. These may be interconnected to form cells or systems.
2. Optimised orchestration: the control system needs to be the most agile aspects. This is achieved by adopting a multi-agent based, distributed control approach with embeded controllers.
3. Adaptability: the modularity allows for stepwise upgradeability and economoic flexibility (it is cheaper & simpler to change a module than modify a system). The actual system may also adapt to minor changes via its control system, which, being skill-based, allows for emergent behaviour to be exploited.
4. Robustness: the equipment is dedicated, small, and includes an own processor. Some modules (robots) may even be reconfigurable. The control system is goal-oriented, and the system is process-oriented. This results in a dedicated system based on an adatable concept with advanced interfaces.

Fundamentally, EAS suggests that true agility/flexibility can only be achieved if the lowest building blocks of a system are those that exhibit the highest rate of adaptability/evolvability. As the clustering of components increases in complexity, so does the agility/flexibility decrease. Hence, in order to build truly agile systems, one must begin by considering the control architecture.

According to the EAS Paradigm, each system should consist of several skill-based and process-oriented units: these elements should be very task-specific in order to accomplish only a simple action. It is possible, in fact, to consider every complex task as the union of several simple actions. Therefore each "shared element" can be used to accomplish the same action in different assembly cycles or in different product generations. Obviously, due to its modularity and unit-by-unit development, such a system is accessible even for small-medium sized companies that can spread the investment over a given timespan. Moreover, as will be detailed in Chapter 3, that the EAS process-oriented approach to the Ontology allows to define the Assembly System requirements for a whole **Class of Products** instead of a single product: the defined assembly processes are common to an entire set of products.

A fundamental condition is the plugability of all components.

One of the most important consequences of this approach relates to its control system: modules are agents, knowing their proper capabilities and possible forms of cooperation with other agents. The principles of emergence can be applied, working with module skills and forming higher capabilities out of it.

Therefore, when a system is created according to the EAS principles, the resulting capability of the sum of the modules will not be so easily predicted. When a multitude of small entities is brought together, new and unexpected capabilities surface from such coalitions [10]: this is called Emergent Behaviour. Of course the lower the level of the device considered, the higher is the emergent behaviour (fine granularity = high emergence).

Evolvable Assembly Systems (EAS) exhibits the following characteristics:

- It is a fully "reconfigurable" system platform that exhibits an emergent behaviour.
- Mechatronically integratable assembly units.
- The reconfigurable system has to be composed of process-oriented components (gives granularity of emergent behaviour).
- A system that can automatically determine its functionality based on the components' skills.
- The change in paradigm is, partly, that we no longer invest in the programming & coding, but, rather, in how to establish and exploit relations.
- Maintenance, documentation and the ability to store information in support of operational stability.

3. METHODOLOGY

The EAS Methodology provides the references architecture, enablers, and modelling formalisms. In the following section brief description of the methodology is given.

3.1. Reference Architecture, RA

The EAS Reference Architecture (EAS_RA) describes the essential features of an Evolvable System which means the reference architecture specifies the necessary features that a system should have to be an evolvable system.

The reference architecture is composed of three main elements: Principles, Technical Positions and Templates.

Principles : EAS has two fundamental principles which lay foundation and guide the development processs of an evolvable system. These principles can be considered as description of the core ideas of the evolvable system paradigm.

Principle 1: *the most innovative product design can only be achieved if no assembly process constraints are posed. The ensuing, fully independent, process selection procedure may then result in an optimal assembly system methodology.*

Principle 2: *Systems under a dynamic condition need to be evolvable, i.e., they need to have an inherent capability of evolution to address the new or changing set of requirements.*

These principles have been described in detail in [11]:

Technical Positions: EAS design and implementation decisions and objectives set at a technical / technological level that describes the ontology, exploited protocols, standards or specifications for use with each major architectural component.

Templates and Partial Models: Reusable diagrams, graphs, objectives and knowledge and rules that address the distribution of system functions and how they relate topologically. Templates use models to show relationships and between components as specified by the Technical Positions and pertinent knowledge units.

3.2. Modeling Formalisms

Modelling formalisms refers to the ontology and the graphical tools used to build models in the reference architecture and the enabling models as described in section 3.3.

The EAS formalised concepts (ontology) and definitions are represented using a set of descriptive tools such as:

- Definitions of the most important concepts: module, process, product, eas module, skills, eas assembly system (which is a composition of modules), etc
- Diagrams (UML, etc) where the interactions between the concepts defined are shown. This enables to show how the EAS architecture generates assembly systems. The interaction may show the global system behaviour
- Formalisation of concepts

The domain ontology indeed captures the concepts in the system with their specifications (consensual semantic) i.e., what the concepts are and how they are related to each other in the domain. However, it does not capture the logic behind the relationships and the how's in the synthesis and functionality of the system.

3.3. Enablers

This part of the methodology provides the necessary models, tools and methods for the development and evolution of an evolvable system.

The enabling models include: the development process model, the business model and the knowledge model. These models are constructed using the formalisms described above and most notably the EAS ontology

The figure below depicts the first proposed EAS design methodology using IDEF0. The is a simplified high level activity model showing the main activities in the development process and their input, output, control and mechanisms needed to generate or modify instances of the architecture.

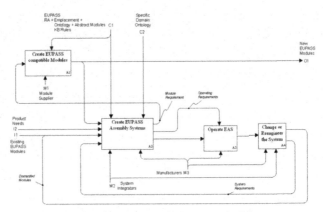

Figure 2. The simplified EAS Methodology

The traditional top-down system design is feasible only in cases where the emergent behaviour is fully describable; (Ueda, 2001). If emergent behaviour has to be investigated even at design and development stages, then a heterarchical or a network approach are the options.

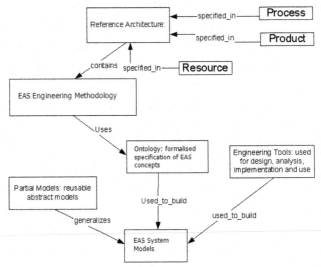

Figure 3. Basic Aspects of the EAS Reference Architecture

Concepts that are formalised in the EAS Ontology are used to capture the stakeholders understanding of their own domain. The EAS knowledge model is thus a structured and formalised collection of such knowledge capturing representations of the domains. The main objective of the EAS knowledge model is to provide an environment that supports the development and operation of evolvable systems.

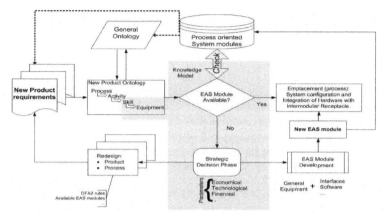

Figure 4. The preliminary EAS approach

The domain knowledge captured using the EAS ontology and the EAS knowledge templates are the two entities used to develop the knowledge model. The knowledge models are used among other things how each module in a system should address for a new set of conditions.

The elements in the EAS knowledge model consist of the following knowledge domains:
1. The enterprise knowledge domain – globalizes knowledge of the system and represents the business, organizational and global knowledge models captured. Enterprise knowledge enables environment recognition and maintenance of organizational associations.
2. The product knowledge domain – captures the knowledge related to product specification and design to assembly tasks.
3. The execution knowledge domain: capturing knowledge elements related to communications, planning and scheduling

The learning knowledge domain: containing knowledge elements that are used to incorporate case based reasoning.

The EAS RA is ultimately viewed from different perspectives addressing the different concerns of the stakeholders. The stakeholders include:
- those who build the system (structure and communication views),
- those who use it (functional view),
- those who are concerned with control (control view).

The architecture should, therefore, address the concerns of every stakeholder, which gives rise to a multiple set of viewpoints concerning the requirements, expected outputs and controlling mechanisms. These may come to include:
- Functional Views, which address the concerns of the users of the system, and describe the functionality of the system, the process flows, quality, logistical issues.
- Communication Views: which address the concerns of how the data and information is to be represented, interpreted, recorded and transmitted.
- Control views: which address the concerns of the control system.
- Structure Views, which address the concerns of the system integrators, and maintenance.

These represent the background work that needs to be carried out in order to develop and establish an adequate EAS_RA. The actual implementation of this architecture, when considering the EAS modules and how they are to be integrated and formed into a system, will also be subject to a set of "views".

3.4. Intermodular Receptacle

One of the most important aspects of developing an Evolvable Assembly system resides in the advanced interfacing requirements.

Every piece of equipment has its properties. They enable the equipment to perform or to assist at technical operations leading to the process goal. On the other side every piece of equipment has constraints on several levels. Moreover aspects like lifetime or maintenance cycles have to be taken into account. The design of assembly systems requires the awareness of both the abilities as well as the constraints. Automating the design process requires therefore a structured knowledge base including the equipments properties, comprehensive for operators or designers as well as for software services. If the technical properties were static and no runtime access to the properties was necessary it would make sense to just save everything in one large database. But modern mechatronic systems require fast and reliable data exchange. Furthermore regarding that the development of assembly systems is leading to more distributed systems, a knowledge base included in the equipment itself should be preferred. This equipment knowledge base can be regarded as a multi-level interface definition. It could be described completely with the contact and channel method , which actually is nothing else than an interface description, or with other more differentiated methods.

EAS is an approach to systemize the design of products and their assembly systems. The reasons mentioned above impose the inclusion of distributed knowledge. The optimisation goal of EAS is adaptability. To assure maximum adaptability, the knowledge bases have to be put at the lowest level available; i.e., at module level.

The module choice, in build time and in runtime, depends on the module's ability to perform skills and constraints imposed by general properties. A skill and its inherent information requires a structure and a place to store. To fit into yet proposed control concepts an implementation into the modules is also to be aimed at. Aiming at agility & adaptability requires that as many components as possible fit together. This imposes standard interfaces, covering all relevant mechatronic aspects. Minimizing the amount of used interface types leads to a higher plugability and, therefore, agility on system design. In order to allow system designers to create new modules, by modifying legacy equipment or by developing something new, the interfaces have to be specified. This way the designers know how to develop a module fitting into the standard. The specification should also describe approaches and show examples.

The here described multi-level interface specification, including inherent module knowledge in form of a template and enabling the module to communicate its abilities with other system modules in form of skills, is called "Intermodular Receptacle"-see Figure 5.

The development of the intermodular receptacle cammot be detailed at present due to pending patent applications, but these advanced interface devices will have embedded processing power. This will allow assembly modules to communicate between each other and attain self-configuration capability.

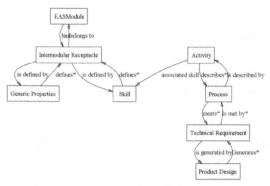

Figure 5. Ontological description of the Intermodular Receptacle

4. APPLICATIONS

Initial evaluations were carried out in the test cell shown below (Figure 6a). More industrially viable evaluations are currently being deployed within a new system being developed at KTH (Figure 6b).

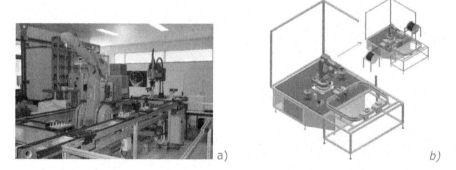

Figure 6. a)The evaluation test case setup; b)Industrial test case setup

5. CONCLUSIONS

At present the EAS paradigm is only just starting to take a practical form, and the control solution, ontologies, and methodologies only partially describe the most recent developments. These ideas are now being put into a real industrial scenario through the participation of Electrolux Home Products Italy SpA and UNINOVA. The layout given in Figure 7b is being setup for two industrial products (self-configuring & reconfiguring).

EAS, as with other similar approaches, offers great opportunities for attaining true agility and cost-effective, stepwise automation. The technologies for achieving this are available and there are several partners willing to partake in this endeavour; however, it is vital to point out that EAS does imply that the manner in which we develop and create projects for the development of assembly systems are radically changed, assuming a more synthesis-based approach.

The experience of this group is that there exists far too strong a resistance to such change in certain academic and industrial circles, and that the creation of new approaches and even new service sectors, all based on EAS and similar approaches, will have to prove their validity through even more elaborate industrial scenarios. Nevertheless, it must be said that at the end of the day it is not the most efficient or technologically advanced solution that may represent the future way of developing assembly systems, but the one that best paves the way to large-scale exploitation.

6. REFERENCES

1. "SMEs in Focus- Main results from the 2002 Observatory of European SMEs", submitted to the Enterprise Directorate-General of the European Commission by KPMG Special Services; Observatory of European SMEs, ISBN 92-894-4878-4.
2. The NEMI Roadmap; NEMI, National Electronics Manufacturing Initiative (USA), http://www.nemi.org/Roadmapping/index.html.
3. "Strategic Research Agenda-assuring the future of manufacturing in Europe"; Manufuture Platform-Executive Summary, Dec. 2005, EC.
4. "MANVIS, Manufacturing Visions-Integrating Diverse Perspectives into Pan-European Foresight"; FP6 Support Action, NMP2-CT-2003-507139.
5. "The Future of Manufacturing in Europe 2015-2020-The Challenge for Sustaninability"; FutMan, Institute for Prospective Technological Studies, European Commission Joint Research Centre, EUR 20705 EN.
6. "First Draft Roadmap-deliverable 1.5b"; Project Report-Public, Document 1.5b, EUPASS-Evolvable Ultra Precision Assembly, NMP-2-CT-2004-507978; October 2005.
7. "Plants prospering from climate change"; Environment News Services; Pegg,J.R.; International daily Newswire, Washington DC, June 6, 2003.
8. Viewpoint; Onori, M. Assembly Automation Journal 2002b; 22: 8-12.
9. Barata, J., Onori, M. and Frei, R. In ISIE'06 - IEEE International Symposium on Industrial ElectronicsIEEE, Montreal - Canada, 2006b.
10. Ueda, K. Journal of Artificial Intelligence in Engineering 2001; 15: 319-320.
11. Semere, D., Barata, J. Onori, M. Evolvable Systems: Developments and Advance., ISAM 2007 IEEE conference, Ann Arbor, Michigan, USA. July 2007.
12. Holland, J. H. Emergence - From Chaos to Order, Oxford University Press,Oxford, 1998.
13. Johnson, S. Emergence, Penguin group, London, 2001.
14. Barata de Oliveira, J.A.;" Coalition Based Approach for Shop Floor Agility- A multi-Agent Approach"; PhD thesis, Universidade Nova de Lisboa, January 2004

23

CONFIGURATION OF AN AUTONOMOUS DECENTRALIZED SDIGITAL FACTORY USING PRODUCT AND MACHINE AGENTS

Michiko Matsuda and Nobuyuki Sakao

Kanagawa Institute of Technology, matsuda@ic.kanagawa-it.ac.jp

The configuration of an autonomous decentralized manufacturing system using multi agent technology is proposed to get more flexibility. In this digital factory, all elements such as machine tool, assembly machine, AGV, and product are installed as agents. The product agents take the initiatives in the system. When a blank workpiece is put on the shop floor, the product agent is dynamically generated with the product model. The product agent can autonomously plan the manufacturing process and the allocation of machines for the production of the final product through negotiations with other product agents and machine agents. The trial implementation of product agents and machine tool agents has been done by structuring a virtual machining system.

1. INTRODUCTION

A high-mix very-low-volume production such as order-made production is accommodated by an autonomous decentralized manufacturing system. In this manufacturing system, a manufacturing activity unit such as a machine tool, assembly machine, robot, AGV (Automatic Guided Vehicle), and/or manufacturing cell has autonomous functionalities. Multi-agent technology is recently being well applied to construct such kind of virtual factory for production planning. In this virtual factory, manufacturing activity units, especially manufacturing devices, are configured as agents and flexible production planning is performed (Brussel et al., 1998) (McFarlane and Bussman, 2000) (Sugimura et al., 2003) (Fujii et al., 2004) In these cases, the system structure is a device oriented structure. To establish more flexible order-made production and to use manufacturing devices more efficiently, the digital factory should be configured by an event driven structure.

This paper proposes the configuration of an autonomous decentralized manufacturing system which is constructed based on an event driven system structure. In a manufacturing system, the occurrence of an event means that a workpiece for the product is input to the machining shop floor or that parts of the product are input to the assembly line. Then, a "product agent" is introduced as an actor for controlling the digital factory, and then the digital factory would be configured using this product agent.

Please use the following format when citing this chapter:

Matsuda, M. and Sakao, N., 2008, in IFIP International Federation for Information Processing, Volume 266, *Innovation in Manufacturing Networks;* ed. A. Azevedo; (Boston: Springer), pp. 215–222.

2. CONFIGURATION OF A DIGITAL FACTORY BASED ON PRODUCT AGENTS

In the proposed digital factory, products such as workpieces, parts, and sub-assembled parts are configured as agents in addition to all factory elements such as machine tools, assembly machines and AGVs. The former one is called a product agent, and the latter a machine agent.

The machine agent can determine which process is to be performed by itself and can schedule its own operations for allocated jobs. The product agent is an intelligent and autonomous software unit attached to the product. The substance of the product changes the form from workpiece to complete product through parts or sub-assembled parts. In the manufacturing processes, the product agent plans the processes and allocates the machine for executing the manufacturing processes required to turn the workpiece into the target product. This means that the product agent takes an initiative in the manufacturing system by communicating with other product agents and machine agents. The conceptual structure of the autonomous decentralized manufacturing system based on product agents is shown in Figure 1.

In Figure 1 there are two components constituting the shop floor. One is the machining line, and the other is the assembly line. The machining line is structured by several agents corresponding to machine tools or machining cells, and AGVs. The assembly line is also structured by several agents corresponding to assembly machines or assembly cells, and AGVs. Usually, at first, a product agent is generated when a workpiece is introduced in the machining line. The product agent plans its own machining processes to output complete parts. One of the agents is placed on the assembly line as the main part of the product. This product agent leads the assembly processes for producing the complete product by associating with the other agents for sub-parts. Some of sub parts are manufactured outside of the factory.

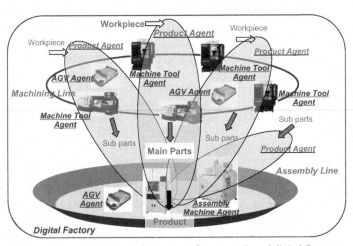

Figure 1. Conceptual structure of an agents based digital factory

3. TYPES OF AGENTS

3.1. Product Agents

The product agent autonomously plans and controls the entire process to evolve itself from workpiece to complete product. The product agent is a dynamic agent. It is created when the workpiece or part is input to the shop floor, and is deleted when the product is completed. Figure 2 shows the structure of a product agent. A product agent consists of a process planner, job allocator, and a transfer and machining requester. When a product agent is created, it has a product model which has the descriptions of the finished product. The process planner in the product agent performs machining process planning and assembly process planning by referring to manufacturing knowledge and machine data from a machine agent. The job allocator of the product agent schedules and allocates jobs according to each manufacturing machine's schedule. Once the job schedule is decided, the product agent requests an AGV to transfer itself and asks a manufacturing machine for execution of the operation.

The product agent is called a workpiece agent in the machining line of the factory and a main parts agent or sub parts agent in the assembly line. In the machining line, a workpiece changes the form of the parts. In the assembly line, parts are integrated into the product.

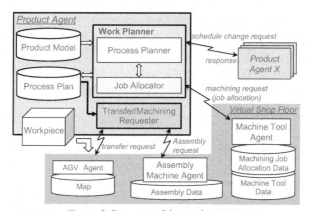

Figure 2. Structure of the product Agent

3.2. Machine Agents

Manufacturing machines in the factory are also agents which are called machine agents. The general structure of a machine agent is shown in Figure 3. A machine agent consists of operation planner, job scheduler, machine model and the machine itself. When the product agent asks whether a requested process can be performed by a machine, the machine agent determines which operations can be processed by the machine itself, generates its own schedule and replies with the possible operations and schedule to the product agent. Sometimes the product agent requests the machine agent to re-schedule the operation schedule because of an urgent job. Once a job is allocated, the machine agent schedules and controls the execution of this job. In this paper, there are two types of machine agents: machine tool agents and assembly agents.

The machine model is referred to by the operation planner and the job scheduler. In the machine model, the capability and specification of the machine is described. For example, the machine tool model consists of machine data and machining knowledge. The machine data consists of specifications of the machine tool itself, specifications of the ATC (Automatic Tool Changer), jig and fixture which are prepared. Machining knowledge is described by means of a parametric operation plan with applicable tools corresponding to feature type and feature size. The tool models are described by means of tool data which the machine tool is holding. Tool types are mill, drill, ream, and so on. The machine tool model is implemented using XML.

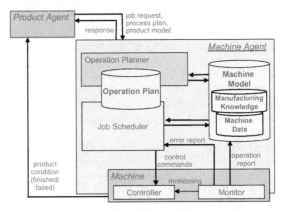

Figure 3. Structure of the machine agent

3.3. Other Agents in The Factory

The other elements of the factory are also agents. In the digital factory, all of the constituent elements are constructed as agents. For example, there are AGV agents, transfer machine agents and material handling tool agents.

4. AN AGENTS BASED DIGITAL FACTORY

4.1. Machining Line

The machining line in the digital factory consists of agents. Figure 4 is an UML sequence diagram which shows the sequence flow in the machining line. In this figure, only sequences for product agents and machine tool agents are drawn by omitting carrier devices such as AGV and transfer machine from a product agent view. A workpiece agent is a product agent in the machining line.

First in the sequence, several possible machining process plans are generated by the workpiece agent by referring to the product model and by communicating with machine tool agents to get machining knowledge and machine tool data. Second, the workpiece agent distributes some of the proposed process plans to all machine tool agents. Each machine tool agent makes an operation plan, schedules them if the plan is processed by itself and feeds back the results to the workpiece agent. Third, the workpiece agent selects the schedule from proposed plans and, if needed, negotiates with the other workpiece agents by requesting schedule changes according to the selected plan. After a successful negotiation, the workpiece agent modifies job allocation and scheduling status, and asks the machine tool agent to verify the machining job allocation schedule. Fourth, the workpiece agent requests an AGV for a transfer and asks the machine tool agent for execution of the machining. During machining job execution, the workpiece agent deliberates the requests from newly input workpiece agents. When the workpiece agent accepts the schedule change request, the agent requests the AGVs and machine tools to follow the new plan.

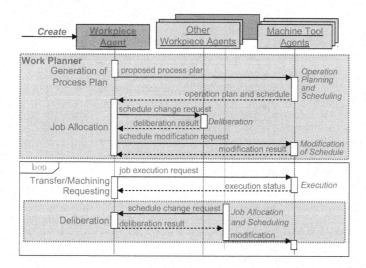

Figure 4. Sequence flow for the machining process

4.2. Assembly Line

The assembly line in the digital factory also consists of agents. Figure 5 is an UML sequence diagram which shows the sequence flow on the assembly line. In this figure, only sequences for product agents and assembly machine agents are drawn from a product agent view. The main parts agent and sub parts agents are product agents in the assembly line.

As in the machining line sequence, the main parts agent leads process planning and job allocation through communication with assembly machine agents. In this sequence, the main parts agents also confirms whether necessary sub parts are ready. Finally in the sequence, the main parts agent requests an AGV for a transfer of itself and any necessary sub parts and asks the assembly machine agent for execution of the assembly. During the execution, the main parts agent monitors the assembly process and asks for additional transfers of parts if necessary.

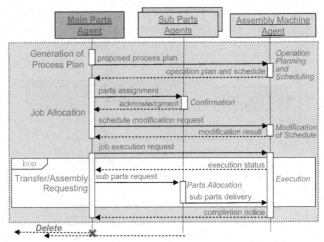

Figure 5. Sequence flow for the assembly process

5. TRIAL IMPLEMENTATION OF PLANNING SYSTEMS

5.1. Machine work planning using the workpiece agent

A machine tool agent for a machine work planning system was implemented. The machine tool model for the machine tool agent was installed using XML. The parametric process plans are listed for machining features in the model. The list of tools belonging to the machine tool and the specification of associated tools such as tool size, cutting speed and feed speed for material types are also described in the model using XML (Matsuda et al., 2006-1).

The machine work planning system using workpiece agents was virtually constructed and simulated on a computer. The workpiece agent is a product agent as mentioned above. The workpiece agent manager controls the timing of workpiece input to the shop floor in the trial system. When a workpiece is input, the corresponding product model is put on the blackboard model. Machine work scheduling is done by one-to-many workpiece agent negotiation after process planning. For example, Workpieces A, B and C are already on the shop floor. Workpiece D is input with some urgency. Machine A and B have the same specification. Before the negotiation, an optimized schedule is generated by applying a genetic algorism. According to this schedule, Workpiece Agent D negotiates with Workpiece Agent A, B and C at same time. If there is no delay in the turnaround time, the negotiation is successful. If the negotiation is not successful, another process plan for Workpiece D is selected and the procedure is repeated. The current schedule is also on the blackboard model. Figure 6 shows the display of this system. The display shows the detailed progress of the simulation. The left side of the window shows the job progress from the workpiece view. The right side of the window shows the job progress from the machine tool view (Matsuda et al., 2006-2) (Matsuda et al., 2007).

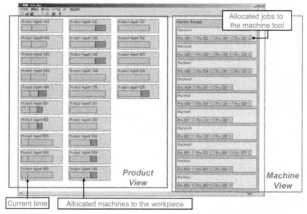

Figure 6. Display of the machining simulation

5.2. Assembly planning using the parts agent

The assembly planning system using parts agents was virtually constructed and simulated on a computer. The parts agent is also a product agent as mentioned above. In this system, assembly machine model in the machine agent and product model in the parts model are implemented using XML. Figure 7 shows the display of this system. In Figure 7, two kinds of cell phones are assembled. The main parts are electronic substrate. The main part agents of the substrate take the initiative in this assembly line. Machine 1 and 2 are for thread fastening. Machine 3 and 4 are adhesive machines. Two workers who supply parts to the machines are shown as Machine 5 and 6. Five lots of product are on the shop floor. The lower part of the display shows their current condition. The upper-left part of the display shows the planed work schedule from the product view and the machine view. The upper-right shows usage rate for each machine and completion rate for each of the products.

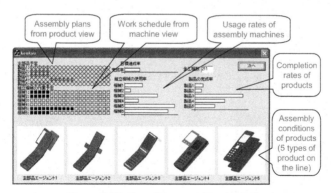

Figure 7. Display of the assembly simulation

6. CONCLUSIONS

An event driven configuration of the digital factory using agent technology is proposed in this paper. In this configuration, all elements of the factory including workpiece and parts are implemented as agents. The product agent which epitomizes workpiece and/or parts has the initiative in the manufacturing process and can autonomously decide on the production process and the allocation of manufacturing machines. The method for structuring a product agent and machine agent were also shown. Trial implementation of the machine work planning simulation systems using machine agents and product agents have shown the possibility for the construction of a more autonomous and flexible virtual manufacturing system. This configuration has the possibility to provide efficient usage of manufacturing machines for environment-conscious manufacturing.

6.1. Acknowledgments

The authors thank Toyota Caelum Inc. for useful assistance in developing the trial system. The authors are also grateful to Dr. Udo Graefe, retired from the National Research Council of Canada for his helpful assistance with the writing of this paper in English.

7. REFERENCES

1. Brussel, H. V., Wyns, J., Valckenaers, P., Bongaerts, L., Peeters, P. Reference architecture for holonic manufacturing systems: Prosa. Computers in Industry 1998; vol. 37, no. 1: 255 274.
2. Fujii, N., Kobayashi, M., Makita, T., Hatono, I., Ueda, K. "Integration of Facility Planning and Layout Planning Using Self-Organization in Semiconductor Manufacturing", Proc. of the 37th CIRP-ISMS, 2004, 175-180.
3. Matsuda, M., Ishikawa, Y., Utsumi, S. "Configuration of Machine Tool Agents for Flexible Manufacturing". Proc. of The 39th CIRP-ISMS, 2006, 351-357.
4. Matsuda, M., Utsumi, S., Ishikawa, Y. "Machine Work Planning Using Workpiece Agents in An Autonomous Decentralized Manufacturing System". In Knowledge Enterprise: Intelligent Strategies in Product Design, Manufacturing and Management, IFIP vol.207, 2006, 869-874.
5. Matsuda, M., Utsumi, S., Ishikawa, Y. "Configuration of an Autonomous Machining System Using Workpiece Agents". Proc. of The 40th CIRP-ISMS, 2007, CD-ROM.
6. McFarlane, D.C., Bussman, S. Developments in Holonic Production Planning and Control. Production Planning and Control 2000; vol. 11, no. 6: 522–536.
7. Sugimura, N., Shrestha, R., Inoue, J. "Integrated process planning and scheduling in holonic manufacturing systems -Optimization based on shop time and machining cost". Proc. of the 2003 IEEE International symposium on Assembly and task planning (ISATP2003), 2003, 36-41.

24

COMPARING WORKLOAD BASED ORDER RELEASE MECHANISMS

N.O. Fernandes
Instituto Politécnico de Castelo Branco
nogf@est.ipcb.pt

S. Carmo-Silva
Universidade do Minho
scarmo@dps.uminho.pt

A variety of orders release mechanisms have been developed for workload control. However, in many situations it is difficult to fully understand the behaviour of these mechanisms due to its complexity. In this paper order release mechanisms are compared by studying the influence of single release strategies. Simulation results show that real world order release mechanisms are likely to benefit from incorporating the workload balancing and the atemporal workload accounting over time strategies.

1. INTRODUCTION

Workload Control (WLC) is a Production Planning and Control (PPC) concept, particularly appropriate for jobbing and flow shops in the make-to-order (MTO) sector of industry (Haskose et al., 2004). It has received much attention both from researchers and practitioners alike, particularly due to its simplicity and similarity to what is done in practice. WLC is an approach applied to control workload in the shop floor. The main principle is to keep the length of queues on the shop floor at appropriate levels to meet the promised deliver dates, taking into account the system capacity and capabilities.

Orders release is a main control element within WLC. It determines the moment and the orders (jobs) to release into the shop floor. Orders arrive from customers over time but they are not immediately released, rather they are collected in a pre-shop pool. The collected orders are assessed periodically and are only released if they fit workload norms for the required capacity groups (e.g. machines). The decision to release an order is usually based on its urgency and influence on the current shop floor situation (Henrich et al., 2004). Once released, a job remains in the shop floor until all of its operations have been completed. Priority dispatching rules determines which orders or jobs in queue, should be selected next for processing in a resource or machine that becomes available. This clearly influences the progress of individual orders through the shop floor. Due to easy handling and general industrial acceptance, a variety of such rules have been devised for application in the shop floor. Ramasesh (1990) makes a review on this topic.

Several order release mechanisms have been developed for workload control. Graves et al. (1995), Bergamaschi et al. (1997) and Fowler et al. (2002) review literature on this matter. Two of the most known mechanisms proposed in the literature are the Load Oriented Order Release (LOOR) (Bechte, 1988) and the Lancaster University Management School (LUMS) approach (Hendry and Kingsman, 1991, Stevenson and

Please use the following format when citing this chapter:

Fernandes, N.O. and Carmo-Silva, S., 2008, in IFIP International Federation for Information Processing, Volume 266, *Innovation in Manufacturing Networks*; ed. A. Azevedo; (Boston: Springer), pp. 223–230.

Hendry, 2006). However, until now no mechanism has shown to be the best for order release and production control over a wide range of conditions. This is due partly to the following:

(1) Order release mechanisms performance highly depends on production control conditions, such as dispatching rules and shop load;

(2) The shop floor operation conditions, i.e. type of manufacturing system, processing times variability, due date tightness when set externally (e.g. by the customer), and machine unavailability, can have a major impact on the mechanisms overall performance; and

(3) Different mechanisms have been evaluated by addressing them as a whole, rather than by setting reference to their inherent structure. This remark have leaded Cigolini and Portioli (2002) to suggest that, comparative analysis should be performed by considering two or more order release mechanisms not as a whole, but by switching single features, each of them related with different characteristics of the release procedure.

To this respect Bergamaschi et al. (1997) classifies order release mechanisms based on eight dimensions that describe the fundamental principles, characteristics and logic of the mechanisms. In this paper, we adopted the above methodology comparing order release mechanisms that only differ by the strategies used in the workload control and the workload accounting over time dimensions. In particular we studied the influence two typical shop configurations on the performance of these strategies. The results of this study should contribute to the choice of the appropriate order release mechanism in practical situations.

The remainder of the paper is outlined as follows: section 2 addresses the overall research methodology and introduces the general structure of the order release strategies tested; section 3 presents, analyses and discusses the results of the simulation study; and finally in section 4, concluding remarks are made and directions for future research work are presented.

2. RESEARCH METHODOLOGY

In order to evaluate the influence of the shop configuration on order release strategies behaviour, a simulation study was carried out using Arena software. During simulation runs, data were collected with reference to the system steady state. The simulation runs last for 27600 time units. For each simulation run 90 independent replications were performed. To avoid initialization bias a warm-up period of 9600 time units was used. Common random numbers were used as a variance reduction technique across all experiments.

This section details the simulation model and the release strategies tested.

2.1. Simulation Model

A job shop without an explicit bottleneck has been the starting point of this investigation. The job shop consists of six work centres each containing a single multi-purpose machine. In the simulation model, the job's routing is randomly chosen from a set of twenty routings each of which with an equal probability of occurrence, see Table 1.

Because most real life job shops exhibit a prevalent flow pattern, Enns (1995) argues that these shops have most in common with the theoretical general flow shop. So, a general flow shop was also considered in the simulation study. Routings for this shop are established in a way similar, only with work centres being visited in order of increasing work centre number. This ensures that the flow between any combinations of two work centres will always have the same direction, as required in general flow shops.

Table 1. Work centre job routing matrix

Routing pattern	Operation number					
	1	2	3	4	5	6
1	2	4	6	1	5	3
2	1	3	5			
3	2	3	5	4		
4	5					
5	4	2	5	6	1	
6	2	5	4	6	1	3
7	1	3	2	6		
8	2	6				
9	2	5	4			
10	3	1	5	4	6	2
11	6	2	3			
12	2	6	1	3	2	
13	2	3	6			
14	4	1	2	5	3	
15	1					
16	4	3	6	5	1	
17	4					
18	3	4	6	5		
19	4	1	6			
20	4	1				

As a result of the number of operations in each of the twenty routings indicated in Table 1, the mean number of operations per routing is 3.6. Processing times for all machines are identical, following a 2-Erlang distribution with a mean of 1 time unit. According to Oosterman et al. (2000) the 2-Erlang distribution approaches well the observations made in real life job shops. An average planned system utilization of 90% is ensured by setting the appropriate time between jobs arrivals. An exponential distribution is used for the jobs inter-arrivals times, as this typically explains the stochastic nature of job arrivals.

Due dates are assigned to jobs on their arrival and are modelled as a random variable. They are established to ensure that, under immediate release, the number of tardy jobs falls between 5% and 10%. This is determined by the jobs arrival time plus a uniformly distributed allowance between 50.8 and 60.8 time units. After the assignment of the due date, jobs are placed in the pre-shop pool, waiting for release. Job release decisions are made periodically, every 8 time units, in the beginning of each *release period*. Each job is considered for release according to the earliest planned release time. Planned release times are determined by backward scheduling from the due date, using the work centres lead times, as follows:

$$r_j = d_j - \sum_{s \in S_j} LT_s \qquad [1]$$

Where LT_s is the work centre lead time, r_j is the planned release time of job j, d_j is the planned job j due date and S_j is the set of work centres in the job's routing. Planned work centre lead times were established through some pilot simulation runs, also using immediate release.

The order release mechanism ensures that a job candidate for release is released only if it fits the established workload norms for the required capacity groups. Every job in the pool with a planned release time within a *time limit* is a candidate. However, it has been shown (Land, 2006) that imposing such a *time limit* tend to deteriorate the performance of order release mechanisms. Thus, in this study no time limit is placed on the release of jobs.

Released jobs follow a first-in-first-out (FIFO) dispatching rule on the shop floor in all work centres. Setup times have been considered sequence independent and assumed as part of the operation processing time.

2.2. Order release strategies

Two strategies for workload accounting over time and three for workload control were simulated. The strategies simulated were chosen because they are frequently used and considered to be important in several order release mechanisms (Oosterman et al., 2000, Cigolini and Portioli, 2002).

Workload accounting over time, defines the method of accounting the load of a released job, establishing when and how much of this load should be allocated to each work centre or capacity group. Workload accounting is simulated at two levels or strategies: (1) atemporal and (2) probabilistic.

The *probabilistic* strategy, accounts for the actual direct load of a work centre (the quantity of work resulting from jobs queued and being processed at the work centre) at the time of release and estimates the input to this load during the release period, resulting from jobs at upstream work centres, using an estimation method called load conversion (Bechte, 1988). This method is detailed by Breithaupt et al. (2002).

Under an *atemporal* strategy a released job is assumed to instantaneously add up load to each work centre or capacity group on the basis of the job processing time. This means that a job is included in the accounted load of a work centre upon release, and excluded as soon as the operation at that work centre is concluded, thus considering the upstream load (the quantity of work resulting from jobs queued and being processed at upstream work centres) in the same way as the direct load. The accounted load under this strategy is based on adjusted aggregated load method (Oosterman et al., 2000).

Workload control influences job release decisions in order to maintain the load on the shop floor under control. Workload control is simulated at three levels or strategies: (1) upper bound, (2) lower bound and (3) workload balancing.

Under an *upper bound* workload control, the release of a job to the shop floor is allowed only if workload in all work centres of a job routing does not exceed an *upper limit*. This means that a job will not be released if, as a result, at least in one work centre of the job routing the workload becomes larger than the upper workload limit established.

The *lower bound* workload control seeks to avoid 'starving' of work centres by ensuring that workload in all the work centres is above the *lower limit*. This means that a job will be released if at least in one work centre in the job routing the workload is lower than the lower workload limit.

Workload balancing releases a job only if it contributes to a better load balancing among work centres even if the upper workload limit is exceeded. However, the load at each work centre in the job's routing is not allowed to exceed the upper limit in more than 20%. This 20% value was established after some pilot simulation runs, ensuring good results. The workload balancing measure employed was the follow index (BI):

$$BI = \frac{\sum_i F_{ij}}{\max_i F_{ij} \ m} \qquad (i = 1, ..., m) \qquad [2]$$

Where F_{ij} represents the accounted workload on work centre i resulting from releasing job j into the shop floor, and m represents the number of work centres. As can easily be guessed the best balancing situation is obtained when BI equals one.

3. SIMULATION RESULTS AND DISCUSSION

This section presents and discusses the results of the simulation study described in the preceding section. We recorded two main performance measures, namely shop flow time and time in system. The former is defined as the time that elapses between job release and job completion. The latter is defined as the time a job spends waiting in the pre-shop pool plus the shop flow time.

Figures 1 and 2 shows the time in system behaviour for each one of the strategies tested. Figure 1 shows the results for the job shop configuration. Figure 2 shows the results for the general flow shop. In these figures, the average value of the time in system is plotted against the average value of the shop flow time. Superior strategies yield a lower time in system for a given shop flow time, i.e. will have a curve which is shifted down and to the left. A point on the curve is the result of simulating an order release strategy at a specific workload level or norm.

For each of the release strategies, appropriate values for the workload norms, have to be determined. In particularly, we want to compare the strategies based on the time in system at different levels of norm tightness. However, norm levels for each of the strategies cannot be compared directly, because they result in different shop flow times. So we use the shop flow time as an intermediate variable. According to Oosterman et al. (2000) norms of two mechanisms or strategies are equally tight, if they result in the same shop flow time.

As can be seen, curves converge at the higher values of the shop flow time. This is the result of an infinite workload norm level, i.e. the upper or lower limits, according to the workload control strategy, are both very large. As could be expect all strategies give the same results if release is not restricted by workload norms, as it happens in this case for very large values of workload norm levels. However, as norms get particularly tighter, i.e. as shop flow time decreases below a certain point, time in system tends to increase substantially. To some extent, the waiting time in the shop floor tend to be replaced, by the waiting time in the pre-shop pool of orders. However, since the time in system is the sum of the pool time and the shop floor time, we can conclude that waiting times in the pool increase more than waiting times in the shop floor decrease.

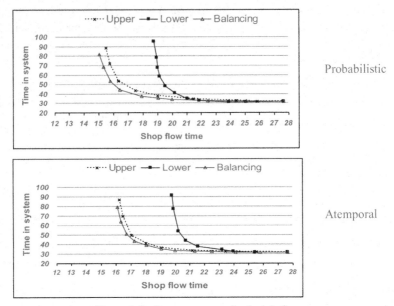

Figure 1. Performance curves for the job shop

Analysis of results of the job shop configuration leads following conclusions.

First, the lower bound workload control strategy does not lend itself to as good control as the upper and balancing strategies do. In fact, it cannot achieve the shop flow time reduction that the others can. This holds for both, atemporal and probabilistic workload accounting strategies.

Second, workload balancing performs slightly better than the upper bound control strategy under both, probabilistic and atemporal strategies, particularly for tighter workload norms, i.e. low values of time in system.

Third, the performance of the workload accounting strategies seems not to be independent of the workload control strategy adopted. Comparing strategies at a shop flow time of 19 time units (i.e. about a 31% reduction of shop flow time relatively to unrestricted periodic release), we may see that under the lower bound workload control, the probabilistic approach performs visibly better than the atemporal one. However, under the balancing or the upper bound workload control strategies, the probabilistic approach performs similarly to the atemporal one.

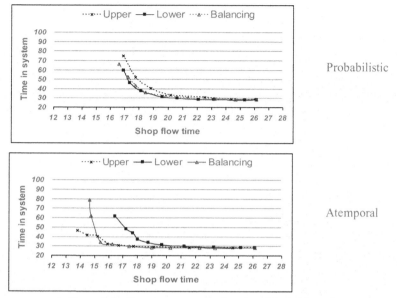

Figure 2. Performance curves for the general flow shop

Analysis of results for the general flow shop case leads to the following conclusions.

First, the performance of the probabilistic strategy deteriorates in the presence of direct work flow, typical of flow shops, both under the upper bound and workload balancing strategies. This can be observed comparing figures 1 and 2.

Second, the performance of the lower bound workload control strategy clearly improves for both, atemporal and probabilistic workload accounting strategies in relation to the job shop case. As work flow becomes more direct, operating differences between workload control strategies become less visible, and similar results may be expected.

Third, consistently with the observation made in the job shop configuration, performance of the workload accounting strategies does not seem to be independent of the workload control strategy adopted.

Fourth, it is not evident that workload balancing improves order release compared with the upper workload control strategy. We may explain this by the fact that as job routing becomes more direct, fewer jobs can be found in the pool that contributes to improve the balance index (BI), reason why the two strategies perform similarly. Note that in our simulation processing times for all machines are identical and balancing opportunities become exclusively dependent on jobs routings.

4. CONCLUSIONS

Order release mechanisms are strategically important for the economic success of companies having a great influence on system operations performance.

In this study computer simulation was used for evaluating the behaviour of several order release strategies related with workload control and workload accounting over time, instead of evaluating order release mechanisms as a whole. Results are based on a job shop and a general flow shop.

Two important conclusions could be drawn. Frist, even if results show that no single workload control strategy performs best in any condition, overall results show that 'workload balancing' is the best overall performer while the 'lower bound' is the worst.

Second, performance of the workload accounting strategies does not seem to be independent of the workload control strategy adopted. Results also suggest that, incorporating 'atemporal' workload accounting over time in combination with 'workload balancing' in order release mechanisms used in practice, it is likely to offer good system operating performance.

Although some insights point out the utility of the study for practical use, it is important to extend it to a wider spectrum of order release strategies and dimensions in order to get an in dept understanding of the full complexity behind order release mechanisms.

5. REFERENCES

1. Bechte W. Theory and practice of load-oriented manufacturing control. International Journal of Production Research 1988; 26(3), 375-395.
2. Bergamaschi D, Cigolini R, Perona M, Porioli A. Order review and release strategies in a job shop environment: a review and classification. International Journal of Production Research 1997; 35(2): 339-420.
3. Breithaupt JW, Land J, Nyhuis, P. The workload control concept: theory and practical extensions of Load Oriented Order Release. Production Planning and Control 2002; 13(7): 625-638.
4. Cigolini R, Portioli A. An experimental investigation on workload limiting methods within ORR policies in a job shop environment. International Journal of Production Research 2002; 13(7): 602-613.
5. Fowler JW, Hogg GL, Mason, SJ. Workload control in the semiconductor industry. Production Planning and Control 2002; 13(7): 568-578.
6. Graves RJ, Konopka JM, Milne RJ. Literature review of materials flow control mechanisms. Production Planning and Control 1995; 6(5): 395-403.
7. Haskose A, Kingsman BG, Worthington, D. Performance analysis of make-to-order manufacturing systems under different workload control regimes. International Journal of Production Economics 2004; 90(2): 169-186.
8. Hendry L, Kingsman BG. A decision support system for job release in make-to-order companies. International Journal of Operations and Production Management 1991; 11: 6-16.
9. Henrich P, Land M, Gaalman GJC. Exploring applicability of the workload control concept. International Journal of Production Economics 2004; 90(2): 187-198.
10. Land, M. Parameters and sensitivity in workload control. International Journal of Production Economics 2006; 104(2), 625-638.
11. Oosterman B, Land M, Gaalman GJC. The influence of shop characteristics on workload control. International Journal of Production Economics 2000; 68: 107-119.
12. Ramasesh R. Dynamic Job shop scheduling: a survey of simulation research. Omega 1990; 18(1): 43-57.
13 Stevenson M, Hendry L. Aggregated Load-oriented workload control: A review and re-classification of a key approach. International Journal of Production Economics 2006; 104(2): 676-693.

25

NEURAL NETWORK MODELING AND
SIMULATION OF THE SCHEDULING

Ricardo Lorenzo Avila Rondon

Facultad de Ingeniería, Universidad de Holguín, Cuba. ricardo@cadcam.uho.edu.cu

Adriano da Silva Carvalho

Facultade de Engenharia, Universidade do Porto, Portugal. asc@fe.up.pt

Guillermo Infante Hernández

Facultad de Ingeniería, Universidad de Holguín, Cuba. guillermo@cadcam.uho.edu.cu

A three layer feed forward neural network was constructed and tested to analyze the scheduling process on single machine. The operating variables studied are the operation, processing time, setup time, deadline time, duedate time, priority, machine, and fabric color. These variables were used as input to the constructed neural network in order to predict the scheduling completion time as the output on a single machine. Three layer feed forward network trained with error back propagation learning rule are used. The constructed network was found to be precise in modeling the scheduling for the operating conditions studied and also, in predicting the scheduling for the new input data which are kept unaware of the trained neural network.

1. INTRODUCTION

Scheduling is a decision making process of allocating limited resources (machines at a workshop, runways at an airport, crews at construction site) to activities (operation in a workshop, takeoffs and landings, stages at a construction project) over time (Pinedo, 2005). Generally resources are identified with machine and activities with tasks or jobs. A schedule is a job sequence determined for every machine of the processing system. Scheduling in the context of manufacturing involves finding a sequential allocation of competing resources that optimizes a particular objective function, subject to certain constrains.

Job shop scheduling has generated a great of research (Johnson 1954), (Adams et al. 1988), (Dell'Amico and Trubian 1993), Foo et al. 1995, Yamada and Nakano 1996). In job-shop scheduling the parts may flow in different directions, also a machine can be visited more than once by the same part, and it's objective might be to minimize the makespan or maximize machine utilization, subject to constraints such as the number of machines, plant capacity, labour availability, and so on.

Another mode of processing in correspondence with the way parts visit machines is known as flow shop, when all parts flow in one direction.

The scheduling models are specified (Pinedo, 2005) according to three field classification $\alpha|\beta|\gamma$ where: α specifies the machine environment, β specifies the job characteristics, and γ specifies the optimality criterion.

Please use the following format when citing this chapter:

Rondon, R.L., Carvalho, A.S. and Hernández, G.I., 2008, in IFIP International Federation for Information Processing, Volume 266, *Innovation in Manufacturing Networks;* ed. A. Azevedo; (Boston: Springer), pp. 231–238.

2. SCHEDULING

2.1. Machine environment

a) Single stage systems.

- If there is a single or dedicated machine (m = 1), each job should be processed by that machine exactly once. Here $\alpha = 1$, and p_j is the processing time of job j.
- If there are several parallel machines $\{M_1, M_2, ..., M_n\}$, each job can be processed by any machine. Here $\alpha = P$, and p_{ij} is the processing time of job j on machine i.

b) Multistage systems

   In this case each job should be processed on each machine from the set $\{M_1, M_2, ..., M_n\}$. Here $\alpha = F$ (for flow shop, a job j is processed first on machine 1, then on machine 2, and finally on machine n), or $\alpha = J$ (for job shop, each job has it own route to fallow), or $\alpha = O$ (for open shop, each job can be processed by the machines in an arbitrary order).

2.2. Job environment

There are n jobs N = {1, ..., n}. For job j there may be given also. Figure1.
   w_j - weight (the importance or priority of the job)
   p_j – process time (the time the job is processed on the system)
   r_j - release time (the time the job arrives at the system)
   s_j – start time (the time the job start on the system)
   c_j - completion time (the time the job end on the system)
   d_j - due date (the time the job is promised to the customer)

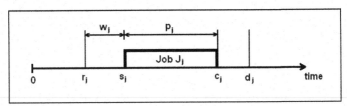

Figure 1. Graphics representation of job parameters

2.3. Optimality criterion

The objective is to construct a schedule that minimizes a given objective function F.
   Usually function F depends on job completion times Cj, j = 1, ..., n, where Cj is the completion time of the last operation of job j.
   Common objective functions are:
   Makespan: $C_{max} = \max \{C_j, | j = 1, ..., n \}$

   Total completion time: $\sum C_j = \sum_{j=1}^{n} C_j$

   Total weighted completion time: $\sum w_j C_j = \sum_{j=1}^{n} w_j C_j$

Other objective functions depend on due date d_j. It is defined for each job j:
Lateness of job j: $L_j = c_j - d_j$. The latest time at which a job j can be completed.
Earliness: $Ej = \max \{0, d_j - c_j\}$. The amount of time between the d_j and c_j.
Tardiness: $Tj = \max \{0, c_j - d_j\}$. The amount of time between the c_j and d_j.

2.4. Approaches to Scheduling Problems

The input size of a typical scheduling problem is bounded by the number of job n, the number of machines m. An algorithm is said to be polynomial if it's running time is bounded by a polynomial in input size. Polynomials algorithms are sometimes called efficient or simply good. The class of all polynomial solvable problems is called class $\mathcal{P}$.

Another class of optimization problems is known as NP-hard problem (NP stand for non-deterministic polynomial). In this case, complete enumeration of all the solutions to identify the optimal one is not practical. Very often technological constrains demand that each job should be processed through the machines in a particular order.

There are many techniques applied to find a solution to the different scheduling models, all of them are in correspondence with model classification, problem size, optimality criteria, and son.

Given a scheduling problem we first need to determine its complexity status. This is done either by designing a polynomial time algorithm for it solution or by proving that the problem is NP-hard. Once it is known the problem is NP-hard, it is necessary to determine the solution type: exact or approximate. It is unlikely that an exact solution can be found by a polynomial time algorithm. In any case, for problems of practical interest only small size instances can be handled by exact methods.

In order to find a good solution within an acceptable amount of time, two types of algorithms can be developed: approximation algorithms and heuristic algorithms.

An algorithm is called an approximation algorithm if it is possible to establish analytically how close the generated solution is to the optimum (either in the worst case or on average). Approximation algorithm produces solutions in polynomial time, but for the price of loss of optimality. The solutions found are guaranteed to be within a fixed percentage of the actual optimum.

The performance of a heuristic algorithm is usually analyzed experimentally, through a number of runs using either generated instances or known benchmark instances. Heuristic algorithms can be very simple but still effective. Most of modern heuristics are based on various ideas of locals search (neighborhood search (Hurink, 1998), tabu search, simulated annealing, genetic algorithms (Dorigo and Stutzle, 2004), (Pinedo, 2005), and so on). Heuristic algorithms produce feasible solutions which are not guaranteed to be close to optimum.

2.5. Case study

The case study considered in this paper is similar to the paper mill mentioned by (Pinedo, 2005). The input to textile mill is cotton, polyester or other fiber the output is finished rolls of cotton fabric, or wool fabric, or synthetic material. At the heart of the textile mill are its textile machines, which are very large and represent a significant capital investment. The end of this process produces various types of fabric which are characterized by their basis weights, grades and colors.

Master production plans for these machines are typically drawn up on an annual basis. The projected schedules are cyclic with cycle times weekly. A particular type of fabric may be produced in every cycle, or every other cycle, or even less often, always depending on demand.

Every time the machine switches over from one combination of grade of fabric to another there is a setup cost involved. During the changeover the machine keeps on producing fabric. Since the fabric produced during a changeover does not meet any of the required specifications, it is either sold at a steep discount or considered wasted into the production system.

The production plan tries to maximize production, while minimizing inventory costs. Maximizing production implies minimizing changeover times. This means longer production runs, which in turn result in higher inventory cost. The overall production plan is a trade off between setup and inventory cost.

2.6. Mathematical Formulation

Consider a single machine and n jobs as it is depicted in (Pinedo, 2005). Job j has a processing time p_j, a release date r_j and a due date d_j. If $r_j = 0$ and $d_j = \infty$, then the processing of a job j is basically unconstrained. It is clear that the makespan C_{max} in a single machine environment does not depend on the schedule. For various other objectives certain priority rules generate optimal schedules. If the objective to be minimized is the total weighted completion time and the processing of the job j is unconstrained, then the Weighted Shortest Processing Time first (WSPT) rule, which schedules the jobs in decreasing order of w_j/p_j, is optimal. If the objective is the maximum lateness L_{max} and the jobs are all released at time 0, then the Earliest Due Date first (EDD) rule, which schedules the jobs in increasing order of dj, is optimal.

Other objectives, such as the total tardiness $\sum T_j$ and the total weighted tardiness $\sum w_j T_j$ are much harder to optimize than the total weighted completion time or the maximum lateness. A heuristic for the total weighted tardiness objective is described in (Dorigo and Stutzle, 2004), (Glover, 1989), (Pinedo, 2005).

In general for this case, n jobs have to be sequentially processed on a single machine. Each job j has a processing time p_j, a weight w_j, and a due date d_j associated, and the jobs become available for processing at time zero. The tardiness of a job j is defined as $T_j = \max \{0, C_j - d_j\}$, where C_j is the completion time of job j in the current job sequence. The goal is to find a job sequence which minimizes the sum of the weighted tardiness given by

$$\sum_{i=1}^{n} w_i T_i$$

When the jobs in a single machine problem have different release date rj, then the problems tend to become significantly more complicated.

2.7. Experimental data

It was considered the follow real data: operation, processing time, setup time, deadline time, duedate time, priority, machine, and color. Initially the data are in worksheet format file. The data are arranged in a 75 by 6 matrix corresponding to one work day in a factory. For convenience the matrix is divided into two data sets, the first 55 rows as training set and the rest as a testing set.

3. NEURAL NETWORK MODELING

Neural network consists of a number of interconnected artificial neurons which are divided into three groups, namely: input, hidden and output layers. To construct the network, following steps are to be followed. First, weighting factors are divided from back propagation learning algorithm. The weighted inputs are summed and transferred through the sigmoid function of neurons to obtain outputs. The output is propagated along the outgoing of connecting weights to become the input of neurons on next layer. In the present study a multiple layer feed forward network with two layers was constructed. Multiple layer networks can approximate any function very well. Feed forward ANN allows signals to flow only in one direction, i.e., from input to output.

The feed forward ANN adjust the transfer function that is associated with the inputs and outputs. In the present study, initially a network with five hidden layer was constructed and was trained to simulate the scheduling process for various operating conditions. The detailed structure of the network and the training strategy of the constructed neural network are shown in Figure 2 and Figure 3 respectively. Figure 3 shows the feed forward network with to hidden layers. P1 is the input vector to the hidden layer, W1 and b1 represents the weight and bias of the hidden layer.

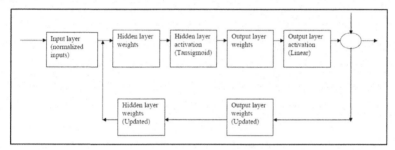

Figure 2. Training strategy of the constructed feed forward artificial network

The information from the hidden layer is transferred to the output layer as shown in Figure 3. The terms P2 represent the output vector and can be determined from the weight, W2 and bias b2 of the output layer. In the present research a *tansig* function and a *purelin* function was used as the propagation functions in the hidden layer and in the output layer respectively.

The training strategy of the network is shown in Figure 2. As shown in Figure 2, the input vectors and the corresponding output vectors are used to train the network until it approximates the propagation function. Thus the bias and the weights can be obtained from the training procedure which is based on the experimental data.

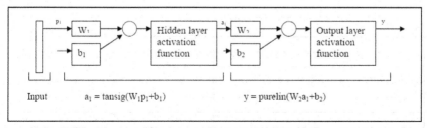

Figure 3. Two layer network structure and the flow of information within the network

In the present study, the operation, processing time, setup time, duedate time, priority, and fabric color treated are as the input vector and the corresponding completion time was defined as the output vector to train the neural network.

The neural network toolbox Version 4 of MATLAB, Mathworks Inc., was used for simulation. The input vectors and the target vector was normalized before training such that they fall in the interval of 0 to 1, so that their standard deviation and mean will below the value of 1. The experimental data used for targets and the experimentally determined target values were pre-processed so that the mean and the standard deviation is 0 and 1.

The experimental conditions and the corresponding experimentally determined completion time were set as the input and the target vectors, respectively. The neural network was trained in a batch mode. The training was made using the Levenberg-Marquardts training strategy.

Training the neural networks by the Levenberg-Marquardt algorithm is sensitive to the number of neurons in the hidden layer. The more the number of neurons, the better is the performance of the neural network in fitting the data. However, too many neurons in the hidden layer may result in the over fitting. During the training process, the number of neurons in the hidden layer was changed during the training process while optimizing the transfer function for the given input and output vectors. In order to avoid the problems due to the over fitting, a Bayesian regularization technique in combination with the Levenberg-Marquardt's algorithm was used during the ANN training process.

The Bayesian algorithm works best when the networks input and output are scaled within range of -1 to +1. After several trials, the neural network with 10 neurons in the hidden layer was found to be excellent in representing the scheduling process. In the hidden layer, initially three types of transfer functions namely the exponential sigmoid, tangent sigmoid and linear functions were tested while training the neural network. The linear function was used at the output layer. A tansigmoid function in the hidden layer and the linear function at the output layer are found to be excellent in predicting the scheduling completion time irrespective of the initial operating variable condition. The training is stopped until the convergence is reached and the network is set ready for the prediction.

The convergence is reached when the sum of the squared errors and the weights and biases reach some constant values. The normalized targets were converted back to the original target values. The training program was terminated when the neural network has truly converged. The network is converged if the sum of the squared errors and the sum of the squared weights are nearly constant over several iterations.

The details of the completely trained neural network used in the present study to design the scheduling completion time are given in table 1. Figure 4 shows a comparison between actual targets and predicted completion time by ANN. From the Figure 4, it can be observed that the developed neural network was found to be excellent in predicting scheduling completion time for various operating conditions.

Table 1. Details of the trained neural network used to predict the completion time in the scheduling on single machine

Type	Value/comment
Layer 1	6 neurons
Layer 2	5 neurons
Layer 3	1 neuron
Number of data used for training	75 (one machine, one work day)
Function in hidden layer	Tansigmoid
Function of output layer	Linear

3.1 Results

The accuracy of the newly constructed neural network was verified using regression analysis and correlation coefficient. The correlation coefficient between the experimentally determined $c_{experiment}$ and the c_{ann} determined by the neural network was found to be 0.886 with slope equal 0.95. The high correlation coefficient confirms that the newly constructed ANN was highly precise in predicting the scheduling completion time solutions.

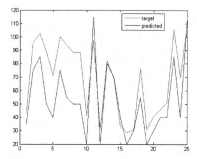

Figure 4. Comparison between actual targets and predictions

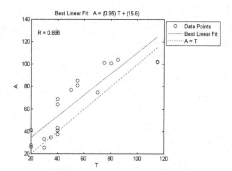

Figure 5. Regression graphic to judge scheduling ANN

From design point of view it would be helpful to use know the amount of data at any time irrespective of the operating conditions. Thus the constructed network was used to simulate the production system for new operating conditions that are kept unaware of the trained neural network. For simulation purpose, new inputs which are not used while training was feed to the trained neural network and the corresponding completion time were determined from the neural network. Figure 5 shows the plot of predicted c_{ann} using the trained network and the $c_{experiment}$ calculated experimentally for various initial operating conditions. From Figure 5, it can be observed that the newly constructed neural network was precise in predicting the scheduling completion time with a higher correlation coefficient of 0.886.

4. CONCLUSIONS

In this study we presented an artificial neural network for the one-machine scheduling problem. This shows the developed neural network model can be precise in predicting the scheduling. Another advantage of the newly constructed neural network model over the theoretical models is its accuracy to predict the completion time for any initial production data. The present study and some of our previous works suggested the strong influence of the operating variables on the scheduling completion time. It is a highly complicate process to propose a generalized expression correlating the operating variables involved in the production system with the scheduling priority. The constructed network was trained considering all the operating variables of the system making the neural network precise enough to predict the scheduling for any operating condition. Though the lab scale study is limited to the range of operating variables studied, it is always possible to introduce new inputs to train the network whenever new experimental data are available. The future work is aimed to extend this idea for the logical link between process planning and scheduling systems.

5. REFERENCES

1. Adams, J., Balas, E., Zawack, D. The shifting bottleneck procedures for job shop scheduling. Management Science 1988; 34 (3): 391–401.
2. Dell'Amico, M., Trubian, M. Applying tabu searches to the job shop scheduling problem. Annals of Operations Research 1993; Vol. 41: 231-252.
3. Dorigo, M., and Stutzle, T. Ant Colony Optimization. A Bradford Book. The MIT Press. ISBN 0-262-04219-3, 2004.
4. Foo, Y.P.S., Takefuji, Y. Integer linear programming neural networks for job-shop scheduling. In: Proceedings of Joint International Conference on Neural Networks 1988; vol. 2: 341–348.
5. Glover, F. Tabu search. Part I. ORSA J. Computing 1989; Vol. 1: 190-206.
6. Hurink, J.L. Memorandum No. 1449. An exponential neighborhood for a one-machine batching problem. ISSN 0169-2690. July 1998.
7. Johnson, S. M. Optimal two-and three stage production schedules with setup times included. Nav. Res. Logistics Q., 1954; 1(1): 61–68.
8. Pinedo, M. L. Planning and Scheduling in Manufacturing and Services. Springer Series in Operation Research. ISBN 0-387-22198-0, 2005.
9. Van Laarhoven, P.J.M., Aarts, E.H.L. Job shop scheduling by simulated annealing. Operations Research 1992; Vol. 40, no 1: 113-125.

26

MANUFACTURING SYSTEMS OF THE FUTURE: A MULTI-DISCIPLINARY APPROACH

Regina Frei and José Barata

Department of Electrotechnical Engineering, New University of Lisbon
{regina.frei, jab}@uninova.pt

Successful manufacturing systems for the future have to be based on know-how
originating from more than the traditional manufacturing domains. Approaches such
as Reconfigurable Manufacturing Systems, the Agile Assembly Architecture and
Holonic Manufacturing Systems go into the right direction; combined with
approaches known from Mobile Robotics, Collective Artificial Intelligence and
Complexity Science, there is considerable potential for creative solutions to the
problems of low volume – high change productions. Systems must be enabled to self-
organize, take profit of emergence and become more autonomous.
More due to human factors than due to technical reasons, system autonomy and
emergence belong to industry's worst nightmares. It is therefore crucial to address
this fear while at the same time working on reliable methods and tools.

Keywords: Evolvable Assembly Systems, Reconfigurable Production Systems, Automation, Autonomous Systems, Emergence

1. INTRODUCTION

The field of manufacturing paradigms targeting at low volume – high change production systems is relatively scattered. There are **Reconfigurable Manufacturing Systems** (ElMaraghy 2006), **Holonic Manufacturing Systems** (Ulieru 2004; Valckenaers and Van Brussel 2005; Colombo, Schoop et al. 2006), **Biological Manufacturing Systems** (Ueda 2006), the **Agile Assembly Architecture** (Rizzi, Gowdy et al. 1997; Kume and Rizzi 2001) and **Evolvable Assembly Systems** (Onori 2002; Frei, Ribeiro et al. 2007). Diverse topics serve to justify their specific focus or orientation of these approaches – be it Biology, Self-Organization, Holarchies or Mobile Robots or **Emergent intelligence in MAS for industry** (Rzevski and Skobelev 2007).

Most of them use nowadays Multi-Agent Systems as their control solution (Monostori, Vancza et al. 2006). It has been broadly recognised that for production systems which require optimality and which rarely undergo changes while producing high volumes of identical products, the hierarchical control approach works in satisfying manner, but the challenges of agile manufacturing for small volumes, many variants, frequent changes and dynamic conditions make it less favorable.

Many research domains are relevant for bringing the manufacturing systems of the future to success. There is abundant know-how available in the scientific world; the challenge is to gather it and combine it into a consistent framework. A corresponding article is to be submitted soon in a journal.

Please use the following format when citing this chapter:

Frei, R. and Barata, J., 2008, in IFIP International Federation for Information Processing, Volume 266, *Innovation in Manufacturing Networks;*
ed. A. Azevedo; (Boston: Springer), pp. 239–244.

After identifying some enabling research domains earlier (Barata, Onori et al. 2007), this article will show the multitude of relevant research areas which can serve as important inspirations for future-oriented solutions to manufacturing systems and will stress what must be done for making the manufacturing systems of the future successful.

System autonomy and emergence are important topics which appear in many of the recent manufacturing paradigms, also due to the inspirations laid out in the first part of this article; however, industry is very reluctant to accept anything which has to do with autonomy or emergence. The second part of this article addresses this is issue.

2. A MULTI-DISCIPLINARY APPROACH

Building manufacturing systems is a domain which, already in the traditional approach, brings together several branches: **Mechanical Engineering**, **Electrotechnical Engineering** and **Production Engineering** as well as **Systems Engineering**. These are certainly core competences, but they are not enough.

Computer Science is another classical discipline which is fundamental for developing innovative control systems. **Cybernetics**[16], itself an interdisciplinary approach which studies all kinds of systems and their unifying control principles, is obviously the right domain to learn more.

That body and brain cannot be considered separately is one of the teachings of **Embodied Cognitive Science** (Pfeifer and Scheier 1999). Hardware and Software need to evolve together, in any context – including manufacturing systems.

Studying issues related to **Complexity Science** in general[17] and Self-Organization and Emergence in particular has lead to the conclusion that these domains can be highly helpful to tackle the problems of production systems (Frei, Barata et al. 2007). The Multi-Agent Community can provide us with mechanisms for Self-Organization which work in reliable fashion (Di Marzo Serugendo, Fitzgerald et al. 2007). This knowledge alone, however, does not lead to success yet. It has to be combined with specific expertise in the application area – namely assembly and production engineering.

Mobile Robotics and **Collective Intelligence / Swarms** often already go together (Mondada, Gambardella et al. 2005). Experiments with robot swarms are highly useful to find out more about engineering methods and the ways predictable results can be achieved.

Natural / biological systems have considerable potential for being useful for manufacturing systems. This potential goes far beyond simply "copying" mechanisms as it is done in ant-inspired algorithms or AGV swarms. Natural systems have a plenitude of highly attractive characteristics which should be achieved in artificial systems – even if sometimes by other means than it happens in natural systems. A deeper analysis will be published soon in a journal.

Figure 7 illustrates the situation of the researcher intending to build the manufacturing systems of the future, standing in the middle of a high number of relevant scientific areas. A multi-disciplinary approach and the ability to communicate with specialists from many different domains are required. How can this overwhelming richness of concepts be managed? Are there useful principles?

---

[16] „Principia Cybernetica Web" : http://pespmc1.vub.ac.be/

[17] The Complexity & Artificial Life Research Concept for Self-Organizing Systems, http://www.calresco.org

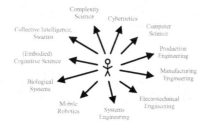

Figure 1. Research areas of influence in an interdisciplinary approach to the manufacturing systems of the future

First of all, it is necessary to very well understand the requirements imposed to the systems of the future in terms of adaptability, reconfigurability and evolvability. Second, it has to be stated that systems designed to correspond to these specifications are not solutions to any kind of manufacturing situation. There are limitations. E.g., systems for mass-production need to be optimal but do not require fast reconfigurability nor the avoidance of re-programming efforts. Third, the key concepts for success have to be identified. Most of them cannot be found in traditional engineering disciplines. Fourth, the concepts and methods taken from non-engineering domains have to be adapted in order to comply with engineering principles.

As a consequence, this highly promising domain needs to be thoroughly studied. The inherent multi-disciplinarity requires researchers able of understanding a broad range of concepts, methods and principles.

3. INDUSTRIAL ACCEPTANCE OF AUTONOMY AND EMERGENCE

As resulted from the discussion above, autonomy and emergence are two important ingredients for the industrial systems of the future. They allow systems to reach much higher levels of service to the user. But unfortunately, autonomy and emergence belong to the industry's worst nightmares. In this chapter, we look into the reasons for this aversion and propose ways out.

3.1. Why autonomy and emergence create fear

At the origin of the fear from emergence and autonomy in industry is probably a deep belief that humans are better at controlling systems than machines or computers ever could be. In some cases, this may be true – but there are many counter-examples. For instance, computers can calculate much faster as humans. They can execute big numbers of processes in parallel – while talented humans are limited to a handful (e.g. talking on the phone while passing the vacuum cleaner and at the same time keeping an eye on the playing children and the dog). Robots can repeat the same task with the same precision for a very long time, but humans get tired much faster and lose precision as well as attentiveness. The reasons for most of the airplane accidents reported recently were human mistakes, not technical defects! So why do people still believe in the absolute human superiority? Why not rely more on machines, also in production systems?

A reason why people try to suppress emergence is that most known examples of emergence are linked to a negative feeling, to the loss of control. When software crashes, the user is rather helpless; restarting is often the only solution.

Popular science fiction movies created a very bad image of "robots ruling the world". A recent example is the musical "Evil Machines" by Luis Tinoco and Monty Python's Terry Jones, where a humanoid robot takes over the role of the human inventor and incites any kind of machine, from electro-domestic gadgets to motorcycles, to revolt against their slavery and take over the power. It is only a logical consequence of such fantasies that everything advancing a little into the direction of autonomous machines causes fears.

These fears unfortunately interfere with the advance of new technology in industry.

3.2. Differences in the understanding of the terms autonomy and emergence

When people hear the word "emergence", they most often think about unexpected problems and trouble. The fact that something happens which was not predicted is naturally disturbing. In engineering, this is even stronger than in our every-day life. Engineering is strongly linked to the feeling that everything was carefully analyzed and designed in order to behave exactly in the expected way. If systems break this law, the user has a reflex to dislike it. It requires a certain mental distance to see that sometimes the unexpected occurrence can also have positive effects.

But is emergence obligatorily linked to surprise or unexpected situations? The intuitive answer mostly heard in industry is "yes". Researchers who have studied the topic are likely to negate. Emergence refers to the fact that system properties or behaviors sometimes appear at the global level without having been designed explicitly at this global level – which is clearly different from being unpredictable. If the local parts are conceived accordingly, they interact in the desired way and it is possible to determine how the global system will behave. Corresponding frameworks to elaborate methodologies exist, e.g. (Auyang 1998).

The term "System autonomy" induces people to think of the above-cited robots that get out of control and take over the power. This has obviously nothing to do with what researchers intend to create. Fist of all, autonomy is never absolute. It is much more appropriate to talk about a certain (modifiable) degree of autonomy. Also a highly autonomous system never gets completely out of control; a vehicle on Mars (one of the popular examples used for illustration of concepts in (Pfeifer and Scheier 1999)) which loses its contact to Earth may be an exception – but even then, the vehicle will not suddenly start doing crazy things. In the worst case it will stand still and do nothing any more, latest when the batteries are empty. Taking care of worst case scenarios are a fundamental aspect of an engineer's work. A simple example is that the designer of an axis has to think of what happens in case of a power cut. Will the axis fall down and by accelerating put into danger equipment and user? Or will the power cut not have any further consequences because the axis has passive breaking devices?

The same design principle applies to autonomy. The engineer will always provide ways of taking over control at any time – simply by including the obligated emergency power interrupter, this system can be stopped in any situation. Besides this, the degree of autonomy has to be adjustable. Every-day standard tasks should be executed without requiring the user's help, but if desired, every action can be confirmed manually. For special cases or safety-critical steps, a suggestion should be given for the user to confirm or modify at wish.

We should keep in mind that we are the creators of these systems, and this means that we choose where to put the limits.

Additionally, if wished, a second system can be implemented separately in order to monitor the first and alert the user in case of problems. With responsible engineers at work, there is no reason for industry to be worried about autonomous systems which might get out of control! This is and stays science fiction.

3.3. Why autonomy and emergence are useful for industry

Besides the aspects addressed in previous chapters, systems with a certain autonomy and emergence also offer other advantages.

Numerous manufacturing companies report that they experience increasing difficulties in recruiting skilled staff to operate production machines. It seems that this kind of profession is not popular any more. In some cases, off-shoring to other countries / continents may be a solution (with the disadvantage to lose business), but especially in the domains which require high-precision, automation is the only alternative. The more autonomous the systems work, the better.

Autonomy is also fundamental for coping with "ghost shifts": in countries with high salaries, it is too expensive to employ staff for supervision the machines during the night. This means that the machines run as long as everything goes well, and in case of minor problems, they simply stop production[18]. Valuable production time is lost every night. Some system autonomy to handle complications could avoid this.

If systems can care for themselves to an important degree and can propose solutions to the type of problem which frequently occur, there is less need for highly specialized staff. Choosing among a few proposals for how to proceed is much easier than having to imagine what to do from zero. In this sense, limited autonomy is a way of assisting the user as much (or as little) as he or she desires.

The more complex the system, the more assistance the user may require. High complexity in the body needs corresponding complexity in the brain[19]; this means that the human user can easily become overburdened with managing systems with many modules, many products and many interactions.

A system which is made to run autonomously also has to be able to cope with changes, be it the addition / removal of modules or the confrontation with new requirements without programming. In other words, autonomy leads to evolvability.

Industry as well as research often asks for reactive systems. This is certainly reasonable, but proactive systems can even offer more – they can put themselves at the service of the user and take the initiative to solve problems.

3.4. Preparing people for emergence and autonomy

The resistance in industry against new approaches is more due to human factors than due to technical problems. This means that to make industry accept, we must work on people. Frightening buzzwords must lose their mystery. They need to be explained, they must get reachable, and people must be able to "touch" them. A way to achieve this is to let customers play with autonomous / emergent systems at manufacturing fairs and when visiting labs at university.

They must be shown how the user always keeps the highest command, even if allowing the system to be proactive and autonomous. Similar to the situation of the robot on Mars, which is explores autonomously while still receiving certain commands from earth – with the difference that the user can stand next to the machine in the shop-floor. Constantly giving orders is neither necessary nor useful.

Understanding the concepts of partial autonomy, controlled emergence and supervised proactivity is fundamental. Nevertheless, we will not try to hide that there are also serious technical challenges to solve on the way towards more autonomous systems with emergence: there is still a lack of tools and methods.

---

[18] Recently heard in a radio report on channel DRS1 about the Swiss Textile Industry

[19] From „Principia Cybernetica Web" : http://pespmc1.vub.ac.be/

To conclude: It is difficult to understand emergence, difficult to implement autonomy, and difficult to convince people, but still worth the effort!

4. CONCLUSIONS

This article has placed current research for manufacturing systems of the future in the context of a plentitude of other relevant scientific areas. They can help manufacturing systems to get useful characteristics found in natural systems as well as artificial systems made for other purposes.

Two fundamental properties are autonomy and emergence. Their advantages for manufacturing have been illustrated, and an attempt to explain and mitigate the reluctance of industry to adopt them has been made.

Obviously, a lot of work is still needed. Without a paradigm-shift from traditional engineering to more flexible ideas, the manufacturing systems of the future will probably never be able to cope with the challenges they are already facing today.

5. REFERENCES

1. Auyang, S. Y. Foundations of Complex -System Theories in Economics, Evolutionary Biology, and Statistical Physics, Cambridge University Press, 1998.
2. Barata, J., M. Onori, et al. Evolvable Production Systems: Enabling Research Domains. CARV, Toronto, Ontario, Canada, 2007.
3. Colombo, A. W., R. Schoop, et al. An Agent-Based Intelligent Control Platform for Industrial Holonic Manufacturing Systems. IEEE Transactions on Industrial Electronics 2006; 53(1): 322-337.
4. Di Marzo Serugendo, G., J. Fitzgerald, et al. A Generic Framework for the Engineering of Self-Adaptive and Self-Organising Systems. CS-TR-1018, Technical Report. Newcastle, UK, School of Computing Science, University of Newcastle, 2007.
5. ElMaraghy, H. A. Flexible and reconfigurable manufacturing systems paradigms. International Journal of Flexible Manufacturing Systems 2006; 17: 261-276.
6. Frei, R., J. Barata, et al. A Complexity Theory Approach to Evolvable Production Systems. ICINCO, Angers, France, 2007.
7. Frei, R., L. Ribeiro, et al. Evolvable Assembly Systems: Towards User Friendly Manufacturing. ISAM, Ann Harbor, Michigan, USA, 2007.
8. Kume, S., A. Rizzi A high-performance network infrastructure and protocols for distributed automation. ICRA - IEEE Int. Conference on Robotics and Automation, 2001.
9. Mondada, F., L. Gambardella, et al. SWARM-BOTS: Physical Interactions in Collective Robotics. Robotics and Automation Magazine 2005; 12(2): 21-28.
10. Monostori, L., J. Vancza, et al. Agent-Based Systems for Manufacturing. BASYS, Canada, Annals of the CIRP 2006.
11. Onori, M. Evolvable Assembly Systems - A New Paradigm? ISR2002 - 33rd International Symposium on Robotics, Stockholm, 2002.
12. Pfeifer, R., C. Scheier Understanding intelligence. Cambridge, Massachusetts, The MIT Press, 1999.
13. Rizzi, A. A., J. Gowdy, et al. Agile Assembly Architecture: an Agent Based Approach to Modular Precision Assembly Systems. International Conference on Robotics and Automation, 1997.
14. Rzevski, G., P. Skobelev. Emergent Intelligence in Multi-Agent Systems. Windsor, Berkshire, UK, Magenta Technology, 2007.
15. Ueda, K. Emergent Synthesis Approaches to Biological Manufacturing Systems. DET, Setubal, Portugal, 2006.
16. Ulieru, M. Emerging Computing for the Industry: Agents, Self-Organisation and Holonic Systems. IECON 2004, Busan, South Korea, 2004.
17. Valckenaers, P., H. Van Brussel. "Holonic Manufacturing Execution Systems." CIRP Annals - Manufacturing Technology 2005; 54(1): 427-432.

27

RELIABILITY EVALUATION OF FAILURE DELAYED ENGINEERING SYSTEMS

Jose A. Faria
Institute for Systems and Robotics
University of Porto, Portugal
jfaria@fe.up.pt

This paper introduces an analytical approach for the evaluation of multi-user engineering systems presenting a failure delayed behaviour pattern, that is, systems whose performance decays progressively after the failures, due to internal fault tolerance mechanisms or to the complacency of the users regarding the temporarily unavailability of the services. The approach is based on the determination of analytical expressions for the reliability measures, e.g. frequency and probability of failure states, which may then be evaluated using general purpose mathematical tools. The paper discusses the rationale and the fundamental algorithms of the approach and presents a set of illustrative examples.

1. INTRODUCTION

This paper presents the results of a research project aiming to develop a systematic approach for the reliability evaluation of systems containing multiple concurrent processes with generalized distributions. The approach was primarily developed to assist the steady-state analysis of failure delayed systems (FDS), i.e. systems whose performance decays progressively in the sequence of a failure. The paper presents a definition of these systems and shows that they present a non-Markovian behavior pattern and that the existing methodologies present a number of shortcomings regarding the evaluation of FDS systems. Then, the paper introduces the fundamental aspects of the new approach and presents a set of numerical results in order to illustrate its practical application and usefulness.

2. FAILURE DELAYED ENGINEERING SYSTEMS

In many situations, the users of an engineering system are complacent about a temporary unavailability of the service provided to them by the system. This means that, at first, the disturbances of a system failure are often negligible. However, if the failure persists for a long time, the system will enter into successive degraded operational modes where its quality of service decays progressively, until a successful repair action is undertaken and the system restores its normal operation, or a catastrophic failure occurs.

Please use the following format when citing this chapter:

Faria, J.A., 2008, in IFIP International Federation for Information Processing, Volume 266, *Innovation in Manufacturing Networks;* ed. A. Azevedo; (Boston: Springer), pp. 245–256.

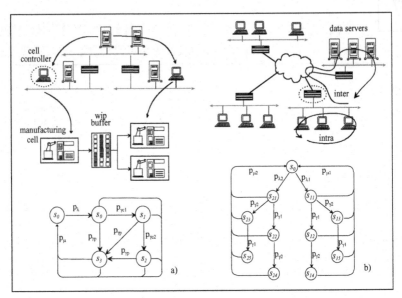

Figure 1. Failure delayed systems examples

As practical examples, consider the two models presented in the next figure. In the two models, s_0 corresponds to the normal operating state of the system, and s_{fi} to the failure states. The failure, repair and propagation (or delay) processes are represented respectively by $p_{\lambda i}$, $p_{\mu i}$ and $p_{\gamma i}$. The model of figure 1.a represents a production system with intermediate work-in-process (wip) buffers between the manufacturing cells. The cells and plant controllers of the manufacturing system get their data from a plant data server. If this server becomes unavailable (process p_λ), the plant will be able to continue producing, because the cell and plant level production plans are frozen some time in advance of the physical production (processes $p_{\gamma c1}$ and $p_{\gamma p}$). However, the plant will enter a sub-optimal mode because it will not be possible to react to production events, such as new urgent orders. If an upstream cell halts its operation, the downstream cells will continue to be fed by the intermediate work in process buffer (processes $p_{\gamma p}$). Only when there is a shortage of products at the output of this buffer, will the consequences of the failure propagate downstream. If this production system belongs to a just-in-time supply chain, the severity of the damages is likely to increase dramatically.

The model in figure 1.b sketches the information system of a business company from the retail sector. End users execute intra and inter-site transactions (which both depend on the availability of a number of remote data servers) and may tolerate a temporary unavailability of the information services. However, this complacency is different regarding intra and inter-sites transactions, and regarding the operations executed in each site (end consumers' point of sales, or logistical support). This behaviour is represented in the model by two concurrent failure propagation processes $p\gamma_1$ and $p\gamma_2$.

These two examples show that a progressive decay of performance after a failure, due to an internal temporal redundancy mechanism, or to the complacency of the users regarding the temporary unavailability of the services provided to them, is a common behaviour pattern in engineering systems. The analysis of these systems also shows that FDS systems present a number of common features that directly impact on their reliability and performance evaluation. Suppose that S is a repairable failure delayed system and M is its behaviour model (figure 2).

In this case, the following assumptions regarding S and M will be considered in the context of this paper:

- S provides services to multiple users (e.g. downstream manufacturing cells, electrical consumers or information systems users) each of which presents its own complacency regarding the unavailability of the services of S.
- S has a regenerative state which is represented in M as s_{up}.
- In s_{up}, one or more failure processes are active. Each one of those processes corresponds to a particular failure.
- The execution of a failure process leads the state of S to one of the initial failure states

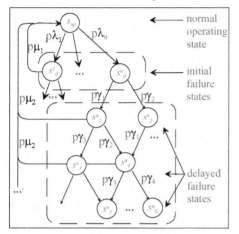 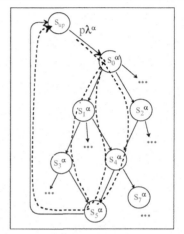

Figure 2. Failure delayed system models   *Figure 3.* Alternative trajectories

where the disturbances for the users will typically be negligible.

- In each failure state, several concurrent delay processes, $p\gamma_\beta$, may be active. Each one of them corresponds to the complacency of a particular type of user regarding the failures of the system.
- The execution of a delay process leads the system to a delayed failure state, e.g. s_n^α with $n \geq 0$, where the severity of the damage will typically increase.
- In each initial or delayed failure state, a repair process $p\mu_\eta$ may be active. The execution of this process leads the system to the s_{up}. In other words, it is assumed that repair is a regenerative process that completely restores the normal operating condition (the extension of the model to non-regenerative repair will be discussed in Section 6).
- Failure, delay and repair processes may present arbitrary distributions (deterministic or stochastic).
- When a transition occurs from a failure state, the other processes that were simultaneously active in that state may be deactivated, reinitialized or remain active (keeping their firing time). Simultaneously, other repair or delay processes may be activated on the arrival at the new state.

3. REVIEW OF EXISTING METHODS

The assessment of non-Markovian systems remains a largely open issue in reliability analysis, despite the significant progress achieved in the last two decades, mostly based on stochastic Petri nets. The device of stages is one of the well proved techniques for the evaluation of non-Markovian systems, which makes it possible to model a large range of experimental probability density functions. For example, a log-normal distribution often found in repair processes may be represented through a combination of a series of states with two states in parallel, as shown in (Singh 77) and (Pages 80).

First introduced in (Cox 65), it has been applied to the reliability evaluation of fault tolerant computer systems (Laprie 75), and to the reliability analysis of electrical power systems (Singh 77). An extension of the method has been proposed in (Haverkort 93), to allow the assignment of a memory policy to any timed transition. One of the important features of the method is the possibility of designing automated tools to support its application, as presented in (Cumani 85). This tool uses Petri nets as the modelling tool and converts the reachability set of the net into a continuous time Markov chain defined over an extended state space. Although very flexible, this method restricts the firing times of the stochastic processes so that they are PH distributed (Neuts 81). Consequently, it presents a major limitation when the systems under analysis contain deterministic or quasi-deterministic processes, because the number n of additional states rises quadratically with the ratio between the standard deviation and the mean of the distribution.

In the past two decades, several evaluation techniques based on stochastic Petri nets (SPN) modelling have been developed in order to support the reliability analysis and the performance evaluation of complex systems. When SPN were first introduced (Molloy 82), all the random variables associated with the transitions were assumed to be exponentially distributed, so that the evolution of a Petri net could be mapped into a continuous Markov chain. Since then, and in order to broaden the field of application of SPN, several classes of Petri nets incorporating non-exponential features in their definition have been proposed. This is the case of the deterministic and stochastic Petri nets defined in (Marsan 87), in which a single deterministic transition may exist in each marking. Subsequently, it was observed in (Choi 95) that the underlying marking process is a Markov regenerative process. This allowed the extension of the model in order to accommodate immediate transitions, exponentially distributed timed transitions and generally distributed timed transitions but with the important restriction that at most one generally distributed timed transition be enabled in each marking (Choi 94). Two evaluation approaches were then developed: one based on the derivation of the time dependent transition probability matrix in the Laplace transform (Choi 94), the other based on the supplementary variables method (German 94). In spite of this progress, several restrictions still apply to the analytical evaluation of non-Markov systems, and no general solution is available

4. NEW APPROACH FUNDAMENTALS

This Section introduces the mathematical foundations of the procedures for the determination of the frequencies and the probabilities of a non-Markovian model M. The analytical expressions for the frequencies will be considered first in paragraph 4.1, then the states probabilities expressions will be addressed in paragraph 4.2. The procedure is based on the notion of *state trajectory*: immediately after a failure, the system occupies one of the initial failure states. Then, it returns to the normal operating state following one of the several possible trajectories, as shown in figure 3. A trajectory is an ordered set of failure states $\{ s_n^\alpha, s_n^\alpha, s_n^\alpha, \dots s_n^\alpha \}$ that starts at one of the regenerative initial failure states s_n^α, and such that, for each pair of consecutive states, s_n^α and s_n^α, there is a delay process $p\gamma_\beta$ in M whose execution causes the transition from s_n^α to s_n^α. In the presentation of the procedure, the following notation will be adopted:

- Λ_M and P_M: two vectors such $\Lambda_M(s)$ and $P_M(s)$ contain the frequency and the probability of state s, respectively;
- s_{up}: the normal operating state,
- $p\lambda_\alpha$: the failure process corresponding to failure mode α,
- s_0^α: the initial failure state corresponding to failure mode α,
- $p\gamma_\beta$ and $p\mu_\eta$: the processes corresponding to the propagation delay β and the repair action η, respectively;
- s_n^α: a delayed failure state subsequent to s_0^α ($n \geq 1$);
- $f_p(t)$: the probability density function of process p.

4.1. Failure states frequency

Suppose that s_n^α is a failure state whose frequency is to be determined and that Ψ_n^α is the set of trajectories starting at s_0^α and ending at s_n^α. The frequency of the failure state $\Lambda(s_n^\alpha)$ results from the sum of the frequencies of each trajectory ψ of Ψ_n^α:

$$\Lambda(s_n^\alpha) = \sum_{\psi \in \Psi_n^\alpha} \Lambda(\psi) \tag{1}$$

The frequency of each trajectory ψ comes from the product of (i) the frequency of s_0^α and (ii) the probability that, once arrived at s_0^α, the system follows the trajectory ψ.

$$\Lambda(s_n^\alpha) = \Lambda(s_0^\alpha) \sum_{\psi \in \Psi_n^\alpha} P(\psi) \tag{2}$$

The determination of $P(\psi)$ will be addressed hereafter, whereas that of $\Lambda(s_0^\alpha)$ will be postponed to paragraph 4.3 because it requires formulae introduced in 4.2.

4.1.1. Probability of a trajectory

The probability of a trajectory comes from the product of the probabilities of each one of its transitions. Consider, as an example, the following trajectory:

$$\psi = \{ s_0^\alpha, s_a^\alpha, s_b^\alpha, \dots s_r^\alpha, s_s^\alpha \}$$

Its probability will be:

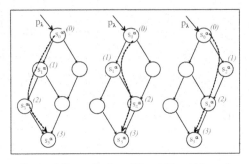
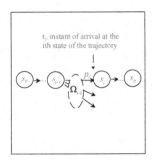

Figure 4. Renumbering of the states within each trajectory

Figure 5. Arrival at the ith state of the trajectory

$$= P(s_0^\alpha \to s_a^\alpha) \times P(s_a^\alpha \to s_b^\alpha) \times \ldots \times P(s_r^\alpha \to s_s^\alpha)$$

For the sake of simplicity of the expressions, it will be considered that, within each trajectory, the states are renumbered according to their order, as exemplified in figure 4 for the three trajectories considered above. If the random variable t_i represents the time elapsed between the arrival at the initial failure state s_0 and the arrival at the ith state s_i, the probability of a trajectory leading to the nth state, s_n, may be expressed as:

$$P(\psi) = P(s_0 \to s_1) \times P_{t_1}(s_1 \to s_2) \times .. \times P_{t_1, t_2, ..t_{n-1}}(s_{n-1} \to s_n) \quad \text{or as:}$$

$$P(\psi) = \prod_{i=1}^{n} P_{t_1..t_{i-1}}(s_{i-1} \to s_i) \tag{3}$$

where $P_{t_1..t_{i-1}}(s_{i-1} \to s_i)$ represents the conditional probability of transition from s_{i-1} to s_i given that the previous transitions of ψ have occurred at $t_1..t_{i-1}$. These conditional probabilities may, in turn, be evaluated from the following expression:

$$P_{t_1, t_2..t_{i-1}}(s_{i-1} \to s_i) = \int_0^\infty \int_{t_1}^\infty ..\int_{t_{i-1}}^\infty T(t_i) \, dt_i..dt_2 dt_1 \tag{4}$$

where $T(t_i)$ is the density function of the random variable t_i. This time depends, in turn, on the set of stochastic processes that are active in state s_{i-1}. If Ω_k is the set of processes that are active in a state s_k, and p_i is the process that causes the transition from i-1th to the ith state of the trajectory (figure 5), then the expression for $T(t_i)$ comes from the product of the density function of this process, $f_{p_i}(t_i)$, and the probability that the other processes p of Ω_{i-1} do not occur before t_i ($p \in \Omega_{i-1}$ and $p \neq p_i$). If p is a process of Ω_{i-1} that became active at a previous instant t_p^0, then the density function for the execution of this process is:

$$f_p'(t) = \frac{f_p(t - t_p^0)}{1 - \int_{t_p^0}^{t_{i-1}} f_p(\tau - t_p^0) d\tau}, \quad t > t_{i-1}$$

where τ is an auxiliary variable with local scope. Therefore, it results for $T(t_i)$:

$$T(t_i) = \frac{f_{p_i}(t_i - t^0_{p_i})}{1 - \int_{t^0_{p_i}}^{t_{i-1}} f_{p_i}(\tau - t^0_{p_i})d\tau} \left(\prod_{\substack{p \in \Omega_i \\ p \neq p_i}} \frac{\int_{t_i}^{\infty} f_p(\tau' - t^0_p)}{1 - \int_{t^0_p}^{t_{i-1}} f_p(\tau - t^0_p)d\tau} d\tau' \right) \tag{5}$$

where:

- t^0_p is the instant of activation of process p, which will always coincide with one of the random variables t_j, with $j < i - 1$;

- $\dfrac{f_{p_i}(t_i - t^0_{p_i})}{1 - \int_{t^0_{p_i}}^{t_{i-1}} f_{p_i}(\tau - t^0_{p_i})d\tau}$ represents the density function of the instant of transition from

s_{i-1} to s_i due to p_i;

- $\dfrac{\int_{t_i}^{\infty} f_p(\tau' - t^0_p)}{1 - \int_{t^0_p}^{t_{i-1}} f_p(\tau - t^0_p)d\tau} d\tau'$ represents the probability that another process p of Ω_{i-1}

does not occur before p_i.

Now, combining (3), (4) and (5) the expression for the probability of the trajectory ψ may be obtained from:

$$P(\psi) = \int_0^{\infty} T(t_1) \int_{t_1}^{\infty} T(t_2) .. \int_{t_{n-1}}^{\infty} T(t_n) \, dt_n ... dt_2 \, dt_1 \tag{6}$$

If a process p stays active from state s_k (i.e., $t^0_p = t_k$) to state s_m, its density function will participate in the expressions $T(t_j)$ for $k \leq j \leq m$. Therefore, the contribution of p to $P(\psi)$ will be:

$$\frac{\int_{t_{k+1}}^{\infty} f_p(\tau' - t_k)d\tau'}{1} \times \frac{\int_{t_{k+2}}^{\infty} f_p(\tau' - t_k)d\tau'}{1 - \int_{t_k}^{t_{k+1}} f_p(\tau - t_k)d\tau} .. \frac{\int_{t_{m+1}}^{\infty} f_p(\tau - t_k)d\tau'}{1 - \int_{t_k}^{t_m} f_p(\tau - t_k)d\tau}$$

Once $\int_{t_{l+1}}^{\infty} f_p(\tau - t_k)d\tau$ equals ($1 - \int_{t_l}^{t_{l+1}} f_p(\tau - t_k)d\tau$), the global contribution of p to $T(t_k)$ will be equivalent to $\int_{t_{m+1}}^{\infty} f_p(\tau - t_k)d\tau$. This means that, if a process p is active from s_k to s_m, it is possible to consider its contribution to $T(t_i)$ only at state s_m. This fact leads to a significant simplification of the density functions:

$$T(t_i) = f_{p_i}(t_i - t^0_{p_i}) \left(\prod_{\substack{p \in \Omega_{i-1} \\ p \notin \Omega_i \\ p \neq p_i}} \int_{t_i}^{\infty} f_p(\tau - t^0_p)d\tau \right) \tag{7}$$

4.2. Failure states probability

Here, the procedure introduced in paragraph 4.1 will be extended in order to address the probability of the failure states. Assuming, as before, that s_n^{α} is a failure state of a model M, that Ψ_n^{α} is the set of trajectories leading to s_n^{α} and that $P(\psi)$ is the probability of the trajectory ψ, then the probability of s_n^{α} may be obtained from:

$$P(s_n^\alpha) = \Lambda(s_0^\alpha) \sum_{\psi \in \Psi_n^\alpha} P(\psi) \times \overline{t_n^\psi} \qquad (8)$$

where the new term $\overline{t_n^\psi}$ represents the mean sojourn time in s_n^α when this state is achieved following trajectory ψ. If p is a processes of Ω_n, the mean sojourn time in state s_n^α when the transition to next state is caused by p results from the product of (i) the mean execution time of p and (ii) the probability that the other processes of Ω_n do not occur before p, that is:

$$\int_{t_n}^\infty (t_{n+1} - t_n) f_p(t_{n+1} - t_{0p}) (\prod_{\substack{p' \in \Omega_n \\ p' \neq p}} \int_{t_{n+1}}^\infty f_{p'}(t' - t_{0p'}) dt') \, dt_{n+1}$$

As the output transition from state s_n^α may be caused by any of the processes belonging to Ω_n, the total sojourn time $\overline{t_n^\psi}$ may be obtained from:

$$\overline{t_n^\psi} = \sum_{p \in \Omega_n} \int_{t_n}^\infty (t_{n+1} - t_n) f_p(t_{n+1} - t_p^0) (\prod_{\substack{p' \in \Omega_n \\ p' \neq p}} \int_{t_{n+1}}^\infty f_{p'}(\tau - t_{p'}^0) d\tau) \, dt_{n+1} \qquad (9)$$

The expression of $\overline{t_n^\psi}$ depends on the instants of the previous transitions of ψ (due to the instants of activation t_p^0 and $t_{p'}^0$ of the processes belonging to Ω_n. Therefore, this expression should be combined the probability of ψ (6), yielding:

$$P(s_n^\alpha) = \Lambda(s_0^\alpha) \sum_{\psi \in \Psi_n^\alpha} \int_0^\infty T(t_1) \ldots \int_{t_{n-1}}^\infty T(t_n) \times$$

$$\times \left[\sum_{p \in \Omega_n} \int_{t_n}^\infty (t_{n+1} - t_n) f_p(t_{n+1} - t_p^0) (\prod_{\substack{p' \in \Omega_n \\ p' \neq p}} \int_{t_{n+1}}^\infty f_{p'}(\tau - t_{p'}^0) d\tau) \, dt_{n+1} \right] dt_{n-1} .. dt_1 \qquad (10)$$

The expressions for the states probabilities (as the previous expressions for the states frequencies) depend on the frequency of arrival at the initial failure state, $\Lambda(s_0^\alpha)$, which is addressed in the next paragraph.

4.3. Initial failure states frequency

Depending on the distributions of the failure and the repair processes, four situations regarding the determination of frequencies of the initial failure states have to be considered: (i) exponential failure processes, and a common repair process, (ii) exponential failure processes, and several repair processes, (iii) non-exponential failure processes, and a common repair process and (iv) non-exponential failure processes, and several repair processes.

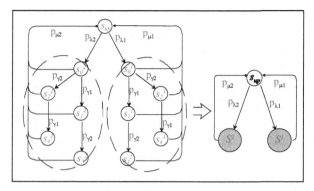

Figure 6. Macro-failure states

Hereafter, just the first one of these situations will be considered. This is the simpler and more common situation found in practical applications regarding FDS systems: the failure processes present exponential distributions; the repair processes are enabled immediately after the occurrence of the failures; and they remain active until the system re-enters the normal operating state s_{up}. In this case, the set of failure states corresponding to a particular failure mode may be grouped in a single macro-state because all of them share the same repair process (figure 6). The mean sojourn time in the macro-state corresponding to failure mode α is:

$$\overline{t}^{\alpha} = \int_0^{\infty} t\, f_{\mu_\alpha}(t)\, dt$$

where $f_{\mu_\alpha}(t)$ is the density function of the repair process. Once the failure rates λ_α are constant and the state probabilities verify:

$$P(s_{up}) + \sum_{s \in F_M} P(s) = 1$$

where F_M is the set of failure states of M, the probability of the normal operating state may be obtained from:

$$P(s_{up}) = \frac{1}{1 + \sum_{\alpha} \lambda_\alpha \int_0^{\infty} t\, f_{\mu_\alpha}(t)\, dt}$$

Now, the frequency of the initial failure state corresponding to a particular failure mode α may be readily obtained from:

$$\Lambda(s_0^\alpha) = \lambda_\alpha\, P(s_{up}) \tag{13}$$

5. NUMERICAL RESULTS

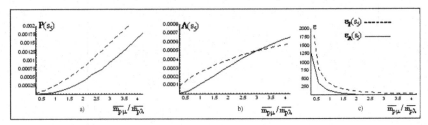

Figure 7. Numerical results

This section presents several results regarding the evaluation of the model represented in figure 1.a. It is assumed that s_5 is a catastrophic failure state and that its probability and frequency are to be evaluated. The analytical expressions for these two measures were already introduced in paragraphs 4.1 and 4.2 Two scenarios will be considered here for illustrative purposes: scenario 1 where all the processes present exponential distributions and scenario 2 where the repair and delay processes present 3rd order Erlang distributions.

For the sake of simplicity, it is also be assumed that the three delay processes are identical and that their mean $\overline{m_{p\gamma}}$ is 3 hours. For the mean of the repair processes, several values will be considered for the mean ranging from $\overline{m_{p\gamma}}/4$ to $4\overline{m_{p\gamma}}$. Figure 7.a and 7.b represent the evolution of the probability and of the frequency of the catastrophic failure state with the ratio $\rho = \overline{m_{p\gamma}}/\overline{m_{p\gamma}}$, for the two scenarios.

Figure 7.c provides another important result. It shows the error that will be introduced in the evaluation of a system presenting the non-Markovian behaviour corresponding to scenario 2, using the Markovian model of scenario 1 (which is something often done in reliability analysis). The error ε in a reliability measure $\mathcal{R}$ is calculated from:

$$\varepsilon = \frac{\mathcal{R}_1 - \mathcal{R}_2}{\mathcal{R}_2}$$

where $\mathcal{R}_1$ *and* $\mathcal{R}_2$ are the values corresponding to the two scenarios. These results reinforce the idea that, when a model contains concurrent processes having non-exponential distributions, the use of non-Markovian techniques becomes mandatory. In fact, even with this simple system, the error may be high then 1000%.

6. DISCUSSON AND CONCLUSIONS

The paper has presented an approach for the reliability and performance evaluation of ergodic repairable systems containing a Markov regenerative state (corresponding to normal operation) and multiple concurrent processes with generalized distributions. There are well established analytical solutions for the transient and steady state evaluation of regenerative Markov systems. These solutions allow immediate, exponentially distributed and generally distributed timed transitions to be considered but they require that all the non-exponential processes be enabled at the same instant.

As it has been shown, the approach presented here does not impose this important restriction. Other approaches for the evaluation of non-Markovian systems require the consideration of additional variables, whose number increases quickly when the model contains several concurrent processes with narrow hyper-exponential distributions, i.e.

deterministic or quasi-deterministic processes, as happens with the device of stages. In these conditions, the approach presented here may offer a more straightforward solution. In fact, the analytical expressions for the relevant reliability measures may be obtained through a systematic procedure directly from the structure of the model and the distributions of the stochastic processes. There is no need for auxiliary variables, and the expressions may be evaluated using general purpose mathematical tools. The approach has been successfully applied to the study of non-Markov industrial manufacturing systems, distributed information systems and electrical power systems, and it constitutes an effective alternative to simulation based techniques. For relatively small models, containing just a few states and processes, the analytical expressions can be evaluated directly using general purpose mathematical tools. For the evaluation of larger models, the use of these general purpose tools may become ineffective, but it is possible to develop specialized evaluation tools.

7. REFERENCES

1. Bobbio, A, Telek, M. Non-exponential stochastic Petri nets: an overview of methods and techniques. Computer Systems Science and Engineering 1998; 13 (6): 339-351.
2. Brehm, E "System Dependability Assessment Tool", Proceedings of the 2nd IEEE International Conference On Engineering of Complex Computer Systems, Montreal, Canada, 1996.
3. Choi, H, Kulkarni, VG, Trivedi, KS. Markov regenerative stochastic Petri nets. Performance Evaluation 1994; v 20, n 1-3: 337-357.
4. Choi H, Kulkarni, V., Trivedi, K. Markov Regenerative Stochastic Petri Nets. Performance Evaluation 1995; 21.
5. Cox, DR and Miller, HD, The Theory of Stochastic Processes, Chapman and Hall, London, UK, 1965. Cumani, A, "ESP – a package for the evaluation of stochastic Petri nets with phase type distributed transition times", Proceedings of the International Workshop Timed Petri Nets, pages 144-151, Torino, Italy, 1985
6. Faria, J, Nunes, E, Matos, M, "Optimal dimensioning of work-in-process buffers", Proceedings of the International Conference on Industrial Engineering and Production, Portugal, May 2003.
7. Faria, J, Matos, M. Availability Analysis and Design of Business Information Systems. International Journal of Business and Information 2006; vol 1, n 1.
8. German, R, Lindemann, C. Analysis of stochastic Petri nets by the method of supplementary variables. Performance Evaluation 1994; v 20, n 1-3: 317-335.
9. Haverkort, BR and Trivedi, KS, "Specification techniques for markov reward models", Discrete Event Dynamic Systems: Theory and Applications, v 3, n 2-3, p 219, Jul, 1993
10. Laprie, JC, "Prévision de la Sûreté de Fonctionnement et Architecture des Structures Numériques Temps Réel Réparables", Ph.D Thesis, Université Paul Sabatier, Toulouse, France 1975.
11. Limnios, N, "Failure Delay Systems Reliability Modelling", in Systems Reliability Assessment, Edited by Colombo, AG, Saiz de Bustamante, A, ECSC Brussels, 1990
12. Marsan, MA and Chiola, G, "On Petri nets with deterministic and exponentially distributed firing times", Lecture Notes on Computer Science, vot 266, pp 132-245, Springer Verlag, 1987.
13. Molloy, M., "Performance analysis using stochastic Petri nets", IEEE Trans Computers 1982; C-31(9): 913-17.
14. Neuts, M.F., Matrix Geometric Solutions in Stochastic Models, John Hopkins University Press, Baltimore USA, 1981
15. Nunes, E, Faria, J, Matos, M "A comparative analysis of dependability assessment methodologies" Proceedings of the $\lambda\mu$13 ESREL Conference, Lyon, France, May 2002
16. Pages, A and Gondran, M, Fiabilité des systèmes. Eyrolles, France, 1980
17. Puliafito, A, Scarpa, M, Trivedi, K. Petri nets with k simultaneously enabled generally distributed timed transitions. Performance Evaluation 1998; 32 (1): 1-34.
18. Scarpa M, Distefano S, Puliafito A, "A parallel approach for the solution of non-Markovian Petri nets", Recent Advances in Parallel Virtual Machine and Message Passing Interface, Lecture Notes in Computer Science 2840: 196-203, Springer Verlag Berlin Heidelberg, 2003
19. Singh, C, Billinton, R, Lee, SY, "The method of stages for non-Markov models", IEEE Transactions on Reliability 1977; vol.R-26, n°2: 135-7.
20. Wu, L. Operational models for the evaluation of degradable computing systems. Performance Evaluation Review (USA) Winter 1982-1983; Vol. 11, Issue 4: 179-85,

PART 4

INTELLIGENT MACHINES AND SENSOR NETWORKS

28

MAS AND SOA:
COMPLEMENTARY AUTOMATION PARADIGMS

Luís Ribeiro, José Barata, Pedro Mendes

UNINOVA / UNL, Quinta da Torre, 2829-516 Caparica, Portugal

{ldr,jab,pcm}@uninova.pt

This document surveys existing research in emergent concepts and technologies supporting the establishment of what are expected to be future automation systems. Multiagent systems (MAS) and Service Oriented Architectures (SOA) are currently the most promising concepts in this matter. The author's experience in the implementation and study of SOA and MAS for distributed automation systems suggests that there are substantial benefits in converging both paradigms and technologies In this context, the goal of the present work is to unveil their strengths and weaknesses and propose the unification of complementary features as a mean to provide unprecedented support to the study, modelling, design and implementation of complex distributed systems.

1. INTRODUCTION

Pushed by market instability and turbulence, modern enterprises are expected to adopt innovative business methodologies to gain flexibility and agility and remain high end competitors in a globalized market.

As customers' demands rise higher in respect to diversity, exclusivity and quality of the goods, the impact of emerging requirements is deeply felt at the shop floor level. Virtually all the recent control approaches and paradigms advocate the use of distributed intelligence to maximize enterprise's agility and flexibility: bionic manufacturing systems (BMS) (Ueda 1992), holonic manufacturing systems (HMS) (Babiceanu and Chen 2006; Bussmann and Mcfarlane 1999; Gou et al. 1998; Van Brussel et al. 1998), reconfigurable manufacturing systems (RMS) (Koren et al. 1999; Mehrabi et al. 2000), (EAS) (Barata et al. 2006b; Frei et al. 2007b; Onori 2002; Onori et al. 2005; Onori et al. 2006) and evolvable production systems (EPS) (Barata et al. 2007a; Barata et al. 2007b; Frei et al. 2007a).

The industrial sector, traditionally conservative in respect to technological changes, is aware of the potential of application of such technologies and paradigms and two concepts seem to be in the research frontline: Service Oriented Architectures (SOA) and Multiagent Systems (MAS). The slow shift to SOA and MAS is accompanied by an increase in the offer of embedded tiny devices that will effectively support the establishment of intelligent automation environments. In fact, there will not be real implemented adaptive and reconfigurable systems without tiny embedded controller able to support MAS/SOA.

The success of the approaches earlier described partially depends on the possibility of having embedded MAS/SOA-ready devices. There are, however, computational limits and constraints to render the use of such technologies and devices cost effective that necessarily need to be overcome. Although is difficult to quantify and access the

Please use the following format when citing this chapter:

Ribeiro, L., Barata, J. and Mendes, P., 2008, in IFIP International Federation for Information Processing, Volume 266, *Innovation in Manufacturing Networks;* ed. A. Azevedo; (Boston: Springer), pp. 259–268.

performance of the different approaches it is the authors' experience-based belief that there are substantial advantages in merging the best of both worlds (MAS and SOA).

The subsequent sections are organized as follows: section 2 details the concept of SOA and surveys existing research; section 3 presents a similar analysis for MAS; section 4 overviews the authors' applied research in distributed manufacturing systems that empirically suggests a favourable outcome of merging the best of MAS and SOA and in section 5 the main conclusions are discussed.

2. SERVICE ORIENTED ARCHITECTURES

The subject of Service Oriented Architectures (SOA) is vast, complex and multidisciplinary.

The definition of SOA is far from being agreed as a search in the literature easily confirms. Contact points between the numerous definitions frequently include the following topics:

- Autonomy: there are no direct dependencies between the services and they are structurally decoupled.
- Interoperability: is achieved by, rather than detailing the operations performed by the service provider, specifying an interface that describes the services being hosted and the interaction patterns considered.
- Platform Independence: ideally the services are described using text-based formats (XML(Bray et al. 2006), WSDL(Christensen et al. 2001), ebXML, etc). These representations are not tied to a particular computer architecture, operating systems, programming language or technology and can be easily decoded by any system.
- Encapsulation: services provide self-contained functionalities that are exposed by user defined interfaces hiding unnecessary details. By composing and orchestrating services a very complex level of functionality can be offered through a clean and simple interface.
- Availability/Discovery: the services can be published in public registries and made available for general use.

As an emerging modelling paradigm for distributed systems SOA is often confused with a wide range of networked information technologies. In this context, Web Services are the preferred mechanism for SOA implementation.

The Web Services Working group of the World Wide Web Consortium (W3C) defines Web Service as(Booth et al. 2004): "a software system designed to support interoperable machine-to-machine interaction over a network. It has an interface described in a machine-processable format (specifically WSDL). Other systems interact with the Web Service in a manner prescribed by its description using SOAP(Box et al. 2000) messages, typically conveyed using HTTP with an XML serialization in conjunction with other Web-related standards." The comparison to SOA is, in this case, immediate and natural as SOA was born through the convergence of several web technologies.

Although a significant share of the research in SOA focus on modelling and supporting inter enterprise relationships, there is a favourable convergence of factors that are rendering it attractive in the establishment of automated networks of devices namely: the availability of affordable and high performance embedded devices, the expansion and low cost of Ethernet based networks and its acceptance in the industrial domain, the ubiquitous nature of the Internet, the existence of lightweight, platform agnostic communication infrastructures, etc.

This has triggered several European projects in the field including industry's heavy weights. Among them one may mention as examples: SIRENA (SIRENA 2006) – award winning project that targeted the development of a Service Infrastructure for Real time Embedded Networked Applications (Jammes and Smit 2005); SODA (SODA 2006) – creation of a service oriented ecosystem based on the Devices Profile for Web Services (DPWS) framework developed under the SIRENA project; SOCRADES (SOCRADES 2006) – development of DPWS-based SOA for automation systems; InLife (InLife 2006) – including a test case that explores service oriented DPWS-based diagnosis on distributed manufacturing systems (Barata et al. 2007c; Barata et al. 2007d).

The DPWS (Chan et al. 2006), whose initial publication dates from May 2004, is especially relevant for automation environments, as it defines the minimal Web Service's implementation requirements for: secure message exchange, dynamic discovery, description and subscribing and eventing. DPWS is in this context directed to tiny low cost computing devices.

In (Papazoglou et al. 2005) a roadmap for SOA is presented and identifies the following research areas: Service Foundations, Service Composition, Service Management, Service Design and development. The main open challenges, also described in the roadmap include: dynamically reconfigurable run-time architectures, services discovery, autonomic composition of services and orchestration, self-* (self-configuring/healing/diagnosing…) services, design principles for engineering service applications. While some of these challenges can be eased by emergent standards such as BPEL4WS (Andrews et al. 2003) and WSCI (Arkin et al. 2002) others, specifically service composition in dynamically reconfigurable run-time architectures, are harder to tackle specially in heterogeneous systems, which are typically SOA's target environments.

Additionally, as stated in (Huhns and Singh 2005) most Web Services specifications do not properly support transactions which constitutes a significant implementation barrier in a wide range of systems. Other frequent limitations include:

- Code explosion – when there exists interaction between many heterogeneous services
- Reprogramming – under those circumstances the introduction of a new service with an unknown service description leads to the reprogramming of every service that interact with it.

3. MULTIAGENT SYSTEMS

Most definitions for agents are of functional nature and relate to their authors' background and the systems under study. Nevertheless, it is possible to isolate a common set of characteristics widely accepted(Camarinha-Matos and Vieira 1999):

- Autonomy – an agent is autonomous when it is able to act alone without help from third parties (like other agents or humans).
- Sociability – an agent must be able to communicate with other agents or even other entities.
- Rationality – an agent can reason about the data it receives in order to find the best solution to achieve its goal.
- Reactivity – an agent can react upon changes in the environment, changing its behaviour accordingly.
- Proactivity – a proactive agent has some control on its reactions basing them on its own agenda and objectives.
- Adaptability – an agent is capable of learning and changes its behaviour when a better solution is discovered adapting itself to changes in the environment.

Furthermore as detailed in (Wooldridge and Jennings 1995) several agent architectures have been categorized according to the prevalence of certain characteristics ranging from purely deliberative to purely reactive and hybrid.

While SOA is attractive for automation in part due to the possibility of seamlessly integrating systems at an interface of proxy level, the MAS contribution has been mainly related with "what lies behind the interface".

The agent characteristics earlier pinpointed allow a Multiagent System to behave as a dynamic social network of problem solvers that provide a result that is often bigger than the sum of individual contributions.

Given the large scope of applicability of such a system numerous environment implementations (A-globe 2007; ABLE 2007; JADE 2007; JATLite 2007) have been developed focusing distinct agent models and communication mechanisms.

A consistent standardization effort in defining agent communication languages (ACL), interaction protocols and overall integration of heterogeneous agents systems has been deployed The Foundation for Intelligent Physical Agents (FIPA)

As shown in (Bussmann et al. 2004; Marik and Mcfarlane 2005; Monostori et al. 2006) automation domain denotes a potential of MAS application with effective advantages over, currently used centralized solution in respect to: feasibility, robustness and flexibility, reconfigurability and redeployability. In (Marik et al. 2005) is shown that at least 25% of industrial automation problems can be efficiently solved by using an agent based approach. In (Monostori et al. 2006) a thoroughly overview of the use of MAS in manufacturing is addressed and the major strategic directions are indicated. In particular, the aspects of support for emergence and embodied intelligence to support highly adaptable and reconfigurable (evolvable) manufacturing systems are emphasized. There are, however, several weaknesses in MAS when applied to industrial systems, namely: rather limited time for the decision making, constraints given by the properties of the physical equipment as well as limited number of acceptable manufacturing structures.

4. MERGING MAS AND SOA

Although there is a lack of measurable evidence on the strengths and weakness of both concepts some issues systematically pop-up during the implementation of distributed control systems for flexible assembly cells. Two installations have been used to test MAS and SOA: the MOFA educational shop floor (Barata et al. 2006a) (Figure 1) and the NOVAFLEX pilot assembly cell (Barata 2003; Barata et al. 2007c; Cândido and Barata 2007; Ribeiro 2007) (Figure 2).

Figure 1. The MOFA educational shop floor

Figure 2. The NOVAFLEX cell Assembly cell

In either case each participant in the assembly process (robot, gripper, conveyor, tool magazine, etc) was abstracted as an agent or a service that interact among in the completion of cooperative tasks.

The implementation work was mainly pc-based (Figure 3) therefore computational power was not a constraint. However, the differences between SOA and MAS were immediately felt. Although both paradigms support the idea of distributed autonomous entities and provide an effective modeling metaphor for complexity encapsulation, SOA emphasizes contract-based descriptions of the hosted services and does not provide a reference programming model. MAS, on the other hand, support well established methods to describe the behavior of an agent. The automation environments considered are typically heterogeneous and the lack of a structured development model/template renders system designing, implementation and debugging harder. The fact that agents are regulated by internal rules that support the implementation of social behaviour is a clear advantage. This is of major importance when considering systems that undergo dynamic runtime changes which is the case of the production paradigms earlier referred. SOA, on the other hand, is typically supported by widely used web technologies and assures interoperability with a wide range of systems and can easily spawn over the internet. Most well known MAS platforms are optimized for LAN use and are restricted to compliance with well defined but less used interoperability standards

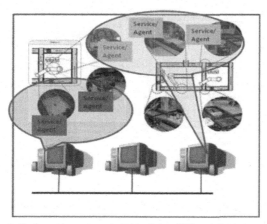

Figure 3. Each service or agent abstracting a different device run on a pc.

Recently in an extension to (Barata et al. 2006a), after successfully running JADE-LEAP (JADE 2007) on a GUMSTIX (GUMSTIX; Wooldridge 2002) device, it was possible to control some of the MOFA shop floor components from an agent inside that device. This experiment is closer to the systems envisioned by the future automation paradigms earlier mentioned where each participant in the process has local processing power (Figure 4).

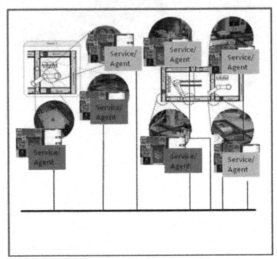

Figure 4. Each service or agent abstracting a different device runs on a local controller on the device itself.

Unfortunately the computational requirements of the java virtual machine in addition to the ones of the JADE-LEAP platform introduced a significant overkill that tremendously reduced the performance of the system. . Emergent frameworks like DPWS provide high performance Web Service support for devices with limited resources without constraining services implementation but the inners describing the behaviour of the service have coded from scratch.

Table 1 presents a comparative analysis between MAS and SOA. The selected characteristics included the conceptual and technology related features that are most relevant for the systems under study.

Table 1. Comparative Analysis between SOA and MAS

Characteristics	SOA	MAS
Basic Unit	Service	Agent
Autonomy	Both entities denote autonomy as the functionality provided is self-contained	
Behaviour description	In SOA the focus is on detailing the public interface rather than describing execution details.	There are well established methods to describe the behaviour of an agent.
Social ability	Social ability is not defined for SOA nevertheless the use of a service implies the acceptance of the rules defined in the interface description	The agents denote social ability regulated by internal or environmental rules
Complexity encapsulation	Again, the self-contained nature of the functionalities provided allows hiding the details. In SOA this encapsulation is explicit.	
Communication infrastructure	SOA are supported by Web related technologies and can seamlessly run on the internet.	Most implementations are optimized for LAN use.
Support for dynamically reconfigurable run-time architectures	Reconfiguration often requires reprogramming	The adaptable nature of agents makes them reactive to changes in the environment.
Interoperability	Assured by the use of general purpose web technologies.	Heavily dependent on compliance with FIPA-like standards.
Computational requirements	Lightweight implementations like the DPWS guarantee high performance without interoperability constraints	Most implementations have heavy computational requirements

The discussion around the fusion of MAS and SOA is not fundamentally new. However the research focus has been in enabling agents in existing systems to request, provide or manage web services (Greenwood and Calisti 2004; LIAO et al. 2004; Lyell et al. 2003; Maamar et al. 2003).

In the work developed by (Shen et al. 2005) an Agent-Based Service-Oriented Integration Framework was implemented in which web services were used as the backbone of some of the agents used in their case study. However, this integration framework is aiming business transactions and e-Business and therefore not targeting low cost computationally limited resources such as the ones under study.

In a first attempt to merge MAS and SOA in a lightweight environment for embedded devices, DPWS has been used to provide Web Services interfacing functionalities, while state control and the execution model has been borrowed from the Agent concept.

The approach taken is currently running as nearly forty independent entities, spread across several computers in the NOVAFLEX's cell, that interact in the completion of assembly tasks. In each entity Web Services are providing:

- Data encapsulation
- Communication support
- Complexity encapsulation

- Service Publishing and Discovery

Behind the Web Services interface the agent inspired code takes care of:

- Structured communication with the adequate semantics
- State control and interactions' monitoring
- Generic execution of process plans

In this manner the entities running in the system denote a memory footprint of few kilobytes and yet deliver the adequate performance in the tasks under execution while being pooled by external system that gather extra information concerning the device (documentation and life cycle parameters). Currently this code is being installed in embedded devices to test its performance.

5. CONCLUSIONS

It is expected that future automation environments denote a complex and distributed nature. Current approaches are on the edge of becoming obsolete in supporting the expected requirements. Researchers are currently structuring the paradigms and technologies that will support these systems and, in this context, the demand and use of network intelligent devices is growing and new systems need to be developed to accompany also that shift in technology. Multiagent systems and Service Oriented Architectures currently align as the main candidates for that purpose. The comparative analysis in the previous section unveiled contact points, weaknesses and strengths. Paradigmatically both concepts target similar systems and are supported by well structured standards and development environments. Nonetheless, each misses significant complementary functionalities provided by the other.

As the number of SOA/MAS ready devices is expected to increase the need for good tools and methods to support the integration of both worlds become mandatory. The authors are currently developing solutions for this goal.

6. REFERENCES

1. A-globe. "A-globe." http://agents.felk.cvut.cz/aglobe/. 2007
2. ABLE. "Agent Building and Learning Environment." http://www.alphaworks.ibm.com/tech/able 2007
3. Andrews, T., Curbera, F., Dholakia, H., Goland, Y., Klein, J., Leymann, F., Liu, K., Roller, D., Smith, D., Thatte, S., Trickovic, I., Weerawarana, S. "Business Process Execution Language for Web Services Version 1.1.", 2003
4. Arkin, A., Askary, S., Fordin, S., Jekeli, W., Kawaguchi, K., Orchard, D., Pogliani, S., Riemer, K., Struble, S., Takacsi-Nagy, P., Trickovic, I., Zimek, S. "Web Service Choreography Interface (WSCI) 1.0 W3C Note.", 2002
5. Babiceanu, R., Chen, F. "Development and applications of holonic manufacturing systems: a survey." Journal of Intelligent Manufacturing, 2006; 17: 111-131.
6. Barata, J. "Coalition Based Approach for Shop Floor Agility," PhD, Universidade Nova de Lisboa, Monte da Caparica, 2003.
7. Barata, J., Cândido, G., Feijão, F. "A multiagent based control system applied to an educational shoop floor." BALANCED AUTOMATION SYSTEMS in Manufacturing and Services, Niagara Falls, Canada, 2006a.
8. Barata, J., Frei, R., and Onori, M. "Evolvable Production Systems Context and Implications." International Symposium on Industrial Informatics, IEEE, Vigo. 2007a
9. Barata, J., Onori, M., Frei, R., and Leitão, P. "Evolvable Production Systems: Enabling Research Domains." International Conference on Changeable, Agile, Reconfigurable and Virtual Production, Toronto, Canada. 2007b
10. Barata, J., Ribeiro, L., and Colombo, A. W. "Diagnosis using Service Oriented Architectures (SOA)." International Conference on Industrial Informatics, IEEE, Vienna. 2007c
11. Barata, J., Ribeiro, L., and Onori, M. "Diagnosis on Evolvable Production Systems." International Symposium on Industrial Electronics, IEEE, Vigo. 2007d
12. Barata, J., Santana, P. F., and Onori, M. "Evolvable Assembly Systems: A Development Roadmap." IFAC Symposium on Information Control Problems in Manufacturing, Saint-Etienne, France. 2006b
13. Booth, D., Hass, H., McCabe, F., Newcomer, E., Champion, M., Ferris, C., and Orchard, D. "Web Services Architecture, W3C Working Group Note 11 February 2004.", 2004
14. Box, D., Ehnebuske, D., Kakivaya, G., Layman, A., Mendelsohn, N., Frystyk Nielsen, H., Thatte, S., Winer, D. "Simple Object Access Protocol (SOAP) 1.1, W3C Note 08 May 2000.", 2000
15. Bray, T., Paoli, J., Sperberg-McQueen, C. M., Maler, E., Yergeau, F. "Extensible Markup Language (XML) 1.0 (Fourth Edition), W3C Recommendation 16 August 2006.", 2006
16. Bussmann, S., Jennings, N. R., and Wooldridge, M. Multiagent Systems for Manufacturing Control: A Design Methodology, Springer, Berlin. 2004
17. Bussmann, S., Mcfarlane, D. C. "Rationales for Holonic Manufacturing." Second International Workshop on Intelligent Manufacturing Systems, Leuven, Belgium, 177 - 184.
18. Camarinha-Matos, L. M., Vieira, M. "Intelligent Mobile Agents in Elderly Care." Journal of Robotics and Autonomous Systems, 1999; 27(1-2): 59-75.
19. Cândido, G., Barata, J. "A Multiagent Control System for Shop Floor Assembly." International Conference on Industrial Applications of Holonic and Multiagent Systems, Regensburg, Germany. 2007
20. Chan, S., Conti, D., Kaler, C., Kuehnel, T., Regnier, A., Roe, B., Sather, D., Schlimmer, J., Sekine, H., Thelin, J., Walter, D., Weast, J., Whitehead, D., Wright, D., Yarmosh, Y. "Devices Profile for Web Services." http://schemas.xmlsoap.org/ws/2006/02/devprof/. 2006
21. Christensen, E., Curbera, F., Meredith, G., Weerawarana, S. "Web Services Description Language (WSDL) 1.1, W3C Note 15 March 2001." 2001
22. Frei, R., Barata, J., Di Marzo Serugendo, G. "A complexity theory approach to evolvable production systems." Internacional Conferecene in informatics and control, automation and robotics, Angers, France. 2007a
23. Frei, R. M., Ribeiro, L., Barata, J., and Semere, D. "Evolvable Assembly Systems: Towards User Friendly Manufacturing." International Symposium on Assembly and Manufacturing, IEEE, Ann Arbor, USA. 2007b
24. Gou, L., Luh, P. B., Kyoka, Y. "Holonic Manufacturing Scheduling Architecture, Cooperation Mechanism and Implementation." Computers in Industry, 1998; 37(3): 213-231.
25. Greenwood, D., Calisti, M. "Engineering Web Service - Agent Integration." 2004 IEEE International Conference on Systems, Man and Cybernetics. 2004
26. GUMSTIX. "GUMSTIX." http://www.gumstix.com.
27. Huhns, M. N., Singh, M. P. Service-Oriented Computing: Key Concepts and Principles. Internet Computing 2005; 9(1), 75-81.
28. InLife. "Integrated Ambient Intelligence and Knowledge Based Services for Optimal Life-Cycle Impact of Complex Manufacturing and Assembly Lines." http://www.uninova.pt/inlife/, 2006.
29. JADE. "Java Agent Development Framework." http://www.jade.tilab.com, 2007.
30. Jammes, F., Smit, H. "Service-oriented architectures for devices - the SIRENA view." International Conference on Industrial Informatics, Perth, Western Australia, 140- 147.

31. JATLite. "Java Agent Template, Lite." http://java.stanford.edu/, 2007.
32. Koren, Y., Heisel, U., Jovane, F., Moriwaki, T., Pritchow, G., Ulsoy, A. G., Van Brussel, H. Reconfigurable Manufacturing Systems. CIRP Annals 1999, 48.
33. LIAO, B.-S., GAO, J., HU, J., CHEN, J.-J. "A federated multi-agent system: Autonomic control of Web Services." Proceedings of the Third International Conference on Machine learning and Cybernetics, Shangai.
34. Lyell, M., Rosen, L., Casigni-Simkins, M., Norris, D. "On software agents and Web services: Usage and design concepts and issues." Proceedings of WSABE 2003.
35. Maamar, Z., Sheng, Q., Benatallah, B. "Interleaving Web services composition and execution using software agents and delegation." Proceedings of WSABE 2003.
36. Marik, V., Mcfarlane, D. C. "Industrial adoption of agent-based technologies." Intelligent Systems 2005; 20(1): 27-35.
37. Marik, V., Vrba, P., Hall, K. H., Maturana, F. P. "Rockwell automation agents for manufacturing." International Conference on Autonomous Agents, The Netherlands, 107 - 113
38. Mehrabi, M. G., Ulsoy, A. G., Koren, Y. Reconfigurable Manufacturing Systems and their Enabling Technologies. International Journal Manufacturing Technology and Management 2000; 1: 113-130.
39. Monostori, L., Váncza, J., Kumara, S. R. T. Agent-Based Systems for Manufacturing. CIRP Annals 2006; 55(2).
40. Onori, M. "Evovlbale Assembly Systems - A New Paradigm?" 33rd International Symposium on Robotics Stockholm, 2002.
41. Onori, M., Alsterman, H., Barata, J. " An architecture development approach for evolvable assembly systems." International Symposium on Assembly and Task Planning: From Nano to Macro Assembly and Manufacturing, Montréal, Canada, 19-24.
42. Onori, M., Barata, J., Frei, R. "Evolvable Assembly Systems Basic Principles." Conference on Information Technology for BALANCED AUTOMATION SYSTEMS in Manufacturing and Services, Springer, Ontario, Canada, 2006.
43. Papazoglou, M. P., Traverso, P., Dustdar, S., Leymann, F., Krämer, B. J. "Service-Oriented Computing: A Research Roadmap." Dagstuhl Seminar Proceedings 05462 (SOC).
44. Ribeiro, L. "A Diagnostic Infrastructure for Manufacturing Systems," New University of Lisbon, Lisbon, 2007.
45. Shen, W., Li, Y., Hao, Q., Wang, S., Ghenniwa, H. "Implementing Collaborative Manufacturing with Intelligent Web Services." Proceedings of the 2005 The Fifth International Conference on Computer and Information Technology, 2005.
46. SIRENA. "Service Infrastructure for Real-time Embedded Network Applications." http://www.sirena-itea.org/Sirena/Home.htm, 2006.
47. SOCRADES. "Service-Oriented Cross-layer infRAstructure for Distributed smart Embedded devices." http://www.socrades.eu/Documents/AllDocuments/default.html, 2006.
48. SODA. "Service Oriented Device and Delivery Architecture." http://www.soda-itea.org/Home/default.html, 2006.
49. Ueda, K. "A concept for bionica manufacturing systems based on DNA-type information." PROLAMAT, IFIP, Tokyo, 1992.
50. Van Brussel, H., Wyns, J., Valckenaers, P., Bongaerts, L., Peeters, P. Reference Architecture for Holonic Manufacturing Systems: PROSA. Computers in Industry 1998; 37: 255-274.
51. Wooldridge, M., Jennings, N. R. Intelligent Agents - Theory and Practice. Knowledge Engineering Review 1995; 10(2): 115-152.
52. Wooldridge, M. J. An Introduction to Multiagent Systems, J. Wiley, New York, 2002.

29

EMBODIED INTELLIGENCE TO TURN EVOLVABLE ASSEMBLY SYSTEMS REALITY

Regina Frei and José Barata
Department of Electrotechnical Engineering, New University of Lisbon
{regina.frei, jab}@uninova.pt

Evolvable Assembly Systems may successfully resolve industry's problems with low volume / high change productions; thanks to Embodied Intelligence, systems can play an active role in the engineering procedure. Modules do not only consist of their physical body including small local controllers, but also represent themselves in Virtual Reality. Interacting with each other, they Self-Organize to fulfill the ever-changing production requirements. Systems become user-friendly, distributed and more autonomous.

This article concretizes the required control solution by detailing the different control-related issues and tasks at hand. Examples of information needed for computer-readable specifications of parts, processes and system modules are given. A navigator system is proposed to transform resource-independent assembly instructions into layout-specific executables.

Keywords: Evolvable Assembly Systems, Reconfigurable Production Systems, Automation, Autonomous Systems, Embodied Intelligence

1. INTRODUCTION

Industry-branches which have to cope with small lot sizes and frequent changes need innovative solutions such as Evolvable Assembly Systems, EAS (Frei et al. 2007; Onori 2002). They are based on a thorough analysis of product properties and production processes; the systems' modularity must be supported by a correspondingly modular control solution (Marik et al. 2007; Rizzi et al. 1997). Solutions consist of agents or other technologies like Service Oriented Architectures (Jammes and Smit 2005) or Function Blocks (Lewis 2001), which however need to be completed with proactivity.

One of the most important remaining questions is how to realize these control systems, which must be easy to use, dependable, flexible and scalable. Specialized and extensive programming must be avoided. Being user-friendly implies the systems to be as autonomous as possible, hiding complexity and providing the user with well-represented, specific information resp. requests. Chances are best for Multi-Agent Systems (MAS) with extended system capabilities, able to organize themselves to a high degree.

Ideally, system modules are plugged together the way a new mouse is plugged into a laptop, which, if necessary, automatically searches for the right driver and installs it, or eventually asks for user interaction in a precise way. Similarly, the module controllers will communicate with each other, verify their compatibility, create complex skills based on their individual simple skills, and offer them to the user. Functionality is readily offered.

Please use the following format when citing this chapter:

Frei, R. and Barata, J., 2008, in IFIP International Federation for Information Processing, Volume 266, *Innovation in Manufacturing Networks;* ed. A. Azevedo; (Boston: Springer), pp. 269–278.

A possible approach towards achieving such a distributed, autonomous control solution with Embodied Intelligence is discussed in this article. Embodied Intelligence is a concept widely used in the area of intelligent and cognitive systems in the Artificial Life (AL) research domain. The main idea is that intelligence requires a body to interact with (Pfeifer and Scheier 2001). Intelligent behavior emerges from the interaction of brain, body, and environment. In the specific case of EAS the idea is not to consider the concept strictly as understood in the AL domain but using an interpretation in which each assembly component has computer power (brain), its hardware (body), and is placed within its external environment. As in the AL domain, the actions of the systems (realizing assembly according to the requirements), which can be regarded as intelligent actions, are the result of the interactions between the components, its onboard computer, and the environment.

Chapter 2 presents control-related tasks in a conceptual overview, chapter 3 details module specifications and chapter 4 takes up the issue of the autonomous generation layout-specific assembly operations and layout improvements and the way it could be achieved. Finally, conclusions and outlook are provided.

2. CONTROL-RELATED TASKS

Automated assembly consists of various phases and / or levels which lead one to another, following the flash upwards, in time as well as in logic (Figure 1). They are often iterative and closely related, like running the assembly operations and monitoring them. The next few paragraphs describe the phases in some detail, starting with the lowest.

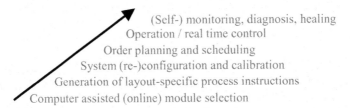

(Self-) monitoring, diagnosis, healing
Operation / real time control
Order planning and scheduling
System (re-)configuration and calibration
Generation of layout-specific process instructions
Computer assisted (online) module selection

Figure 1. Control-related tasks in EAS

2.1. Module Selection with Embodied Intelligence

Embodied Intelligence opens up much more possibilities for interactive system design. All available standard modules, i.e. those present on the shop floor, those stored in the repository and eventually those offered for rent or sale by a network of system suppliers, also exist in a "second world", a Virtual Reality (VR). This is not a simple user interface with simulation. Modules represent themselves and their current or future interactions in the Module Pool. The user specifies the types of products to be treated. According to the product class, suitable module class will propose itself to the user, based on a well-elaborated ontology of processes, products and systems, as explained in (Barata et al. 2007a; Onori et al. 2004). The user can then select the wished modules.

If there is no suitable module available for a certain task, the user is advised to reconsider the product and its processes in order to solve the problem with standard modules, or could otherwise ask a module supplier to create the required special module. The modules guide the user in this selection procedure, giving indications about their compatibility, performance, emplacement constraints, etc.

2.2 From resource-independent assembly instructions to specific executables

A product to be assembled brings generic assembly instructions, which determine how the parts shall be joined to each other. This description is not specifically made for a certain system layout; most products could even be assembled by hand. It does not mention, neither, how the parts get from their storage place to the assembly location.

In the scenario considered here, the "navigator" (Figure) will then combine the generic assembly plan with the existing layout or the chosen modules and generate concrete steps to realize the assembly. This means that the instructions will now be interpreted for the actual layout and thus transformed into executable programs, using the modules' skills. Such programs must, however, stay easily modifiable in case the layout is changed again later or in case one or several modules should become unavailable.

The way this navigator is realized could be similar to the navigating systems used in cars: a dynamically created system map (Embodied Intelligence!) is compared with the initial situation, i.e. the parts as fed into the system, and the goal, which is the completely assembled product. The paths to bring the parts from their initial location to their final target position are then calculated (chapter 4).

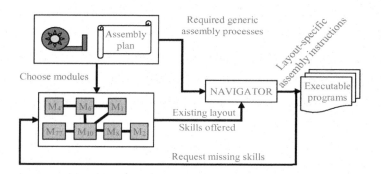

Figure 2. From generic assembly instructions to layout-specific operations

2.3. System (re-)configuration, layout improvements and calibration

When the modules are being connected to each other, they will announce their presence and contact their immediate "geographical" neighbors. Each module provides one or several functions (simple skills). The user can decide about the complex skills to be formed, but even better, the modules know themselves with whom they can collaborate (or not) and know in which way their skills can be combined (chapter 3). Thanks to the matching between the requirements of the tasks to be executed on one hand, and the skills offered by the layout on the other hand, discrepancies will be detected. Also unsuitable module combinations or locations will cause a user alert, asking for a layout change (chapter 4).

The modules will be able to autonomously calibrate themselves and their interactions with others. This requires that a module, e.g. a basis axis, can identify if there are other modules fixed on top of it, e.g. second or third axis including a gripper. Calibration data will be stored and used for monitoring effects of fatigue and other deviations from the original values.

CoBASA (Barata 2005) can already today fulfill most of these tasks. An increased version with more functionality is currently under construction.

2.4. Order planning and scheduling

Many agent-based planning and scheduling algorithms are available in literature, e.g. (Valckenaers and Van Brussel 2005), or even already implemented in industry, such as the "Truck Scheduler" (Magenta Technology) described in (Rzevski and Skobelev 2007); therefore, this issue is not further detailed in the scope of this work.

2.5. Operation / run-time control and Orchestration

Real-time control must be highly efficient and robust. Tiny controllers to include in modules allow truly distributed operation. The challenge is to develop MAS for those small real-time controllers, to be used at fine levels of granularity – i.e. as an integrated part of modules. Hardware as well as software is required. MAS environments such as JADE is computationally too heavy for tiny controllers, which will not be full PCs but something smaller, lighter.

Agent-oriented Architectures (AoA) as well as Service-oriented Architectures (SoA) are suitable choices for autonomous, adaptive, decoupled and distributed systems as required for EAS. In AoA and SOA, the logical and physical aspects of an entity are uncoupled, enabling a Holonic approach.

The main question is how to make two devices, with no previous knowledge of each other's type, recognize each other and start interacting. To solve this problem, devices need knowledge processing capabilities. Using semantic web services, knowledge is explicit through machine-interpretable semantics and can be inferred by machine-reasoning. Applying this approach to the manufacturing domain, components previously unknown can be recognized straightforward and be ready to interact with existing ones. It could be also possible to select the best available service following search parameters, such as QoS (Quality of Service), supplier, past activities, etc. After identifying the services, it is possible to compose them to complex processes through orchestration and choreography. Combining AoA with SoA, a new paradigm (or evolution of an existing two) can arise by joining "the best of two worlds", allied to crescent technology improvements that allow to put even more intelligence in ever tinier devices.

2.6. System (self-)surveillance, (self-)diagnosis, (self-)healing

Autonomous systems are able to maintain themselves in good condition. Self-monitoring is required at the level of each individual module as well as on cluster level and (global) system level. The modules locally manage their maintenance and service schedules and inform the user about forthcoming events.

Creating a way of autonomously supervising and diagnosing higher (emergent) system levels is not easy in a situation characterized by frequent changes. Of course the monitoring / diagnosis system could be manually adapted whenever the layout has changed – but this would be a breach with the goal of creating autonomous systems with minimal user interaction. Methods for system self-diagnosis are currently being developed (Barata et al. 2007b).

In certain cases, the system will be able to "heal" itself, e.g. by restarting a blocked controller or exchanging a problematic gripper. If the failure is more serious, the shop floor staff will be alerted. In the meantime, the navigator reconsiders the requirements and the current layout (now with unavailable modules) and tries to find alternative ways of fulfilling the current tasks, eventually delegating the operations to modules which have the same skills but work slower or which are already executing other tasks. What counts is keeping production running.

3. MODULE, PART AND OPERATION SPECIFICATIONS

Embodied Intelligence means that agents must know themselves, their physical bodies, their workspace and their interactions with others. This implies specifying parts, modules and operations / skills in a computer-readable way.

3.1. Module specifications

Modules need an internal functional model of themselves and their working space, in the geometrical sense, as well as specifications of their pneumatic, electric and electronic interfaces. They could then match with each other much in the way jigsaw puzzle pieces match with each other.

When modules come together, their workspaces merge. This may result both in an expansion or in a limitation; modules can give each other more freedom or constrain each other. Generally, the consequences may be calculated by the agents, using vector addition (Figure 3). Doing this properly is crucial for collision avoidance by the means of the control software.

Besides their interface descriptions, the modules may also carry a changeable list of preferable partner modules, and accordingly establish a "black list" of modules which are known for causing trouble or being unsuitable. Similarly, modules will carry rules for forming complex skills in collaboration with their partners. The most frequent combinations might be explicitly stated – while more compositions may emerge when encountered. Such a mechanism prepares the system for the eventual emergence of functions or combinations which the system designer did not originally plan.

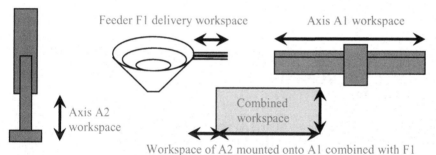

Workspace of A2 mounted onto A1 combined with F1
Figure 3. Example of individual and combined workspaces (symbolic representation)

3.2. Part specifications

In order to be treated by autonomous agents (or alternatively, to be autonomous agents themselves), parts must be precisely specified, analogous to the module specifications. There is plenty of potentially useful information, including:
- Geometry: plate, sphere, hemisphere, cylinder, cube, bar, stick, triangle, etc.
- Material: steel, cupper, aluminum, rigid plastic, rubber, composite fiber, etc.
- Properties: insulating, conducting, magnetic, transparent, etc.
- Mass
- Rigidity (or stiffness), elasticity
- Conditioning: in bulk, on pallet, in band, etc.
- Way of gripping

Even a CAD file for every part might be included in the part specifications. This would allow graphically specifying the locations of assembly operations, of gripping points and other relevant spots (example: Figure 4).

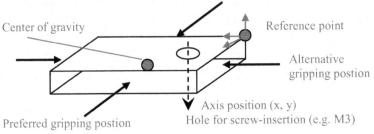

Figure 4. Specifications of a plate with hole

3.3. Operation specifications

On the resource side, the operations a module can do are called skills; on the requirement side, they correspond to the processes needed to assembly a product. The goal of specifying them generically is to describe operations independent from the concrete part to be treated and independent from the resource (modules) which will execute the tasks. This gives the system a certain level of abstraction and thus the liberty to attribute any module with suitable skills to the operation in question. The execution of a certain task will not be blocked if a certain module is unavailable or out of service; having the abstract description, the agents may find one or several other modules corresponding to the requirements and able to do the task at hand. Neither will a part stay untreated in case a certain (maybe composite) process becomes unavailable; knowing the part and its needs allows finding alternative processes.

4. FROM RESOURCE-INDEPENDENT ASSEMBLY INSTRUCTIONS TO SPECIFIC EXECUTABLES

A simplified scenario will serve to explain the concept mentioned in section 2.2. We imagine the automated and autonomous assembly of a tape roller, consisting of four parts and a carrier, as symbolically shown on Figure 85. The main input to the system are part specifications including precise but layout-independent assembly instructions. The part descriptions indicate where the parts come from, i.e. if they are contained in a feeder or stored on pallets, and how they are preferably grabbed by which kind of gripper. The already existing system layout is as schematically represented in Figure 107 a).

Two different approaches are possible: Either the assembly plan is an agent, which has the task to procure the (passive) parts and assemble them, or the parts themselves are agents which must find their destined "neighbors" according to the plan, which is a passive piece of information. An intermediate solution could be that both assembly plan and parts are agents and collaborate in reaching their common goal.

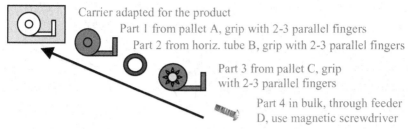

Carrier adapted for the product
    Part 1 from pallet A, grip with 2-3 parallel fingers
    Part 2 from horiz. tube B, grip with 2-3 parallel fingers

        Part 3 from pallet C, grip
        with 2-3 parallel fingers

            Part 4 in bulk, through feeder
            D, use magnetic screwdriver

Figure 5. Symbolic representation of assembly instructions

The fact that each module knows its neighbors allows implicitly knowing the system composition; this is knowledge can easily be made explicit by forming a kind of map in Virtual Reality. This makes it easy to form routing tables based on those used in telecommunications. This VR could then be used in a similar way as a navigator in modern cars. Parts are located on their storage spot and can calculate their possible trajectories to the carrier resp. the final assembly (Figure 9). This can imply the transfer over a series of conveyors and the handling by several robots on the way – partners which all must be interacted with. Obstacles need to be avoided, and timing respected – the before-mentioned orchestration of the assembly modules. Based on the assembly instructions and these calculations, a resource usage plan (Table 1) is generated. The specific control programs for the modules to execute all these actions are then derived automatically; asking the user for confirmation is obviously necessary.

Table 1. Resource usage plan (P&P= "Pick & Place", R = robot, g = gripper)

	Operation plan	Resource
1	Bring carrier	Conveyor
2	P&P part 1	R1 G1
3	Pick part 2	R1 G1
4	Insert part 2 into part 1	R1 G1
5	Pick part 3	R1 G1, R2 G3
6	Place part 3 on part 1, align +/- 2°	R1 G1, R2 G3
7	P&P part 4, screw part 4: 5x 360°	R2 G1
8	P&P finished product (unload)	R2 G3, R1 G1

In case of difficult, long or impossible handling paths, the system may propose layout changes, based on a set of relatively simple rules such as:
- Check if a part is sent from a point to another and back again; if yes, try moving the storage location or the assembly place.
- Check if a part has a long trajectory compared to the size of the system; if yes, try moving the storage location or the assembly place.
- Check if all the axes / robots are used at least at (e.g.) 60% of their time; if not, try replacing the ones with lower usage. Try to equally distribute the work charge to all the robots, eventually requesting the addition of suitable grippers or other supplementary modules from the storage.

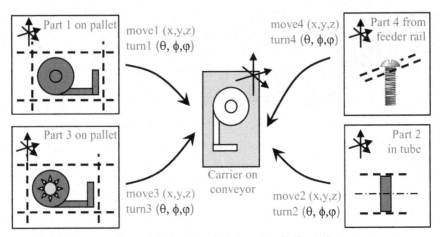

Figure 6. Trajectory calculations done by the navigator

As an example, the layout in Figure 10 a) could be improved as shown in b). It could mean that robot R1 has a parallel 2-finger gripper (G1) and can do all the needed movements, but it is a rather slow robot. Robot R2 has a magnetic screw-driver (G2) and is fast. A compatible parallel 2-finger gripper (G3) is available in the storage, as the system detects in the list of available modules. It would thus propose to add G3 and to move pallet C as well as the unloading station from R1 to R2.

Obviously, the system is neither capable of moving modules and pallets nor should it be allowed to take such decisions autonomously – at least not before the system has been proven absolutely dependable. The right approach is to inform the user about the detected possibility for improvement and letting her decide.

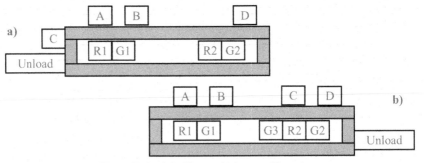

Figure 7. a) original layout, b) improved layout

5.　CONCLUSIONS AND OUTLOOK

The control-related tasks in EAS require innovative solutions. The realization of user-friendly, evolvable and more autonomous control systems for EAS relies on the use of Embodied Intelligence. It implies the computer-readable specification of parts, modules and processes. System modules consist of their physical body, their local controller and their software agent, representing them in Virtual Reality. They thus need thorough knowledge of themselves and their interaction characteristics. A well-founded ontology for EAS is currently being made and will soon be available. This article structured the different steps and suggests solutions such as the automatic creation of a dynamic system map in VR and the use of a "Navigator", similar to the navigation systems in cars. Generic, layout-independent assembly instructions can thus be transformed into layout-specific operations (i.e. executable programs) which will lead to the assembly of the product.

Most ideas presented in this article are still in theoretical form; their implementation has just begun. The authors are aware of the fact that many difficulties and complications will only surface when the ideas are put into practice. Nevertheless, the concepts are expected to turn out to be highly useful for future systems and make their handling user-friendly and fast.

It is well-known that production industry is a very traditional business and requires systems to be predictable, reliable and traceable. System autonomy is for most old-school engineers a red flag. However, the world is moving fast, and especially in Swarm Robotics great advances are being made. Even if not directly applicable to production systems with heterogeneous agents / modules and complex, specific tasks, such advances foster the development of new ideas and approaches. In order to convince the research departments of innovative industrial companies to collaborate in such futuristic research, a careful and stepwise approach is necessary.

6. REFERENCES

1. Barata, J. Coalition Based Approach For ShopFloor Agility, Amadora - Lisboa, Edições Orion, 2005
2. Barata, J., Frei, R., Onori, M. "Evolvable Production Systems: Context and Implications". In ISIE'07 - IEEE International Symposium on Industrial Electronics, Vigo - Spain, IEEE, 2007a
3. Barata, J., Ribeiro, L., Onori, M. "Diagnosis on Evolvable Production Systems". In ISIE'07 - IEEE International Symposium on Industrial Electronics, Vigo - Spain, IEEE, 2007b
4. Frei, R., Ribeiro, L., Barata, J., Semere, D. "Evolvable Assembly Systems: Towards User Friendly Manufacturing". In ISAM'07 - IEEE International Symposium on Assembly and Manufacturing, Ann Arbor - Michigan - USA, IEEE, 2007, pp 288-293.
5. Jammes, F., Smit, H. Service-oriented paradigms in industrial automation. IEEE Transactions on Industrial Informatics 2005; v1, n1: 62-70.
6. Lewis, R.W. Modelling control systems using IEC 61499 - Applying function blocks to distributed systems, IEE, 2001
7. Marik, V., Vyatkin, V., Colombo, A.W., eds. Holonic and Multi-Agent Systems for Manufacturing. Heidelberg, Springer, 2007
8. Onori, M. "Evolvable Assembly Systems - A New Paradigm?". In ISR2002 - 33rd International Symposium on Robotics (Stockholm), 2002, pp 617-621.
9. Onori, M., Lastra, J.L.M., Alsterman, H. "Evolvable Assembly Platforms - Definitions, Approaches and Requirements". In IPAS (Bad Hofgastein, Austria), 2004
10. Pfeifer, R., Scheier, C. Understanding intelligence. Cambridge, MA, MIT Press, 2001
11. Rizzi, A.A., Gowdy, J., Hollis, R.L. "Agile Assembly Architecture: an Agent Based Approach to Modular Precision Assembly Systems". In International Conference on Robotics and Automation, 1997
12. Rzevski, G. and Skobelev, P. Emergent Intelligence in Multi-Agent Systems. Windsor, Berkshire, UK: Magenta Technology, 2007.
13. Valckenaers, P., Van Brussel, H. Holonic Manufacturing Execution Systems. CIRP Annals - Manufacturing Technology 2005; v54, n1: 427-432.

30

NEXT GENERATION OF FLEXIBLE
ASSEMBLY SYSTEMS

Rolf Bernhardt, Dragoljub Surdilovic, Volker Katschinski, Gerhard Schreck and
Klaus Schröer

*Rolf Bernhardt, Dragoljub Surdilovic, Volker Katschinski and Gerhard Schreck are with the
Fraunhofer Institute for Production Systems and Design Technology (IPK), Pascalstraße 8-9, D-
10587 Berlin, Germany
(e-mail: {rolf.bernhardt / dragoljub.surdilovic / volker.katschinski}@ ipk.fraunhofer.de).
Klaus Schröer is with Volkswagen AG, PP-F2, Planung-Karosseriebau, Brieffach 1619/4, D-38436
Wolfsburg, Germany.
(e-mail: klaus.schroeer@volkswagen.de).*

*In September 2006 an integrated European project was launched entitled "Flexible
Assembly Systems through Workplace-Sharing and Time-Sharing Human-Machine
Cooperation (PISA)". PISA belongs to the research area "next generation of flexible
assembly technology and processes". The general aim of the project is to develop
intelligent assist systems (IAS) in order to support the human worker instead of
replace him. Thus, flexibility should not be reached through fully automated assembly
systems but should instead support the better integration of human workers.*

1. INTRODUCTION

The growing number of product variants, smaller lot sizes, accelerated time to market and
shorter product life cycles have led to increasing demands on assembly equipment and
concepts. They must achieve a high degree of flexibility with respect to variants, low-cost
adaptability of products and quick amortisation within a sustainable equipment concept. In
order to master these challenges, innovative approaches and technologies are required
(Butala et al., 2002). The performance of existing automation techniques is often
insufficient. As a solution to this problem, hybrid, i.e. human-integrated, approaches are
proposed. The idea is to combine human flexibility, intelligence and skills with the
advantages of sophisticated technical systems. Such systems should help the human
worker instead of replace him. Intelligent assist systems (IAS) offer a rational, advanced
method for the assembly of complex products on demand and at significantly reduced cost
(Surdilovic et al. 2003). Since today neither the technology nor the tools for planning and
managing IAS are available, the aim of the project is their prototypical development,
including demonstration based on use cases [3]. One breakthrough of this project will be
to bridge the gap between manual and automated assembly by introducing novel IAS
technology and providing planning and integration tools to make this new technology
applicable. A second breakthrough will be the reconfigurability of assembly systems and
the reusability of assembly equipment. On the one hand, this is related to a modular
structure of assembly systems including standard hardware and software interfaces for
assembly equipment. On the other hand, methods and tools are needed for reconfiguration
planning, reprogramming, life cycle and equipment management and knowledge bases for

Please use the following format when citing this chapter:

Bernhardt, R., Surdilovic, D., Katschinski, V., Schreck, G. and Schröer, K., 2008, in IFIP International Federation for Information Processing,
Volume 266, *Innovation in Manufacturing Networks*; ed. A. Azevedo; (Boston: Springer); pp. 279–288.

assembly solutions. Each breakthrough will lead to an increase in production capacity and productivity, to reduce the cost of investment and rearrangement and to react more quickly to market demands.

2. PISA OBJECTIVES

A skilled and motivated workforce still provides the most capable and reliable resource for the flexible (or customised) assembly of complex products. Recent studies have demonstrated clearly that flexibility can be improved by combining the benefits of human capabilities with sophisticated automation equipment in so-called hybrid flexible automation systems, providing a rational advanced concept for producing high-tech products with growing complexity at significantly reduced cost (Hägele et al., 2002). However, a reliable technological basis for hybrid systems does not yet exist, and the performance of existing flexible automation techniques (e.g. industrial robots) is quite limited in their ability to cooperate with and assist the human worker in a shared and reconfigurable assembly space (Karlsson, 2002). The existing standards do not permit workspace-sharing and cooperation.

Therefore, the prime objective of PISA is to establish a new generation of modular flexible assembly methodology by developing concepts, formal methods, standards and safety frameworks, tools and underlining technologies to allow the integration and cooperation between human workers and highly flexible devices and equipment in a qualitatively new and efficient manner. The main idea is to break from traditional paradigms regarding flexibility, cost, accessibility and applicability of high-tech assembly solutions, as well as conventional human-machine interaction. The project development concerns the following next-generation flexible assembly equipment and planning tools:

- A new generation of passive collaborative robots (COBOTS) and intelligent assist devices. These combine the benefits of industrial robots with those of passive handling devices. They also provide low-cost, operator-friendly solutions for the assembly of complex and variable volume products.

- Modular assembly robots representing the next generation of sensor-based robotic systems. These integrate visual and compliance control feedbacks, reconfigurable control systems and sophisticated grasping and tooling devices. They are capable of time-sharing with human workers and provide an efficient solution for capacity flexibility when workforce availability is lower or product volume varies.

- Assistant robots based on standard robotic systems. These are equipped with additional sensors and control functions and are capable of sharing a workspace and assembly process operations with a human worker. This approach offers a promising short-term solution for the flexible, reconfigurable assembly of highly customised products.

- Assembly process design and simulation tools involving the knowledge base of standardised processes and environmental models; interactive robots and human-in-loop models enabling a realistic conception of the assembly, planning and the optimisation of assembly system structures and process variations (virtual assembly system). These tools will also be very useful for the training and skill improvement of assembly workers.

- Reusable and reconfigurable electro-mechanical and control equipment; design and planning tools, including tight interfaces to assembly processes and parameters. This includes concepts and methods to support the planning and reconfiguration of new-generation hybrid flexible assembly lines for specific production systems and market demands.

3. PISA STRUCTURE AND APPROACH

Humans are the most flexible "components" of assembly systems, offering many advantages over machines (Tichem). Rather than remove human workers and develop fully automated solutions, PISA aims to keep human workers in the loop and to support them with qualified tools. Such an integrative approach combines human creativity, intelligence, knowledge, flexibility and skill with the advantages of sophisticated technical systems and tools, such as electronic and physical power, speed and accuracy.

The project is divided into nine interrelated subprojects (SP), as outlined in figure 1. The technical subprojects are SP1 to SP5; SP6 to SP8 handle innovation-related activities – IPR & Exploitation, Training & Dissemination and Occupational Safety & Standards – and SP9 comprises the project management.

The technical objective is to implement prototypical systems for the subprojects SP1 to SP4. Based on the use cases defined in SP5, integrated prototypes will be implemented to demonstrate the functionality, performance and novelty of the overall approach. Use cases will be selected from three different branches: the automotive, the home appliance and the aircraft industries. All prototypes will also be used for training purposes. Additional applications which are specifically interesting for SME will also be considered. This demonstrates one further advantage of the planned human-integrated solutions: not only can they be easily integrated into large assembly lines in the automotive and home appliance industries, but also into batch production in the aircraft industry.

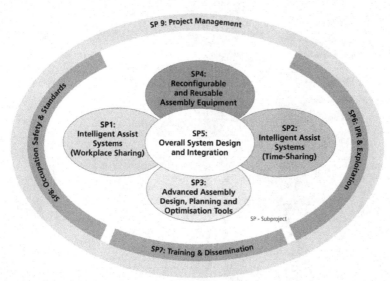

Figure 1. PISA Structure

4. PISA TECHNICAL SUBPROJECTS

SP1 Intelligent Assist Systems concerns two novel IAS for assembly processes. One is based on new industrial robot technology capable of sharing a workplace and operations with a human worker as outlined in figure 2 (ROBOT-IAS). The other, referred to as collaborating robot (COBOT), shown in figure 3, is capable of working jointly in direct physical contact with the human operator.

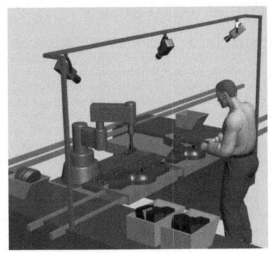

Figure 2. IAS Workplace-Sharing

Figure 3. Cooperative Robot (COBOT)

Within SP1, control algorithms and prototypes are under development which will allow workplace-sharing as well as pure collaboration with human workers in assembly processes. This includes the design of a new intelligent COBOT prototype that integrates power assistance, motion guidance functions, advanced interaction control and programming algorithms into a reliable, efficient and ergonomic assembly system. Thereby it is important that sophisticated human-machine interfaces are developed which will ensure efficient cooperation and easy integration into assembly lines. A particular objective is to establish a technological and functional basis for safe operation (OSHA) and standardisation of the new assist systems. The advantages of the first European COBOT developed in SP1 in comparison to the pilot systems developed in the USA will be appreciably lower cost, significantly improved ergonomics, simpler intuitive operation, higher-precision rapid movements and considerably reduced stress during manipulation and assembly of complex and heavy loads.

The results of SP1 after one year are the user requirements for IAS. Based on a system analysis of actual needs within the considered branches (aerospace, automotive, household industry and SME assembly sectors), and on an analysis of the state-of-the-art and research technology, critical development needs and problems were identified and specified. These requirements provide the basis for the further development of the novel assist technology for human-centred assembly. Additionally, a first prototype was implemented, demonstrating some COBOT functions. This system was demonstrated at the 26th international MOTEK fair in September 2007 in Stuttgart, Germany.

In **SP2 Intelligent Assist Systems** will be developed which will enable the time-sharing of work between robots and humans (figure 4), depending on the lot size, required accuracy, complexity of assembly operation, etc. In order to apply these innovative human-machine systems efficiently, related planning tools will be developed.

Figure 4. Time-Sharing Transportable Robot System

The specific objectives are the development of concepts, control algorithms and prototypes of intelligent assembly assist systems capable of time-sharing with human workers, i.e. replacement of humans when workforce availability is reduced or product volume changes during the product life cycle. This includes the design of a modular, easily programmable and transportable multi-arm robotic system which can work in an assembly workplace designed for human workers. The new assembly robot should represent the next generation of robotic systems integrating human dexterity and manipulation capabilities, visual and compliance control feedbacks, reconfigurable control systems and interfaces, as well as grasping and process-specific tooling devices. Additionally, a multi-modal human interface is in development which ensures efficient and skill-oriented programming by means of off-line programming and simulation tools, as well as virtual and augmented reality. Further aspects are related to occupational safety functions and systems as well as guidelines for the standardization of the new system.

The work began with the refinement of requirements (specifics from flexible assembly systems and end-user views) and the definition of the system architecture considering the assembly process and workplace environment. As a starting base system, existing anthropomorphic robots were considered. Based on the requirements, a system specification was worked out covering all subsystems such as mechatronic components, visual and force sensors, real-time controller, assembly task-level programming and safety functions. In the next step the software and hardware components will be designed. A simulation environment including kinematic and dynamic models will be developed and implemented in order to allow an analysis of component and overall system design. Based on these results the initial design will be revised and the components will be implemented.

The current results of SP2 are the user requirements on workplace-sharing robots capable of replacing the human operator in future assembly lines (referred to as an assembly robot). The concept of time-sharing robots for assembly processes is based on a dual-arm robot and focuses mainly on the improvement of capacity flexibility of advanced assembly. The main points are the overview of existing solutions and system requirements, the analysis and specification of the human-robot interface regarding the assembly process and safety issues and the specification of interfaces and requirements for simulation systems.

In **SP3 Advanced Assembly Design Planning and Optimisation Tools** are under development. An important feature of these tools will be their application in training purposes.

The specific objectives are to develop methods and tools based on concurrent engineering approaches which enable the use of virtual assembly for process design and system planning. Geometrical and non-geometrical features and knowledge of the product and assembly process must be integrated. The tools should also contain models of human-machine collaboration for assembly system planning purposes.

Specifically, a toolset architecture based on open technologies and communication standards (figure 5) is in development. Thereby the novel collaborative human-machine approaches play a dominant role. The research work covers physical feature models of assembly process related components as well as tolerance and tolerance chain models. This includes the specification of a vendor-neutral structure and the development of a repository of these models. Regarding the human-robot cooperation, skill-oriented assembly planning tools will be developed, considering sequencing and scheduling based on manual and automatic assembly. Furthermore, an open knowledge base will be developed in order to ensure future access to assembly structures (product, process and system knowledge). Finally, a toolset prototype will be implemented, tested and evaluated using the IAS prototype environment.

The results of SP3 so far include the analysis of current technology used in planning and optimisation tools, as well as the definition of the technology development roadmap for SP3. This includes the input from end users gathered during the industrial workshops. The result summarises the state-of-art and describes the development necessary to meet the future demands in the area of assembly simulation, planning, scheduling and optimisation. Further work was done to introduce tools and methods to solve knowledge exchange challenges between the design, process planning, simulation and actual execution of manufacturing systems.

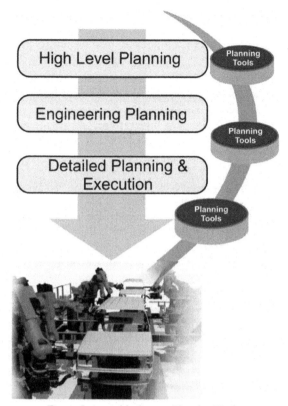

Figure 5. Assembly System Planning Tools

SP4 is dedicated to **Reconfigurable and Reusable Assembly Equipment**. Tools for the management of components, configuration, design, planning and control, as well as for simulation and testing will be developed.

The specific objectives are to develop reconfiguration concepts that support the rearrangement and reuse of assembly devices and systems considering generalised organisational, planning and technical requirements, as well as specific aspects of novel hybrid assembly technology. Thereby standardised hardware and software interfaces and tools enabling reconfigurability and reusability of assembly equipment will be considered. Based on the results, reconfigurable and reusable assembly system components will be designed, considering in particular the mechanical interfaces, condition monitoring systems and condition prediction algorithms. Finally, distributed control system hardware, software, and IT infrastructure for reconfiguration and reuse will be prototypically implemented.

The work began with a survey of end-user and system integrator companies in order to quantify the benefit/potential of reusability and reconfigurability of assembly equipment. Based on this survey an analysis of the strengths, weaknesses, opportunities and threats (SWOT-Analysis) was performed. The result is the requirements definition, which has been adapted to the specific needs of the industrial branches involved in PISA. In the next step a component knowledge base for life cycle assessment and reuse/reconfiguration management will be specified. This includes a formal description of tasks, equipment and life cycle information. A further important issue is related to the hardware of assembly system components, i.e. mechanical interfaces, condition monitoring and condition prediction algorithms. Related interface design rules as well as monitoring and prediction methods/tools will be developed and implemented. Additionally, assembly system controllers along with their hardware, software and IT infrastructure will be analysed. Based on this, a reusable/reconfigurable controller structure will be specified. Wherever applicable, these specifications are tested via simulation. The knowledge base and a distributed controller will be implemented.

In **SP5 (Overall System Design and Integration)**, user requirements will be defined, the results of SP1-4 will be tested and evaluated and a demonstrator combining all results will be specified, implemented and evaluated.

The specific objectives are:

- to develop assembly system concepts that meet and balance the demands in terms of flexibility, cost-efficiency and technology level,
- to specify requirements on the performance and safety of new human-assisting assembly technology and on the planning methods and design tools supporting the novel technology and concepts,
- to assess prototype systems according to established demands,
- to integrate subproject prototypes and design overall demonstration systems, testing scenarios and evaluation criteria,
- to test the project demonstrators and examine the benefits considering reliability, flexibility, reusability and economical aspects and
- to define product design guidelines to optimally support new technology.

The work began with the consideration of bottlenecks in flexible assembly automation and defined research directions for the design of concepts for next-generation assembly systems. In figure 6 a COBOT prototype is shown which was specified and analysed for aircraft assembly.

The current results are the user requirements for reconfigurable and reusable assembly equipment. Based on a systematic analysis of standard hardware and software interfaces and control architectures, critical assembly problems were identified from the viewpoint of end-users and novel assembly technology developers, taking into account also the development of future assembly processes in European industry.

In particular, requirements have been specified for the further development of industrial robots to support power-assist applications in assembly processes. Furthermore, the deficiencies of existing assembly solutions in automotive-industry suppliers' assembly lines were analysed, and the requirements for new IAS for flexible assembly were specified, specifically from the point of view of system integration.

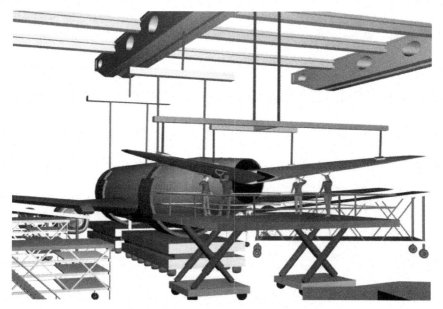

Figure 6. COBOT for Aircraft Assembly

5. SUMMARY

It is worth mentioning that the development of new concepts will be strongly supported by industrial research centres and SMEs. After the specification of requirements in the technology development subprojects, the work continues with the design of a detailed system architecture and the development of systems demonstration and testing scenarios. In order to reach the project goals, broad know-how in various scientific, engineering and technology areas from different branches is necessary. Partners selected for their practical and scientific perspectives provide this knowledge. The project involves four large companies, seven SME and seven research institutes from seven European countries. The integrated project approach enables parallel work on all subprojects and is therefore most efficient. The breakthrough of this IP will be the development of innovative intelligent assist systems (IAS) technology and the related methods and tools for planning, integration and reusability of assembly equipment. The results are flexible, cost-effective and highly productive solutions.

6. CONCLUSION

The IP-PISA targets an ambitious goal to develop a new generation of modular flexible assembly production concepts, formal methods, standards and safety framework tools and underlying technologies to allow the integration and cooperation between human workers and truly flexible, responsive devices in a qualitatively new and efficient manner. To reach this objective, the project is reasonably divided into four subprojects concerning assembly technology and tools development; one subproject dealing with the development and integration of assembly concepts and the evaluation of new technology; and three subprojects handling innovation-related activities. For SP1 to SP4 a duration of 36 months is planned. For SP5, which sets requirements for and integrates the results of SP1-SP4, and for the innovation-related subprojects, a duration of 48 months is planned.

6.1. Acknowledgment

The article reports on a research and technical development project partly funded by the EU as an Integrated Project in the 6th Framework Programme.

7. REFERENCES

1. P. Butala, J. Kleine, S. Wingen, H. Gergs. "Assessment of assembly processes in European industry," in Proc. 35th CIRP-International Seminar on Manufacturing Systems, Seoul, May 2002.
2. D. Surdilovic, R. Bernhardt, and L. Zhang. New intelligent power-assist systems based on differential transmission. Robotica 2003; vol. 21: 295–302.
3. http://www.pisa-ip.org
4. M. Hägele, W. Schaaf, E. Helms, "Robot assistants at manual workplaces," in Proc. 33rd International Symposium on Robotics, 2002.
5. A. Karlsson. Assembly-initiated production – a strategy for mass-customisation utilising modular, hybrid automatic production systems. Assembly Automation 2002; vol. 22, no. 3: 239–247.
6. M. Tichem, "Position Report on Flexible Assembly Automation," Delft University: Laboratory for Production Engineering and Industrial Organisation, Delft University of Technology. Available: http://www.ocp.tudelft.nl/pto/research/publications/reports/KTHReport.pdf
7. OSHA: http://europe.osha.eu.int/

31

INTELLIGENT OPTICAL SENSORS USING ARTIFICIAL NEURAL NETWORK APPROACH

Ireneu Dias, Rui Oliveira, Orlando Frazão

INESC Porto, Rua do Campo Alegre, 687, 4169-007 Porto, Portugal.
INEGI,, Rua do Barroco, 174, 4465-591 Leça do Balio, Portugal.
idias@inescporto.pt, ofrazao@inescporto.pt,roliveira@inegi.pt

This work present and demonstrated an applications of artificial neural network approach in optical sensing. The conventional matrix method used in simultaneous measurement of strain and temperature with optical Bragg gratings is compared with artificial neural network approach. The alternative method is proposed for reduced the error.

1. INTRODUCTION

According to (Culshaw, 1996), a smart structure can be defined as one that monitors itself and/or its environment in order to respond to changes in its condition. Fibre Bragg grating sensors (FBG) can be very useful in applications where layered materials, such as composites, are involved. Due to the fact that fibre optic sensors are small, multiplexable, electrically isolated and immune to electromagnetic fields, they can give engineers the possibility to incorporate a fibre optic nervous systems into their composite material designs. These sensors allow measurement of parameters such as load/strain, vibration, temperature and detection of cracks and delamination phenomena (Culshaw, 1996). When FBGs are applied to the measurement of strain their cross-sensitivity to temperature is an issue that needs to be addressed.

One approach to solve this problem it is to design sensing heads insensitive to temperature. Another one is the conception of structures with sufficient degrees of freedom to permit the simultaneous discrimination of these two parameters. However, when the sensing head contains two devices, the error increases due to the cross component of the physical parameter. Usually, the matrix method to solve the problem is acceptable, but when the instability of the matrix is high, it is necessary to apply other alternative solutions. Other disadvantage of the matrix method is when the response of the sensors is non linear. This problem appears when the sensors are characterized in temperature or embedded in laminated composites.

In this work the authors present an alternative solution using an artificial neural approach to reduce the errors obtained by the matrix method in optical fibre Bragg grating embedded in laminated composite. The optical sensor presents linear response for strain and non linear response for temperature.

Please use the following format when citing this chapter:

Dias, I., Oliveira, R. and Frazão, O., 2008, in IFIP International Federation for Information Processing, Volume 266, *Innovation in Manufacturing Networks;* ed. A. Azevedo; (Boston: Springer), pp. 289–294.

2. ARTIFICIAL NEURAL NETWORK APPROACH

An artificial neural network (ANN) approach is proposed to improve the strain and temperature measurements. ANN has been applied to temperature and strain measurements in the case of large cross-sensitivity sensors, whose matrix inversion causes significant errors due to the nonlinear evolution of the matrix coefficients as function of ΔT and $\Delta \varepsilon$

To avoid the matrix inversion, an ANN was trained to perform a nonlinear input-output mapping. The variations $\Delta \lambda_1$ and $\Delta \lambda_2$ were given as inputs to the ANN which provides values of ΔT and $\Delta \varepsilon$ as outputs.

An ANN is an interconnected group of simple processing units (neurons) that uses a mathematical or computational model for information processing based on a connectionist approach to computation (Fig. 1). Despite the simplicity of each processing unit, the use of many neurons guarantees the execution of multiple tasks.

The links between neurons are characterized by weights, w_{ki}, which modulate the effect of the associated input, x_i, to a neuron, k. A pondered sum of the weighted input is then performed. The neuron transmits an activity level transduced by a function of activation, φ.

ANN is an adaptive model that can learn from the data and generalize it. It extracts the essential characteristics from the numerical data. This offers a convenient way to create an implicit model.

The chosen network was a multilayer perceptron (MLP) trained in supervised learning with the *Levenberg-Marquardt* algorithm. The MLP is based on an input, a hidden and an output layers interconnected in a feed-forward way (Haykin, 1999). Each neuron has directed connections to all the neurons of the subsequent layer (Fig. 2). The neurons activation function in the hidden layer is the non-linear sigmoid function whereas in the output layer it is the linear function. The network output is thus a linear combination of the outputs of the hidden neurons with α_{jk} defining the synaptic weights of output layer.

The MLP outputs are compared to the pretended predefined target using an error-function. This error is then fed back through the network. Using this information, the algorithm adjusts the weights of each connection in order to reduce the error value. The process is repeated until the network converges to some state where the error is small. In this case the network has learned a certain target function.

The universal approximation theorem for ANN states that every continuous function that maps intervals of real numbers to some output interval of real numbers can be approximated arbitrarily closely by a MLP with just one hidden layer (Bishop, 1995). ΔT and $\Delta \varepsilon$ can thus be approximated as follows:

$$\begin{cases} \left| \Delta T - \sum_{k=1}^{m} \alpha_{1k} \varphi \left(w_{k1} \lambda_{conv} + w_{k2} \lambda_{sat} + b_k \right) \right| < \epsilon_1 \\ \\ \left| \Delta \varepsilon - \sum_{k=1}^{m} \alpha_{2k} \varphi \left(w_{k1} \lambda_{conv} + w_{k2} \lambda_{sat} + b_k \right) \right| < \epsilon_2 \end{cases} \qquad (1)$$

where φ is the sigmoid function, b_k the bias, the approximation errors and m the number of neurons in the hidden layer.

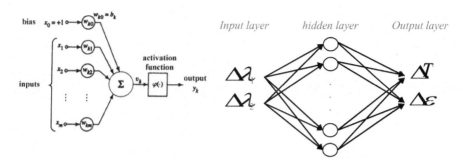

Fig. 1. Model of a neuron.   *Fig. 2.* Architectural graph of a MLP with one hidden layer.

The hidden layer of the chosen MLP is constituted of 10 neurons. Classical back-propagation training algorithm is based on the gradient descent method. This method is often too slow for practical problems. The Levenberg-Marquardt back-propagation algorithm is then used here instead of MLP training because of having a faster convergence (Bishop, 1995). The performance of the trained ANN is measured using the mean square error.

Data analysis was performed using MATLAB® Neural Network Toolbox (Demuth and Beale). The network inputs consist of pairs of ($\Delta\lambda_1$, $\Delta\lambda_2$). During the training the MLP is adjusted to relate these input pairs to their respective target pair (ΔT, $\Delta\varepsilon$).

The training efficiency highly depends on the data used for training. This data must be representative of the underlying model. Training data consisted of 3400 pairs of (ΔT, $\Delta\varepsilon$) values generated, within a range of 0-2700 $\mu\varepsilon$ and 0-45 °C, by interpolation of the experimental values. The respective pairs of ($\Delta\lambda_1$, $\Delta\lambda_2$) were obtained applying the equation (1). To improve the training efficiency the data was pre-processed. Inputs and targets were normalized to have zero mean and unity standard deviation to guarantee that they have the same relevance.

The generalization ability of the trained MLP network was then verified with a set of another 100 pairs of simulated data.

3. RESULTS

Two fibre Bragg gratings were embedded between layers of pre-impregnated carbon fibre/epoxy resin to produce a smart laminated composite. One of the Bragg gratings is located between two layers. The other Bragg grating is positioned between four layers. The smart composite was characterized concerning stain and temperature. The characterization consisted in temperature measurements holding strain constant ($\varepsilon = 0$) and strain measurements induced by strain holding the temperature constant (T = 20°C).

The sensing head presents different strain sensitivities of the Bragg grating when embedded in different number of layers and when the smart composite is subjected to strain. Relatively to the temperature, a nonlinear response is obtained. These results allow to write a well-conditioned system of two equations for ΔT and $\Delta\varepsilon$, given in a matrix form as:

$$
\begin{bmatrix} \Delta\lambda_{FBG1} \\ \Delta\lambda_{FBG2} \end{bmatrix} = \begin{bmatrix} b_1 & 0 \\ b_2 & 0 \end{bmatrix} + \begin{bmatrix} \kappa_{T1} & \kappa_{\varepsilon1} \\ \kappa_{T2} & \kappa_{\varepsilon2} \end{bmatrix} \begin{bmatrix} \Delta T \\ \Delta\varepsilon \end{bmatrix} + \begin{bmatrix} a_1 & 0 \\ a_2 & 0 \end{bmatrix} \begin{bmatrix} \Delta T^2 \\ \Delta\varepsilon^2 \end{bmatrix}
\tag{2}
$$

and the solution obtained for ΔT and $\Delta\varepsilon$ is:

$$
\Delta T = \frac{-\left(\kappa_{T2} - \kappa_{T1}\frac{\kappa_{\varepsilon2}}{\kappa_{\varepsilon1}}\right) \pm \sqrt{\left(\kappa_{T2} - \kappa_{T1}\frac{\kappa_{\varepsilon2}}{\kappa_{\varepsilon1}}\right)^2 - 4\left(a_2 - a_1\frac{\kappa_{\varepsilon2}}{\kappa_{\varepsilon1}}\right)\left(\frac{\kappa_{\varepsilon2}}{\kappa_{\varepsilon1}}(\Delta\lambda_{FBG1} - b_1) - (\Delta\lambda_{FBG2} - b_2)\right)}}{2\left(a_2 - a_1\frac{\kappa_{\varepsilon2}}{\kappa_{\varepsilon1}}\right)}
$$

$$
\Delta\varepsilon = \frac{1}{\kappa_{\varepsilon1}}\left[\lambda_{FBG1} - \kappa_{T1}\Delta T - a_1\Delta T^2\right]
\tag{3}
$$

Replacing all the coefficient parameters, we obtained the following results:

$$
\begin{bmatrix} \Delta\lambda_{FBG1} \\ \Delta\lambda_{FBG2} \end{bmatrix} = \begin{bmatrix} 4.63 & 0 \\ 3.34 & 0 \end{bmatrix} + \begin{bmatrix} 1.74 & 1.14 \\ 1.59 & 0.55 \end{bmatrix} \begin{bmatrix} \Delta T \\ \Delta\varepsilon \end{bmatrix} + \begin{bmatrix} 0.14 & 0 \\ 0.13 & 0 \end{bmatrix} \begin{bmatrix} \Delta T^2 \\ \Delta\varepsilon^2 \end{bmatrix}
\tag{4}
$$

and the solution is:

$$
\Delta T = \frac{-0.755 \pm \sqrt{+0.24\Delta\lambda_{FBG2} - 0.11\Delta\lambda_{FBG1} - 0.31}}{0.12}
\tag{5}
$$

$$
\Delta\varepsilon = 0.87\Delta\lambda_{FBG1} - 1.51\Delta T - 4.03\Delta T^2
$$

The system performance was evaluated when the sensing head was simultaneously subjected to strain and temperature changes over strain and temperature ranges of 2700 $\mu\varepsilon$ and 45 °C, respectively. The results are shown in Fig. 3. The *rms* deviations were found to be ±1.47 °C and ±5.7 $\mu\varepsilon$ for temperature and strain measurements, respectively.

Usually the matrix method presents good performance when the sensing head shows linear response in all physical parameter characterization. In our design, the sensing head presents non linear response due to the optical fibre being embedded in laminated composite and presents a thermal differential between the optical glass and the polymer used in the pre-impregnated. In these cases alternative solutions are required and this work presents the results using ANN.

The performance of the two techniques (matrix method and ANN) was evaluated when the sensing head undertook strain variations in a range of 2700 $\mu\varepsilon$ at a fixed temperature ($\Delta T = 20$ °C) and the other way around, i.e., temperature variations in a range of 50 °C for a specific applied strain ($\Delta\varepsilon = 1250$ $\mu\varepsilon$). See Figure 4. For the ANN method a satisfactorily generalization of data was achieved. The resulting maximum errors for the

ANN method were found to be ± 0.2 °C and ± 1.9 με for temperature and strain measurements, respectively.

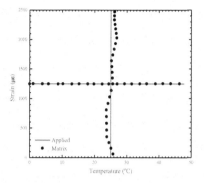

Fig. 3. Sensor output as determined by matrix method.

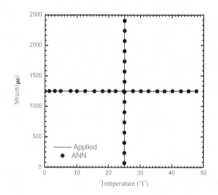

Fig. 4. Sensor output as determined by ANN.

4. CONCLUSIONS

In this work, the authors presented an intelligent composite based on optical Bragg grating structure embedded between of layers of pre-impregnated carbon fibre/epoxy resin. Due to its geometry, the smart composite can be simultaneously discriminate the strain and the temperature. To reduce the errors of the matrix methods, an artificial neural network (ANN) approach is proposed to improve the strain and temperature measurements cross-sensitivity. The authors concluded that the ANN approach is an alternative method when the optical sensor presents non linear response to the physical parameters. The problem of the sensing head embedded in composite laminated is the non linear temperature response and the matrix method presents a high error for the temperature measurement. The results show that, for a particular sensor with large cross-sensitivity, temperature and strain measurement accuracy can be increased by 7 and 3 times, respectively, when compared with the matrix inversion method.

5. REFERENCES

1. Culshaw, B. Smart structures and Materials, Artech House Publichers, 1996.
2. Chan, CC.; Jin, W., Rad, A.B., Demokan, M.S. "Simultaneous measurement of temperature and strain: an artificial neural network approach". IEEE Photonics Technology Letters, 1998; 10: 854 – 856.
3. Haykin, S. Neural Networks: a comprehensive foundation - Chapter 4: Multilayer Perceptrons, Prentice Hall, 156, 1999.
4. Bishop, C. "Neural Networks for Pattern Recognition" - Chapter 4: The Multi-layer Perceptron, Oxford: University Press, 116, 1995.
5. Demuth H., Beale M., "Neural Network Toolbox User's Guide", Version 4.

32

INTELLIGENT PRODUCTS: INTELLIGENT BEINGS OR AGENTS?

Paul Valckenaers and Hendrik Van Brussel
K.U.Leuven, Mechanical Engineering, Belgium
Paul.Valckenaers@mech.kuleuven.be

*This paper introduces a novel concept, **the intelligent being**, as a vehicle to achieve suitability for integration. The paper argues for a role of the intelligent being that is analogous to what maps contribute in navigation systems (and may become as important). The concept is applied to intelligent product instances, intelligent product types and intelligent resources alike.*

1. INTRODUCTION

This paper focuses on suitability for integration. It identifies which components and subsystems can be designed such that they are highly suited for integration. And, the paper discusses how to design such components. The motivation to present this research in an intelligent product context resides in its aptness as a foundation for components that are suited for integration.

The quest for system components suited for integration dates back to the CIM era and its "islands of automation." The disappointing performance of those early-day integration efforts triggered a search for the root causes. Thus, research in Intelligent Manufacturing Systems has been looking at the fundamental science of the artificial, addressing complex adaptive systems, holonic systems, etc. A major insight is that manmade system components incorporate varying degrees of choice, and that conflicting choices are a necessary condition for integration problems.

Intelligent beings avoid these choices – at least in their application domain, not in the ICT dimensions. The full set of these in-depth insights distinguishes more levels and nuances (e.g. inertia build-up by these choices) but the intelligent being concept covers the most important part from a practical point of view. It is a clean concept delivering hard integrate-ability guarantees. The intelligent being inherits those guarantees from the real world, which it reflects.

This paper first discusses intelligent products as a composition of an intelligent being and an intelligent agent. Next, it addresses the intelligent products architecture. This includes a list of services offered by the intelligent being within the intelligent product. Finally, conclusions are given.

Please use the following format when citing this chapter:

Valckenaers, P. and Brussel, H.V., 2008, in IFIP International Federation for Information Processing, Volume 266, *Innovation in Manufacturing Networks;* ed. A. Azevedo; (Boston: Springer), pp. 295–302.

2. INTELLIGENT PRODUCTS

This section identifies what intelligence may be added to a product without losing the ability to integrate the resulting intelligent product into any overall system. It also introduces the concept of an intelligent being.

2.1. Products are "beings"

Since the 1980s, software engineering recognizes that, to create long-lived information systems, the foundations of a system have to reflect the corresponding reality (Jackson, 1995). The design of an intelligent product – whose main function is to reflect a real product – naturally applies and exploits this principle.

The real world possesses a much sought-after property by software and system designers: it is a (very large) coherent and consistent collection of components and subsystems. This is the reason why the above software engineering principle is so effective. Software components reflecting reality are protected by this reality. Any design conflict involving such a protected component simultaneously has a conflict with reality. Consequently, solutions of such conflict leave these reality-reflecting software components intact (Valckenaers, 2003).

The oldest information artifacts that reflect some part of reality are maps. Maps add intelligence to reality. Maps are top-performing artifacts concerning integration issues. People have no problems using multiple maps even if they overlap geographically or deliver overlapping information (e.g. a tourist map, navigation map and topological map of the same area). Conflicts between maps indicate erroneous implementations and are easily corrected by checking with the corresponding reality.

For software designers, this may seem utopia. Indeed, a complete functional software system cannot be developed through exclusively reflecting reality such that this reality protects all the software components as effectively as it protects maps. However, navigation software hints that a major part of the software system may benefit from such protection in applications that are closely connected to parts of the real world. Intelligent products certainly are suitable candidates.

2.2. Intelligent Beings

Intelligent Beings are software components that
1. are sufficiently sophisticated to be considered *intelligent* and
2. *reflect some part of reality in a choice-free manner that offers protection* as discussed above

---

Actually, these intelligent software artifacts emphasize and mirror existence (being) in their world-of-interest. In contrast, intelligent agents emphasize action and decision-making on behalf of such an existence in their world-of-interest (analogous to the relation between an artist and his/her agent).

To illustrate the distinction between the protection enjoyed by an intelligent being and the exposure endured by intelligent agents, the following story may help. It is the actual transcript of a US naval ship with Canadian authorities off the coast of Newfoundland in October, 1995. This radio conversation was released by the Chief of Naval Operations on 10-10-95:

- Canadians: "Please divert your course 15° to the South to avoid a collision."
- Americans: "Please divert your course 15° to the North to avoid a collision."
- Canadians: "We Repeat. Recommend you divert YOUR course 15 degrees to the South to avoid a collision."
- Americans: "This is the captain of a US Navy ship. I say again, divert YOUR course."
- Canadians: "No, I say again, you divert YOUR course."
- Americans: "THIS IS THE AIRCRAFT CARRIER USS ABRAHAM LINCOLN, THE SECOND LARGEST SHIP IN THE UNITED STATES' ATLANTIC FLEET. WE ARE ACCOMPANIED BY THREE DESTROYERS, THREE CRUISERS AND NUMEROUS SUPPORT VESSELS. I DEMAND THAT YOU CHANGE YOUR COURSE 15 DEGREES NORTH. THAT'S ONE-FIVE DEGREES NORTH, OR COUNTER MEASURES WILL BE UNDERTAKEN TO ENSURE THE SAFETY OF THIS SHIP."
- Canadians: "This is a lighthouse. Your call."

The Canadians are enjoying the role/situation of an intelligent being. The Americans are enduring the role/situation of an intelligent agent, erroneously interacting with the intelligent being as if it were an agent.

What the above story illustrates is that in conflicts, the solution cannot be expected from adaptations of the intelligent being, especially when the intelligent being is able to track its corresponding reality. Solutions only involve the intelligent agents and reality itself. Integration and collaboration issues affecting the intelligent being in the story are limited to the radio conversation itself: frequency, modulation, language and jargon spoken, etc. These are minor compared to the real-world stakes.

2.3. Intelligent product = "intelligent being + intelligent agent"

An intelligent product will be a combination of an intelligent being and an intelligent agent. The intelligent being is restricted to functionality and services for which the corresponding reality provides adequate protection. This requirement cannot be compromised in any way since the intelligent being would loose its most attractive property, which it shares with old-fashioned maps. Any functionality or service that requires decision-making, not covered by reality, is delegated to the intelligent agent (cf. figure 1).

In nature (i.e. in humans and animals), the functionality of the intelligent agent is included within the intelligent being. Such implementation of multiple functions in a single embodiment is characteristic for natural systems. For instance, birds combine lift and propulsion in their flapping wings. In contrast, successful manmade artifacts often have separate embodiments for every main function. Aircraft have fixed wings for lift that are separate from the engines providing propulsion. A key motivation for this separation in artificial systems is specialization in the design and production of these components (separate organizations are responsible). Separate embodiments effectively serve much larger user groups over longer periods of time than a single combined embodiment.

For the intelligent being and intelligent agent, this motivation most strongly applies since they have radically different domains – concerning life cycle, location and service type – across which they remain functional. In fact, the intelligent being is functional whenever its reflected reality is. In contrast, the intelligent agent is functional wherever its decision-making capabilities provide adequate service. Techno-economic pressures call for two separate embodiments. In comparison, a hardwired combination of an intelligent agent and its intelligent being would lack critical user mass and would be short-lived.

The stability and suitability for integration of intelligent beings makes them the prime candidates for the foundation of the overall system. Therefore, the following section discusses what services and functionality can be delivered by intelligent beings within intelligent products.

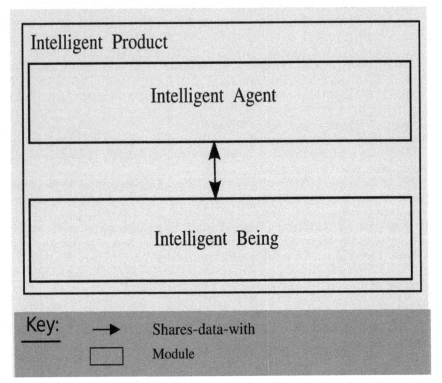

Figure 1. Intelligent product architecture

3. INTELLIGENT PRODUCTS ARCHITECTURE

An intelligent product has two main modules: the intelligent being and the intelligent agent. The intelligent agent performs all decision-making tasks. It accesses the real world exclusively through the intelligent being. In environments for multi-agent systems, as discussed in (Valckenaers, 2007), the agents interact with the real world through environment entities. Intelligent beings are prime candidates for this environment entity role (cf. figure 2). The intelligent being reflects a real-world entity, while delegating all decision-making to the intelligent agent.

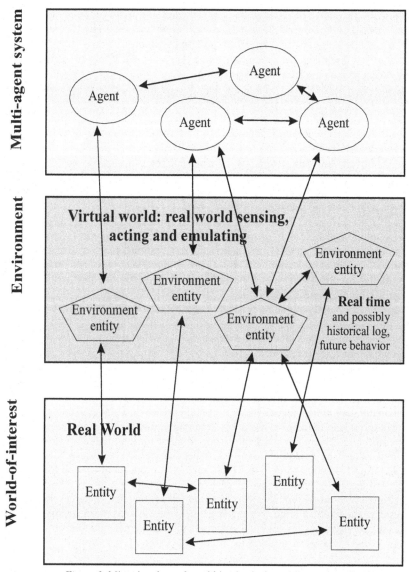

Figure 2. Mirroring the real world in physical-world-rooted applications

An intelligent agent exchanges information with its corresponding intelligent being. The agent can perform actions in the environment (for instance, the agent can request actuation of the physical machine). The agent can also perceive the intelligent being (for instance, it can observe its capabilities or check if a certain task can be performed on the machine the intelligent being reflects).

Intelligent beings may offer decision-free reality-reflecting services belonging to the following categories:

- *Self-models (static)*. The intelligent being informs about product properties (technical specifications). It is knowledgeable about the current state of the product instance and the possible states of instances of its product type.

- *Self-models (dynamic)*. The intelligent being provides information on how the product evolves or may evolve over time. It is knowledgeable about the possible transitions between possible states and the properties of these transitions.
- *Emulation*. The intelligent being supports emulation of its real-world counterpart that, among others, can be used for plan verification.
- *Acquaintances network*. The intelligent being is able to contact its surrounding entities and to provide their contact coordinates to virtual visitors. This includes the resources on which the product resides, its owner, its customer, its intelligent agent, and the links to its real-world counterpart. This feature creates *a network across which intelligent agents and beings may travel virtually*.
- *Stigmergie*. Intelligent beings offer the cyber-counterpart of tagging (post-its) in the real world. This permits virtual visitors to deposit, observe and modify information attached to the intelligent being. A refresh-or-forget mechanism may be applied to cope with a dynamic environment.
- *Access to the real world*. Raw sensor data needs processing (filtering, aggregation, fusing, interpreting) before it provides useful information. Moreover, sensor data often is only available at given instances and state estimators need to compensate (resulting in virtual sensors). In the reverse direction, raw actuating needs encapsulating by proper services. The intelligent being provides this service while delegating possible choices to its agent.
- *Traceability*. The intelligent being provides tracking and tracing. It provides access to information about the current state of the product instance as well as the trajectory leading to this state. The intelligent product may provide a high-quality time base against which the trace is recorded.
- *Forecasting (reflecting agent intentions)*. The emulation/modeling services provided by intelligent product support some simple forecasting. For instance, the models may indicate how a heat treatment is likely to affect product properties. To move beyond this, the intelligent being extends the part of reality that it reflects. It extends this part of reality to include the known intentions and commitments of agents that affect its short-term future. This produces a short-term forecast for the product itinerary and a load forecast for the resources involved. Valckenaers (2005) discusses a Holonic Manufacturing Execution System in which intelligent products offer such forecasting service. Parunak (2007) uses a similar principle to generate short-term forecasts in a self-organizing fashion. Both designs produce predictions for resources loads and user/product trajectories. Note that the intelligent beings only need agents that are capable to take decisions in the actual situations in order to generate forecasts. Agents must not possess models themselves to produce forecasts.

These responsibilities reflect the experience of the authors in building intelligent beings. Variations on this architecture, depending on the requirements of the application, are possible. Importantly, the functionality provided by an intelligent being can be expanded and enhanced without causing an avalanche of software maintenance or validation efforts. This situation is analogous to enhancing maps, indicating perhaps where the one-way streets are, and expanding maps to cover maybe a wider geographic area. This does not necessarily apply to the associated intelligent agents. Indeed, a more accurate and detailed representation of reality often renders a decision mechanism inadequate. Intrinsically, intelligent beings (inside intelligent products) are maintenance-free until the corresponding reality changes in a manner that the intelligent beings are unable to track.

4. CONCLUDING REMARKS

This paper introduces a new software concept – the intelligent being – that delivers the suitability for integration. Furthermore, the paper addresses which components and services can be developed in this manner. The discussion argues that intelligent products and intelligent beings are a natural match. Furthermore, intelligent beings are attractive components for the development of a system foundation since they are capable of surviving changes and confrontation with other systems unscathed.

Concerning work-by-others, McFarlane (2003) discusses the application of RFID technology in intelligent manufacturing control. His team has been generalizing the concept of an Intelligent Product to cover intelligent resources (Wong 2002). To shed some light on this, it is useful to understand how intelligent products correspond to three main categories depending on which part in the world-of-interest they reflect and/or correspond to:

1. A product type (non-material, virtual, knowledge only)
2. A product instantiation (the activity of producing a product instance)
3. A product instance.

Each of those categories should have its own intelligent being/product. The main motivation to demand separate intelligent products is similar to the motivation to cleanly separate intelligent being from intelligent agents: their user communities and markets are different. Having separate intelligent products increases critical user mass versus the software component complexity.

The first two categories are self-explaining. An intelligent product types is knowledgeable about a product design and process plans. An intelligent product instantiation is knowledgeable about the activity that is producing a product instance (i.e. production). The intelligent product instance covers the remainder of the life cycle for the result of a successful product instantiation.

An interesting category of intelligent product instances are intelligent resources. Indeed, production equipment and other production means are themselves products. In this manner, intelligent resources are a subcategory of intelligent product instances (in the usage phase of their life cycle). Such a unifying view on intelligent components/products is likely to benefit from cross-fertilization. For instance, emulation services, commonly provided for production equipment, may become more commonplace and become available on ordinary products. This opens perspectives of virtual eco-audits, virtual assessment of accessibility by users with special requirements, etc.

Overall, the analysis and discussion on how to design and structure the *internet of things* has only just started. This paper demonstrates that significant innovation opportunities are present and that fundamental rethinking may yield significant benefits.

4.1. Acknowledgments

This paper presents work funded by the Research Fund of the K.U.Leuven – Concerted Research Action on Autonomic Computing for Distributed Production Systems.

5. REFERENCES

1. Jackson, M. Software requirements and specifications. Addison-Wesley, 1995.
2. McFarlane, D., Sarma, S., Chirn, JL, Wong, CY, Ashton, K. Auto ID systems and intelligent manufacturing control. Engineering Applications of Artificial Intelligence Jun 2003; 16 (4): 365-376.
3. Parunak, HVD, Brueckener, S., Weyns, D. Holvoet, T., Verstraete, P., Valckenaers, P., E Pluribus Unum: PolyAgent and Delegate MAS Architectures, Eight International Workshop on Multi-Agent Based Simulation at AAMAS 2007, Honululu, Hawaii, 15 May 2007, forthcoming in the proceedings
4. Valckenaers, P., Van Brussel, H., Hadeli, Bochmann, O., Saint Germain, B., Zamfirescu, C. On the Design of Emergent Systems: an Investigation of Integration and Interoperability Issues. Engineering Applications of Artificial Intelligence 2003; 16: 377-393.
5. Valckenaers, P. and Van Brussel, H. Holonic Manufacturing Execution Systems. CIRP Annals - Manufacturing Technology 2005; 54/1: 427-432.
6. Valckenaers P., Sauter J., Sierra C., Rodriguez-Aguilar J.A. Applications and environments for multi-agent systems. Autonomous Agents and Multi-Agent Systems Feb 2007; 14 (1): 61-85
7. Wong, C.Y., McFarlane, D., Zaharudin, A., Agarawal, V. The intelligent product driven supply chain. Proceedings of IEEE Systems Man and Cybernetics, Hammamet, Tunisia, 2002.

33

A BIO-INSPIRED SOLUTION FOR MANUFACTURING CONTROL SYSTEMS

Paulo Leitão

Polytechnic Institute of Bragança, Quinta Sta Apolónia, Apartado 1134, 5301-857 Bragança, Portugal, pleitao@ipb.pt

Manufacturing is nowadays facing with markets trends that ask for more customized products, shorter product life-cycles, best quality and shorter prices. Addressing these requirements, manufacturing systems need to be more responsive and reconfigurable, adapting their behaviors to changing conditions. The concepts inherited from biology and nature seem suitable to design reconfigurable manufacturing systems. In this paper, a bio-inspired solution, where self-organization and multi-agent systems play key roles, is described, contributing to achieve an adaptive and evolvable reconfigurable manufacturing control system.

1. INTRODUCTION

Cost, quality and responsiveness are the three foundations on which every manufacturing company stands, to be competitive in the current global economy (ElMaraghy, 2006). Increasingly, traditional centralized and sequential manufacturing systems are being found insufficiently flexible to respond to changing production style and highly dynamic variations in production requirements. Under these circumstances, companies are forced to have manufacturing systems that exhibit innovative features to support the agile response to the emergence and changing conditions by the dynamic re-configuration on fly, i.e. without stopping, re-programming or re-starting the process. Briefly, re-configurability can be defined as the ability to repeatedly change and re-arrange the components of a system in a cost-effective way (Setchi et al., 2004). In manufacturing domain, reconfiguration implies a change in the control software or hardware of industrial automation and control systems, allowing the shop floor to adapt automatically to change while maintaining predictable and stable system behavior. Typically, a change would be required if the system is upgraded (e.g. new software components, hardware drivers or the hardware itself) or as a contingency to some event (e.g. the failure of a piece of hardware or a systematic error in the software). Re-configurability plays a key role in the new generation of production control systems, providing a way to achieve a rapid and adaptive response to change, which is a key enabler of competitiveness.

This idea is reinforced by two studies, one elaborated by the US Committee on Visionary Manufacturing (CMV, 1998) and another sponsored by the European Commission (Manufuture, 2004), which have identified reconfigurable manufacturing as the highest priority for future research in manufacturing. In fact, the first study states that the reconfigurable manufacturing is one of the six key manufacturing challenges for the year 2020, and the second one points out the need to have adaptive, digital, networked and knowledge-based manufacturing processes. They propose that manufacturing processes,

Please use the following format when citing this chapter:

Leitão, P., 2008, in IFIP International Federation for Information Processing, Volume 266, *Innovation in Manufacturing Networks;* ed. A. Azevedo; (Boston: Springer), pp. 303–314.

components and systems have to be re-adaptable and re-configurable for a wide range of customer requirements for products, features and services.

Reconfigurable Manufacturing Systems (RMS) are "designed at the outset for the rapid change in its structure, as well as its hardware and software components, in order to quickly adjust its production capacity and functionality within a part family in response to sudden market changes or intrinsic system change" (Koren et al., 1999). RMS possesses characteristics of modularity, integrability, customization, scalability, convertibility and diagnosability (ElMaraghy, 2006), which impose, among others, strong requirements to the control solution, with manufacturing systems built on centralized structures becoming unsustainable due to its intrinsic rigidity. These characteristics can be applied to the design of whole manufacturing systems, as well as to some of its components, i.e. reconfigurable machines, their controllers and also to the control system software. A typical RMS has several of these characteristics but not necessarily all.

The concept of RMS is a step ahead of the concept of Flexible Manufacturing Systems (FMS), presenting different goals. FMS aims at increasing the variety of parts produced, and RMS aims at increasing the speed of responsiveness to changing conditions. RMS instead of incorporating all the flexibility once at the beginning of their life-cycle should incorporate basic process models – both hardware and software – that can be rearranged or replaced quickly and reliably (Mehrabi et al., 2000). In other words, in a FMS it is necessary to install in the beginning all functionalities that can be used in the future, while in a RMS the functionalities are added during its life-cycle according to the needs (Mehrabi et al., 2000). Biology and nature are suitable sources of inspiration for the development of RMS, mainly addressing the development of adaptive and evolvable systems. For this purpose, some theories inherited from biological systems, such as artificial life, chaos theory, swarm intelligence and complexity behavior may be applied. However, at the time, significant proofs about the applicability of reconfigurable solutions in industrial environments are missing, since only very few implementations of reconfigurable solutions have been reported in the literature. Additionally, the implemented functionalities are normally restricted. This requires the implementation of bio-inspired solutions in real scenarios to proof its real applicability. This paper illustrates the applicability of bio-inspired theories to build reconfigurable manufacturing (control) systems. In this context, a bio-inspired solution is discussed, presenting evolving mechanisms based on self-organization, supervision and learning concepts and on ant-based communication, supported by the use of multi-agent principles.

The paper is organized as follows: first, Section 2 overviews the concept of self-organization and how it can be applied in manufacturing systems. Section 3 discusses the foundations of a bio-inspired solution for manufacturing control and Section 4 describes the adaptive control system working in practice by presenting how the control structure evolves dynamically and how the task allocation is performed. Finally, Section 5 rounds up the paper with the conclusions.

2. APPLYING SELF-ORGANIZATION TO MANUFACTURING SYSTEMS

Fundamental works to provide control architectures to solve RMS requirements are Multi-agent Systems (Wooldridge, 2002) and Holonic Manufacturing Systems (HMS) (Koestler, 1969), (Brussle et al., 1998), (Deen, 2003). Multi-agent systems, derived from distributed artificial intelligence, suggest the definition of distributed control based on autonomous agents that account for the realization of efficient, flexible and robust overall plant control, and consequently the disturbance handling component. In a similar way, HMS translates into the manufacturing world the concepts developed by A. Koestler for living organisms and social organizations. Holonic manufacturing is characterized by holarchies of holons (i.e., autonomous and cooperative entities), which represent the entire range of manufacturing entities. A holon, as Koestler devised the term, is a part of a (manufacturing) system that may be made up of sub-ordinate parts and, in turn, can be part of a larger whole.

The capability of adaptation and evolution to face emergence, crucial in RMS, requires the implementation of complex adaptive algorithms within distributed control approaches, e.g. the MAS and HMS. A suitable approach is to translate some mechanisms and concepts founded in the biology and nature to build adaptive reconfigurable systems. In fact, biology and nature offer powerful mechanisms built on entities that exhibit simple behaviors and have limited cognitive abilities, where a small number of rules or laws can generate systems of surprising complexity (Holland, 1998). Complex behavior may then emerge from interactions among entities exhibiting simple behavior (Bonabeau et al., 1999), being the behavior of the whole much more complex than the behavior of the parts (Holland, 1998). The emergence only occurs when the resulted whole is more than the sum of its parts (Holland, 1998).

The swarm intelligence concept, also inherited from biology, can be defined as the emergent collective intelligence of groups of simple and single entities. It offers an alternative way of designing intelligent systems, in which autonomy, emergence, and distributed functioning replace control, pre-programming and centralization (Bonabeau et al., 1999). As an example, a social insect colony is a decentralized system composed of cooperative, autonomous units that are distributed in the environment, exhibit simple probabilistic stimulus-response behavior, and have access to local information (Bonabeau et al., 1999). The system exhibiting these characteristics operates in a very flexible and robust way (Bonabeau et al., 1999), where flexibility allows adaptation to changing environments and robustness endows the colony with the ability to work even if some individuals may fail to perform their tasks.

In biological systems there are two different approaches to adaptation to the dynamic evolution of the environment (Vaario et al., 1996): evolutionary systems and self-organization. In the evolutionary approach, the nodes of the control structure are encoded as genetic information and are subject to the application of evolutionary techniques by selecting gradually a better system. Well known examples of this approach are neural networks, where learning occurs in an evolutionary way, and genetic algorithms, where problems are solved by an evolutionary process. In the self-organizing approach, the network of nodes that represents the control system is established by the nodes themselves. The driving forces drive the re-organization process according to the environment conditions and to the control properties of the distributed entities. In other words, the self-organization is viewed when the evolution is determined by the re-organization of the structure through the addition/removal of the relationships among entities and through the addition/removal of the goal-oriented activities lead by the entities.

Self-organization is not a new concept, being applied in different domains such as computing and robotics. Several distinct definitions, but not necessarily contradictory, are found in the literature. The Intelligent Manufacturing Systems (IMS) consortium defines a self-organized system as a system which is not coordinated or regulated by the exterior, and Massote (Massotte, 1995) defines self-organization as the integration of autonomy and learning capabilities within entities to achieve, by emergence, global behavior that is not programmed or defined a priori. Thamarajah (Thamarajah, 1998) defines self-organization as the ability of an entity/system to adapt itself to prevailing conditions of its environment and Bousbia and Trentesaux (Bousbia and Trentesaux, 2006) defines self-organization as the ability of an entity to look after and ensure its optimal functioning with minimum help or intervention by external or internal component of the system.

A possible way to integrate self-organization capabilities is to move from fixed and centralized architectures to distributed ones (Bousbia and Trentesaux, 2006), that does not follow a rigid and estimated organization. In fact, autonomous systems, as our brain, have to constantly optimize their behavior, involving the combination of non-linear and dynamic processes. These characteristics imply the management and control of behavioral complexity as well. The application of self-organization allows the dynamic self-configuration (i.e. adaptation to changing conditions by changing their own configuration permitting the addition/removal of resources on fly and without service disruption), self-optimization (i.e. tuning itself in a pro-active way to respond to environmental stimuli) and self-healing (i.e. capacity to diagnose deviations from normal conditions and take proactive actions to normalize them and avoid service disruptions).

The self-organization of each distributed entity can be defined as the capability to organize by itself into different structures, according to its perception of the environment. The emergence of the global control or organizational structure is a result of the capability of local entities to change dynamically and autonomously their properties. In such system, the network of control entities is coordinated towards a unique goal or objective to evolve, with a new solution for the re-organization achieved by emergence. During the re-organization process it is necessary to evaluate, according to a specific criteria, if the achieved solution is better than the previous one (Pujo et al., 2001).

When dealing with reconfigurable systems, in which distribution and emergence play key roles, it is crucial to have regulation mechanisms to introduce order and stability, avoiding the increase of entropy and consequently the chaotic or instable states. Here, it is important to remark the analogy with the 2nd Law of Thermodynamics that states that the total entropy of any isolated thermodynamic system tends to increase over the time, approaching a maximum value.

Self-organization can contribute to adaptive manufacturing systems in the main following areas (Vaario et al., 1997):

–   Shop floor layout, where the manufacturing entities present in the shop floor are movable, e.g. to minimize the transportation distances;
–   Adaptive control, in which the goal is to find out an adaptive and dynamic production control strategy based in the dynamic and on-line schedule, adapted in case of occurrence of unexpected disturbances;
–   Product demand, in which the manufacturing system re-organizes itself in order to adapt to the changes in the product demand, increasing or reducing the number of manufacturing resources, or modifying their capabilities.

The work presented in this paper focuses the adaptive control, with self-organization contributing for the dynamic re-organization of the control system.

3. BIOLOGICAL-INSPIRED CONTROL SOLUTION

The Darwin's theory of the evolution of species tell us that species change over a long period of time, evolving to suit their environment, and that the species that survive to changes in the environment are not the strongest or the most intelligent, but those that are more responsiveness to change. Translating into the manufacturing domain, the manufacturing companies better prepared to survive are those that better respond to emergent and volatile environments.

3.1. Basic Concepts

Having this idea in mind, the ADACOR (ADAptive holonic COntrol aRchitecture for distributed manufacturing systems) holonic manufacturing control architecture introduces an adaptive and evolvable approach, considering bio-inspired theories, that addresses the system re-configurability and evolution, especially in emergent environments. The proposed adaptive architecture intends to be as decentralized as possible and as centralized as necessary, i.e. evolving from a centralized approach when the objective is the optimization, to a more heterarchical approach in presence of unexpected scenarios.

ADACOR architecture is based on concepts inherited from biology, social organizations and artificial life, namely self-organization and swarm intelligence, translating into the manufacturing world the way how complex biological entities and systems behave in a simple way. It is based on the following main foundations: holonic manufacturing principles, supervisor entities and self-organization.

In analogy to insect colonies, ADACOR architecture is built upon a community of autonomous and cooperative holons, representing the manufacturing components, such as robots, conveyors, pallets, products and orders. Using HMS principles, the manufacturing control functions are distributed among holons, taking advantage of modularity, decentralization, agility, flexibility, robustness and scalability.

In social society colony, an individual usually does not perform all tasks, but rather specializes in a set of tasks (Bonabeau et al., 1999). In fact, the division of labor is used to have specialized individuals performing simultaneously different activities, which is believed to be more efficient than sequential task performance by unspecialized individuals (Bonabeau et al., 1999). Following this idea, ADACOR architecture identifies four manufacturing holon classes (Leitao, Restivo, 2006), product (PH), task (TH), operational (OH) and supervisor (SH), according to their roles and functionalities. The product holons represent the products (and sub-products) available in the factory catalogue, containing all knowledge related to the product. The task holons represent the production orders launched to the shop floor to execute the requested products and the operational holons represent the physical resources available at shop floor, such as operators, robots and conveyors. Operational holons are also specialized to perform physical tasks, namely machining and moving. The supervisor holons represent the logical coordination of a group of holons, providing co-ordination and optimization services to the holons under their supervision, and thus introducing hierarchy in an otherwise decentralized system.

The product, task and operational holons are quite similar to the product, order and resource holons defined in PROSA reference architecture (Brussel et al., 1998), while the supervisor holon, inspired in biological systems, presents characteristics not found in the PROSA staff holon, namely the possibility to coordinate other supervisor holons in a federation architecture and the responsibility to manage the dynamic evolution of groups of holons according to the environment context (Leitao, Restivo, 2008). ADACOR holons are of the plug and produce type, being possible to add a new element without the need to re-initialize and re-program the system, thus allowing high flexibility in system adaptation and re-configuration on fly.

The self-organization exhibited by each distributed holon allows the dynamic evolution and re-configuration of the organizational control structure, combining the global production optimization with the agile reaction to unexpected disturbances. As in biological systems, where the evolution of the species or the groups results from the self-organization of local entities, the adaptive ADACOR mechanism, as illustrated in *Figure 1*, emerges from a bottom-up approach, built upon the individual self-organization of manufacturing holons. Here, the dynamic adaptation of each holon to unexpected situations contributes to the adaptation of the system as a whole to the emergent contexts and to the quick reaction to the occurrence of unexpected disturbances.

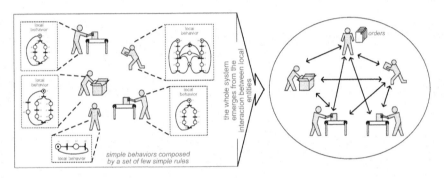

Figure 1. Global System Emerged from the Behavior of Local Holons

3.2. Individual Driving forces

The self-organization mechanism requires local driving forces to support the adaptation. In ADACOR architecture, the driving forces are the autonomy factor and the learning capability, which are inherent characteristics to each ADACOR holon.

An ADACOR holon is autonomous, since it can operate on its own, without the direct intervention of external entities, and has full control over its behavior. Having its own objectives, knowledge and skills, each holon has the capability to reason in order to take decisions about its activities. Each ADACOR holon possesses only a partial view of the system, needing to cooperate with the other holons in order to achieve its goals or to get additional information about the system.

Aiming to achieve an adaptive and evolvable behavior, ADACOR introduces the autonomy factor concept, designated by α, that is a parameter associated to each holon reflecting its degree of autonomy (Leitao, Restivo, 2006). The autonomy factor is regulated by a decision mechanism that evolves dynamically in order to adapt the holon behavior to changes in the environment where it is placed. The evolution of the autonomy factor is regulated by a fuzzy rule-based engine, illustrated in

Figure 112, which takes into consideration the reestablishment time (τ), which is the estimated time to recover from the current disturbance, and the pheromone parameter (ρ), which is an indication of the level of impact of the disturbance.

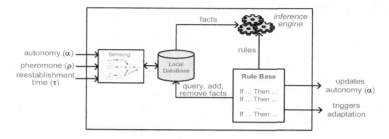

Figure 2. Rule-based Mechanism to Regulate the Holon's Autonomy

The cardinality of the numerical set associated to the autonomy factor may have strong impact in the dynamic of the adaptation mechanism: on one hand, the higher the number of values, the more gradual will be the adaptation procedure, but, on the other side, a high number of values makes the adaptation mechanism more complex and the response times longer (Leitao, Restivo, 2006). In this study, it was considered that the autonomy factor is a discrete binary variable comprising the states {Low, High}.

The set of simple rules that regulates the adaptation behavior of the holon is illustrated in *Figure* 3. Normally, the operational holons have a low autonomy factor, following the supervisor holon coordination and accepting its schedule proposals. In case of {Low} autonomy factor, the emergency, normally the occurrence of a disturbance and represented by the {High} value associated to the pheromone parameter (ρ), triggers the change of the autonomy factor to {High} and the re-organization process.

```
IF ρ == High AND α == Low
    THEN α = High AND ReorganiseIntoNewStructure

IF ρ == High AND α == High AND τ == Elapsed
    THEN α = High AND Reload τ

IF ρ==Low AND α==High AND τ == Elapsed
    THEN α = Low AND ReorganiseIntoNewStructure
```

Figure 3. Set of Simple Rules that Regulates the Adaptive Mechanism Behavior

When the reestablishment time elapses, if the autonomy factor is {High} and the pheromone is still active, which means that the disturbance is not completely recovered, the reestablishment time is re-loaded. If the pheromone has already dissipated, which means that the disturbance is already solved, the holon can return to the original structure, changing the autonomy factor to {Low}.

The degree of efficiency of the self-organization capability, and consequently the improvement of the holon's behavior performance supporting its adaptation to the environment emergency, is strongly dependent on how the learning mechanisms are implemented. The learning capability associated to ADACOR holons allows the acquisition of new knowledge, improving the holon's ability to act in future and to support the dynamic evolution of the environment where it is placed. The learning capability is dependent on the decision mechanisms and on the learning algorithms. As an example, in case of neural networks, the learning is associated with the adjustment of the nodes coefficients, but in case of expert systems, the learning is associated with the addition of new facts or to the generation of new rules. The elaboration of new rules is more complex than the simple acquisition of new factual knowledge, and requires a special attention to verify dynamically the possible contradiction between the new knowledge rules and the initial behavior knowledge.

3.3. Global Driving Forces to Achieve Evolvable Systems

The driving forces associated to each individual entity aiming to achieve adaptation were analyzed in the previous section. The global self-organization of the system is only achieved if the distributed entities have stimulus to drive their local self-organization capabilities. The behavior recalls the stimergy concept, which is often used in biology to describe the influence on behavior of the persisting environmental effects of previous behaviors.

The global self-organization requires global mechanisms that allow the interaction between local individual holons, supporting the propagation of the emergence, which constitutes the event-driven mechanism to trigger the evolution of the control system into different structures. ADACOR approach proposes a pheromone-like spreading mechanism to propagate the emergence, triggering the evolution process. The entities cooperating with this type of mechanisms (Brussel et al., 2000):

- Dissipate the information to the other entities, in a similar way to the ant that deposits pheromones;
- Sense the information dissipated by the other entities (like ants sense the odors) to take their own actions; sometimes they reinforce the odor.

In the ADACOR architecture, when an emergence or an unexpected disturbance occurs, the need for re-organization is propagated through the deposit of a certain quantity of pheromone in the neighbor supervisor holons, as illustrated in *Figure*4. This quantity is proportional to the estimated reestablishment time, forecasted according to the type of disturbance and to the historic data.

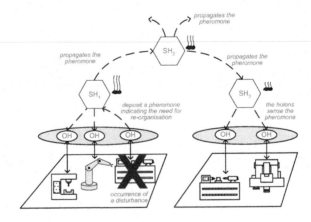

Figure 4. Propagation of the Emergence using Pheromone-like Techniques

The holons associated to each supervisor holon receive the need for re-organization by sensing the pheromone and propagating this need to neighbor holons. The intensity of the odor associated to the pheromone becomes smaller with the increase of the number of the levels of supervisor holons (similar to distance in the original pheromone techniques), according to a defined flow field gradient, which is characterized by the reduction of the intensity of the odor and increase of the entropy. With this mechanism, holons positioned near of the disturbance epicenter will be more sensitive to the self-evolution than the holons positioned far from the epicenter. While the emergence is still active, e.g. because the disturbance was not completely solved, the holon reinforces the odor associated with the pheromone indicating that the problem still remains. The holon stops to reinforces the odor when the problem is solved.

The propagation of the emergence and the need for re-organization using pheromone-like techniques is suitable for the dynamic and continuous adaptation of the system to disturbances, supporting the global self-organization, reducing the communication overhead and improving the reaction to disturbances (Leitao, Restivo, 2006).

4. ADAPTIVE CONTROL WORKING IN PRACTICE

The control architecture is the key factor for the performance of the manufacturing control system, playing a critical role in the system performance in terms of response to change and capability to learn. The proposed dynamic and adaptive control approach improves the agility and reaction to unexpected disturbances without compromising the global optimization. In this section, the adaptive control approach will be further analyzed, mainly the dynamic evolution of the control structure and the task allocation mechanism.

4.1. Dynamic Evolution of the Control Structure

The ADACOR adaptive control balances between a more centralized approach and a more flat approach, passing through other intermediate forms of control (Leitao, Restivo, 2006), due to the adaptive and dynamic evolution of the autonomy factor of each ADACOR holon. The control is shared between supervisor and operational holons, and is splited into two alternative states (Leitao, Restivo, 2006): a stationary state, in which the system control uses coordination levels to get global optimization of the production plan, and a transient state, triggered by the occurrence of disturbances and presenting a behavior quite similar to the heterarchical approach in terms of agility and adaptability.

In stationary state the holons are organized in a hierarchical architecture, with supervisor holons interacting directly with the task holons during the task allocation process. Supervisor holons, as coordinators, elaborate optimized schedule plans that are proposed to the task holons and to the operational holons under their coordination domain. In this state, each operational holon has a low autonomy factor and sees these proposals as advices, following the proposals, although they have enough autonomy to accept or reject the proposed schedule (Leitao, Restivo, 2006).

If, for any reason, the system deviates from planned, due for example to a machine failure or a rush order, the operational holon which detects the disturbance increases its autonomy factor parameter and propagates the need for re-organization to the other holons in the system using pheromone-like techniques. The neighbor holons also sense the pheromone and will increase their autonomy factors according to the intensity of the pheromone and their local knowledge, entering in a transient state. In this state the holons evolve to a new control structure aiming to achieve an agile reaction to the emergency, with the self-organization capability playing a crucial role. The task holons interact directly with the operational holons in order to achieve an alternative schedule plan and the supervisor holons can continue elaborating and proposing the allocation of operations to the operational holons, but since these have now high values of autonomy factors, they will probably reject the proposals (Leitao, Restivo, 2006). The holons remain in the transient state during the reestablishment time, τ, which is typically a short period of time estimated by the operational holon that detected the disturbance for its recovery.

After the recovery from the disturbance, the holon ends the reinforcement of the pheromone. When the other holons don't sense the pheromone odor anymore, they reduce their autonomy factors and the system evolves to a new control structure (often returning to the original one), according to the learning capabilities embedded in each holon. The supervisor holon returns to its coordination function, re-scheduling the non-optimized schedule, reached during the transient state.

4.2. Task Allocation

A result of the proposed dynamic evolving mechanism is the presence of a scheduling approach that distributes the scheduling functions over several entities, combining their calculation power and local optimization. In this scheduling approach, the objective is to achieve fast and dynamic re-scheduling using a scheduling mechanism that evolves dynamically to combine centralized strategies and distributed strategies, improving its responsiveness to emergence, instead of the complex and optimized scheduling algorithms. The idea is that a global optimized schedule should be generated whenever possible, and a fast re-scheduling should be used in case of disturbances, because, in this case, this is preferable than waiting a significant amount of time for an optimized schedule, which is likely to be not optimized again soon (Leitao, Restivo, 2008).

In the distributed scheduling model the computational complexity is related to find an optimal determination problem in combinatorial auctions, with the presence of two specialized types of holons: task holons that have operations to be executed and operational holons that have skills to execute operations. The motivation of ADACOR holons to execute the manufacturing control functions is regulated by a credits system. Table 1 summarizes the evolution of the credits of task and operational holons during their life cycles.

Table 1. Evolution of Credits During the Holon's Life Cycle

Phase	Task Holon	Operational Holon
Initially.	π credits to execute the order	None credits
Operation allocation process.	Contracts the operation execution by φ and the penalty by ξ.	Contracts the operation execution by φ and the penalty by ξ.
End of an operation with success.	Pays the value φ to the OH ($\pi \leftarrow \pi - \varphi$).	Increases the total credits by φ ($\mu \leftarrow \mu + \varphi$).
End of an operation with delay.	Pays the value φ and receives the value ξ from the OH ($\pi \leftarrow \pi + \xi - \varphi$).	Decreases the total credits by ξ and increase by φ ($\mu \leftarrow \mu - \xi + \varphi$).
Operation cancelled (delay, failure, etc.).	Receives the value ξ from the OH ($\pi \leftarrow \pi + \xi$).	Decreases the total credits by ξ ($\mu \leftarrow \mu - \xi$).

When the task holon is launched, it receives a fund to execute the production order (π) and a penalty value for delay. The task holon manages the costs to execute its production order in order to guarantee that they never exceed the initial fund. During the interaction to allocate the operations, the task holons try to pay as less as possible and the operational holons try to receive as more as possible.

Initially, the task holons announce, in an open market basis, the execution of the operations belonging to the order. In presence of operation announcements, each operational holon decides, based on its skills and capacity, its availability to execute the operation. Since each operation has a set of requirements, each operational holon verifies if it can perform the operation by matching the requirements of the operation with the resource's skills, using a rule-based function. In case of availability, the operational holon calculates the price to be proposed to the task holon, p_{jik}, that may be calculated according to the following function:

$$p_{jik} = C_s + C_p \times d_{ik} + C_b \times \left(-e^{-\sigma \times \beta} \times \left(-\gamma\right)\right)$$

where C_s is the cost associated to the setup execution, C_p is related to the cost associated to maintain the machine working, d_{ik} is the duration of the operation execution and C_b reflects the investment done to buy the machine. In order to have a dynamic price, this expression models the market laws, increasing or decreasing the final price in function of the actual load of the resource (reflected by the parameter β) and of the actual bid acceptance rate (reflected by the γ parameter, with $0 \le \gamma \le 1$). The operational holon uses the knowledge learned from the previous bids to adjust the final price: decreasing the γ parameter if the acceptance rate is low or increasing it in the opposite case.

The decision to select the best proposal, taken by the task holon, is achieved by minimizing a heuristic function that takes in consideration, among others, the proposed price, the location of the resource and the confidence degree of the proponent operational holon. The confidence degree reflects the trust that the task holon has in an operational holon and is based on the knowledge learned in previous interactions, considering a percentage of operations successfully executed by the resource. In case of an inconclusive evaluation, the task holon can start another iterative negotiation, re-formulating the bid parameters, for example the due date and announcement specifications. After the negotiation, the task holon accepts to pay a price of φ credits (i.e. p_{jik}) to the operational holon that will execute the operation and to receive a penalty of ξ credits from the operational holon if it does not fulfill the contracted due date.

The global performance of the operational holons in terms of credits is given by the sum of rewards received minus the penalties paid for the delays.

5. CONCLUSIONS

Reconfigurable manufacturing systems appear as an emergent paradigm to face the challenge for agile, adaptive and evolvable systems, where re-configurability and responsiveness play key roles. In fact, these systems should exhibit agile response to emergence by providing dynamic re-configuration on fly, i.e. without stopping, re-programming or re-starting the process. Biological and nature inspired concepts and theories, namely artificial life, chaos theory, swarm intelligence and complexity behavior, seem suitable for the design of reconfigurable manufacturing systems.

This paper illustrates the applicability of these concepts in manufacturing world by introducing a bio-inspired solution for reconfigurable manufacturing control systems, using concepts derived from holonic manufacturing, swarm intelligence and self-organization. The proposed approach introduces an adaptive control approach based on self-organization, supervision and learning concepts and on ant-based communication, supported by the use of multi-agent principles.

The preliminary experimental results have proved the applicability of the proposed bio-inspired solution (Leitao, Restivo, 2006). Future work is related to the introduction of powerful biological and intelligence mechanisms to support better the dynamic reconfigurability of the control system, namely learning mechanisms to identify the situations and the way to evolve.

6. REFERENCES

1. Bonabeau, E., Dorigo, M and Theraulaz, G., "Swarm Intelligence: From Natural to Artificial Systems", Oxford University Press, 1999.
2. Bousbia, S., Trentesaux, D., "Self-organization in Distributed Manufacturing Control: State-of-the-art and Future Trends", Proc. of the International Conference on Systems, Man and Cybernetics, vol5, 2002.
3. Brussel, H.V., Valckenaers, P., Wyns, J., Peeters, P. and Bongaerts, L., "Holonic Manufacturing Systems, Architectural and Manufacturing Control Issues", Proceedings of 2nd CIRP Int'l Seminar on Intelligent Computation in Manufacturing Engineering, 2000, pp. 19–29.
4. Brussel, H.V., Wyns, J., Valckenaers, P., Bongaerts, L. Reference Architecture for Holonic Manufacturing Systems: PROSA. Computers In Industry 1998; 37(3): 255–274.
5. CMV, "Visionary Manufacturing Challenges for 2020", Committee on Visionary Manufacturing, 1998, National Academic Press: Washington DC, USA.
6. Deen, S. (editor), Agent-Based Manufacturing: Advances in the Holonic Approach, Springer Verlag Berlin Heidelberg, 2003.
7. ElMaraghy, H. Flexible and Reconfigurable Manufacturing Systems Paradigms. International Journal of Flexible Manufacturing Systems, 17, 2006, pp. 261-271.
8. Holland, J., "Emergence: from Chaos to Order", Oxford University Press, 1998.
9. Koestler, A. "The Ghost in the Machine", Arkana Books, London, 1969.
10. Koren, Y., Heisel, U., Jovane, F., Moriwaki, T., Pritchow, G., Ulsoy, G. and Brussel, H.V., "Reconfigurable Manufacturing Systems", CIRP, 48 (2), 1999, pp. 527-540.
11. Leitão, P. and Restivo, F. ADACOR: A Holonic Architecture for Agile and Adaptive Manufacturing Control. Computers in Industry 2006; 57(2): 121-130.
12. Leitão, P., Restivo, F. "A Holonic Approach to Dynamic Manufacturing Scheduling", accepted for publication in Robotics and Computer Integrated Manufacturing, 2008.
13. Manufuture, "Manufuture, A Vision for 2020, Assuring the Future of Manufacturing in Europe", Report of the High-level Group, European Commission, 2004.
14. Massotte, P., "Self-organization: A New Approach to Improve the Reactivity of the Production Systems", Proc. of the International Conference on Emergent Technologies for Factory Automation, 1995, pp. 23-32.
15. Mehrabi, M.G., Ulsoy, A.G., Koren, Y. Reconfigurable Manufacturing Systems: Key to Future Manufacturing. Journal of Intelligent Manufacturing 2000; 11: 403-419.
16. Pujo, P., Ounnar, F., "Decentralized Control and Self-organization in Flexible Manufacturing Systems", Proc. of the International Conference on Emergent Technologies for Factory Automation, vol.2, 2001, pp. 659-663.
17. Setchi, R., Lago, N., "Reconfigurability and Reconfigurable Manufacturing Systems – State of the Art Review", 2nd IEEE International Conference on Industrial Informatics 2004, pp. 529-535.
18. Thamarajah, A. A Self-organizing Model for Scheduling Distributed Autonomous Manufacturing Systems. Cybernetics Systems 1998; 29 (5): 461-480.
19. Vaario, J., Ueda, K., "Self-Organisation in Manufacturing Systems", In Japan- USA Symposium on Flexible Automation, 1996, pp. 1481-1484.
2. Vaario, J., Ueda, K., "Biological Concept of Self-organization for Dynamic Shop Floor Configuration", Proc. of Advanced Product Management Systems (APMS'97), 1997, pp. 55-66.
21. Wooldridge, M., "An Introduction to Multi-Agent Systems", John Wiley & Sons, 2002.

PART 5

INNOVATION AND ENTREPRENEURSHIP

34

AN INNOVATIVE PATTERN TO DESIGN NEW BUSINESS MODELS IN THE MACHINE TOOL INDUSTRY

Giacomo Copani
Politecnico di Milano, giacomo.copani@polimi.it
Silvia Marvulli
Institute of Industrial Technologies and Automation-CNR, silvia.marvulli@itia.cnr.it
Lorenzo Molinari Tosatti
Institute of Industrial Technologies and Automation-CNR, lorenzo.molinari@itia.cnr.it

Since some years, European machine tool companies are facing a turbulent market, where Asiatic competitors are becoming more and more aggressive. In such context, technology improvement is not anymore sufficient to preserve their market position: the evolution of their business model towards the offer of value added services will be a fundamental key for future success. This paper, realised within "Next Generation Production Systems" FP6 European Project, proposes an innovative operative pattern guiding machine tool companies in the business model innovation decisions.

Keywords: Business model, Machine tool industry, customer-supplier relationships

1. INTRODUCTION

Business model innovation is an innovative concept in the European machine tool industry, which represents more than 40% of the worldwide value of machine tools' production and counts about 150,000 employees (Cecimo, 2006). In this sector, equipment suppliers are traditionally oriented to the offering of production systems with a limited number of additional product related services (e.g. installation, training, etc.). The relationship between customers and suppliers are mainly limited to the sales operative phase (transaction based relationship) and machine tool builder core competencies are related to the engineering and production of machines. In the past, such an approach allowed European machine tool companies to get and preserve a strong position in their sectors (Mathe-Portioli Staudacher, 2004). In recent years, the European industry competitiveness has been strained by the increased turbulence of the business arena, determined by new aggressive competitors from emerging Countries (Windahl et al. 2004, Gebauer et al., 2005).

To cope with this situation, companies should innovate their business models establishing more collaborative long-term relationships with their customers and offering value added services beyond the traditional technical ones (Windahl et al., 2004). In fact, the technological innovation does not represent anymore a differentiating strength point which companies can base their offer on (European Manufacturing Survey, 2005). Instead, the integration of value added services with the physical products (i.e. production systems) could guarantee a stable source of revenues, an increasing market demand and a competitive weapon not easily imitable (Cohen-Whang, 1997, Oliva-Kallenberg, 2003).

Please use the following format when citing this chapter:

Copani, G., Marvulli, S. and Tosatti, L.M., 2008, in IFIP International Federation for Information Processing, Volume 266, *Innovation in Manufacturing Networks;* ed. A. Azevedo; (Boston: Springer), pp. 317–324.

Furthermore, service offerings incentivize the creation of sustainable long-term relationships with customers (Frambach et al., 1997).

Despite the unanimous agreement on the described innovation need, European machine builder companies are still far from reaching this goal (Lay, 2007). The main reasons have been identified in the lack of specific managerial culture and of operative tools supporting this complex change, which requires market, organizational, financial, and supply chain innovation (Copani et al., 2007 a). Current literature offers general theoretical addresses about business models, but available results are mainly derived from the world of internet based companies and, apart some recent exceptions, no structured managerial tool supporting strategic decisions exists. To cover this lack, a new frame to shape the relationships between machine tool builders and their customers, consisting of a multi-step methodology for the selection and design of the most appropriate business models, has been designed and presented in this paper.

In the next section the research methodology is briefly described. The third section is dedicated to the review of the existing literature on New Business Models in the machine tool industry, while the fourth and fifth sections describe the designed methodology and the results of the testing phase. In conclusion, some guidelines for future research in this field are provided.

2. RESEARCH METHODOLOGY

To develop the decision tool supporting the business model selection, a preliminary literature review on New Business Models has been carried out. The tool has been then designed, identifying the main decision phases that a company should face while selecting a business model. For each phase, the main possible variables that should be evaluated by a machine builder, together with their possible options, have been made explicit using the knowledge acquired from literature review on one side, and involving in the research some leading European machine builders on the other. Finally, the decision support tool has been tested in some real business case.

3. LITERATURE REVIEW

The topic of New Business Models referred to the machine tool sector has gained the attention of industrialists and management researchers only in recent years. Up to the beginning of the 2000's, technology was thought to be the main answer to respond to market needs and evolution. As a consequence, the research focus was mainly addressed to the development of production systems able to efficiently support companies in their production activities. The introduction and conceptualization of Reconfigurable Manufacturing Systems (Koren et al., 1999) paved the way for different collaborative approaches beyond the only production system technology. The "selling use" approach, where the supplier owns and operates the machine and the customer pays only for its use, was conceived by Franke et al., 2002 as the alternative to the traditional selling of the production system in case of high reconfigurability. Seliger et al., 2004 argued that adaptation services (e.g. maintenance, enlargement, rearrangement, modernization, etc.) are needed to enable the re-use of the system and "align" it to the exigencies of different customers. In line with this view, a specific strategy to implement and develop such services has been proposed in recent years (Scholz et al., 2007).

Focused on a customer-supplier relationship perspective, a new research stream on the service based supply of manufacturing capacity emerged (Urbani et al., 2002, Molinari

Tosatti et al., 2002). Based on the possible scenario evolutions and on the different drivers determining the supply chain relationships (ownership, location, operating personnel, maintenance personnel, payment mode), a categorization scheme allowing the structured representation of different business models options has been proposed (Lay et al., 2003). Such scheme has been further detailed and enriched during the Mantys Project (Mantys, 2005) with the scope to supply machine builders with a matrix supporting the negotiation phase with customers.

The organizational transition from product to service in the value proposition of machine tool suppliers was the focus of the study of Oliva and Kallenberg, 2003, that provided a process model for developing service capabilities. The combination of products and services has also been taken into account by Windahl et al., 2004, referring to it as "integrated solution" as part of the growth strategies of companies in this sector. In the last years these research trends, and especially the shift from the technology to its use, have been integrated in the wider research stream of the Industrial Product Service System (IPS2). Different IPS2 for the machinery sector have been proposed, together with some criteria to differentiate them (revenue model, operating personnel, production responsibility, maintenance personnel, service request) (Meier-Kortmann, 2007).

As it can be noticed, the research results currently available to companies are mainly at strategic and conceptual level. The link between strategy and concrete operation practices is still missing, and this partly explains the slow adoption rate of New Business Models by European companies (Copani et al., 2007 a). One of the first attempts to overcome this lack has been the definition of specific financial guidelines supporting machine tool builders to identify the proper revenue model to be offered within an innovative service oriented value proposition (Copani et al., 2007 b). Unconventional financial methods, such as pay per part or per availability mechanisms, have been theorised in order to start a cultural change in the industry.

4. PATTERN TO DESIGN NEW BUSINESS MODELS

The main scope of the methodology presented in this paper is to support machine tool suppliers in the definition of potential innovative offerings to be proposed to their customers in a New Business Model environment. The methodology represents thus a powerful operative instrument guiding machine builders to take strategic and commercial decisions in order to gain competitiveness through non-technical innovation. The methodology consists of three sequential analysis-decision phases. For each of them, a pre-built database of options and of analysis criteria has been designed, so that the methodology is populated with a-priori defined contents. Such contents have been developed assessing the main possible market situations that a machine builder could face, both derived from the surveyed literature and, especially, from the involvement of leading European machine builder companies experienced with New Business Models.

The sequential phases are described in the following paragraphs.

4.1. Identification of customers' business needs

In the first phase the machine builder customer's needs are identified according to his specific company situation. In order to support such analysis, the following possible business needs have been recognized as the most frequent in the market:
- Reduction of costs, referred to production, logistics and maintenance.
- Increase of quality of the production process and of the final products.

- Reduction of the lead time, including production, maintenance and logistics (procurement and delivery) time.
- Increase of productivity, defined as the ratio between the produced output and the inputs necessary for it.
- Increase of flexibility, defined as the capacity of the company to respond in a timely and costly effective manner either to internal or external changes, as variations in market requests.
- Reduction of risk, related to the production process (operating risk) or the logistic activities.

To detect which are the real customer business needs among those listed, the specific company situation has to be analyzed. A checklist has been made available for this, composed of 29 customer indicators in the following areas:

- Production process situation (low productivity, high production lead time, high scrap rates, low operational availability, high production costs, alternating capacity requirements, presence of bottle-necks).
- Workforce situation (skilled service workforce missing at customer's plant, low operational know-how).
- Production system situation (long reinvestment period, low flexibility, no or low exploitation of available machine features).
- Final Product situation (huge amount of product variants, small amount of product variants, short product cycles, low retooling frequency, cyclical industry, customer is a make-to-order manufacturer, production of prototypes/sample/trial parts, production of spare parts in end of service (life) cycle, unpredictable market prospect).
- Logistic process situation (high procurement costs, high delivery costs, high procurement time, high delivery time, high logistic risk).
- Maintenance process situation (high maintenance costs, high repair frequency, high repair time).

Starting from the indicators, criteria permitting to identify which are the possible customer's business needs have been imbedded in the methodology and are graphically represented with the coloured cells in Figure 1, which is an extract from the overall data base of indicators, business needs and criteria.

			Business needs				
			Increase of quality		Reduction of costs		
			Product	Process	Production	Maintenance	...
Indicators	Production process	Low productivity					
		High production lead time					
		High scrap rates at customer's					
		Low operational availability					
		High production costs					
		Alternating capacity					
		Bottle-neck					
	Workforce	Skilled service workforce missing at customer's plant					
		...					

Figure 1. Extract from the table supporting customer's business needs identification

Since the customer condition is outlined by more than one indicator, multiple business needs among those described can be identified at the same time. Nevertheless, the value of this first phase consists of the restriction of the attention of the machine builder to some real problems of the customer, which are detected considering its whole productive and organisational situations.

4.2. Definition of the value propositions

In the second step, the machine tool supplier has to define his value proposition to the customer in order to innovatively respond to the business needs detected in the previous phase. A value proposition represents the intentions of the machine builder while fulfilling customer requests; thus, it should include the technical proposition (the production system) and the additional value added services.

Nine innovative value propositions have been thought as a quite significant set of the existing industrial realities:

- offering concepts for levelling irregular and temporary customer capacity requirements;
- offering complete production service;
- offering procurement management;
- offering delivery management;
- providing availability guarantee;
- solving customer qualification deficits;
- continuous modernization concepts;
- lean machine business concepts;
- towards reconfigurable production systems.

The machine builder has available a table (see Figure 2), where the identified value propositions are reported on the columns and the business needs on the lines. All the business needs fulfilled by each value proposition are highlighted by a coloured box and, among them, the prior ones that can be satisfied through that value proposition have been marked with "x". For example, if the customer business need is "increase process quality", the most appropriated value proposition to cover this need is "continuous modernisation concepts", as suggested by industrialists. Nevertheless, also "providing availability guarantee" may have impact in the business need response to some extent. As it can be noticed, the proposed methodology does not aim to provide any automatic answer or solution. It constitute a structured support for a conscious decision taking, where resulting options have to be at the end evaluated by machine builder through its experience and according to the specific market situation he is assessing.

| | | VALUE PROPOSITIONS | | | | | | | | |
		A — Offering concepts for leveling irregular and temporary customer capacity requirements	B — Offering complete production service (outsourcing)	C — Offering procurement management	D — Offering delivery management	E — Providing availability guarantee	F — Solving customer qualification deficits	G — Lean machine business concepts	H — Continuous modernisation concepts	I — Towards reconfigurable production system
Increase of quality	Product						x		x	
	Process									
Reduction of costs (production, logistics, etc.)	Production							x		
	Maintenance					x				
	Procurement			x						
	Delivery				x					
Reduction of lead time	Production								x	
	Maintenance					x				
	Procurement			x						
	Delivery				x					
Increase of productivity		x	x						x	
Increase of flexibility		x	x							
Reduction of risks	Operative	x								x
	Logistic			x	x					

Figure 2. Table supporting the identification of value propositions

4.3. Definition of cooperation scenarios

Once identified the value propositions able to respond to customer business needs, the methodology provides some operative addresses to the machine builder in order to shape the relationships and the technology in the business model. With this purpose, the available categorization schemes to configure a business model have been improved and the results are shown in Figure 3. The business model can be graphically identified by a line connecting the different options that are chosen for each configuration dimension. The business model configuration dimensions are: responsibility for operating personnel, responsibility for maintenance personnel, production location, payment model, production equipments ownership, production equipment utilization rate, responsibility for raw material procurement, responsibility for final products transportation, equipment technology. Based on the existing literature and on the judgements of machine builder companies, the methodology suggests which are the different types of business models (lines in the table) corresponding to each value proposition, in terms of the possible options for the business model configuration dimensions. As in the previous phase, it is possible that more than one type of business models is associated to a single value proposition. Nevertheless, the attention of machine builder will be restricted on a limited number of possibilities to be evaluated in cooperation with the customer.

4.4. Testing of the methodology

The methodology has been applied in real market scenarios that are faced by two leading European machine tool companies. One case was related to a large customer
in the railway sector and the other to a small customer in the moulds and dies industry. The methodology allowed companies to select 3-4 potential cooperation scenarios that will be proposed to the customers and negotiated. Machine tool companies appreciated the structured approach that permitted them to consider all relevant customers' variables in order to identify innovative responses to their needs.

Characteristic features		Options			
Operating personnel		Equipment producer	Operating Joint Venture	Third party	Customer
Maintenance personnel		Equipment producer	Operating Joint Venture	Third party	Customer
Location		Equipment producer	Third party	"Fence to Fence" to the customer	Customer
Payment modus		Pay per Part	Pay per Use (Rent)	Pay for availability	Fixed rate / Pay for equipment?
Ownership	During phase of use	Equipment producer	Leasing bank		Customer
	After phase of use	Equipment producer	Leasing bank		Customer
Utilization rate		High		Low	
Procurement of raw materials		Equipment producer	Operating Joint Venture	Third party	Customer
Transport of end products		Equipment producer	Operating Joint Venture	Third party	Customer
Technology	Automation level	High		Low	
	Performance level	High		Low	
	Reconfigurability level	High		Low	
	Availability (MTTR/MTBF)	High		Low	
	Complexity level	High		Low	
	Efficiency level	High		Low	

Figure 3. Table supporting the business models configuration

5. CONCLUSIONS AND FUTURE RESEARCH

In order to contribute to the development of instruments that can support machine builder companies in the adoption of innovative business models, this paper presented a methodology for the identification of the suited value added cooperation scenarios to be established between customers and equipment suppliers. The starting points of the methodology are customer needs, based on which value propositions and cooperation scenarios are identified. Such a methodology dictates the sequential decision phases that should be faced, it offers diagnostic checklists, some lists of possible options that a machine builder should evaluate, and basic decision criteria that should support the decisions in each phase. The methodology has been developed starting from the literature and involving in the research some leading European machine tool companies. For this reason, it is deeply customised for the application in the machine tool sector. The approach has been tested in two real business cases, whose data and information have been provided by two European machine builders. The results have been very useful to better define their strategic market approach and their commercial action.

According to industry needs, further research is needed to continue developing operative tools supporting new strategies implementation. In particular, the development of quantitative instruments assessing the impact of strategic decisions in an economical and environmental life cycle perspective, will be an important goal to be reached in the near future.

5.1. Acknowledgments

This work has been partly funded by the European Commission through Project "Next - Next Generation Production Systems" (IP 011815 FP6). The authors acknowledge the Commission for its support and Next project partners for their contribution during the development of various ideas and concepts here presented.

6. REFERENCES

1. Cohen MA, Whang S. Competing in Product and Service: A Product Life-Cycle Model. Management Science 1997; Vol. 43, No 4: 535-545.
2. Copani G, Molinari Tosatti L, Lay G, Schroeter M, Bueno R. "New Business Models diffusion and trends in European machine tool industry". Proceedings of the 40th CIRP International Manufacturing Systems Seminar, 2007.
3. Copani G, Molinari Tosatti L, Marvulli S, Groothedde R, Palethorpe D. "New Financial Approaches for the Economic Sustainability in Manufacturing Industry". Proceedings of the 14th CIRP Conference on Life Cycle Engineering, 2007.
4. European Committee for Cooperation of the Machine Tool Industries (Cecimo), www. cecimo.be, 2006 data.
5. Frambach RT, Wels-Lips I, Gündlach A. Proactive Product Service Strategies An Application in the European Health Market. Industrial Marketing Management 1997; Vol. 26: 341-352.
6. Franke C, Seliger G, Hu SJ, Koren Y. "A new paradigm of manufacturing: selling use instead of selling systems". Proceedings of JUSFA Japan-USA Symposium on Flexible Automation, Hiroshima, Japan, 2002.
7. Gebauer H, Fleisch E, Fredli T. Overcoming the Service Paradox in Manufacturing Companies. European Management Journal 2005; Vol. 23, No 1: 14-26.
8. Koren Y, Heisel U, Jovane F, Moriwaki T, Pritschow G, Ulsoy G, Van Brussel H. "Reconfigurable Manufacturing Systems". Annals of the CIRP 1999; Vol. 48/2/1999.
9. Lay G, Meier H, Schramm J, Werding A. Betreiben statt verkaufen – Stand und Perspektiven neuer Geschäftsmodelle für den Maschinen- und Anlagenbau. Industrie Management 2003; 19-4.
10. Lay G., Betreibermodelle fur investitionsuter – Verbreitung, chancen und risiken, erfolgsfactoren, working paper Fraunhofer ISI, Karlsruhe, 2007
11. Mathe H, Portioli Staudacher A. "Innovative Service that Reinvent Manufacturing". IMS International Forum 2004 Global Challenges in Manufacturing, May 17-19, Italy, 2004.
12. Meier H, Kortmann D. "Leadership – From technology to use Operation fields and solution approaches for the automation of service processes of industrial Product-Service Systems". Proceedings of the 14th CIRP Conference on Life Cycle Engineering 2007, pp. 159-163.
13. Oliva R, Kallenberg R. Managing the transition from product to services. International Journal Of Service Industry Management 2003; Vol. 14, No 2: 160-172.
14. Scholz-Reiter B, Krohne F, Severengiz S. "Adaptation Service Manager for Manufacturing Equipment". Proceedings of the 40th CIRP International Manufacturing Systems Seminar, 2007.
15. Seliger G, Consiglio S, Zettl M. "Selling use instead of selling products – Technological and educational enablers for business in ecological product life cycles". In Product Life Cycle Quality Management Issues, 2004.
16. Stollt G. "Development of a Generic Business Model for the European Machine Tool Industry - As part of the foresight activity by Mantys". Mantys report 2005, pp. 8-27.
17. Urbani A, Molinari Tosatti L, Pasek Z. "Manufacturing practices in dynamic markets: reconfigurability to enable a service-based manufacturing capacity supply". Proceedings of the ASME-IMECE International Mechanical Engineering Congress and Exposition, New Orleans, Louisiana, November 17-22, 2002.
18. Urbani A, Molinari Tosatti L, Pierpaoli F, Jovane F. "New frontiers for manufacturing in Mass customization". The 35th CIRP, May 12-15, Korea, 2002.
19. Windahl C, Andersson P, Berggre C, Nehler C. "Manufacturing firms and integrated solutions: characteristics and implications". European Journal of Innovation Management 2004; Vol. 7, No 3: 218-228.
20. www.european-manufacturing-survey.eu

35

ENTREPRENEURIAL POTENTIAL IN ENGINEERING AND BUSINESS COURSES ... WHY WORRY NOW?

Aurora A.C. Teixeira

INESC Porto, Faculdade de Economia do Porto (FEP), CEMPRE, Universidade do Porto,
ateixeira@fep.up.pt; aurora.teixeira@inescporto.pt

In this paper we analyze the magnitude of this propensity in engineering and economics/business courses. The reason for such focus is that traditionally these courses are viewed as the ones concentrating individuals that are more likely to create new ventures. The empirical results, based on a large-scale survey of 2430 final-year students, reveal that no statistical difference exists in entrepreneurial potential of economics/business and engineering students, and that these two latter groups have lower entrepreneurial potential than students from other courses. This result proves to be quite unfortunate given the focus that previous studies have placed on these two majors, and the fact that a substantial part of entrepreneurial education is undertaken in business and engineering schools.

1. INTRODUCTION

Several recent trends have sparked renewed interest in entrepreneurship: the European Commission's recognition that "[e]ntrepreneurial activity underlies the creation of wealth and employment (...) Europe needs more entrepreneurs, to raise the number of competitive enterprises in Europe" (European Commission, 2000); the discontent of many employees with the structure of Europe's large businesses; emerging business opportunities due to technological, ecological, and social changes (for example, computerization, pollution, energy shortages, the increase in two-worker families, the growing elderly population, and geographical shifts in population) (McFarlane, 1981); and the problems of current European and Portuguese businesses related to low productivity, lack of innovative flexibility, and increased international competition (GEE, 2005).

The idea of becoming an entrepreneur is more and more attractive to students because it is seen as a valuable way of participating in the labor market without losing one's independence (Martínez et al., 2007).

The most common values amongst graduates facing the new labor market are linked to those of the self-employed: independence, challenge and self-realization (Lüthje and Franke, 2003).

While there has been significant research on the causes of entrepreneurial propensity (Greenberger and Sexton, 1988; Learned, 1992; Naffziger et al., 1994; Brandstatter, 1997), only a limited number of studies have focused on the entrepreneurial intent among students. Those that exist tend to focus on US and UK cases and are mainly restricted to small samples of business related majors.

Please use the following format when citing this chapter:

Teixeira, A.A.C., 2008, in IFIP International Federation for Information Processing, Volume 266, *Innovation in Manufacturing Networks;* ed. A. Azevedo; (Boston: Springer), pp. 325–336.

While new venture opportunities exist within nearly all academic disciplines (e.g., graphic arts, nursing, computer science), the majority of entrepreneurship initiatives at universities are offered by business schools (Ede et al., 1998; Hisrich, 1988) and for business students (e.g., Roebuck and Brawley, 1996). In fact, most studies that have been conducted to explore entrepreneurial intent among university students have focused on business students (e.g., DeMartino and Barbato, 2002; Ede et al.; Hills and Barnaby, 1977; Hills and Welsch, 1986; Krueger et al., 2000; Lissy, 2000; Sagie and Elizur, 1999; Sexton and Bowman, 1983). However, Hynes (1996) advocated that entrepreneurship education can and should be promoted and fostered among non-business students as well as business students. Consequently, if a goal in designing entrepreneurial programs is to assist students within and outside the business school, it is important to understand the similarities and differences between business school students and their non-business counterparts. In the present paper we examine the entrepreneurial characteristics among students of business/economics and engineering and the relationships between academic major and interest in entrepreneurship. The focus is thus on two groups of students: business/economics majors and engineering majors.

Despite the heterogeneity of sampling methods and target population, the existing studies on the issue (see Table 1) report that, on average, one quarter of students surveyed claimed that after their graduation they would like to become entrepreneurs (starting their own business or being self-employed).

It is not widely known (and is currently subject to intense debate) whether contextual founding conditions or personal traits drive the students' career decision towards self-employment (Luthje and Franke, 2003). In order to design effective programs, policy makers have to know which of these factors are decisive (Scott and Twomsey, 1988). In the next section we discuss this issue in greater detail.

The paper is structured as follows. In the following section a brief review of the literature on students' entrepreneurial intentions is presented. Then, in Section 3, we detail the methodology and describe the data. The estimation model and results are presented in Section 4. Some conclusions are summarized in Section 5.

2. STUDENT ENTREPRENEURSHIP POTENTIAL. A BRIEF REVIEW OF THE LITERATURE

The traditional mainstream view of the entrepreneur is as a 'risk-taker' bringing different factors of production together. The Austrian school takes a more dynamic perspective with entrepreneurship crucial for economic development and as a catalyst for change. In particular the Schumpeterian entrepreneur is an innovator who introduces new products or technologies. Frequently the notion of entrepreneurship is associated with predominant characteristics such as creativity and imagination, self-determination, and the abilities to make judgmental decisions and coordinate resources (Henderson and Robertson, 1999).

Adapting Carland et al.'s (1984: 358) definition of "entrepreneur", we define 'potential entrepreneur' as "an individual [final year student] who [admits] establish[ing] and manag[ing] a business for the principal purposes of profit and growth".

According to several authors (e.g., Carland et al., 1984; Hatten and Ruhland, 1995), entrepreneurs are characterized mainly by innovative behavior and employment of strategic management practices in the business.

A relevant body of literature on entrepreneurial activities reveals that there is a consistent interest in identifying the factors that lead an individual to become an entrepreneur (Martínez et al., 2007). Several pieces of evidence show that these are similar, with the most frequent analyzed as age, gender, professional background, work experience, and educational and psychological profiles (Delmar and Davidsson, 2000).

Broadly, three factors have been used to measure entrepreneurial tendencies: demographic data, personality traits (Robinson, 1987), and contextual factors (Naffziger et al., 1994). Demographic data (gender, age, region) can be used to describe entrepreneurs, but most of these characteristics do not enhance the ability to predict whether or not a person is likely to start a business (Hatten and Ruhland, 1995). The second method of assessing entrepreneurial tendencies is to examine personality traits such as achievement motive, risk taking, and locus of control. McClelland (1961) stressed need for achievement as a major entrepreneurial personality trait, whereas Robinson (1987) asserted that self-esteem and confidence are more prominent in entrepreneurs than the need for achievement. Several authors (e.g., Naffziger et al., 1994), however, argue that the decision to behave entrepreneurially is based on more than personal characteristics and individual differences. Accordingly, the interaction of personal characteristics with other important perceptions of contextual factors needs to be better understood.

Dyer (1994) developed a model of entrepreneurial career that included antecedents that influenced career choice. Antecedents to career choice included individual factors (entrepreneurial traits), social factors (family relationships and role models), and economic factors. This author asserted that children of entrepreneurs are more likely to view business ownership as being more acceptable than working for someone else. Baucus and Human (1995) studied Fortune 500 firm retirees who started their own business and found that networking, their view of departure, and prior employment experience positively affected the entrepreneurial process. Carroll and Mosakowski (1987) asserted that children with self-employed parents likely work in the family firm at an early age. That experience, coupled with the likelihood of inheriting the firm, led the individuals to move from a helping situation to full ownership and management. Van Auken et al. (2006) found that the importance of family owned businesses and the influence of family (including parental role modeling) in Mexico suggests that Mexican students may be more interested in business ownership than US students. Earlier, Scott (1988) also found that children of self-employed parents have a much higher propensity to become self-employed themselves. He conjectured that perhaps the influence of parents was twofold: first, as occupational role models, and second, as resource providers.

In general, the results indicate that being a man aged between 25 and 40 with self-employed parents, a higher education degree, need for achievement, risk taking propensity, and preference for innovation are the factors that favor the decision to undertake entrepreneurial activities (Storey, 1994; Reynolds, 1997; Stewart et al., 1998; Delmar and Davidsson, 2000; Martínez et al., 2007).

In Section 4, for the selected students, we assess which of the three groups of determinants of entrepreneurial intention – demographic, psychological, and contextual – emerges as more relevant. Before embarking on this analysis, the next section details and describes the methodology and data gathered.

3. METHODOLOGY AND DESCRIPTIVE STATISTICS

A questionnaire was developed and pre-tested during spring 2006. Final year students of all subjects at the largest Portuguese university were surveyed regarding their entrepreneurial potential. The survey was mainly implemented in the classroom, but when that was impossible (some final year students did not have classes as they were in internship training) the survey was implemented through an online inquiry. The final year students totaled 3761 individuals, spread over 60 courses, offered by 14 schools/faculties. The survey was carried out from September 2006 up to March 2007. A total of 2430 valid responses were gathered, representing a high response rate of 64.6%. Of these responses, 490 were from economics and business students and 495 from engineering (totaling 985 individuals). The response rates of these groups were, respectively 51.6% and 71.7%.

The questionnaire contained 17 questions, which include specific demographic descriptors (such as gender, age, student status, and region); participation in extra curricula activities, professional experience, academic performance, and social context; statements designed to measure fears, difficulties/obstacles and success factors concerning new venture formation to which students responded using a 5-point Likert scale. The entrepreneurial potential was directly assessed by asking students which option they would choose after completing their studies: starting their own business or being exclusively self-employed; to work exclusively as an employee; to combine employment and self-employment.

Analyzing responses by courses within Economics and Engineering Schools we observe that almost 35% are from Economics course and 15% from Business. In engineering the most representative courses are Computing, Electronics and Civil engineering, encompassing, respectively, 11%, 9% and 8% of the total number of selected students.

On average, 24% of economics/business and engineering students surveyed claim that they would like to start their own business after graduation. Metal and Industrial and Management Engineering are the most entrepreneurially driven courses with over 30% of students desiring to start a new venture. It is interesting to note that, in general, male students are more entrepreneurially driven than their female counterparts - 29% of male students would like to start their own business after graduation, whereas in the case of female students, that percentage is around 18%. Differences by course are particularly acute in Mining, Economics and Computing. In Business and Civil engineering, male and female students have a similar entrepreneurial propensity.

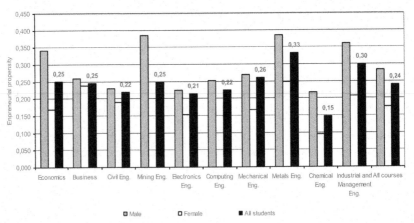

Figure 1. Entrepreneurial propensity by gender and courses

Excluding Industrial & Management Engineering, in general, older students (over 26 years old) are more entrepreneurial than their younger colleagues.

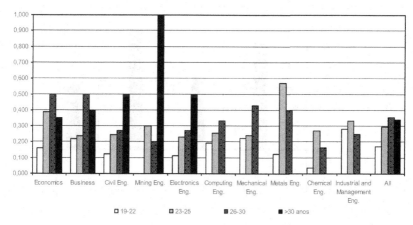

Figure 2. Entrepreneurial propensity by age and courses

At first sight, there seems to be a relationship between the status of the student, namely to be involved in academically related issues (student association members) and the desirability to be an entrepreneur. Notwithstanding, there is considerable heterogeneity among the courses analyzed, with Electronics, Computing and (utmost) Mechanical Engineering presenting the highest entrepreneurial potential by student association members. In sharp contrast, in Business the highest potential is associated with 'ordinary' enrolled students.

Correlating entrepreneurial potential with some psychological attributes associated with an entrepreneur (cf. Section 2) – risk taking, no fear of employment instability and uncertainty in remuneration; leadership wishes; creative focus; and innovative focus – we obtain an interesting picture by course.

Risk taking behavior was computed by considering the scores of the four items regarding the fear associated with new business formation – uncertainty in remuneration; employment instability; possibility to fail personally; possibility of bankruptcy. Firstly, dummies were computed for each item attributing 1 when the student responded small or no fear. Then we added up the four dummies and computed a new one which scored 1 if the sum variable totaled 3 or 4.

Leadership variable was computed based on the response to the question on which occupation the student would choose in the case of employment by a third party or combining self and third party employment. We consider those that answered directors (of firms and other organizations) as having potential 'leader' behaviors.

In the case of creativity and innovation focus, the computations were based on students' answers to, respectively, desired occupation and industry where he/she would start the new business. We categorize occupation in terms of creativity potential (e.g., architecture, design, arts) and sectors by degree of technology intensity (cf. OECD, 1981) and knowledge intensity.

As is apparent in Figure 3, the highest entrepreneurial potential is associated with entrepreneurial traits such as risk, leadership and creativity but not so much for innovativeness.

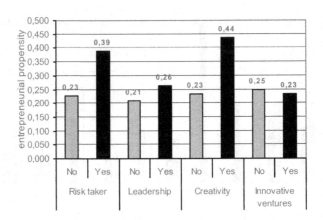

Figure 3. Entrepreneurial propensity by student psychological traits

In courses such as Economics, Civil Engineering, Electronics, and Industrial and Management Engineering, students presenting higher risk behavior, leadership traits, focus on creativity and innovative sectors reveal, on average, higher entrepreneurial potential. Nevertheless, risk behavior is associated with low entrepreneurial propensity in Mechanical and Metal courses; in Business and Metal Engineering leadership traits are essentially associated with non entrepreneurs; creativity is negatively associated with entrepreneurial potential in Mining, Mechanical, Metal and Chemical industries, which, given their business focus, is not really surprising. More surprising is the fact that focus on innovative sectors is not associated with entrepreneurial propensity in the Computing course.

The role of experience at the level of associations, and other extra curricula activities, having international experiences and professional activity experience is mixed with regard to entrepreneurial potential. On the whole, international experience is associated with higher entrepreneurial potential, whereas professional experience emerges negatively related to that potential – the only exceptions are Economics, Mining and Industrial and Management Engineering. Other extra curricula activities do not seem to impact on entrepreneurial potential, though there seems to be a strong positive correlation between these two variables in Mining, Mechanical and Metal Engineering. As stressed in the literature, other context variables, such as family background, emerge here as an important factor associated with entrepreneurial potential – particularly in Mining, Electronics, Chemical and Industrial and Management Engineering.

4. ESTIMATION MODEL AND RESULTS

Considering all (2430) final year students, on average, 26.5% stated that after graduation they would like to start their own business or be exclusively self-employed. Around 56% are female and have an average age of 23. The vast majority (over 80%) are ordinary students and live in the North region. Only a small percentage of students (8%) may be classified as risk prone (no or little fear of employment instability, uncertainty in remuneration, and failure). Over a third (35.7%) present a leadership conduct, admitting that if they could choose an occupation, they would like to be firm or other organization's directors/CEOs. Although 51.3% would invest in high-tech or high knowledge intensive industries in the event of starting a new business, only 14.2% would invest in creative industries. On average, students present a reasonable academic performance (with an expected grade of 13 out of 20), the majority (53.3%) have or had some professional activity, 29.4% were or are involved in extra curricula activities, and a few (17%) had some sort of international experience (e.g., Erasmus mobility program). More than half (54.5%) have close relatives that are entrepreneurs. Economics/Business and Engineering encompass around 40% of total students, with similar shares (20%).

In both models (Table 2 - Model I, which includes students from 60 majors, and Model II, which restricts the analysis to economics/business and engineering students), females reveal a much lower propensity for entrepreneurship. This ties in with other studies (e.g., Martínez et al., 2007), which indicate that entrepreneurship activities are more related to males. Nevertheless, it contrasts, to a certain extent, with the study of Ede et al. (1998), who found no difference between male and female African American students in their attitudes toward entrepreneurship education. All other characteristics and determinants being constant, and similarly to Ede et al. (1998), more senior students are more likely to be a potential entrepreneur. Student status only emerges as a relevant determinant of entrepreneurial propensity for the restricted model. However, the estimate indicates that among business/economics and engineering students, normal or ordinary students (i.e. full-time students) tend to be more entrepreneurially driven. Regional origin of the student does not seem to impact on the propensity which might be at least in part be explained by the fact that the vast majority (almost 90%) live in the North (the region where the University of Porto is located).

Table 1. Descriptive statistics

	Mean	SD	Min	Max	1	2	3	4	5	6	7	8	9	10	11	12	13	14
Entrepreneurial propensity					-0.091***	0.113*	-0.011	-0.004	0.104***	-0.035*	0.024	0.051*	-0.030	-0.039*	-0.046**	0.035*	-0.015	-0.011
(1) Gender (Fem=1)	0.564	0.496	0	1	1.000	-0.128	0.056	-0.029	-0.111	-0.031	-0.042	0.024	0.007	-0.057	-0.042	-0.074	-0.043	0.002
Individual characteristics																		
(2) Age	3.156	0.143	2.9	4.1		1.000	-0.362	-0.028	0.068	0.034	-0.060	0.073	-0.109	-0.047	-0.026	0.266	0.011	-0.090
(3) Student status (Normal=1)	0.813	0.390	0	1			1.000	0.003	-0.025	-0.024	-0.099	-0.007	0.114	-0.139	0.002	-0.281	-0.075	-0.086
(4) Region (North=1)	0.884	0.321	0	1				1.000	-0.059	-0.005	0.019	-0.030	0.035	0.021	-0.011	0.031	-0.006	0.016
(5) Risky	0.079	0.269	0	1					1.000	-0.025	0.022	-0.003	0.004	0.039	0.013	0.045	0.018	-0.004
(6) Innovative	0.513	0.500	0	1						1.000	-0.059	-0.159	0.038	0.035	-0.019	-0.055	0.038	-0.033
Psychological characteristics																		
(7) Leadership	0.357	0.479	0	1							1.000	-0.303	-0.195	0.063	0.013	-0.006	0.106	0.521
(8) Creativity	0.142	0.349	0	1								1.000	0.072	-0.041	0.060	0.101	-0.056	-0.159
(9) Academic performance	2.591	0.106	2.3	3.0									1.000	0.077	0.082	0.048	-0.058	-0.318
(10) Extra curricula activities	0.294	0.456	0	1										1.000	0.103	0.083	0.061	0.094
(11) International experience	0.170	0.375	0	1											1.000	0.088	0.027	-0.044
Context																		
(12) Professional experience	0.533	0.499	0	1												1.000	0.059	-0.041
(13) Family background (entrepreneurs=1)	0.545	0.498	0	1													1.000	0.149
(14) Economics Business	0.202	0.401	0	1														1.000

*** significant at 1%; ** significant at 5%; * significant at 10%. N=2359

Table 2. Determinants of students' entrepreneurial propensity (Logistic model)

		Model I	Model II
Individual characteristics	(1) Gender (Fem=1)	-0,437***	-0,630***
	(2) Age	1,440***	1,978***
	(3) Student status (Normal=1)	0,209	0,471**
	(4) Region (North=1)	0,047	0,279
Psychological characteristics	(5) Risky	0.700***	0,576**
	(6) Innovative	-0,104	-0,064
	(7) Leadership	0,277**	0,580***
	(8) Creativity	0,291**	1,152***
	(9) Academic performance	-0,623	-1,421*
Contextual factors	(9) Extra curricula activities	-0,143	0,063
	(10) International experience	-0,277**	-0,305
	(11) Professional experience	0,054	0,110
	(12) Family background (entrepreneurs=1)	-0,063	0,250
(13) Economics/Business		-0,270*	-0,039
(14) Engineering		-0,381***	
Constant		-3,438*	-4,089
N		2359	971
Entrepreneurs		623	237
Others		1710	734
Goodness of fit statistics			
% corrected		73.9	75.8
Hosmer and Lameshow test (p-value)		4.359 (0.823)	2.635 (0.955)

Psychologically related factors, namely risk propensity, leadership behavior and creativity focus, emerge as critical for explaining students' entrepreneurial intent. The main differences between potential entrepreneurs and other students are observed in risk bearing, leadership, and creativity focus. In these competences the scores of potential entrepreneurs are much higher than those of the remaining students. The expected average grade depicts a negative relation with entrepreneurial propensity in Model II. This means that, all else being equal, on average, for economics/business and engineering students, those that evidence better academic performance are less likely to become an entrepreneur. In part this might be explained by the fact that in Portugal, the traditional employment hunt by firms is based on grades, making those 'good' students not so eager to pursue their own venture.

Surprisingly, none of the contextual factors turn out to be relevant. In contrast to some previous evidence (e.g., Martínez et al., 2007), potential entrepreneurs do not differ from other students in the time they spend on other activities. Controlling for individual and psychological factors, potential entrepreneurs and others spend a similar amount of time working to acquire professional experience, and on extra curricula activities. Moreover, the role model stressed by the literature concerning the importance of family and contextual background does not prove to be important in this study. We do not confirm, therefore, the results of other entrepreneurship studies (Brockhaus and Horwitz, 1986; Brush, 1992; Cooper, 1986; Krueger, 1993), which found that students from families with entrepreneurs have a more favorable attitude toward entrepreneurship than those from non-entrepreneurial backgrounds.

Finally, controlling for all the variables likely to impact on entrepreneurial propensity, Model I shows that Economics/Business and Engineering students are less prone to entrepreneurial intents than students from other majors such as arts, life sciences or sports, to name but a few. This result proves to be quite unfortunate given the focus that previous studies on entrepreneurship placed on these two majors, and the fact that a substantial part of entrepreneurial education is undertaken in business schools (Levenburg et al., 2006). Additionally, no differences emerge (Model II) between Economics/Business and Engineering majors with regard to entrepreneurial propensity.

5. CONCLUSIONS

In this paper, the entrepreneurial intentions of undergraduates in Portugal are examined along with their related factors. The findings have insightful implications for researchers, university educators and administrators as well as government policy makers. First, the entrepreneurial propensity of undergraduates in Portugal is reasonably high (around 25%) and mirrors the findings of their European counterparts (e.g., Germany, Austria).

Although a reasonable amount of students in Portugal would like to run their own businesses, their intentions are hindered by inadequate preparation. They recognize that their business knowledge is insufficient.

Second, two demographic factors - gender, age – and four psychological traits – risk, leadership, creativity and academic performance - are found to significantly affect interests in starting one's own business, while contextual factors, such as family background, are found to have little independent effect.

Notwithstanding these results, we do agree with Hatten and Ruhland (1995) and Kent (1990) when they claim that more people could become successful entrepreneurs if more potential entrepreneurs were identified and nurtured throughout the education process. The former authors demonstrate that students were more likely to become entrepreneurs after participation in an entrepreneurially related program. In this context, and as Kolvereid and Moen (1997) suggest, entrepreneurship, at least to some extent, might be a function of factors which can be altered through education.

5.1. Acknowledgments

The author would like to thank the Rector of the University of Porto (UP), the Deans of the 14 Schools of the University, and professors/lecturers for their support for this research. Thanks to José Mergulhão Mendonça (FEP Computing Center) and André Rosário (MIETE Master Student) for their valuable assistance in the implementation of the survey. A word of profound recognition to all students of UP.

6. REFERENCES

1. Baucus, D., Human, S. Second-career entrepreneurs: A multiple case study analysis of entrepreneurial processes and antecedent variables. Entrepreneurship Theory and Practice 1995; 19(4): 41–72.
2. Brandstätter, H. Becoming an entrepreneur - a question of personality structure?. Journal of Economic Psychology 1997; 18: 157-177.
3. Brockhaus. R. H.. Jr., Horwitz, P. S. "The psychology of the entrepreneur". In The art and .science of entrepreneurship, D. L. Sexton & R. W. Smilor (Eds.), Cambridge. MA: Ballinger, 1986, pp. 25-48.
4. Brush, C. Research of women business owners: past trends, a new perspective, future directions". Entrepreneurship Theory and Practice 1992; Vol. 16: pp.5-30.
5. Carland, J. W.. Hoy, F.. Boulton. W. R., & Carland. J. Differentiating entrepreneurs from small business owners: A conceptualization. Academy of Management Review 1984; 9: 354-359.
6. Carroll, G., Mosakowski, E. The career dynamics of self-employment. Administrative Science Quarterly 1987; 32: 570–589.
7. Cooper, A. "Entrepreneurship and high technology". In The art and science of entrepreneurship, D. Sexton & R. Smilor (Eds.), Cambridge, MA: Ballinger Publishing, 1986, pp. 153-180.
8. Delmar, F., Davidsson, P. Where do they come from? Prevalence and characteristics of nascent entrepreneurs, Entrepreneurship & Regional Development 2000; 12: pp. 1–23.
9. DeMartino. R., Barbato. R. An Analysis of the Motivational Factors of Intending Entrepreneurs. Journal of Small Business Strategy 2002.
10. Dyer, W.G. Toward a theory of entrepreneurial careers. Entrepreneurship, Theory and Practice 1994; Vol. 19 No. 2: pp. 7-21.
11. Ede, Fred O., Panigrahi, Bhagaban, Calcich. Stephen E., African American students' attitudes toward entrepreneurship. Journal of Education for Business 1998; May/Jun98, Vol. 73, Issue 5.
12. European Commission. Toward enterprise eEurope: work programme for enterprise policy 2000–2005: Commission staff working paper. Document No., 2000.
13. Franke, N., Lüthje, C. Entrepreneurial Intentions of Business Students: A Benchmarking Study. International Journal of Innovation and Technology Management 2004; vol. 1(3): 269-288
14. GEE. Temas Económicos. Empreendedorismo, Lisboa: Ministério da Economia e da Inovação, Gabinete de Estratégia e Estudos, 2005.
15. Greenberger. D. B., & Sexton. D. L. An interactive model of new venture creation. Journal of Small Business Management 1988; 26(3): 107.
16. Greene, W.H. Econometric Analysis, Prentice Hall, 2000.
17. Gürol, Y. ve Atsan, N. Entrepreneurial characteristics amongst university students: some insights for enterprise education and training in Turkey. Education and Training 2006; Vol. 48, No. 1: 25-39.
18. Hatten, T.S., Ruhland, S. K. Student attitude toward entrepreneurship as affected by participation in an SBI program. Journal of Education for Business 1995; 70(4): 224-227.
19. Henderson, R., Robertson, M. Who wants to be an entrepreneur? Young adult attitudes to entrepreneurship as a career. Education & Training 1999; 41(4/5): 236-246.
20. Hills, G. E., Barnaby, D. J. Future entrepreneurs from the business schools: Innovation is not dead. In Proceedings of the 22nd International Council for Small Business, Washington, DC: International Council for Small Business, 1977, pp. 27–30.
21. Hills, G.E., Welsch, H. "Entrepreneurship behavioral intentions and student independence, characteristics and experiences". In Frontiers of Entrepreneurship Research: Proceedings of the Sixth Annual Babson College Entrepreneurship Research Conference, Babson Park, MA: Babson College, 1986, pp. 173–186.
22. Hisrich, R. D. Entrepreneurship: Past, present, and future. Journal of Small Business Management 1988; 26(4): 1–4.
23. Hosmer, D., Lemeshow, S. Applied Logistic Regression, New York: John Wiley & Sons, 1989.
24. Hynes, B. Entrepreneurship education and training: Introducing entrepreneurship into non-business disciplines. Journal of European Industrial Training 1996; 20(8): 10–17.
25. Kent, C. A. "Introduction: Educating the heffalump". In Entrepreneurship education: Current developments, future directions, C. A. Kent (Ed.), New York: Quorum, 1990, pp. 1-27.
26. Klapper, R., Léger-Jarniou, C. Entrepreneurial intention among French Grande École and university students: an application of Shapero's model. Industry & Higher Education 2006; April: 97-110.
27. Kolvereid, L., Moen, Ø. Entrepreneurship among business graduates: does a major in entrepreneurship make a difference?. Journal of European Industrial Training 1997; Vol. 21(4): 154.
28. Kourilsky, M.L., Walstad, W.B. Entrepreneurship and female youth: Knowledge, attitudes, gender differences and educational practices. Journal of Business Venturing 1998; 13: 77 - 88.
29. Krueger, N. The impact of prior entrepreneurial exposure on perceptions of new venture feasibility and desirability. Entrepreneurship theory and practice 1993; Fall: 5-21.
30. Krueger, N., Reilly, M., Carsrud, A. Competing models of entrepreneurial intentions. Journal of Business Venturing 2000; Vol. 15: 411–432.
31. Learned, K.E. What happened before the organization? A model of organization formation. Entrepreneurship theory and practice 1992; 17(1): 39–48

32. Lena, L., Wong, P.K. Attitude towards entrepreneurship education and new venture creation. Journal of Enterprising Culture 2003; Vol. 11 (4): 339-357.
33. Levenburg, N., Lane, P., Schwarz, T. Interdisciplinary Dimensions in Entrepreneurship. Journal of Education for Business 2006; May-June: 276-281.
34. Lissy, D. Goodbye b-school. Harvard Business Review 2000; 78(2): 16–17.
35. Lüthje, C., Franke, N. The 'Making' of an Entrepreneur: Testing a Model of Entrepreneurial Intent among Engineering Students at MIT. R&D Management 2003; 33, p. 2.
36. Martínez, D. Mora J.-G., Vila, L. Entrepreneurs, the Self-employed and Employees amongst Young European Higher Education Graduates. European Journal of Education 2007, Vol. 42, No. 1, pp.
37. McClelland, D.C. The Achieving Society. Van Nostrand, Princeton, NJ, 1961.
38. McFarlane, Carolyn. Stimulating Entrepreneurship Awareness in High School Students. Journal of Career Education 1981, pp. 135-144.
39. Naffziger, D.W., Hornsby, J.S., Kurtako, D.F. A proposed research model of entrepreneurial motivation. Entrepreneurship Theory and Practice 1994; 18(3): 29-42
40. Oakey, R., Mukhtar, S-M., Kipling,M. "Student perspectives on entrepreneurship: observations on their propensity for entrepreneurial behaviour". 2002, Vol. 2 (4/5): 308-322
41. OECD. Science and Technology Policy for the 1980s. Paris, 1981.
42. Reynolds, P.D. Who starts new firms? Preliminary explorations of fFirms-in-Ggestation. Small Business Economics 1997; 9: 449–462.
43. Robinson, P.B. Prediction of entrepreneurship based on attitude consistency model. Unpublished doctoral dissertation, Brigham Young University. Dissertation Abstracts International 1987, 48, 2807B.
44. Sagie, A., Elizur, D. Achievement motive and entrepreneurial orientation: a structural analysis. Journal of Organizational Behavior 1999; Vol 20 No. 3: 375-87.
45. Scott, A. J. New Industrial Spaces. London: Pion, 1988.
46. Scott, M.G., Twomey, D.F. The long-term supply of entrepreneurs: students' career aspirations in relation to entrepreneurship. Journal of Small Business Management 1988, pp.5-13.
47. Sexton, D.L., Bowman, N.B. "Comparative entrepreneurship characteristics of students: preliminary results". In Frontiers of Entrepreneurship Research, Hornaday, J., Timmons, J., Vesper, K. (Eds). Babson College, Wellesley, MA, 1983, pp.213-32.
48. Stewart Jr., W.H., Watson, W.E., Carland, J.C., Carland, J.W. A proclivity for entrepreneurship: a comparison of entrepreneurs, small business owners, and corporate managers. Journal of Business Venturing 1998; 14: 189–214.
49. Storey, D. J. Understanding the Small Business Sector. London, Routledge, 1994.
50. Teixeira, A.A.C. "Beyond economics and engineering: the hidden entrepreneurial potential", mimeo, Faculdade de Economia, Universidade do Porto, 2007.
51. Teixeira, A.A.C. "From economics, business and engineering towards law, medicine and sports: a comprehensive survey on the entrepreneurial potential of university students", Seminar at EEG, Universidade do Minho, 30 March 2007.
52. Van Auken, H., Stephens, P., Fry F., Silva J. Role model influences on entrepreneurial intentions: A comparison between USA and Mexico. Entrepreneurship Management 2006; Vol. 2: 325–336

36

CO-INNOVATION NETWORKS IN INDUSTRY

Joana Vilhena

NeeaConsulting Portugal, Project Manager - joanav@neeaconsulting.com

We are living in a world of on-demand communication.
Today's turbulent business world, require companies to continually update their skills and capacities. Companies are exploring ways to align and integrate technology-based learning into business processes and strategy. On-demand collaboration is a new trend that is driving higher levels of connectedness than ever before, and which is greatly affecting the way people collaborate and negotiate, since people want to work together anyone, anywhere, anytime. The collaboration market is so crowded, it becomes imperative to select a viable vendor that will survive the consolidation.

1. INTRODUCTION

In the turbulent business world of today, technological advancements, elevated competition and the shifting demands of business require companies to continually update their skills and capacities.

Trends in areas such as demographics, technology, globalization, branding, consolidation/privatization, and outsourcing will greatly affect the way people collaborate and negotiate.

Nowadays, companies are exploring ways to align and integrate technology-based learning into business processes and strategy. They also want to provide employees, clients and partners with the information and skills they need to solve immediate business problems.

Competition today is driving firms to introduce products with a higher degree of novelty. Consequently, there is a growing need to understand the critical success factors behind more novel product innovations. Empirically we can analyze the role of different types of collaborative networks in achieving product innovations and their degree of novelty. Studies (Cotton and Brehm, 2005) (Barbier et al, 2007) show that technological collaborative networks are of crucial importance in achieving a higher degree of novelty in product innovation. Continuity of collaboration and the composition of the collaborative network are highly significant dimensions. Collaboration with suppliers, clients and research organizations— in this order— has a positive impact on the novelty of innovation. The greatest positive impact on the degree of innovation novelty comes from collaborative networks comprising different types of partners.

On-demand collaboration is a new trend that is driving higher levels of connectedness than ever before. People want to work together on tasks, activities, and projects with anyone, anywhere, anytime, and on any connected device. As the environment for collaboration is changing, IT is coming under increased pressure to view on-demand collaboration as part of the infrastructure of their organizations. Over the last decade collaborative solutions have mostly been departmentally focused, but with the drive towards globalization, enterprise-wide solutions are now on IT's agenda. (Howard, 2005)

Please use the following format when citing this chapter:

Vilhena, J., 2008, in IFIP International Federation for Information Processing, Volume 266, *Innovation in Manufacturing Networks;* ed. A. Azevedo; (Boston: Springer), pp. 337–344.

To meet the needs of the enterprise, and with quality of service expectations approaching 99.999%, IT must take a close look at the infrastructure needed to support on-demand collaboration. Top level infrastructure decisions need to be made on Software-as-a-Service vs. premise-based environment, and Performing collaboration activities over a public vs. private network.

In addition to these decision points, there's some criteria that can be used by IT management in evaluating and selecting an infrastructure solution that can support the high service level requirements of on-demand collaboration in an enterprise environment. Security, reliability, accessibility, and scalability are just a few.

We are living in a world of on-demand communication. Cell phones, PDA's, etc. have transformed us into a mobile, connected society where people never want to be out of touch with one another. Many in the younger generation tend to be network-centric and always scanning for opportunities to connect. They don't want to miss anything! We see this desire to be connected having implications in the business world and helping to drive on-demand collaboration in the workplace.

With a myriad of collaboration solutions on the market today, IT management in global organizations is faced with a dilemma on how to make the best decision for the enterprise. (Achrol, 1990)

2. THE MARKET ON-DEMAND COLLABORATION

We can defined On-demand collaboration as the ability for people to work together around tasks, activities, or projects "with anyone, anywhere, anytime, on any connected device." (Coleman and Sayle, 2006) On-demand collaboration can occur among parties in a real time, synchronous environment or in a distributed, asynchronous environment where individuals are working independently of one another.

Growing usage of on-demand collaboration has resulted from several market drivers that are pushing it to the forefront.

• The need for users in disparate geographic locations to interact with each other more efficiently and make timely business decisions is becoming more critical due to increasing competition in the marketplace.

• The complexity of doing business is increasing. Outsourcing has become a way of life for companies. The ability to communicate and collaborate efficiently with outsourcing partners who are integrated into mission critical business processes requires on-demand collaboration technologies.

• The globalization of business has introduced significant challenges in managing a global workforce and working with customers, suppliers, and partners all over the world.

• The emergence of the "human-based computing" trend places the individual as the focus of the interaction rather than the technology.

This is impacting the design of technologies so people can work naturally and don't have to change their behaviors or work habits to accommodate particular hardware or software requirements.

• Telecommuting is a growing trend in business. Employees engaged in team activities are looking to on-demand collaboration to improve their productivity in communicating and collaborating with their teammates who are in disbursed locations. (Coleman and Sayle, 2006)

The SaaS environment offers advantages in that it minimizes IT resources needed to manage and maintain the collaboration infrastructure. These resources can be deployed on other critical activities within the IT organization. Often the cost is low, and it provides a good environment to trial on-demand collaboration solutions before scaling them to the enterprise level. There are some criteria that must be considered when making a decision on the infrastructure for enterprise-scale collaboration. Below there´s a checklist of criteria Table (Table 1) that can be used in developing the requirements in an organization.

Table 1. Checklist of criteria Table used in developing the requirements in an organization.

Check Box	Criteria	Description
✓	Security	Support end-to-end data encryption to prevent unauthorized access
✓	Reliability	Support 99,999% reliability among parties engaged in collaboration activities located anywhere in the world
✓	Availability	Support 100% availability on 24x7x365 basis
✓	Interoperability with different platforms	Support users working on different operating platforms such as Windows, MAC, Unix, etc.
✓	Scalability	Support user growth seamlessly without any degradation in service.
✓	Multimedia Support	Support voice, data, streaming and video conferencing
✓	Connectivity	Support user connectivity from anywhere in the world within a language-friendly interface. Provide technical support 24x7x365 on global basis
✓	Global access, support and localization	Support speedy user access from anywhere in the world within a language-friendly interface. Provide technical support 24x7x365 on a global basis
✓	Integration with critical business processes	Support ability to launch conferencing sessions from within mission critical applications to streamline the business process
✓	Ease of use	Support an intuitive user interface that requires no training of first time users
✓	Operational Support Systems	Support comprehensive OSS features for provisioning, monitoring and troubleshooting the network to deliver a 99,999% service level.
✓	Total Cost of Ownership	Support a pricing structure that eliminates hidden costs and makes the Total Cost of Ownership completely visible to the customer

One of the trends we are seeing is a consolidation of collaborative technologies in use in the enterprise being driven by IT. Since on-demand collaboration has evolved as a departmental solution in many organizations, it has resulted in a myriad of different solutions in use across the enterprise.

There is often pressure from IT to consolidate these collaborative applications down to one or two to reduce usage and support costs. As usage and adoption increases at the enterprise level, IT management must think of on-demand collaboration as part of the infrastructure. Service level expectations of users of these technologies are also growing.

This is placing IT management under significant pressure to deliver service levels approaching 99.999%, similar to or even higher than telephony service.

In addition to IT organizations looking to consolidate the number of collaborative solutions in use across their organizations, we also see a consolidation in the number of vendors offering on-demand collaboration solutions in the market. The collaboration market is very crowded. There are approximately 200 vendors offering real-time, synchronous collaboration solutions today.

Collaborative Strategies predicts this consolidation will continue over the next few years, which can be good for the market, because it weeds out the weaker vendors. However, it makes the market a minefield for IT management. It becomes imperative to select a viable vendor that will survive the consolidation.

The table below (Table 2) provides a list of the top vendors of real time collaborative solutions based on revenue generated from their data/web conferencing solutions:

Table 2. List of the top vendors of real time collaborative solutions based on revenue generated from their data/web conferencing solutions (Coleman and Sayle, 2006)

Company Name	2004 Est. Revenues	2005 Est. Revenues
WebEx	$249M	$308M
IBM/Lotus	$200M	$240M
Citrix (Online)	$75M	$95M
Genesis Conferencing	$78M	$85M
Microsoft	$69M	$80M
Cisco (Latitude)	$50M	$75M
Oracle	$15M	$75M
Adobe (Macromedia Breeze)	$28M	$40M
Polycom	$30M	$33M

Additional research shows there are only few solution providers offering an enterprise-level solution built upon a private network infrastructure supporting on-demand collaboration.

• **WebEx** — offers a **comprehensive SaaS solution supporting** both **real time, synchronous and asynchronous activities** that are built upon its MediaTone network.

• **Cisco** — offers collaboration appliances and a service offering that integrates Web conferencing with its IP phones and network products. (Coleman and Sayle, 2006)

3. INNOVATION EXECUTION FRAMEWORK ARCHITECTURE

Achieving innovation productivity requires an architecture that accommodates some important capabilities, thus creating a 'borderless' enterprise. Aligning the evolution of the architecture with the company's framework priorities can drive an investment commensurate with a calculated ROI. For instance, implementing a Consumer Insight Network would align with specific IT investments. The full architecture is highlighted in the next Picture (see Figure 2).

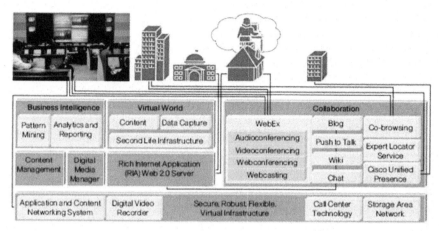

Figure 2. Innovation Execution Framework Architecture (Barbier et al., 2007)

4. REAL TIME COLLABORATION WITH WEBEX

WebEx is the leader in real-time communications infrastructure for Web meetings.

WebEx built a service that could handle massive concurrent connections while maintaining exceptional response times to support live video, shared applications, presentations, documents, and Web pages in highly interactive meetings. WebEx's challenge was to continue to offer the same high level of response time and reliability, while rapidly expanding its customer base and the number of meetings held on its worldwide network. WebEx used Forte Developer 6 to implement the expansion of the WebEx Interactive Platform (WIP), its real-time, multithreaded, multipoint data/audio/video communications platform.

WebEx offers a comprehensive SaaS solution supporting real time collaboration which represented for companies as Sun Microsystems (for example), extraordinary results in productivity efficiency and real time collaboration.

5. CURRENT INNOVATION PROCESSES IN COLLABORATIVE NETWORKS

Nowadays, a more knowledgeable customer is driving the industry.

The companies implementing on-line collaboration services are requiring a system that integrates with their ERP/CRM systems. This market is also putting higher demands and quality expectations on the on-line collaboration industry. These companies have found they have been able to do more with less since their reliance on online delivery have increased. (Lamming, 1993)

6. CASE STUDY

Sun Microsystems strengthens collaboration over distance with WebEx online platform. by Chris Saleh - Program Manager, Open Work Services Group, Sun Microsystems

Case study context

Established in 1982, Sun Microsystems, Inc. is the global supplier of network computing solutions that power the world's most demanding businesses. Among Sun's many breakthrough technologies are the Solaris Operating System and Java. Today, Sun conducts business in 100 countries around the globe. Sun Microsystems required an enterprise-wide collaboration tool to meet the needs of a widely distributed workforce. WebEx helped Sun create an open work environment, bridging geographies while enabling employees to work conveniently from anywhere, any time. Enterprise-wide use of WebEx has significantly reduced operating costs, increased productivity, and opened new business opportunities for the company.

The challenge

At Sun Microsystems, the *Open Work Services Group* plays a critical role in maximizing both corporate productivity and employee satisfaction. In the last few years, a number of significant developments at Sun resulted in a new set of challenges for the Group. As Sun grew globally, the company became more geographically dispersed. Sun's engineering teams, for instance, suddenly spanned five sites including Bangalore, St. Petersburg, and Beijing. In addition, the acquisition of other companies and consequent reorganizations resulted in a surplus of real estate, and Sun began to close campuses. In 2006, Saleh's group conducted a corporate-wide survey that confirmed Sun was deficient in collaboration tools enabling employees to work over distance.

The solution

Chosen by the IT department years before, WebEx was already in place at Sun but wasn't used much. Saleh says, *"When we realized we needed an enterprise-wide collaboration tool, we decided to re-examine our WebEx deployment."*

Sun stopped billing individual departments for WebEx usage and converted to an unlimited plan, providing each seat with 24-hour-a-day access to all five WebEx solutions. Today, Sun primarily uses WebEx Meeting Center across the organization to communicate with, train, and support internal and external customers located around the world. The solution's intuitive capabilities facilitate remote sales calls, demonstrations, installations, and product trainings. WebEx registration and automatic notifications make the sessions easy to plan, while the application sharing feature enables effective visual demonstrations.

WebEx also facilitates program and product development for global teams by providing highly interactive online meetings. For the IBIS Spares Team at Sun, WebEx enables colleagues to provide input to documents the team is creating or editing in real time. Using WebEx, the PDM project, a multi-year effort touching many organizations at Sun, conducts online workshops, presentations, application demos, and document reviews.

The benefits

WebEx helped the Open Work Services Group deliver on its initiative to enable Sun employees to work from anywhere, anytime - reducing costs, increasing productivity, and opening new business opportunities for the company. Sun has increased employee satisfaction and saved on energy and real estate costs.

The future

Since implementing the unlimited WebEx usage, Sun has received a very positive response from her WebEx user community. The Education Services Department at Sun was unhappy with the previous online solution used to provide online product training to its customers. Saleh comments, *"When they found out that WebEx was available at Sun, they switched over and are now very happy users."* Saleh is extremely satisfied with the benefits achieved with this real time collaborative solution and is expecting to grow its usage more and more in the years to come.

7. CONCLUSIONS

Productivity is a key reason for deploying new technology today. To accurately measure the productivity-based returns from a technology requires a structured approach.

Organizations are striving to achieve global connectivity in a dynamic environment where travel is becoming more difficult and expensive, employees are more dispersed, and business boundaries are constantly being extended. People are discovering and inventing new methods to share relevant information with lightning speed. As the Internet pervades all aspects of communications, markets are getting smarter with each passing day. To harness the benefits of the new work order, organizations are looking to achieve true collaboration with customers, partners, suppliers and employees. Simply put, the focus is to improve productivity while lowering costs. Increasing numbers of companies, are discovering the practical and very tangible benefits of online collaboration, and how it can make product training and the sales process more efficient, cost-effective, persuasive and ultimately, more successful. Companies now are able to rollout new products in days, rather than weeks or months. The result has been a dramatic improvement in responsiveness, to both customer needs and market changes. Web collaboration is becoming imperative in reaching this fundamental goal by offering anytime anywhere communications that impacts the bottom line and improves profitability.

Beyond the core benefits of travel cost and time savings are even more significant ways in which web collaboration is providing maximum value.

In addition to the hard benefits, the consensus is that web collaboration delivers increased speed, reduced time to market and increased team productivity. Online collaboration represents the leading edge in workforce communications, but at the same time, the upfront capital expenditures of this method are minimal. Without costly investments in additional computer equipment and software, online communications allow companies to quickly communicate with employees, customers and sales prospects, by sharing their best, time-honored practices via an online environment. (Cotton and Brehm, 2005) According to *Wainhouse Research*, an oston-based communications research and consulting firm that specializes in "rich media," the demand for rich-media communications will grow at a compound rate of 90% a year, for the next three years.

8. REFERENCES

1.   Achrol, R. et al. Designing successful trans-organizational marketing alliances. Cambridge, MA: Marketing Science Institute, September, 1990
2.   Ettlie J., Product-process development integration. Management Science, v.41, n.7, July, 1995.
3.   Kanter, R., Collaborative advantage: The art of alliances. Harvard Business Review, 1994
4.   Lamming, R., Beyond partnership: Strategies for innovation and lean supply. United Kingdom: Prentice-Hall, 1993
5.   Porter, M., Estratégia competitiva: Técnicas para análise da indústria e da concorrência. Rio de Janeiro: Campus, 1991
6.   Amaral D. - Escola de Engenharia de São Carlos, Toledo J. - Universidade Federal de São Carlos, Washington R., Modelo para avaliação da integração na colaboração entre empresas, 2006.
7.   Barbier J., Wysocki M., Du Mont S., Finke S., Kirby S., Macaulay J., McLaughlin M., Sheikh W., Stine J., Van Zanten R., Improving innovation productivity in the consumer packaged goods industry - Cisco Internet Business Solutions Group (IBSG), 2007
8.   Coleman D., Sayle R., The drive towards on-demand collaboration: Criteria and analysis for making a well-informed decision on web collaboration and collaborative strategies, 2006
9.   Howard C., Impacting Business with online training: Case studies on the next generation of e-learning, September 2005
10. Cotton B., Brehm J., Measuring the true business benefits of web collaboration, San Antonio, 2005

37

CREATIVE ENTREPRENEURIAL ABRASION IN HIGHER EDUCATION

João José Pinto Ferreira
INESC Porto, Faculdade de Engenharia, Universidade do Porto, Rua Dr. Roberto Frias, s/n 4200-465 Porto, Portugal; jjpf@fe.up.pt
Milton Sousa
SPI, MIETE teacher miltonsousa@spi.pt
José Oliveira
Auto Sueco, MIETE teacher, jooliveira@autosueco.pt

In a group setting, the exposure to different thinking styles and people promotes what is called creative abrasion, which, if properly managed, can greatly enhance the innovation potential. This is the philosophy behind MIETE, which was conceived in 2004 to promote innovation and entrepreneurship with multidisciplinary teams. With this in mind, MIETE aims at adapting itself to the profiles of candidates from different areas including, amongst others, Management, Engineering, Biotechnology, Sciences and Design.
In this paper the authors, report their experiences during the feedback sessions of the last two years with MIETE students, particularly in the 'Implementation and Strategies for Technology Comercialisation' workshops.

1. INTRODUCTION

Much has happened since the early years of the first "T-group" learning experiences of the 1940s started by Kurt Lewin. In such groups, "learning is best facilitated in an environment where there is dialectic tension and conflict between immediate, concrete experience and analytic detachment" (Kolb, 1984). This conceptual framework, which is a cornerstone of modern management training, forms a key pillar of MIETE's approach to learning. In MIETE, groups are formed with students from different backgrounds (all highly entrepreneurial and ambitious individuals) with the mission of developing a complete business plan based on an existing technology with the ultimate goal of bringing that technology to the market. Taking Yalom's (1995) four key elements of the T-group, one can clearly identify the basic characteristics of the MIETE's group learning experience:

- Feedback: groups are provided feedback on a regular basis about intermediate goals, outcomes, team dynamics and steps to follow. This feedback can be positive, expanding the group's energy, or negative, focusing the group's energy (in MIETE this is done through bi-weekly feedback sessions with dedicated coaches);
- Unfreezing: within the context of MIETE, this process refers to the need of demystifying the field of entrepreneurship and alerting for the needed sacrifices, persistence and patience that entrepreneurs must face. It is important that individuals understand their values and beliefs and how that relates to an entrepreneurial path (MIETE tries to "unfreeze" students through personality tests, continuous dialogue and by bringing "real" entrepreneurs to share their experiences);

Please use the following format when citing this chapter:

Ferreira, J.J.P., Sousa, M. and Oliveira, J., 2008, in IFIP International Federation for Information Processing, Volume 266, *Innovation in Manufacturing Networks;* ed. A. Azevedo; (Boston: Springer), pp. 345–352.

- Participant observation: members need to get emotionally involved in the group's mission and observe each others' behaviour while reflecting on what needs to be improved (MIETE tries to structure this by instilling peer evaluation and inter-group feedback. Feedback sessions also stimulate this by involving several groups in the dialogue process, inducing self-reflection);
- Cognitive aids: in order to structure the work process, students get several seminars with external experts on the relevant subjects for the work at hand (in this case, MIETE provides several seminars on subjects important for building a business plan).

One other important aspect of MIETE is group diversity. This is a key element of creativity and innovation. As described by Leonard and Swap (1999, p. 20) on producing creative options: "… you must select group members who, in combination, will provide you with requisite variety…. these group members must somehow be induced to do something with that variety, including debating – sometimes vigorously – the options. Group members will need to challenge one another and to welcome differences in intellectual background. Through this process, dubbed "creative abrasion" by Henry Hirshberg, the group can unleash the creative potential that is latent in a collection of unlike-minded individuals". In MIETE, as technologies from the University "given" for groups to work on are usually "raw", fuzzy and deprived of a clear market use, creativity and diversity are essential in order to make sense of that technology with a clear and innovative business rational.

One final element of the MIETE program is the role that coaches, in this case the authors of this paper, play in the guiding process of students and groups. While the coaches provide a mix of academic and professional experience that can be used to structure discussions, they also provide a means of reflection and continuous evaluation. The MIETE coaches act as change agents during the personal unfreezing process mentioned before and as facilitators towards optimized group behaviour. With this change agent perspective, self-awareness is paramount. As change agents, the MIETE coaches need to have a high level of awareness about the impact they make and their ability to make choices to direct and modify that impact (Curran, Seashore and Welp, 1995).

Such a learning environment, with high diversity and interaction, raw and fuzzy technology and ambitious entrepreneurial students, raises effectiveness and real learning, but provides also a seedbed for unexpected challenges. This paper tries to highlight some of these challenges that emerge mostly during the feedback sessions with MIETE students.

2. BACKGROUND: THE MIETE COURSE

2.1. In a Nutshell

In a group setting, the exposure to different thinking styles and people promotes what is called creative abrasion, which, if properly managed, can greatly enhance the innovation potential. This is the philosophy behind MIETE, which was conceived to promote innovation and entrepreneurship with multidisciplinary teams.

With this in mind, MIETE aims at adapting itself to the profiles of candidates from different areas including, amongst others, Management, Engineering, Biotechnology, Sciences and Design.

Throughout the program, the teams develop key integrated competencies on innovation, entrepreneurship and technology that will ultimately enable the students to create and develop new technology-based businesses.

2.2. Target

MIETE is designed for highly qualified people with a strong will to start new technology-based businesses, regardless of their educational and professional background.

People attending MIETE are usually middle managers from the private sector, faculty staff and researchers or recent graduate students wishing to major on innovation and entrepreneurship. Students applying to MIETE should have completed at least their bachelor degree (or the 1st cycle as defined in the Bologna treaty).

2.3. MIETE Unique Offer

Master programs that take their participants through the entire venture creation process are rare in Europe[20], especially when compared with the United States, where this kind of formal "hands-on'" training is very much advanced. MIETE started with the support of the North Carolina State University during its 1st Edition (2004/06) in the implementation of the so-called "Technology Commercialization Sequence".

MIETE tries to take its participants through the entire venture creation process, by combining real training in the innovation process and technology commercialization with the interaction of its students with researchers from different fields at the University of Porto (UP) and external experts and entrepreneurs.

2.4 Entrepreneurial Project

2.4.1. Training in New Business Construction

MIETE promotes an innovative combination of training in technology (any topic from the different faculties of the University of Porto), Creativity, New Product Development and Management, promoting, whenever appropriate, the valorisation of technologies through the construction of commercialisation strategies and their implementation through licensing or through the creation of new businesses.

In this context, where innovation is approached as a conscious and consistent effort for identifying new opportunities, MIETE aims at bridging the gap between the technology discovery – conducted at Faculties, Research Institutes and Enterprises – and the commercialisation of innovative technology-based products and services, both through the construction of new businesses or through the transfer of technology to existing companies.

2.4.2. MIETE as Pivot in the Technology Transfer Process

The model with which MIETE started in September 2004 relied heavily on the interaction of MIETE teams and R&D groups at the University of Porto. In September 2006 the new MIETE students were offered additional training in the usage of creative processes and techniques to support the early ideation phases. In parallel, the course started establishing bridges with enterprises. This connection to the private sector is crucial for the role that MIETE wants to play in the modernization of the Portuguese economy. The picture below illustrates the current operational model in which MIETE, through training of multidisciplinary teams, plays an interface role between the University, established enterprises, potential investors and new businesses.

---

[20] We would highlight the Innovation and Entrepreneurship Master program at the University of Oslo

By promoting this close relationship with R&D groups in the University and enterprises, MIETE wishes to explicitly position itself as a Pivot in the innovation process, stimulating technology transfer and new venture creation.

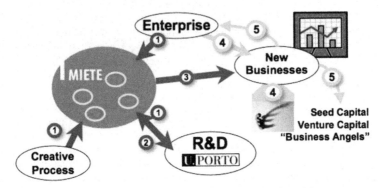

Figure 1. MIETE operational model

3. MIETE 2006/2008 EXPERIENCE

In this section, the authors bring some of their experiences during the feedback sessions held with the MIETE groups.

3.1 Interaction with students

The three authors of this paper have been engaged in MIETE since its 1st edition. João José Ferreira as Course Director, and both Milton Sousa (strategy, organization and innovation classes) and José Oliveira (financial and accounting classes) as MIETE teachers. This paragraph focus in the experience the latter had while supporting the students during the so-called Technology Commercialization (TEC) Sequence and, in particular, on the last course "Implementation Strategies for Technology Comercialisation", which occurs on the 3rd semester. Throughout the whole TEC Sequence, which aims at developing a complete business plan based on a technology from the University, the students should acquire the following competencies

1. Be able to identify technologies with potential for economic valorisation;
2. Be able to drive the creative process to generate business opportunities from existing technologies;
3. Be able to implement the process of technology valorisation;
4. Be able to evaluate a technology's commercial feasibility;
5. Be able to build a business plan based on: opportunity analysis, implementation strategy, investment needs and implementation plan.

During the "Implementation Strategies for Technology Comercialisation" course, students and the authors have the opportunity to meet, twice a month during a semester, to share views on each group's business plan progress.

The course also includes 6 special sessions with invited speakers, covering subjects such as legal procedures, finance, putting business plans to practice, new product development and several soft skills (e.g. presentation techniques, negotiation, team management)..

During this course, students have the opportunity to further develop their business plans, on which they have been working since the beginning of the TEC sequence within their groups (with a particular technology selected during the 1st semester). The feedback sessions are open to all the groups, but interaction is focused and done sequentially on a group by group basis, addressing their specific needs.

During the feedback sessions, the groups need to make a short presentation on their progress. The 'Implementation Strategies for Technology Comercialisation' course ends up with a formal presentation and evaluation of the business plan.

3.2. The challenges of the feedback sessions

The two main questions that need to be answered during this course are:
1. "What is the Product Value Proposition?" That is, what is the value of this product/technology for a particular market?
2. "What is the Business Value Proposition?" At this point in time students should have a very good idea of the market size, the need for the product/service and, finally, the business value for the investor.

To answer these two questions, several others arise that pose many challenges as described below:
1. **'Who will sell what to whom?'** This is probably the most common question asked to students during the 1st semester classes of the TEC Sequence. It is however frequent, as students often loose their focus, to come back to this question during the 3rd semester feedback sessions.
2. **Sizing the market:** Students often struggle to estimate their product/service market size, and usually delay this exercise as much as they can. Most powerful research databases, such as 'Datamonitor^{TM} are not freely available at the University, which means that students need to use other sources and techniques to get market data, including cold calling and direct interviews. While this is on its own a great learning experience, it demands more time and energy from the students as they need to build a picture of the market from scattered bits and pieces.
3. **Defining the product as the client wants it to be:** This involves a very structured iterative process applied to tuning product features to the actual market needs. 'Engineering background driven' groups are usually less careful about what their future customers/clients really want. It is sometimes hard to take these groups out of the 'laboratory view'.
4. **Technology patent issues:** When using technology developed by the University of Porto researchers and students need to come to terms on the legal support and IP rights of the technologies. This only happens when the students are indeed interested in starting a company, which is often the case. These negotiation processes can take a long time, demanding a lot of attention from both the students and the group coaches (the authors). The process itself is a great opportunity to learn from a real example on how to negotiate IP rights, but if taken too long, it can linger the commercialization process.
5. **Realistic expectations about product development, financing and market entry:** Most of the students don't have a clear idea of how much time they need until their projects are ready for take off. Most of them underestimate the timing needed to get the first customer, and usually don't know when to start the fund

raising process. Other problems concern the product development plan, mainly when students don't have a strong product development background, limiting their ability to clearly develop an objective and realistic timeline.

6. **Lack of seed capital:** Students often find interesting technologies or develop interesting concepts that still need a "proof of concept". Students can get frustrated as there is a clear lack of seed capital in Portugal from both Business Angels and the University to support this early-stage projects. Other financing sources include private companies that could become a future supplier, customer or even shareholder of the new company to be created. This is again usually a long process that can lead to frustration and disappointment. This is nothing different from what entrepreneurs face on a daily basis. While this is again a great learning experience, it is important to motivate students to overcome the frustrations associated with these issues.

7. **Is this work academically acceptable?** Most of MIETE teachers combine some working experience in private companies with some academic background and try to bring real live examples to classes. However, MIETE is formally a MSc Course and consequently the students' evaluation is formal. For some of the students this mix of academic content and evaluation with practical entrepreneurship can be quite confusing. Our understanding is that this mix, albeit potentially confusing, is of great value as it brings real hands-on experience with solid academic foundations. It is important that the coaches keep this message clear throughout the whole course.

8. **From producers to consultants:** Students that are 'building' a new product, often expect to build the entire 'factory' to produce it. Students are taught about the importance of keeping fixed costs low and of following asset-light strategies in a new start-up, where cash is vital. However, even asset-light strategies based on outsourcing can prove expensive and hard to finance. Students often finish the course in a position where they can only sell or license the knowledge about the product and technology they worked on. It is important for the coaches to make students alert about their added value in the process and of the importance of networking and outsourcing. This can help them to clearly define their position in the market.

9. **From a Group to several subgroups:** The existing money restrictions to hire and pay for the necessary skills needed to complete the product development process, require groups to seek help from undergraduate or PhD students that receive grants from the State. Students often become project coordinators, and are usually not 'hand on' technicians. This allows students to get project management skills. There are however several challenges to this as students don't have enough authority over project team members to guide the development process within the schedule and specifications defined by them. The coaches often advise students on how to improve their ability to exercise influence and power in those circumstances.

4. CONCLUSIONS

The MIETE experience proves that technology based entrepreneurial teaching in higher education is more effective under the following circumstances:

- Students are from different backgrounds and organized in diverse groups, inducing creative abrasion.

- The groups work on existing technologies from the University (or from enterprises) with the aim of brining that technology to the market. This allows students to get confronted with real-life situations and to face the frustrations entrepreneurs face when starting their companies. Even if students are not able to start a company at the end of the MIETE program, their learning experience is far more valuable than pure academic or case study teaching.

- There are structured feedback sessions that allow students to discuss and understand how they are progressing.

- There are cognitive aids based on seminars or classes that provide a solid academic foundation, guiding this way the learning process.

- The groups are coached by professionals with a mix of solid academic foundations and professional experience. These coaches need to act as change agents, motivating students, facilitating discussions, stimulating students to participate and supporting them through the different challenges posed to them. With this respect, the coaches need to "unfreeze" students from their pre-conceptions so that they understand what it takes to be an entrepreneur. Coaches also need to be highly aware of their impact in the students' progress.

The difficulties and challenges associated with this learning model are far greater than those in more traditional programs. The teachers and team coaches need to be highly skilled in their profession and academic theory, but also in managing team dynamics and the relation between different stakeholders. However, the benefits of this approach reflected on the learned skills and knowledge and successful technology transfer (often with the creation of new companies), outweigh by far the necessary sacrifices that students, teachers and coaches need to endure throughout the program. As the proverb goes: "No pain, no gain!"

5. REFERENCES

1. Leonard, D., Swap, W. When Sparks Fly: Igniting Creativity in Groups, Harvard Business School Press, Boston, 1999.
2. Kolb, D. Experiential Learning. Experience as the source of learning and development, Englewood Cliffs, NJ.: Prentice-Hall, 1984.
3. Yalom, I. The Theory and Practice of Group Psychotherapy 4th edition, New York: Basic Books, 1995.
4. Curran, K., Seashore, C., Welp, M. Use of Self as an Instrument of Change, ODN National Conference, Seattle Washington, 1995.

38

INNOVATION AND ENTREPRENEURSHIP: WHAT PROFESSORS FROM LEADING UNIVERSITIES SAY?

Manuel Oliveira
Faculdade de Economia, Universidade do Porto, Rua Dr. Roberto Frias, 4200-464 Porto, Portugal;
manueloliv@gmail.com

João José Pinto Ferreira
INESC Porto, Faculdade de Engenharia, Universidade do Porto, Rua Dr. Roberto Frias, s/n 4200-465 Porto, Portugal; jjpf@fe.up.pt

Hortênsia Barandas
Faculdade de Economia, Universidade do Porto, Rua Dr. Roberto Frias, 4200-464 Porto, Portugal;
barandas@fep.up.pt

As innovation is essential for the competitiveness of enterprises and economic development there is a question which has been raised with some insistence: Do teaching practices make a difference to innovation and entrepreneurship in the work place? Experts were contacted for their views. They say yes, as long as the teaching method is adequate. So, in the USA, a naturally innovative society, a new concept of integrated teaching was developed - "hands-on" to increase innovation ever more in North America. This concept proved also to be successful in a non-innovative society as is demonstrated by the case of MIETE (a partnership between FEUP and FEP, University of Porto) in Portugal.

1. INTRODUCTION

Innovation enhances employment and society through its improvement of competitiveness. "The importance of promoting innovation has been elevated up to a status of official standard since the Lisbon European Summit in 2000" and "the strategic goal was put forward for Europe to become the most competitive and dynamic knowledge-based economy in the World over the next ten years" Teixeira (2004, p.1-p.2).

However, concerning innovation and entrepreneurship Europe does in fact lag behind the USA. Europe is made up of smaller and more diverse national cultures than the USA, which has achieved a higher rate of technological progress than Europe, and universities of international excellence are seen to play a major part in this (Mateus, 2006).

So, we can ask *"What role does the formal teaching of innovation and entrepreneurship play?* Indeed, top managers in organizations and industry consistently identify that innovation management and the creation of new products and services is one of their priorities. How then should business and engineering schools go about the teaching of innovation and entrepreneurship?

Please use the following format when citing this chapter:

Oliveira, M., Ferreira, J.J.P. and Barandas, H., 2008, in IFIP International Federation for Information Processing, Volume 266, *Innovation in Manufacturing Networks;* ed. A. Azevedo; (Boston: Springer), pp. 353–362.

We begin the article by reviewing the most salient insights from the literature on innovation and entrepreneurship. Then we move on to interviewee comments. Finally we discuss the case of MIETE, at the University of Porto – a Master's degree which has been a success in an environment with a poor track record concerning innovation and technological entrepreneurship – making reference to the new model adopted by North American universities.

2. INNOVATION, TECHNOLOGY AND ENTREPRENEURSHIP - SOME INSIGHTS FROM THE LITERATURE

Inventions are connected to novel ideas for new products or processes, innovation is seen to be the first attempt to put an invention into practice (Fagerberg *et al.*, 2005); as Schumpeter (1934) said, innovation signifies entrepreneurship; and Drucker (1985) defended that innovation and entrepreneurship go hand-in-hand, all successful entrepreneurs are committed to systematically practicing innovation. So, we can't speak of innovation without speaking of entrepreneurship.

Throughout this article entrepreneurship is discussed in view of Shane and Venkataraman's (2000, p.218) definition: "[Entrepreneurship is] a field of business that seeks to understand how opportunities to create something new (e.g., new products or services, new markets, new production processes or raw materials, new ways of organizing existing technologies) arise and are discovered or created by specific persons, who then use various means to exploit or develop them, thus producing a wide range of effects". And, according to COTEC, those persons must have the capability to implement. The authors were thus motivated to contribute to the understanding of the mechanisms that can contribute to its development and with this paper we seek to reflect specifically upon the role of teaching in the development of innovation and entrepreneurship.

Innovators and entrepreneurs – are they born or made? And what is the role of personality? These questions don't cease to incite controversy in the literature.

It may well be that entrepreneurs have special characteristics determined at birth but there seems to be a widespread view in the literature that they can be nurtured, especially through education. An earlier paper published some years ago by Ulrich and Cole (1987) stated that to want to learn throughout one's life and to be interested in education is essential for any entrepreneur. Gorman, Hanlon, and King (1997) indicate that their ten year literature review found considerable support for the teaching of entrepreneurship – educational programs can influence entrepreneurial characteristics. Kolvereid and Moen (1997) confirm this. Later, Henderson and Robertson (1999) found that educationalists can affect students and subsequently entrepreneurship as a career choice. More recently, Peterman and Kennedy (2003) confirmed with their research that exposure to entrepreneurship education makes a positive difference to perceptions of desirability and feasibility. Teixeira (2007) agrees also that more successful entrepreneurs could result if they were better targeted by the education system and then nurtured accordingly.

Teaching entrepreneurship is even more relevant in the case of technology-based entrepreneurs, as stated by Storey and Tether (1998, p.1057) who wrote that "The characteristics of technology-based entrepreneurs are also fundamentally different from those in conventional sectors – they are much more likely to be highly educated" and "new technology-based firms have the potential to fundamentally transform the ways in which societies and markets operate. They are, quite simply, crucial to the long term development of an economy and in this sense deserve special treatment... There is a case for governments to take new technology-based firms more seriously... European policymakers... look enviously at the experience of the United States." (ibid.).

The literature points to the consensus of the importance of education to stimulate entrepreneurship. The same can't be said of the importance of an entrepreneurial personality type, where views diverge. In actual fact, personality, despite being important, is not in itself a sufficient condition to be entrepreneurial. A number of studies have identified an array of important characteristics and we can't confirm that there is a specific type of profile for the entrepreneur.

For example, authors such as Drucker (1985) and Gartner (1988) believe that the personality of the entrepreneur is not relevant and that literature on personality characteristics of the entrepreneur since McClelland (1961) has been unfruitful. In the quest to understand the phenomenon, so many traits related to the entrepreneur have been identified, such as the need for achievement, locus of control, risk taking, values and age, that a sort of generic "Everyman" has been the result; so "Who is an entrepreneur?" may well be the wrong question (Gartner, 1988). We need, according to this latter author, to focus on what entrepreneurs do, the behavioural approach – how they unite means of production.

Johnson (1990) and Cromie (2000) disagree with Gartner (1988) saying that the study of the individual's psychological traits and motivational inclinations shouldn't be abandoned. Entrepreneurship is a multidimensional process but "it remains worthwhile to carefully study the role of the individual, including his or her psychological profile (Johnson, 1990, p.48).

It is amidst this debate that this article is written - can teaching practices on courses of innovation and [technological] entrepreneurship make a difference, especially at the university level where personality characteristics will be more stable?

3. THE OPINION OF RENOWNED EXPERTS

It is generally accepted that there are situations and conditions in society which stimulate innovation. There is, for instance, a popular saying that states that "the need stimulates ingeniousness and art". Going back to the 15th century Portugal had as a national objective to sail to the Orient by sea and then Prince Henry the Navigator created a centre for scientific research calling a group of mathematicians together to search for a new method of determining latitude (North, 1981); simultaneously the shipping industry was developed in practice to enable to achieve that national objective. At the time the Portuguese Navigation School at Sagres played a major role in the nation's development, as was emphasized also by interviewee José Mendonça. In effect, according to the literature it is possible to positively influence innovation and entrepreneurship if the philosophy is that the objective of teaching is not just to cover subject matter - teaching is for producing change in behaviour, through increased understanding and attitude and skill development (Ulrich and Cole, 1987). This is best achieved if the student is an active participant in which case role plays, simulations and field projects are pedagogical techniques which will work well for innovation and entrepreneurship students (ibid.).

Back to our question – "Can innovation and entrepreneurship be taught?" several experts on teaching, innovation and entrepreneurship were contacted for their views (Table 1).

Table 1. Experts contacted for their views on teaching, innovation and entrepreneurship (an advanced draft of the paper was sent to the interviewees for veracity confirmation)

Name	Affiliation and some career information
Alan MacCormack	Harvard Business School Associate Professor in the areas of technology and innovation; as a researcher has received awards for excellence; internationally recognised
Arménio Rego	Assistant Professor at the University of Aveiro; Expert on organizational behaviour, with 27 books published (author and co-author). His papers have appeared in journals such as Journal of Business Review, Creativity and Innovation Management Journal, Thunderbird International Business Review, Business & Society, Management Research and Journal of Happiness Studies
Chris Brewster	Full Professor at the Henley Management College and at the University of Reading Business School – has over 20 books published; one of the most published authors in the international business journals according to a survey by the University of Chicago (2005)
José Mendonça	INESC Porto CEO (INESC Porto is a research laboratory with 300 employees, 100 of whom have PhDs) and Full Professor at the Faculty of Engineering, University of Porto; has extensive international experience
V. Srinivasan	Adams Distinguished Professor of Management and Director of the Strategic Marketing Management Executive Program at the Graduate School of Business, Stanford University; has won best-teacher awards and has also received numerous awards for research contributions

Harvard Business School Professor Alan MacCormack stated that "there are lots of very simple mistakes that entrepreneurs make that we can correct. You know, all that stuff which you might call kind of the science of management we seem to have made progress in. We can certainly teach people concepts that would help them be better at considering all of the possible issues that they might meet if they are an entrepreneur. Over the years we've been very good at finding ways to make business more efficient. If I've got one version of Microsoft Office, here are all the techniques I use to understand how to make a better version of Office, here are the new features, here's how to manage developers so that their programming productivity increases. The concepts of flexibility and adaptability, being able to change as you progress - those things can be taught."

Professor Chris Brewster, of the University of Reading Business School and Henley Management College, stated that "as there are a lot of people teaching innovation obviously it can be taught. Whether that is successful is another matter. Given that innovation depends on two factors: the personality and the system, it may make a difference. The personality cannot be taught; but the systems that allow innovation to flourish can be and if the teaching enables companies to understand and change them it will be useful."

Interviewee V. Srinivasan, of Stanford University, which is well known for its link to Silicon Valley start-ups, created a new concept of teaching, hands-on, and with theory given on an as-needed basis, stated that "Our courses as a whole do have an effect on our students, I think. Certainly the U.S. culture is conducive for innovation, and this is particularly true in the Silicon Valley". Lovejoy and Srinivasan (2002) speak of ten years of experience teaching a multidisciplinary product development course, unique in so far as they use the "hands-on manufacture of customer-ready prototypes executed by cross-disciplinary teams of students in a simulated economic competition against benchmark products and against each other." (ibid., p.32). Concerning course content interviewee V. Srinivasan stated that "both the production of coded scientific and technical knowledge versus experience-based know-how (e.g. learning by doing) play a role on innovation courses."

Interviewees also commented on institutions. The USA has an infrastructure which allows them to rapidly experiment in a variety of new fields as they emerge. And cheaply experiment with a whole bunch of different potential opportunities to find out which ones are profitable and which ones are not. And this is associated with a variety of different kinds of institutions. For instance, Alan MacCormack said that "I personally don't think that people on average are any smarter here [in the USA]. And I don't actually think they're necessarily any more entrepreneurial. I just think the infrastructure has been set up in a way that you get thousands of experiments. And out of those experiments comes a Google or you know comes an E-bay... And then another thing that America does have going for it is the scale that allows these companies to get big and somewhat dominant and take advantage of network effects. So if you're a Portuguese entrepreneur and you come up with a great idea your first worry probably once you start to get the seeds of success and see some success is you know how do I actually migrate this to a bigger market where I can really take advantage of network effects and not be stuck within a single country within Europe" (Alan MacCormack).

4. INNOVATION, TECHNOLOGY AND ENTREPRENEURSHIP IN PORTUGAL

Contrary to North American society, which is culturally innovative and entrepreneurial, Portugal is very badly classified concerning these two characteristics. Portugal had, in 2005, 858 patents in force whilst in the USA there were 1,214,556 patents in force at the same time (World Intellectual Property Organization at http://www.wipo.int/portal/index.html.en). Comparing Resident Patent Filings per Million Population Portugal had, in 2005, 14.97. The USA had 701.08 for the same year (ibid.). And comparing Resident Patent Filings per \$Billion GDP Portugal had, in 2005, 0.82; and the USA had 18.82 for the same year (ibid.). Also and for Total Entrepreneurship Activity (TEA), in 2005, the USA had a figure of 12.4% while Portugal had a figure equal to 4% (or three times less (International Entrepreneurship.com at http://www.internationalentrepreneurship.com/)).

In order to explain the above we focus on three of House *et al.*'s (2004) nine dimensions of culture, as revealed in their study of 62 societies – Performance Orientation, Power Distance and Humane Orientation.

House *et al.* (2004) report that the USA has a high Performance Orientation society practice of 4.49 (Type A) versus that of, for example, Portugal, which scored 3.60 (leaving it in the lowest category of Type C countries on this dimension). "Performance Orientation reflects the extent to which a community encourages and rewards innovation, high standards, and performance improvement" (ibid., p.239). Professor Arménio Rego is of the same opinion and during our interview commented that in Portugal "we have really to focus more on merit and on results... Evidently that this has, I believe, some implications for innovation, in the *latu sensu*."

Power Distance (PDI) is "the extent to which the less powerful members of institutions and organizations within a country expect and accept that power is distributed unequally" (Hofstede, 2001, p.98). In high PDI cultures, such as Portugal (House *et al.*, 2004; Hofstede, 2001), employees are afraid to disagree with their managers (Çakar, 2006). It is, however, divergent thinking that will contribute to innovation capability (ibid.). Again, Arménio Rego, of the University of Aveiro, stated that "Cultures which are very strong in Power Distance, and that is the case of Portugal [unlike the USA], are cultures where innovation can also be less frequent. Why? Do you know what strong Power Distance cultures are? They are cultures where there is difficulty on the part of the subordinates to question their superiors and to collide with the opinions of their superiors. You understand that in a culture with these characteristics it is more difficult for the organizational members to make themselves available to present innovative suggestions which collide with the status quo... cultures with high Power Distance, where people feel inhibited to express themselves to their collaborators with the fear of retaliation and/ or so as to not hurt susceptibilities, are cultures which will eventually have smaller propensity for innovation."

José Mendonça, of the University of Porto and CEO of INESC Porto, spoke about the humane orientation and stated that "primarily there may be a cultural and motivation problem in Portugal. In our Mediterranean culture the family structure protects children. It is the parents who pay for the degrees... not banks. And if our children fail a year it will not be another year they would have to pay the bank back for. So the attitude is different." José Mendonça continued to say that "in Portugal we have risk adverse companies... The State, the government has a very important role to play, especially when they say that thousands of millions of Euros in support etc. are on their way over from the European Commission, etc. of the so-called QREN – National Strategic Reference Framework for the development of Portugal 2007-2013. So, we need a clear, very strict framework to be established of stimulus and orientation which really promote innovation. Not make believe. It is not to cover up support for other types of companies that should go bankrupt." The above examples (parents protecting children in Portugal, and Portuguese government funding being used to avoid unemployment) are reflections of a Humane Orientation, which makes itself evident in caring, altruistic behaviour; being friendly, generous and kind to others (House *et al.*,2004). Schwartz (1992) goes further to mention protection of all people in such Humane societies, including strangers. Portugal is more Humane than Spain (House *et al.*, 2004) which "managed to, obviously going through hard years and high levels of unemployment, etc. managed to reform the industrial sector and to reform the civil service sector. We didn't do one or the other" (interviewee José Mendonça). These facts have a huge weight on the economy and will mean that companies will not be as innovative and competitive as others.

Cultures which lack a Performance Orientation, are high in Power Distance, and in Humane Orientation, may be less innovative and experience greater problems in companies which abide by more benevolent, conflict-avoiding values.

5. MIETE: A BRIEF DESCRIPTION. THE CASE OF PORTUGAL

First of all a brief reference to the new model adopted by North American universities – Stanford University (early 1990s) and the University of Michigan (five years later than in Stanford) both offer courses in innovation – Integrated design for marketability and manufacturing (IDMM at Stanford); and Integrated product development (IPD at Michigan). A project is undertaken; student teams have to perform well in each of the Marketing, Manufacturing, Engineering and Design dimensions; hands-on manufacture of customer-ready prototypes is performed; a tradeshow occurs at the end; projects are subjected to a market-based performance test. Of note and concerning results is the fact that commercial firms have purchased the rights for two of the new products developed by student teams over a period of ten years. This model however is not only possible in the USA, as MIETE (a two year Master's course (dissertation included) in Innovation and Technological Entrepreneurship), in Portugal, shows. The objective at MIETE, a similarly hands-on cross-disciplinary course, is to give real training in the innovation process and technology commercialization involving the assembly of a sound and solid business plan (with real commercialization problems) ready to be analysed by investors by the end of the course – the emphasis is on learning by doing taking its participants through the entire venture creation process even if the technology is not commercialized in the end – though two companies have already been set up as a result of the course in only three years since it started in 2004 (Oliveira, 2008).

Despite Portugal having been in the past an example of entrepreneurship and a centre of excellence for innovation (Martins, 1901, 1983) currently Portugal, according to The European Commission, in its study *Targeted Socio-Economic Research – Strategic Analysis* of the European Science and Technology Policy Intelligence, coordinated by R. Barre (Mateus, 2006, p.512), which classified regions according to number of patents per inhabitant, number of scientific papers per inhabitant and GDP per capita, concluded that in the Iberian Peninsula, comprising Portugal and Spain, there are only two regions of Type B – Madrid and Barcelona. Spain and Portugal don't have any regions of Type A, such as London, for example. The most advanced region in Portugal is Lisbon, which is Type C. All other Portuguese regions are of the lowest level possible – Type D.

It is in this context that MIETE, a new concept of teaching, appears in the North of Portugal – in a region of low gross domestic product per capita, with a low number of patents per inhabitant, as well as few scientific publications per inhabitant (Mateus, 2006). And yet MIETE has managed to produce innovative technological companies in just three years. What does MIETE count on to achieve this success?

The MIETE course is a partnership between two faculties and thus resides in the Faculty of Engineering and the Faculty of Economics, both of the University of Porto, in the North of Portugal. Cross-disciplinary teams of students are formed, indeed MIETE is a cross-disciplinary course – it involves faculty from several academic units (Business, Engineering and Design, and any other technological course of the student's choice (thus providing the flexibility to adjust the technical training to the students' needs)) - the course requires faculty with broad interests and experience with real practitioner innovation. Theory is given only when necessary and to support the practical hands-on innovation process. Contact with area specialists Worldwide and cold-calling are encouraged.

The emphasis is on products and corresponding markets. Interaction of its students with researchers from different fields at the University of Porto is promoted. Technologies are chosen by students in contact with the University of Porto R&D groups. Students are also allowed to follow their own path, their own ideas, and considering interaction with enterprises.

Until now this course has been demonstrated to be a success and two companies have been started as a result of the MIETE course, since its inception, in 2004: Tomorrow Options Microelectronics S.A. (the revolutionary first ever portable product for the prevention of foot diabetes complications, such as foot amputation, WalkinSense, marked the launch of this company. The WalkinSense mechanism may well be used in other areas such as sport, industry, and rehabilitative medicine. Portugal, the UK and then the USA and the rest of Europe are the target markets. An ambitious sales plan has been drawn out – through the year 2012, 20,000 units or more are to be sold, at 2,000€ per unit. The term "pocket multinational" best describes its activities (http://www2.inescporto.pt/uitt/noticias-eventos/nos-na-imprensa/tomorrow-options.html on 05-02-2008).), and IDEAVITY (Mingle is their first project, a unique proposal in mobile social networking, virtual Worlds and communication at an affordable cost).

According to this model MIETE's teaching is based on both theory and practice, on management as a science, giving assignments which broaden, on overcoming uncertainty by promoting uncertain situations requiring flexibility and adaptability to be surpassed, encouraging contact with knowledge leaders, and above all by boosting energy levels of its participants.

6. DISCUSSION

The teachers interviewed for this study are of the opinion that innovation and entrepreneurship can be taught and certainly the literature shows some evidence of this (Ulrich and Cole, 1987; Gorman, Hanlon, and King, 1997; Kolvereid and Moen, 1997; Henderson and Robertson, 1999; Kennedy, 2003; Teixeira, 2007; Storey and Tether, 1998). Lots of very simple mistakes that entrepreneurs make can be corrected and flexibility and adaptability, being able to change as you progress, can also be taught, stated interviewee MacCormack, of Harvard Business School. The influence of market size, institutions and infrastructure, allowing cheap and rapid experiments with potential opportunities, will also be important, MacCormack went on to say. Interviewee Brewster, a prominent author from a leading research university in the UK, pointed to personality and systems as playing a major role in innovation, the systems being able to be taught but the personality being more difficult to change. Interviewee Srinivasan, of Stanford University, says that their courses make a difference, where experience-based know-how (e.g. learning by doing) and theory both play a part.

Interviewee Rego, author of 27 books and numerous scientific articles, of the University of Aveiro, emphasized the importance of culture and having a low power distance and high performance orientation, in society and in organizations. Divergent thinking, being able to disagree with your boss and aiming for results is paramount for innovation to occur. Mendonça, INESC Porto CEO, Full Professor and expert on innovation indicated that more humane societies such as Portugal (and in comparison to its neighbour Spain) which don't want to go through the pain of unemployment will burden the economy with low innovation levels; a strict government framework, of stimulus and orientation, which really promotes innovation, will be needed to remedy this.

Concerning the teaching of entrepreneurship however, interviewee MacCormack, of Harvard Business School, stated that "one of the key elements clearly to a successful entrepreneurial company is associated with the personal characteristics of the founders, their drive and motivation and passion... And you know by definition an entrepreneur has to be somewhat irrational because if an idea was blindingly obvious and didn't require a lot of effort and time it probably would have been done. So an entrepreneur in the initial days probably has to be a bit of a contrarian too... And those are things which, you know, frankly you don't really teach in a classroom." But what if the teaching of innovation and entrepreneurship started earlier, at primary school? If we start encouraging an entrepreneurial spirit earlier, certainly before university (when personalities are more stable and difficult to change) and using the right pedagogical techniques, we may increase the level of entrepreneurship in society. Education can always have an impact but we can also modify personalities to a certain extent if we start early enough. Dreaming of becoming a famous pianist or an accomplished sportsperson may be deemed normal in our youth but why shouldn't children dream of becoming a successful entrepreneur too? Having the right image of what we want to be is essential and this can be encouraged by educators and family members, who, if aided by the media, can create the right messages and long term goals. "Starting earlier offers a lifetime edge" states Goleman (1995, p.79); and as setting up a company that thrives in the global marketplace means being at world class level, as interviewee José Mendonça commented, there may be a parallel between entrepreneurship and the discipline of innovation and other activities (such as violin virtuosos who start at age five and chess champions who start playing chess at age seven (Goleman, 1995)) – the promotion of an entrepreneurial spirit before the personality solidifies may bring benefits to society and as such this may be an issue calling for deeper reflection by policy makers.

We uphold that innovation and entrepreneurship, as taught by the MIETE course, a program founded on initial cooperation with the North Carolina State University, is a good example of how even in a high power distance society with a relatively low performance orientation the teaching of innovation and entrepreneurship can have a positive impact. MIETE, in an environment which is very different as compared to the USA, focuses on learning-by-doing which goes hand-in-hand with its deep theoretical basis of how innovation can be successful in a small society, where the innovation capability has improved satisfactorily over the last 40 years and especially from 1995-2001 (Teixeira, 2004). MIETE has had speedy results and this may be due to its requiring adaptation to immediate circumstances as Ulrich and Cole (1987) advocate. Entrepreneurs should be good at implementing plans and engaging in new action-oriented experiences so the learning style of the entrepreneur (ibid.) is catered to by MIETE. Innovation and entrepreneurship can be taught, we believe, if the right pedagogical techniques are used.

7. REFERENCES

1. Çakar, Nigar Demircan. Enhancing innovation capability through human resource practices: an empirical study in Turkish SMEs. South-East Europe Review 2006; 4: 109-126.
2. Cromie, Stanley. Assessing entrepreneurial inclinations: some approaches and empirical evidence. European Journal of Work and Organizational Psychology 2000; 9(1): 7-30.
3. Drucker, Peter. The discipline of innovation. Harvard Business Review 1985; May-June: 67-72.
4. Fagerberg, Jan; Mowery, David, Nelson, Richard (editors). The Oxford handbook of innovation. Oxford University Press, 2005.
5. Gartner, W.B. Who is an entrepreneur? is the wrong question. American Journal of Small Business 1988; 12(4): 11-32.
6. Goleman, Daniel. Emotional Intelligence – Why it can matter more than IQ. Bloomsbury, 1995.
7. Gorman, G., Hanlon, D., King, W. Some research perspectives on entrepreneurship education, enterprise education and education for small business management: a ten-year literature review. International Small Business Journal 1997; 15 (3), April-June: 56-78.
8. Henderson, Roger and Robertson, Martyn. Who wants to be an entrepreneur? Young adult attitudes to entrepreneurship as a career. Education and Training 1999; 41(5): 236-245.
9. Hofstede, Geert (2001). Culture's consequences: comparing values, behaviours, institutions, and organizations across nations. 2nd edition. Sage Publications.
10. House, R.J., Hanges, P.J., Javidan, M., Dorfman, P.W., Gupta, V. (editors). Culture, leadership and organizations – The GLOBE study of 62 societies. Sage Publications, 2004.
11. Johnson, B.R. Toward a multidimensional model of entrepreneurship: the case of achievement motivation and the entrepreneur. Entrepreneurship Theory and Practice 1990; 14(3): 39-54.
12. Kolvereid, Lars, Moen, Oystein. Entrepreneurship among business graduates: does a major in entrepreneurship make a difference? Journal of European Industrial Training 1997; 21(4): 154-160.
13. Lovejoy, W.S., Srinivasan, V. Ten years of experience teaching a multidisciplinary product development course, Journal of Product Innovation Management 2002; vol. 19: 32-45.
14. McClelland, D.C. The achieving society. The Free Press, 1961.
15. Martins, J. P. Oliveira. História de Portugal, 6th edition, Parceria António Maria Pereira, Livraria Editora, Lisboa, 1901.
16. Martins, J. P. Oliveira. Os filhos de D. João I, Lello e Irmão – Editores, Porto, 1983.
17. Mateus, Abel M. Economia Portuguesa (3rd edition). Editorial Verbo, 2006.
18. North, Douglass C. (1981). Structure and change in economic history. W.W. Norton & Company, Inc.
19. Oliveira, Manuel Teaching innovation – a comparison between courses in Europe and in the USA. Research Seminar article published in the Conference Proceedings of the 18th Luso-Spanish Conference on Management, held at the Faculty of Economics of the University of Porto (7-8 February, 2008).
20. Page, M. The first global village – how Portugal changed the world. 9th edition, Casa das Letras, 2002.
21. Peterman, Nicole E., Kennedy, Jessica. Enterprise education: influencing students' perceptions of entrepreneurship. Entrepreneurship Theory and Practice. Winter, 2003, 129-144.
22. Schumpeter, J.A. "The theory of economic development: an inquiry into profits, capital, credit, interest and the business cycle", (trans. R. Opie), Cambridge, Mass: Harvard University Press, 65-94, in Entrepreneurship (1990), Mark Casson (Ed.), Edward Elgar Publishing Limited, 1934, 105-134.
23. Schwartz, S.H. Universals in the structure and content of values: Theoretical advances and empirical tests in 20 countries. In M. P .Zanna (Ed.), Advances in experimental social psychology, Orlando, FL: Academic Press, 1992; 25: 1-65.
25. Shane, S., Venkataraman, S. The promise of entrepreneurship as a field of research. Academy of Management Review 2000; 25(1): 217-226.
26. Storey, D.J., Tether, B.S. Public policy measures to support new technology-based firms in the European Union. Research Policy 1998; 26: 1037-1057.
27. Teixeira, Aurora C. How has the Portuguese innovation capability evolved? Estimating a time series of the stock of technological knowledge, 1960-2001. Working paper n° 153, Faculdade de Economia, Universidade do Porto, September 2004.
28. Teixeira, Aurora C. Entrepreneurial potential in business and engineering courses – Why worry now? FEP Working Paper n° 256, December. INESC Porto, CEMPRE, Faculty of Economics, University of Porto, 2007.
29. Ulrich, T.A., Cole, G.S. Toward more effective training of future entrepreneurs. Journal of Small Business Management 1987; 25(4): 32-39.

AUTHOR INDEX